An X/Motif
Programmer's Primer

An X/Motif Programmer's Primer

FINTAN CULWIN

PRENTICE HALL

New York   London   Toronto   Sydney   Tokyo   Singapore

First published 1994 by
Prentice Hall International (UK) Limited
Campus 400, Maylands Avenue
Hemel Hempstead
Hertfordshire, HP2 7EZ
A division of
Simon & Schuster International Group

Typeset in 10/12 pt Garamond ITC light
by Columns Design and Production Services Ltd, Reading

Printed and bound in Great Britain by
Redwood Books, Trowbridge, Wiltshire

Library of Congress Cataloging-in-Publication Data

Available from the publisher

British Library Cataloguing in Publication Data

A catalogue record for this book is available from
the British Library

ISBN 0-13-101841-8 (pbk)

1 2 3 4 5   98 97 96 95 94

'For Maria . . .'
. . . or else!!

Contents

Preface

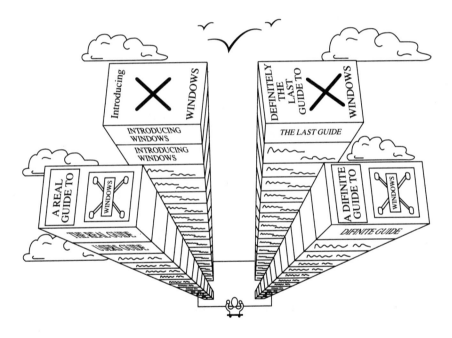

The digital webster application running on my workstation defines *primer* as:

> *...elementary school-book for teaching children to read;...*
> *...a small introductory book...*

Contemplating the estimated size of this book when it is published, I am concerned that I may be guilty of commercial misrepresentation in describing it as a *small introductory book*. However if the other books which have been published on the X Windowing system are considered the title is defensible.

The definitive guide to the X Window system, is the O'Reilly series of reference manuals. My set of these manuals comprises 9 volumes, stands 36 centimetres high and contains an estimated 6000 pages. On top of this I might place the 4 volume OSF/Motif official documentation, adding a further 10 centimetres and 2000 pages. A selection of the most useful books which have already been published on X and Motif, would add 6 volumes, 10 centimetres and another 2000 pages!

I feel I have to justify adding further to this plethora of pages, which already includes other introductory books on X/Motif. The best way in which I can do this is by making an analogy to books that have been published on introductory programming over the last thirty years.

In the early history of programming, introductory programming books were concerned mainly with the syntax and semantics of the programming language which they were introducing. Although books which take this approach are still written and published, they are now targeted only at experienced programmers. Modern introductory books no longer attempt to be comprehensive concerning the programming language, but have changed to emphasize program design and software development in the context of realistic applications. The objective of this approach is that if fundamental skills in design and development can be introduced, together with a useful subset of the language syntax, then the novice programmer will be able to use the reference manuals to extend their language specific knowledge as the applications which they are developing require it. However, what is more important is that the skills of program design, software development and independent study will still be useful when the novice has to cope with revisions and extensions to the language, or even transfer the knowledge to other computer language environments.

In general the existing books on X and Motif have assumed that as the readership is already experienced in programming, a book dealing with the syntax and semantics of the X Window system and the Motif toolkit would be appropriate. It is my belief that this assumption is invalid. My own experience of learning X/Motif, teaching students, impressions gained from talking to other X developers and observations made when visiting sites where X applications are being developed, have convinced me that X application development causes even very experienced programmers undue difficulty.

This difficulty is caused not only by the complexity of the X Windowing system, but also because the design skills possessed by most programmers are not useful in the production of X applications. Furthermore many of the books already published have attempted to offer a comprehensive coverage of the X Windowing system. This expresses itself most clearly in a single introductory book attempting to introduce X application programming and X system programming.

Consequently this book will attempt to introduce only a representative subset of X/Motif facilities within the context of X application programming. In doing this it will also introduce a set of design and development techniques which are appropriate for applications which have a graphical user interface. The intention is that once the material in this book has been assimilated, the reader will be able to extend their knowledge by using more technical books. In keeping with the objective of introducing X in the context of applications, the book evolves towards the last two chapters where the construction of a small application is described and explained.

The book commences in Chapter 1 with an introduction to operating and configuring X running on a workstation. This knowledge is essential to a novice X software developer for two reasons. Firstly they will require the knowledge in order to develop X applications and secondly they have to design their own applications to provide the same customization facilities to the user. Chapter 2 includes some trivial applications which are used to introduce techniques for the systematic development of applications, which will be extended in the remainder of the book. In particular an object based style of programming known as object encapsulation is introduced, together with a usability design technique using state transition diagrams and an implementation technique based on a three-layer (presentation, translation and application) partition. Chapter 2 also introduces the widget application hierarchy and the lifecycles of widgets within an executing program. Chapter 3 concludes the introductory section of the book with a more detailed introduction to usability and application design, together with techniques which can be used to control the visual appearance of applications.

Chapters 4 and 5 apply the techniques which have been introduced to application level main menus, and a selection of standard interfaces which all applications are expected to provide. The emphasis in these chapters, and in Chapter 7, is on engineering interfaces for reusability. Chapter 6 introduces an application, called *graphplot*, which makes use of the interfaces from Chapters 4 and 5. Chapter 7 returns to standard interfaces, introducing interfaces for the selection of colors, the selection of fonts and the entry of text, illustrating how they can be incorporated in the *graphplot* application from Chapter 6.

At the time of completing this book the current releases of the X toolkits are Motif 1.2 and X11R5. I have chosen to use some facilities from these releases which are not available in Motif 1.1 and X11R4. Where such facilities are used I will always comment on their non-availability in previous releases, and where possible suggest a work-around. The vast majority of the facilities used are common to both releases. Appendix C contains listings of the significant sections of code from chapters 1 to 7, which are not included within the main body of the text.

In writing this book I had to make a choice between using a personal style, as in this preface, or using an impersonal style. It is generally agreed that a personal style, where the author addresses the reader directly by the use of 'I', is easier to read. Except when writing a preface I find this style too egotistical and refuse to use it. The alternative personal style which uses 'we' is also fraught with difficulties. Where a book is written by more than one author this can refer to the authors. Where the book is written by a single author, the 'we' can only refer to the author and the reader. I often find myself reacting against the 'we' when reading any book which uses it. When I read '.. *and now we do this* ..'; I often find myself reacting with '*Well you might, but I would never do that!*'

As I find both possible styles of personal writing unacceptable, I am left with using an impersonal style. This style also has its problems, requiring many sentences to be written with a passive verb. The previous sentence is a passive sentence (as indeed this is). The personal style allows an active verb as in: 'When writing in an impersonal style, I often have to use a passive verb'. Although the impersonal style which I have used to write this book may make the text awkward in places, I would ask the reader to ignore this, as the alternative personal styles provide equivalent problems.

The other aspect of writing which I must comment upon is the manner in which I write C code. It is possible for C code to be written in a *write only style*, producing terse statements which exploit every trick of C's semantics. The justification for this style is that it will optimize the performance of the compiled program. I firmly believe that optimization is the responsibility of the compiler, not of the programmer, and also that it is only possible to optimize a program which is known to work. As this is an introductory book, I am more concerned with making the operation of the code obvious to the reader, rather than hiding its meaning behind exotic operators and compact unintelligible identifiers.

In a similar manner I have chosen to make extensive use of code modules. This is in part to employ C's limited information hiding facilities to their best advantage. More importantly it is a consequence of design techniques which divide the components of an interactive graphical interface into three parts: presentation components containing the program objects which are visible to the user, support components containing the program variables which store the state of the interface and translation components containing the behaviour of the interface. As the design produces specifications for each of these components, the implementation process respects this division and realizes each component as an independent C module.

It would be possible to rewrite all the code included in this book in order to produce equivalent code which would take less space, compile faster, use less data storage, execute faster, use fewer modules, etc., and be much more difficult to understand, maintain or extend. As I am more concerned with the engineering of applications, I will defend the decisions expressed above and the style of implementation used within the book.

The X Window toolkits are implemented using an initial capital naming convention. This style uses long multi-word identifiers, with the first character of each word capitalized, for example *XmStringDrawImage*. The toolkits also use an all capitals embedded underscore convention for manifest values, for example *XmSTRING_DEFAULT_CHARSET*. I have chosen to use a lower case embedded underscore convention for identifiers which I have introduced, for example *text_entry_pushbutton_callback*. The intention of using this convention is to allow the reader to easily distinguish application identifiers from toolkit identifiers.

For the curious the applications used in this book were variously developed on Apollo 3500 workstations, Next workstations and a no-name box-engineered 486 pc. Details of the software environment used on the pc are given in Appendix A for those who might wish to obtain the cheapest route into X/Motif development.

This book has taken about 18 months to produce during which I have had support, encouragement, criticism and assistance from a large number of people. The greatest in number are the hundred or so students who have suffered from the draft versions. At South Bank I also have to thank Terry Baylis for keeping my timetable light, Pete Chalk and Anna Pollard for reading and commenting upon each chapter as it was drafted, and John Shanks and John Murphy from computer services for keeping obsolete and cantankerous machines up and running while we were waiting for upgrades. At Prentice Hall, Helen Martin had the misfortune to suffer for a second time my attempts at authoring, a task which I am sure she gladly gave up to Vikki Williams half way through. The final stage of production involved Christine Channon who applied the final polish during copy-editing, catching all manner of faults.

I would like to believe that all errors and inconsistencies have been eliminated, however that would be as naive as claiming that any software I have authored is free of all bugs. Instead I will apologize in advance to any reader who encounters one and ask them to report it to me. All I can promise in return is that they will at least be read.

Finally, three people at home kept me going at times when I had longing thoughts of what I might be able to do with a heavy duty shredding machine. Maria, who is also to be thanked for many cups of coffee carried precariously up a steep ladder into the loft, Leah, who also provided the cartoon at the top of this preface, and Seana, for the help system text in Chapter 5.

FINTAN CULWIN
School of Computing,
Information Systems and Mathematics
South Bank University
London SE1 0AA
England

fintan@uk.ac:sbu.vax

I would have liked to have added another five or more chapters illustrating the construction of a realistic application; fortunately I was persuaded that it would make the book over-long. Instead I have prepared a case study of the design and construction of an application called *yaged* (*y*et *a*nother *g*raphics *ed*itor). Details of how to obtain a copy can be obtained by contacting me at the above address, preferably by e-mail.

\\

CHAPTER ONE

An introduction to using an X environment

1.1 Introduction to using X

This chapter will attempt to introduce the fundamentals of using an X environment, for the production of applications, using the Motif toolkit. There are many potential pitfalls in this chapter which are caused by some of the design features of X, primarily, the requirements that X be operating system independent and that it be extensively customizable by the user to their requirements.

The first pitfall is easily dealt with: although implementations of X for operating systems other than Unix exist they are comparatively rare, and consequently only a Unix based environment need be considered. However, if possible, the construction of an application which is dependent upon a particular operating system should be avoided. The second pitfall is more difficult to deal with: the only way to proceed is to assume a fairly minimal '*factory gate*' X environment is in use. The information presented in this chapter can be applied to a more customized environment. But if an already customized environment were to be assumed, the features of such an environment might not be applicable to the minimal environment.

As explained in the preface, the assumption of this book is that it will be used as a basis for practical exploration of *X/Motif* application development. Because of the possibility that the X environment has been customized, it is not possible to give any general guidance regarding how to start an X session. The assumed starting point for the book is consequently the stage where the *X server* and the Motif window manager have been started. Additionally it is assumed that an initial *xterm* window is available from which system commands can be given. If this environment is not immediately available all that can be suggested is that the Unix system administrator, or the system manuals, should be consulted to obtain such an environment.

Further potential pitfalls are contained within the language which is used when the *X window system* is being discussed. One of the first stumbling blocks is the use of the word *client* to identify an X application; it is called a *client* as X is based upon a *client/server* network architecture. This means that the entire environment consists of at least two parts, a *client* and a *server*, which may be running on different machines. Initially what causes the most confusion is that the *server program* runs on the user's local machine, and the *client program* may be running on the remote machine. This is exactly the opposite meaning to that which many new X Window users already have, where experience of *file servers* or *print servers*, which are always remote, is common.

The server program, known as the *X server*, runs on the user's local machine and is responsible for processing the user's inputs from the keyboard and/or mouse, transmitting the inputs over the network to the client, receiving replies from the client and updating the local display in response. The major advantage of X compared with other windowing systems, is that it was constructed from the start as an operating system independent, networked, windowing environment. Figure 1.1 illustrates a situation where a single *X server* is running one local client and several remote clients simultaneously. A simpler environment is equally possible where the server and the client are running on the same machine, although the communication between the server and the client still takes place as if there were a network link between them.

Each client has its own window on the server's display. The control of the positioning and size of the windows is controlled by the user interacting with a

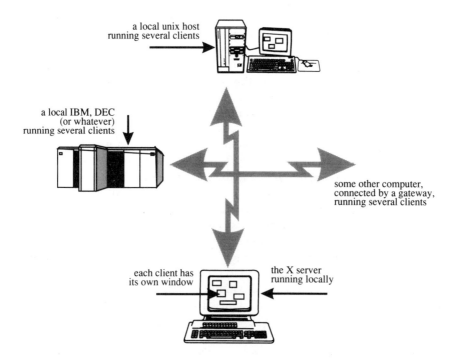

Figure 1.1   The *X Window* client/server architecture.

client called a *window manager*. The window manager usually runs locally and is largely responsible for the *'look and feel'* which the user experiences when operating an X session. The window manager used by the *X Motif* environment is most commonly the *Motif Window Manager*, known as *mwm*.

In order to construct X Window applications the facilities of the operating system to edit, store and maintain source code and other files, to compile, link and execute programs constructed from source code and standard libraries, to obtain printouts of the program listings, and other facilities which an application developer would expect to have available in a production environment, must be available and understood. Within a Unix environment these facilities are fairly standard; Appendix A lists several books which provide a suitable introduction.

For Chapter 2 and subsequent chapters a knowledge of ANSI standard C and object oriented design is assumed. Again there are many other books which have been devoted solely to these considerations, some of which are recommended in Appendix A. In Chapter 2, where some simple *X Motif* programs are introduced, a brief introduction to the design notation and the subsequent implementation in ANSI C will be given.

1.2 Window manipulation operations

A typical screen dump from an X session is given in Figure 1.2. It shows five client windows, an iconified client and the *Motif Window Manager* (*mwm*) root window menu. Only four of the client windows are directly visible, those labelled *xterm*, *xclock*, *Calculator* and *ifs6.c*. The fifth window is mostly hidden underneath the *ifs6.c* window; part of its border is just visible to the bottom left of the *ifs6.c* window; The iconified client is labelled *xedit* and is visible in the middle right. All of these windows are child windows of the *root window* which occupies the entire screen.

The *xterm* window contains an *xterm* (*Xterminal*) client. In this environment *xterm* is used to launch and control other clients, and to interact with the underlying operating system. The *ifs6.c* window contains an *xedit* (*Xeditor*) client, which is currently editing a file called *ifs6.c*. The icon labelled *xedit* contains another instance of *xedit*, editing an unknown file. The *xclock* and the *Calculator* windows contain an *xclock* and an *xcalc* (*Xcalculator*) client respectively. These are all examples of *standard clients* which are provided as part of the X Window system and their use should be obvious. The *mwm* root window menu is only transiently visible under user control; the contents and use of this window will be introduced later in this chapter.

All the windows have identical window borders and decorations. These borders are provided to the client by the window manager (*mwm*), and are used by the user to control the positioning and state of the window. Figure 1.3 shows the *xcalc* client with the component parts of the window border isolated and identified.

The *title bar* component is used to identify the window and/or its client, and to

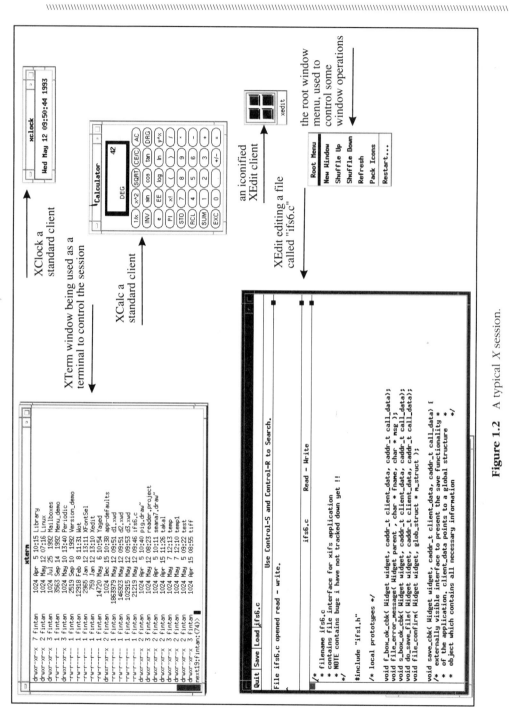

Figure 1.2 A typical X session.

move the entire window around the screen. To move the client window the mouse pointer should be placed within the title bar and the first mouse button pressed. The mouse pointer will then change to a four-pointed arrow and the window can be dragged to a new location. While the window is being dragged, the new location of the window is outlined and a small box containing the *x,y* co-ordinates of the top left corner of the window relative to the *root window* is visible. When the mouse button is released the client window will move to the new location.

The *resize handles* can be used to resize a window. The horizontal and vertical resize handles can be used to resize the window either horizontally or vertically respectively. The corner resize handles can be used to resize a window horizontally and vertically at the same time. To use any of the resize handles the mouse pointer first has to be placed within the handle and the first mouse button pressed. The mouse pointer will then change to indicate the direction in which to drag. While the window is being resized the new size of the window is outlined and the new dimensions indicated. When the mouse button is released the window will resize to the new dimensions.

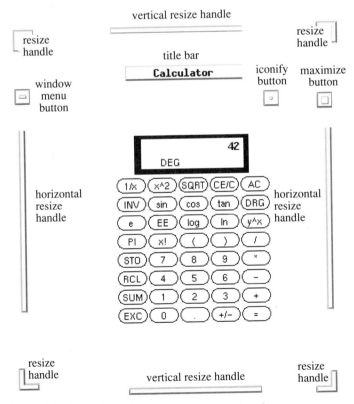

Figure 1.3 The Motif window manager, window frame components.

Resizing a window may, or may not, have a sensible effect upon the client which it contains. When the window border is resized the window manager sends a message to the client indicating the new size; it is up to the client to respond to this message. With the *xcalc* client, if the window is too large it will occupy the same amount of space in the top left corner of the window. With the *xclock* client it will occupy the same amount of space centred within the window. The *xedit* client will make some sensible use of the new size displaying more of the file which is being edited, although the editing controls will still remain at a fixed size at the top left of the window. In all cases if the window is too small only a proportion of the client can be displayed.

The *iconify button* can be used to iconify a client. A client can be iconified by a single click of the mouse button when the pointer is within the iconify button. An icon can be positioned on the root window by dragging it when the mouse pointer is within its boundaries. An icon can be deiconified by double clicking when the mouse pointer is within it. The deiconified client will be placed on the screen with the same position and size as when it was iconified. It is possible that the window manager has been configured so that icons are placed within an *icon box* rather than on the *root window*. This facility will be explained later in this chapter.

The *maximize button* can be used to resize an application so that it occupies the entire *root window*. To maximize a client single click the mouse pointer within the maximize button. As with the resize operation described above, not all clients may be able to make sensible use of a large window. A maximized window can be restored to its original size and position by clicking within the maximize button. The maximize button of a maximized window has a different visual appearance to indicate that clicking it will cause the window to be restored to its previous size and position.

The *window menu button* provides a *pull down menu*, which appears when the mouse pointer is clicked within it. The appearance of the menu is illustrated in Figure 1.4. It contains duplicates of all the controls which are present in the

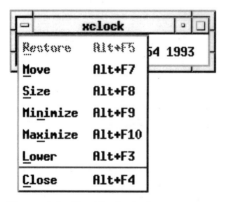

Figure 1.4   The Motif window menu.

\\\

window's border (*Move*, *(re)Size*, *Minimize* (iconify), *Maximize*, *Restore*), and two further operations, *Lower* and *Close*. The *Restore* operation is only available when the window is iconified or maximized. To indicate when *Restore* is not available it is shown, as in Figure 1.4, in a greyed-out state. A button in this state is described as being *insensitive*; a button which can be used is described as *sensitive*.

The *Lower* operation is rarely used and causes the window to be hidden behind all other windows which occupy the same location on the *root window*. The *Close* operation can be used to 'kill' a client stopping the execution of the program and destroying its window. The *Close*, and other *kill* operations, should not be used if there are other ways of terminating a client, as they provide no notification to the client before termination and thus there is no way in which the client can tidy up before termination. There is a mouse *shortcut* for the *Close* operation: if the mouse pointer is double clicked within the menu button the *Close* operation will be performed.

To operate the window menu the mouse pointer is single clicked within the menu button. The window menu is then posted and remains posted until a menu option is chosen, or the menu is cancelled. An option is chosen by single clicking upon it, and the menu can be cancelled by single clicking outside the menu or clicking on an inactive option.

Alternatively the menu can be operated by pressing and holding the mouse button while the mouse pointer is within the menu button. This causes the menu to be posted. A highlight can then be dragged up and down the menu; releasing the mouse button when an active option is highlighted causes the operation to be performed. The menu can be cancelled by dragging the mouse pointer outside the menu and releasing the button, or releasing the button while an inactive option is highlighted.

As indicated on the menu there are two other ways in which the menu can be operated. If the menu has been posted using a single mouse click an operation can be selected pressing the underlined *mnemonic* key on the keyboard. Alternately the operation can be activated, without posting the menu, by using the keyboard <ALT> [F] *accelerator* key shortcut shown on the menu. This can be done at any time when the application has *keyboard focus*, a concept which will be explained below.

In practice most users perform most operations using the window border controls and by double clicking upon the window menu button to *kill* a client. Only very sophisticated users use the *keyboard* accelerators, and very few users use the window menu and its associated *mnemonics*.

One final point needs to be made concerning general window operations. At any instant only a single window can be the recipient of keyboard input. This window is indicated to the user by having a darker border. In Figure 1.2 it can be seen that the *xterm* window border is darker than the other window borders, indicating that it has *keyboard focus*. To select which window receives keyboard input the mouse pointer has to be clicked while it is within the window or its borders. This will also have the effect of raising the window above any other windows which might be occluding it.

1.3 Using the help system (*xman*)

There are many more features of the X Window system than possibly can be explained in this book. Several books which attempt to give a more comprehensive coverage are listed in Appendix A. Rather than continue with a detailed description of a selection of these features, a description of the help system will be given. The intention is that the help system can be used to obtain additional detail of the features which are introduced throughout the book.

The X Window help system is a standard client called *xman* (*xmanual*), which conforms with the Unix help system which is called *man* (*manual*). In a Unix environment the *xman* client can be launched from a terminal with the command line "*xman &.*". The *&* is required in order to launch *xman* as a background process, allowing the user to switch between the *xman* and other clients at will. If the ampersand is omitted then other clients may be 'locked out' until the *xman* client terminates.

When the *xman* client is launched there will be a delay, following which the *xman* window will appear. The initial appearance of the *xman* client is shown in the first illustration on Figure 1.5. Clicking upon the '*Manual Page*' button will cause another window containing an index of help topics to appear. The appearance of this window is shown in the last illustration of Figure 1.5. The list of help topics is organized alphabetically by ASCII sequence, with all uppercase letters listed before lower case letters.

To move through the list the *scroll bar* to the left of the list can be used. The entire length of the scroll bar indicates the whole list, the shaded portion of the scroll bar indicates the currently visible portion of the list and its relative position. Thus in Figure 1.5 approximately one fifth of the list is currently visible, starting approximately half-way through the list. To move down the list the mouse pointer can be positioned in the unshaded part of the scroll bar at the approximate point required and a single mouse click will cause the list to scroll up to the point indicated. Alternatively the shaded part of the scroll bar can be dragged down, causing the list to scroll up.

Once the name of the topic required is visible in the window clicking upon it will replace the list with the manual page for the requested topic. The middle illustration of Figure 1.5 shows the start of the manual page for *xman* itself. This could also have been obtained by clicking the *Help* button from the initial window. The manual page can be browsed using the scroll bar just as the index could be scrolled through.

When the manual page is no longer required, a single mouse click anywhere within the page will cause the display to revert to the help topic index. When the index page is no longer required it can be iconified separately from the initial window using the iconify button, or closed by double clicking upon the window menu button. When exploring manual pages it is sometimes convenient to be able to have two or more help topics simultaneously visible. This can be accomplished by further clicks upon the *Manual Page* button of the initial window. Each click

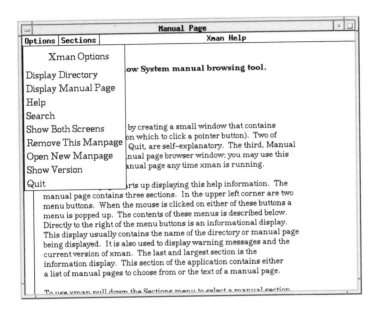

Figure 1.5 The *xman* standard client.

causes a separate manual browser window to be created, each of which can be used to display a separate help topic allowing different topics to be cross-referenced.

The middle illustration in Figure 1.5 also shows the *pull down* menu which is attached to the *options* menu button. The details of the options offered by this menu, and those offered by the *sections* menu, are given in the manual pages for *xman* itself.

This provides only a brief introduction to the operation of the *xman* standard client; for further details the *xman* manual page for *xman* can be used. Table 1.1 contains a list of and brief notes about other standard clients which may be of some interest or use in the rest of this book. Each of these clients has a manual page which can be consulted, using *xman*, for further information.

1.4 Customizing clients from the command line

As was mentioned in the introduction, one of the design goals for the *X window system* was to provide an extensively customizable environment for the user. There

Table 1.1   A selection of standard X clients

bitmap	simple bitmap editor, used to create icons, pointers and graphical labels
oclock	analog clock
xcalc	calculator
xclipboard	displays the contents of the clipboard
xclock	analog or digital clock
xdpr	dump window directly to printer
xdpyinfo	display information of Xserver
xedit	simple text editor
xev	illustrates the contents of various event structures
xfd	displays X windows font
xfontsel	interactively select X windows font
xgc	demonstrates various graphics primitives
xhost	access control to the server, allowing remote machines to be used
xkill	interactively kill an xclient
xload	displays system load
xlogo	displays X logo
xlsclients	list running clients
xlsfonts	list available X window fonts
xmag	magnify a portion of the screen
xman	interactively select and display manual pages
xmodmap	display and alter the keyboard key allocations
xpr	print an X window dump
xrefresh	refresh all or part of a screen
xset	set various display and keyboard preferences
xsetroot	set appearance of the root window
xterm	VT102 & Tektronix 4014 terminal emulator
xwd	dump an X window
xwud	undump an X window

are two major methods which can be used to set the values of *resources* which are used to customize clients. Resource values can be set from the command line when the client is launched, or resource values can be set in *resource default files* and will be applied to clients as they are launched. This section of the chapter will introduce the setting of resource values from the command line and the next section, the use of resource files.

There are a small number of resources which are common to all clients and a larger number of resources which are particular to a single client or shared by a small number of clients. The manual page for each client describes the particular resources which can be set for it. The resources which are common to all clients are listed in Table 1.2.

To set these resources from the command line the name of the resource is specified after the client name with any argument to the resource following it. Thus, for example, to launch the *xman* client with an alternative *font* the command line '*xman-fn *charter-bold*19* &*' could be used. The appearance of the *xman* top level window when this command line is used is illustrated in Figure 1.6, which can be compared with Figure 1.5 to identify the effect which the font resource specification has had.

The font specification string, *charter-bold*19*, has to be quoted on the command line to prevent the command processor from attempting to interpret and substitute the asterisks which it might regard as command wildcards. The font specification string uses wildcards to omit parts of the full font specification. In the

Table 1.2   X standard command line options

-bg **-background**	background color e.g. blue
-bd **-border**	window border color e.g. red
-bw **-borderwidth**	border width of window in pixels e.g. 8
-display	display for the client to show output upon e.g. zeus:0.0
-fn **-font**	font for text display e.g. "*times*bold*14*"
-fg **-foreground**	foreground color e.g. yellow
-geometry	position and size of the window e.g. 400x300+100+50
-iconic	launch client in iconified state
-name	resource name for client e.g. XEdit
-rv **-reverse**	reverse foreground and background colors
-synchronous	run client synchronously, for debugging purposes
-title	title to display on window border e.g. "ifs6.c"

Figure 1.6   The *xman* standard client, alternative font.

example above only the font family (*charter*), weight (*bold*), and pixel size (*19*) have been explicitly specified. The *X server* will use the string to select the first font from its list of available fonts which satisfies the specification. If no font satisfying the specification is located an error message will be output on the terminal, and a default font will be used.

The list of fonts which is available to the server can be obtained by using the *xlsfonts* standard client. The command *xlsfonts* by itself will list all the fonts which are available, a list which will typically contain hundreds of entries. The *xlsfonts* command can take an optional parameter *-fn(fonts)* followed by a font specification string. Only those fonts which match the specification supplied will be listed. Figure 1.7 illustrates the output of *xlsfonts* with the font specification **charter-bold**. It can be seen from this list that there are two possible matches for the string **charter-bold*19**. The *X server* will choose the first font from the list (*19–140*) rather than the second (*19–180*) for the *xman* client above.

Figure 1.7   The *xlsfonts*, list fonts, standard client.

The precise appearance of a font can be examined using one of two standard clients, *xfd* (*fontdump*) or *xfontsel* (*font selector*). The client *xfd* will display all printable characters of a single selected font; an example of *xfd* in use is shown in Figure 1.8. The client *xfontsel* will allow wildcard font specifications to be interactively explored. An example of *xfontsel* in use is shown in Figure 1.9.

An illustrative list of some of the fonts which are available with the standard X distribution is presented in Appendix B, which also explains the meaning of all parts of the full font specification string.

The color resources controlling foreground, background and border color (*-fg, -bg, -bd*) can be specified using English colornames (e.g. *green*). A list of the colornames which are recognized is presented in Appendix B. When a colorname is specified it is not guaranteed that the exact color will be provided. Colors can be a scarce resource on an *X server* and may have to be shared between all active clients. For example, if the user requests *powderblue* as a color resource and

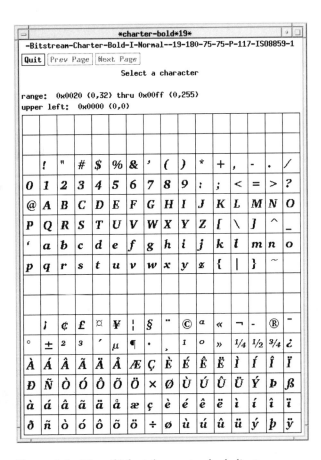

Figure 1.8 The *xfd*, font dump, standard client.

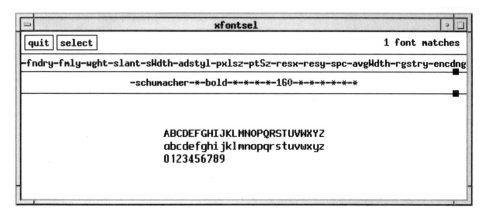

Figure 1.9   The *xfontsel*, *x* font select, standard client.

lightblue is already available the server may provide *lightblue* in response. Once all available color spaces are in use, some apparently strange colors may be allocated upon request. For example, a request for *lilac* may actually return a shade of blue.

A monochrome (black and white) terminal will use a similar mechanism to map all color resource requests onto either *black* or *white*. Thus the command line "*xclock -fg yellow -bg blue &*" can be used on a monochrome *X server*, and will hopefully use white for yellow and black for blue.

The default foreground and background colors of a client can be reversed with the *-rv* (reverse) command line option. Figure 1.10 shows the *xclock* client in normal, black foreground and white background, and reversed colors.

The *-geometry* resource can be used to specify an initial position and/or size for a client. The position and size are specified in an argument to the option which has the form *widthxheight+x+y*. The first two parts of the argument are the *width*

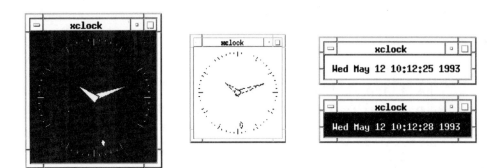

Figure 1.10   The *xclock* standard client in analog, digital, normal and reverse format.

\\

and *height* of the client; the units which these numbers represent are interpreted by the client. For most clients the *width* and *height* specify the size in pixels, but for some clients they are interpreted as units which make more sense to the client. For example some text based clients would interpret them as character units.

The *x* and *y* values in the geometry string specify the position of the client on the *root window.* Positive values indicate an offset from the left or top of the window, negative values from the right and bottom of the window. As with the resize operation described above, some clients may not be able to make effective use of an oversized window and some experimentation may be necessary to determine an optimal combination of font and size. Two different geometry sizes were used to launch the two analog *xclock* instances shown in Figure 1.10.

The *-name* resource will be explained in the next section of this chapter. The *-title* resource can be used to specify a string which will be used in the title bar component of the window border and to identify the client when it is iconified. If no title is specified by the user then a default title, usually the name of the client, will be used.

The default *title* can sometimes be confusing; for example, the *xeditor* uses the name of the client (*xedit*) as the default title. When multiple files are being edited, a number of edit windows and icons may all have the title *xedit.* This can cause problems for a user when several instances of the *xedit* client are active, each of which is editing a different file. By using the *-title* option and specifying the name of the file which is being edited, a more meaningful window and icon title can be specified. The non-iconified *xedit* window shown in Figure 1.2 specified the title resource *ifs6.c* when it was launched. The iconified *xedit* window in the same figure made no title resource specification. The *xfd* window in Figure 1.8 specified the title resource *charter-bold*19* when it was launched.

The *-iconic* command line option can be used to launch the client in an iconic state. The *-synchronous* command line option is used to cause the client to wait for a reply from the server every time a communication is made. This will cause the client to run more slowly, but will allow run time errors to be more precisely located when a client is being debugged.

In addition to the standard command line resource options which have been described above, it is possible for a client to have other resource specifications which are particular to itself. For example, the *xclock* client defaults to an analog clock; however, a digital clock can be specified by using the *-digital* command line option as shown in Figure 1.10. The client specific resources which are available are listed on the relevant manual page for standard clients and should be specified in the documentation of other clients.

1.5 Customizing clients from resource files

The customization of clients described in the previous section can become cumbersome. A user may decide that they would always like their terminals to use a courier 14 point bold font, yellow foreground, blue background, have a scroll bar and maintain a 256 line buffer. To specify this set of resources the required command line would be:

```
xterm -fn "*courier-bold*14*" -fg yellow -bg blue -sb -sl 256
```

which is hardly convenient to type. The resources *-sb* (*scrollbar*) and *-sl* (*save lines*) are particular to the *xterm* client.

The X Window system provides a mechanism by which user preferences expressed as resources can be specified in a series of resource files, which are consulted as a client is launched. The most accessible of these files, in a Unix environment, is a file normally called *.Xdefaults* and usually located in the user's home directory.

The format of an entry in the resource file consists of two strings: a resource identification string, and a value string, separated by a colon. For the resources which were introduced in the previous section the format of a resource string is straightforward. As a minimum it consists of the name of the client, an asterisk and the name of the resource. Thus the *xterm* resources expressed on the command line above could be installed in a resource file in the format:

```
! xterm settings
xterm*font:                         *courier-bold*14*
xterm*foreground:                   yellow
xterm*background:                   blue
xterm*scrollBar:                    true
xterm*saveLines:                    256
```

The first line of this resource file fragment commences with an exclamation mark symbol ('!'), which identifies it as a comment line. The remaining lines identify the client by its default name *xterm* and the resource which is to be set. Some care should be taken when entering resource specifications in a resource file, particularly the use of capitalization within resource names. The resource converter is not very intelligent and may not issue any warnings for resource settings it cannot interpret. For example: if the specification of *yellow* is followed by a space before the end of line, some versions of the resource converter will interpret it as *yellow<space>*. The color *yellow<space>* will not be located in the server's color resources and consequently the request will not be honoured.

The resources which are expressed in the resource file will override any default resources which would have been applied, but they themselves can be overridden by a resource specification on the command line. Thus if the *xterm* resources illustrated above are in a resource file, then an *xterm* client launched with the command line "*xterm &*" will have a 256 line buffer. If a larger buffer is required for a particular terminal instance this can be requested on the command line (e.g. "*xterm -sl 512 &*"). The command line specification will be honoured in place of the resource file specification, giving a 512 line buffer.

There may be situations where two or more differing sets of resources are required by a user. For example, a user may find it useful to have a different visual appearance for *xterm* clients which are being used to access the local host computer and those which are being used to access a remote computer. One way to accommodate this requirement is by using the *-name* command line resource option.

If a client is launched with a *-name* resource specified, then the value of the *name* will be used to locate resources in the resource files. Thus using the example above a user may decide to use the name *rxterm* (remote xterm) for *xterm* clients which will be used to access remote computers, and decide to use a lilac background to distinguish it. The appropriate entries in the resource file would be:

```
! rxterm settings
! rxterm is a '-name' option for remote xterm clients
rxterm*font:                    *courier-bold*14*
rxterm*foreground:              yellow
rxterm*background:              lilac
rxterm*scrollBar:               true
rxterm*saveLines:               256
```

Thus *xterm* clients which are launched with no *-name* option will use the yellow on blue resources specified in the first set of resource specifications. Those *xterm* clients which are launched with the "*-name rxterm*" option will use the yellow on lilac resources specified in the second set of resource specifications. It would also be sensible for the user in this situation to complete the customization by establishing a command alias for the command line "*xterm -name rxterm*". If the alias is "*rxterm*", the command "*rxterm &*" can be used to launch remote *xterm* clients. Details of how to establish an alias are dependent upon the underlying command interpreter.

One source of confusion is the distinction between the *-title* and the *-name* resources. The *-title* option is used solely to specify a string which will be used in the client's title bar and icon; it has no effect upon the name used to identify resources within resource files. The *-name* option is used solely to specify the name which is used to identify resources within resource files; it has no effect upon the window or icon title.

This situation is still not satisfactory; the resource difference between an *xterm* and an *rxterm* client is only in one setting, the background color. All the other resource settings are identical but have been duplicated in each set of resource specifications. There is a mechanism which can be used to avoid this unnecessary duplication.

As explained above each client has an *instance name*, which can be used to identify a particular instance of the application. By default every instance of a client will have the same instance name, but a particular instance name can be established by using the *-name* option. Every client also has a *class name*, which cannot be changed by the user and is identical for all instances of the client, even if they have different instance names. The class name for a client is usually the same as the default instance name with the first letter of the name capitalized, unless the first letter is an *x* in which case the first two letters are capitalized. Thus the default instance name of an *xterm* client is *xterm*, and the class name is *XTerm*. Class names can also be used in resource files to specify resources. Thus the two sets of resources expressed above can be better expressed as:

```
! XTerm settings
XTerm*font:                         *courier-bold*14*
XTerm*foreground:                   yellow
XTerm*background:                   blue
XTerm*scrollBar:                    true
XTerm*saveLines:                    256
! rxterm settings, used for remote xterm clients
rxterm*background:                  lilac
```

As suggested in this example a setting for an instance "*rxterm*background*" will override a setting for a class "*XTerm*background*". It is not the position in the resource file which causes the *rxterm* setting to override the *XTerm* setting, but the general rule that a more precise (*instance*) specification will override a less precise (*class*) specification.

In addition to setting client wide resources, the resource mechanism can be used to set particular resources within a client. The *xedit* client shown in Figure 1.2 has a number of *push buttons* at the top. A user may decide to customize their use of *xedit* by specifying a larger font and different colors for the push buttons, and to change the button label *Quit* to *Exit*.

This can be accomplished by using the class identifier *Command* within the resource identifier string to specify all the buttons in the client, and the instance identifier *quit* to identify the particular button labelled *Quit*. These identifiers are given in the *xedit* manual page. Using this information the relevant portion of the resource file would be:

```
! xedit general settings
xedit*font:                         *courier-bold*14*
xedit*foreground:                   yellow
xedit*background:                   blue
! xedit command button settings
xedit*Command*font:                 *charter-bold*16*
xedit*Command*foreground:           blue
xedit*Command*background:           yellow
xedit*quit*label:                   Exit
```

The first three settings specify resources which are to be applied to the entire client. The next three settings apply to all components of the client of the class *Command* (*button*). Using the rule expressed above that a more precise setting will override a less precise setting, the command buttons will have inverted colors with respect to the rest of the client and their labels will use the charter bold 16 point font. The last setting will apply to the component which has the class or instance name *quit*; the only component which will match is the button labelled *Quit*. The resource specified for this button is the *label* resource and the value specified is *Exit*. This setting will have the effect of changing the label displayed from *Quit* to *Exit*.

\\

If the *.Xdefaults* file were the only file which could be used to specify resources then it would soon become unusably large. Resources for a particular class of clients can be set in a file which has the same name as the class name of the client. Thus settings for the *xterm* client could be specified in a file called *XTerm*. Application specific resource files can be located in one of two places. If the environment variable XAPPLRESDIR (application resources directory) is defined, then its value indicates the directory where the class resource files should be located. If XAPPLRESDIR does not have a value then the class resource files should be located in the home directory. (From release 5 of X the environment variable XFILESEARCHPATH is preferred to XAPPLRESDIR, but the obsolete XAPPLRESDIR will still be recognized.)

The same rule expressed above is used to resolve conflicts between resource setting conflicts in the *.Xdefaults* file and class resource files. As the class resource file is more specific than the *.Xdefaults* file then its settings will override any conflicting settings in the *.Xdefaults* file. However, in the unlikely circumstance of a more specific setting for an individual resource in *.Xdefaults*, the setting in *.Xdefaults* will override the setting in the class resource file.

This introduction to resource file usage is necessarily only an overview. If the changes to the *.Xdefaults* file or the class resource files have no apparent effect, than it could be that the X environment has been customized by the system administrator to look in different places. In this situation the system administrator, or the system manuals, should be consulted for advice.

The setting of resources for a client is an important topic which will be returned to in subsequent chapters when the construction of clients is introduced. The description of the customization of standard clients given in this section provides a guide for the application developer, who should construct and document their clients to offer the same customization possibilities to the user.

1.6 Customizing the Motif window manager

It is not immediately obvious that the Motif window manager (*mwm*) is itself a client and thus can be customized to the user's requirements. Among many other things the window manager provides the borders for client windows, controls the placement, iconification, deiconification and size of windows, and controls the keyboard input focus.

One of the most convenient customizations which can be accomplished is to provide an *icon box* within which an icon is maintained for each active client. This can simplify window management in several ways, the first of which is to collect all icons in a window where they can be quickly located. The icon box window can itself be iconified causing the amount of screen space occupied by icons to be reduced. A typical icon box is shown in Figure 1.11.

The icon box maintains an icon for every client, even those which are not currently iconified. The appearance of icons within the icon box which represent non-iconified clients differs from icons which represent iconified clients. The *xclock* icon in Figure 1.11 illustrates the appearance of a non-iconified client; the

\\

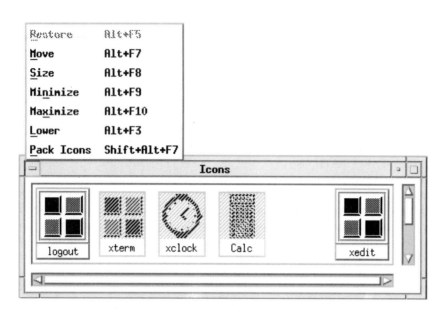

Figure 1.11   The Motif window manager icon box.

xedit icon illustrates the appearance of an iconified client. Non-iconified icons differ from iconified icons by being shown with a lighter less well-defined appearance. An iconified client can be deiconified with the customary double click on the icon in the icon box. A non-iconified client's icon in the icon box can be double clicked to cause the client's window to be raised to the top of the window stack and to have input focus.

When the number of icons required is greater than the number of icons which are visible in the icon box window, the hidden icons can be viewed by using the scroll bars within the window. The window manager menu of the icon box window differs from the window menu of other windows. The option to close the window is replaced by an option to pack the icons within the window. When an active client is killed the corresponding icon in the icon box is removed leaving a space. The *pack icon* operation will rearrange the icons within the icon box window to occupy the minimum space.

The icon box resource is activated by setting the *mwm* resource *useIconBox* to true. This can be best accomplished by setting a resource in the *.Xdefaults* file, or the *Mwm* class resource file:

```
Mwm*useIconBox:              true
Mwm*iconBox*geometry:        8x1+0-0
```

The second resource setting determines the initial size and placement of the icon Box window. Notice that the units for width and height are expressed in terms of icons, the units for *x* and *y* position are expressed in pixels. This resource value will place an icon Box window along the entire width of the bottom of the screen, although some adjustment to the value of the width component may be necessary for different screens.

The changes in the *mwm* resource values will not take effect until the window manager is restarted. One way to do this is to close the X Window session, possibly by logging out from the host and then logging on again. A more convenient method would be to use the *root window* menu to restart the window manager. The default *root window menu* was illustrated in Figure 1.2. It is posted by pressing the mouse button when the cursor is on the *root window*. The last option of the menu is *Restart ..* which when selected will lead to a *dialog* which asks for confirmation of the operation. If confirmation is given the current instance of the window manager client will terminate and a new instance will be started. As the new instance is started any changes made in the resource files will take effect.

The root window menu is another place where user customization of their window manager environment can be usefully effected. The window manager's default behaviour is modified by a system wide *configuration file* called '*system.mwmrc*', normally located in a directory called '*/usr/lib/X11*'. To customize the window manager to a user's requirements this file should first be copied to the user's home directory, renamed to *.mwmrc* and then edited.

The *.mwmrc* configuration file contains three major sections: the menu definitions, the key bindings definitions, and the button binding definitions. To illustrate the usage of this file, the changes required to attach a sub-menu to the *root window menu* will be described. The existing root window menu will be extended by having an additional option inserted between *New Window* and *Shuffle up*. The new option will be labelled *Applications*, be separated from the existing options by horizontal separators, and when selected will post a *sub-menu* which will offer a choice of several clients. The extended root menu is illustrated in Figure 1.12.

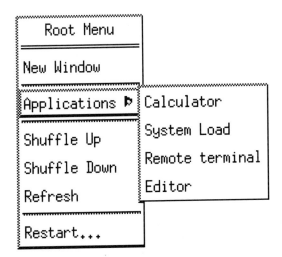

Figure 1.12   The extended root window menu.

The existing root window menu is defined in the *.mwmrc* configuration file as:

```
Menu RootMenu
    {
            "Root Menu"          f.title
            no-label             f.separator
            "New Window"         f.exec "xterm &"
            "Shuffle up"         f.circle_up
            "Shuffle down"       f.circle_down
            "Refresh"            f.refresh
            no-label             f.separator
            "Restart ..."        f.restart
    }
```

The menu definition commences with the word *Menu*, followed by the name of the menu, in this case *RootMenu*. This is followed by a list of the menu labels and their associated actions enclosed between curly braces ('{','}'). The label is a simple string or the literal *no-label*; the actions are expressed as functions which are known to *mwm* and in some cases are followed by parameters. Thus the action '*f.exec "xterm &"*' specifies that the *mwm* function *f.exec(ute)* with the argument *xterm &* should be executed when the *New Window* option is selected from the menu.

The activation of the menu is defined in the button bindings definitions as:

```
    <Btn1Down>          root          f.menu  RootMenu
```

which can be interpreted as 'when the first mouse button is depressed and the mouse pointer is over the root window, invoke the *mwm f.menu* action to post the *RootMenu*'.

The changes required can now be seen to be a two-stage process: first the description of the new sub-menu has to be provided and then this menu has to be introduced into the default root menu. A suitable definition of a sub-menu could be expressed as:

```
    Menu     SubRootMenu
    {
            "Calculator"         f.exec "xcalc &"
            "System Load"        f.exec "xload &"
            "Remote terminal"    f.exec "rxterm &"
            "Editor"             f.exec "xedit &"
    }
```

To introduce this as a sub-menu option from the root menu, the root menu definition will have to be changed as follows:

```
    Menu RootMenu
    {
            "Root Menu"          f.title
            no-label             f.separator
            "New Window"         f.exec "xterm &"
            no-label             f.separator
```

```
"Applications"          f.menu SubRootMenu
no-label                f.separator
"Shuffle up"            f.circle_up
"Shuffle down"          f.circle_down
"Refresh"               f.refresh
no-label                f.separator
"Restart ..."           f.restart
}
```

As before the changes introduced by these redefinitions will not take effect until the window manager is restarted.

It is possible that because of the precise configuration of the X Window environment these changes will have no effect. If this is the case the most probable cause is that the window manager is looking in the wrong place for its configuration file. This can be corrected by including a direction to *mwm* in the *.Xdefaults* or *Mwm* resource file, telling *mwm* where to look for its configuration file. To inform *mwm* that the configuration file is called '*.mwmrc*' and is located in the home directory, the entry in *.Xdefaults* would be:

```
Mwm*configFile:         .mwmrc
```

If this does not accomplish the customizations, then the system manager or the system manuals should be consulted.

One final customization which can make starting an X session more convenient is to use a *login* file to automatically execute commands when the user logs on. This can be accomplished by including the commands in a file called either "*.xsession*" or "*.xinitrc*" located in the home directory. The name of the file depends upon whether the X server is started using *xdm* or a script such as *startx;* the system manager or manuals should be consulted to determine which. However some care should be taken with this file as any errors in it may cause the system to hang.

This section has introduced only a small number of the customizations which are possible with the window manager. The *mwm* manual pages should be consulted for details of the many other customizations which are possible.

1.7 Some standard clients

The intention of this book is to introduce *Motif* application development. Consequently it is assumed that the reader will be using a workstation running X to produce and compile *Motif* programs written in C. To accomplish this, the terminal will have to be used to interact with the underlying operating system and an editor will have to be used to produce program listings.

By default the *xterm* standard client emulates a VT100 terminal. It is at its most useful if a *scroll bar* is available and if a *save lines* buffer has been established. The contents of the buffer can be scrolled using the *scrollbar*. Selections of the text in the buffer can be made using the mouse. Clicking in the left margin will select a line from the buffer; dragging or double clicking in the text will select a word or multiple words; The selected text is displayed in inverted colors and can be pasted to the current insertion point, usually the command prompt, by use of the second mouse button.

The *xedit* standard client can be used as a simple click and point text editor. The operations available from the keyboard are listed in Table 1.3. The selection and pasting of text within *xedit* is accomplished in the same manner as that described for *xterm* above. It is possible to select and paste text between different clients. Thus a selection can be made in one instance of an *xterm* or *xedit* client and pasted into another instance of *xedit* or *xterm*, or indeed into any other well behaved text based clients.

The editing capabilities of *xedit* are rudimentary. Standard text editors, such as the Unix *vi* or *emacs* editor, can be used instead. The best way of accomplishing this is to launch an *xterm* instance with a suitable title and run *vi* or *emacs* exclusively within the terminal window, saving from the editor when appropriate. Neither the editor nor the terminal need be exited in order to return to the original terminal window to attempt a compilation, or whatever other system actions are required.

Alternatively the functionality of the *xedit* client can be reconfigured, using the resource mechanism, in order to make it emulate part of the functionality and

Table 1.3   Xedit default keyboard bindings

<ctrl> a	move to start of line
<ctrl> b	move backwards one character
<ctrl> d	delete next character
<ctrl> e	move to end of line
<ctrl> f	move forward one character
<ctrl> h	delete previous character
<ctrl> j	newline and indent
<ctrl> k	kill rest of line
<ctrl> m	newline
<ctrl> n	move down one line
<ctrl> o	split line at insertion point
<ctrl> p	move up one line
<ctrl> r	replace text
<ctrl> s	search for text
<ctrl> v	move down one screen
<ctrl> w	kill selected text
<ctrl> y	undo last deletion
<meta>b	move back one word
<meta>f	move forward one word
<meta>d	delete next word
<meta>h	delete previous word
<meta>i	insert file
<meta>v	move up one page
<meta>y	insert current selection
<meta><	move to start of file
<meta>>	move to end of file

keybindings of *vi* or *emacs*, or any other text editor. This approach may make *xedit* more acceptable but will not extend its functionality to that of *vi* or *emacs*.

One other standard client deserves mention. Figure 1.13 illustrates the release 5 version of the *bitmap* client being used to edit a '*warning triangle*' bitmap. The release 3 and 4 versions of the bitmap client have a different appearance but offer similar capabilities. Motif programs are graphical by nature and to be maximally effective should employ graphical communication in favour of text communication where possible and appropriate. The *bitmap* client can be used to prepare bitmaps, which can subsequently be incorporated into clients. The bitmap instance shown in Figure 1.13 was launched with the command line '*bitmap -size 40x40 -basename warning &*', which indicated that a 40 pixel by 40 pixel bitmap called *warning* was to be edited. The operation of the controls on the left of the client, and those on the pull down menus, largely should be obvious apart from the *hot spot* controls. The *hot spot* is used when the *bitmap* editor is being used to edit a

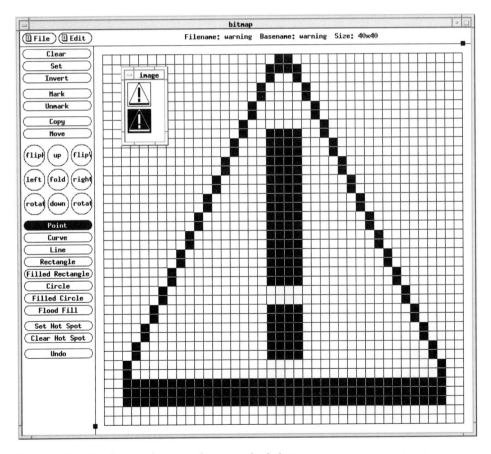

Figure 1.13   The bitmap, bitmap editor, standard client.

\\\

cursor bitmap, and the active point (*hot spot*) of the cursor needs to be defined. The small window contained within the main window shows the appearance of the bitmap being edited in normal and inverted colors.

The output of the *bitmap* client, obtained from the *Write Output* option of the *file menu*, is illustrated in Listing 1.1. It can be seen that this is a textual representation of the bitmap which is suitable for *#inclusion* into a C source code file.

This has necessarily only been a whistle stop tour of the *xterm*, *xedit* and *bitmap* clients. For more details of these and other standard clients which are available the *xman* reference pages, or Volume 5 of the O'Reilly reference set could be consulted.

Listing 1.1   The edited warning.h file from the bitmap client

```
1    /* Filename warning.h contains the warning triangle bitmap.        *
2     * This file was produced by the bitmap client shown in Figure     *
3     * 1.13. These comments were added.                                *
4     */
5
6    #define warning_width   40
7    #define warning_height  40
8
9    #define warning_hot_x   20
10   #define warning_hot_y   35
11
12   static char warning_bits[] = {
13      0x00, 0x00, 0x00, 0x00, 0x00, 0x00, 0x00, 0x18, 0x00, 0x00, 0x00, 0x00,
14      0x24, 0x00, 0x00, 0x00, 0x00, 0x24, 0x00, 0x00, 0x00, 0x00, 0x42, 0x00,
15      0x00, 0x00, 0x00, 0x42, 0x00, 0x00, 0x00, 0x00, 0x81, 0x00, 0x00, 0x00,
16      0x00, 0x81, 0x00, 0x00, 0x00, 0x80, 0x00, 0x01, 0x00, 0x00, 0x80, 0x3c,
17      0x01, 0x00, 0x00, 0x40, 0x3c, 0x02, 0x00, 0x00, 0x40, 0x3c, 0x02, 0x00,
18      0x00, 0x20, 0x3c, 0x04, 0x00, 0x00, 0x20, 0x3c, 0x04, 0x00, 0x00, 0x10,
19      0x3c, 0x08, 0x00, 0x00, 0x10, 0x3c, 0x08, 0x00, 0x00, 0x08, 0x3c, 0x10,
20      0x00, 0x00, 0x08, 0x3c, 0x10, 0x00, 0x00, 0x04, 0x3c, 0x20, 0x00, 0x00,
21      0x04, 0x3c, 0x20, 0x00, 0x00, 0x02, 0x3c, 0x40, 0x00, 0x00, 0x02, 0x3c,
22      0x40, 0x00, 0x00, 0x01, 0x3c, 0x80, 0x00, 0x00, 0x01, 0x3c, 0x80, 0x00,
23      0x80, 0x00, 0x3c, 0x00, 0x01, 0x80, 0x00, 0x3c, 0x00, 0x01, 0x40, 0x00,
24      0x3c, 0x00, 0x02, 0x40, 0x00, 0x3c, 0x00, 0x02, 0x20, 0x00, 0x3c, 0x00,
25      0x04, 0x20, 0x00, 0x00, 0x00, 0x04, 0x10, 0x00, 0x3c, 0x00, 0x08, 0x10,
26      0x00, 0x3c, 0x00, 0x08, 0x08, 0x00, 0x3c, 0x00, 0x10, 0x08, 0x00, 0x3c,
27      0x00, 0x10, 0x04, 0x00, 0x00, 0x00, 0x20, 0x04, 0x00, 0x00, 0x00, 0x20,
28      0xfc, 0xff, 0xff, 0xff, 0x3f, 0xfc, 0xff, 0xff, 0xff, 0x3f, 0xfc, 0xff,
29      0xff, 0xff, 0x3f, 0x00, 0x00, 0x00, 0x00, 0x00};
```

1.8 Activities for Chapter 1

1. The use of an X environment is essential to the production of Motif programs. The activities of this chapter should be reviewed, extended and practised using an X Window environment before proceeding to the next chapter.

2. A useful facility provided by the X environment is one where the contents of an X Window can be printed. The first stage in this process is to obtain an X Window dump using the standard client *xwd*. Taking this as a starting point use *xman* and any other available documentation to obtain a printed image of an X Window.

3. The customization capabilities of an X can make operating within an X environment difficult. The large number of caveats in this chapter are caused by the need to allow for the possibility of local customization. Consider several of the standard tools which you expect to be available in a developmental environment, and consider to what extent the user should be allowed to customize them. Develop this consideration into a policy for application developers who are required to decide which parts of an application should be customizable by the user and which parts should be fixed during production.

\\

CHAPTER TWO

An initial exposure to Motif programming

2.1 An initial client – *xdate*

As with learning to program in other environments, the initial programs which are used to illustrate Motif programming are necessarily short and simple. However, such programs do contain a kernel of concepts which are essential for the comprehension of more complex programs. This chapter will introduce two very simple programs and illustrate the techniques by which they were developed; it is intended that the same development techniques will be used with the more complex programs which follow. Consequently, it is important not to skimp upon the detail which is contained within the simplistic programs in this chapter.

The visual design of the *xdate* client is illustrated in Figure 2.1. The visual design of a client's final appearance is the starting point for any **g**raphical **u**ser **i**nterface (GUI) design process. The visual appearance of a client is important for two reasons. Firstly, the user will be confronted by the graphical nature of the client and will form their initial judgement of the client from it. Secondly, the visual appearance of the client can be used to design the *application widget hierarchy* which is the first stage of developing a Motif GUI for an application.

The *xdate* client is used to display the system date within an X window. It supports no user interactions and thus has no behaviour. More complex clients, which support interactions with the user, require their behaviour to be designed at this stage. Using the visual design of the client as a guide, the *application widget hierarchy* which will be used to implement the client can be produced.

All Motif applications are constructed from *widgets* (***wi***ndow ga***dgets***). A widget is a program object which exists within the client program. Most, but not all,

Figure 2.1   *xdate*, visual design.

widgets have an associated window on the server's screen within which the
widget can display itself. In simple terms a widget consists of its window, a set of
resources which controls its appearance and behaviour, and a set of *methods*
which implement its behaviour. Different *classes* of widgets have different sets of
resources and behaviours, allowing them to implement different user aspects of
interface functionality.

For the *xdate* client the most obvious widget is the one which displays the date.
A suitable widget class to implement this functionality would be the *Label* widget
class. The *Label* widget class allows a string (or an image) to be displayed within
its window. Widgets of the *Label* class do not offer any behaviour to the user.

What is not immediately visually apparent from Figure 2.1 is that there is
another widget behind the label widget. A *label* widget itself cannot interact with
the server or the window manager; only widgets which are derived from a *Shell*
widget class have that functionality. The existence of the *shell* widget can be
visually deduced from the Motif window manager border which is visible in Figure
2.1. This *shell* widget is the *parent* of the *label* widget, and is the top level widget
of this application. The *shell* widget is responsible for any interactions with the
server and window manager. As this shell widget is used to contain an entire
application a suitable class for it is *ApplicationShell*. There are no other widgets
required by this application, so the *application widget hierarchy* can now be
designed. A suitable hierarchy is illustrated in Figure 2.2.

Each widget in an application widget hierarchy requires its widget class to be
identified and requires a name by which it will be known. For most applications
the widget at the top of the hierarchy will be of the *ApplicationShell* widget class
and by convention the name of this widget is *toplevel*. All other widgets used
within the application are descended, directly or indirectly, from this widget. In
the *xdate* application there is only one other widget required, a *label* widget called
date label, which is a *child* of *toplevel*. In an application widget hierarchy each
widget, apart from *toplevel*, has one and only one *parent*; however some widgets
may have more than one *child*.

The C code which implements this widget hierarchy is given in Listing 2.1.
Following the comments at the start of the code, the first line of any interest is the
first *#include* where a programmer supplied header file called *string date (sdate.h)*
is *#included*. This module contains a single function whose prototype is:

toplevel
ApplicationShell

date label
Label

Figure 2.2   *xdate*, application widget hierarchy.

\\\

Listing 2.1   xdate application code

```
1    /* filename xdate.c                                         *
2     *                                                          *
3     * Introductory X/Motif program to display the system      *
4     * date within a label widget.                             *
5     *                                                          *
6     * Fintan Culwin June 93 v1.0                               *
7     */
8
9    #include "sdate.h"
10
11   #include <Xm/Xm.h>
12   #include <X11/Shell.h>
13   #include <Xm/Label.h>
14
15   #define MAX_ARGS      10
16
17   void main ( int argc, char *argv[]){
18
19   char * application_class = "Xdate";
20
21   char          the_date[ MAX_DATE_LENGTH ];
22   XmString      x_the_date;
23
24   XtAppContext  context;
25
26   Widget        toplevel, date_label;
27   Arg           args[ MAX_ARGS ];
28   int           num_args;
29
30       num_args = 0;
31       XtSetArg( args[num_args], XmNallowShellResize, True );
32       num_args++;
33       toplevel = XtAppInitialize( &context,
34                                   application_class,
35                                   NULL, 0,
36                                   &argc, argv,
37                                   NULL,
38                                   args, num_args );
39
40       /* get the date */
41       sdate( the_date );
42       /* convert to XmString */
43       x_the_date = XmStringCreateLtoR( the_date,
44                         XmSTRING_DEFAULT_CHARSET);
45
46       /* create the label widget */
47       num_args = 0;
48       XtSetArg( args[num_args], XmNlabelString, x_the_date );
49                                                 num_args++;
50       date_label = XmCreateLabel( toplevel, "date label",
51                                   args, num_args);
52       XtManageChild( date_label );
53       XmStringFree( x_the_date );
54
55       /* realize the widgets then get and dispatch events */
56       XtRealizeWidget( toplevel );
57       XtAppMainLoop( context );
58   } /* end fun main */
```

```
extern int sdate( char * buffer );
/* function to return the calendar date in the form    *
 * "Day nn Mon yyyy" (e.g. "Tue 18 May 1993").          *
 * buffer is a 16 character string within which the     *
 * string is to be placed.                              *
 * Returns true (1) if successful and the date in the   *
 * buffer, or false (0) if unsuccessful and a null      *
 * string in the buffer.                                *
 */
```

The module also provides a manifest value called MAX_DATE_LENGTH, which defines the number of characters in a date string. The definition of this prototype is contained within the file *sdate.c*, which can be located in Appendix C. The method by which the function *sdate* obtains and formats the date is of no concern to this program; only the calling convention and the logical actions of the function should be considered relevant.

The listing continues by *#including* two X header files called *"Shell.h"* and *"Label.h"*. These header files contain the public details of the *ApplicationShell* and *Label* widget classes. Each widget class supplied by Motif has a header file containing the declarations of its public aspects. Any program which uses a widget of a particular class must include the relevant header file in order to obtain access to that class's public aspects. The class header files also ensure that the general Motif header file (*Xm.h*), the intrinsics header file (*intrinsic.h*) and the protocol header file (*X11.h*) are also *#includ*ed. The distinctions between these different layers will be made clear later in this chapter.

The *main()* function of the program commences with the declaration of the required variables. The first of these is a constant string which contains the application's class name. As explained in Chapter 1 an X client can be identified by its instance name (*xdate*) or by its class name (*XDate*). It is a useful documentation feature to have the class name explicitly declared at this point in the program. The asciiz string variable which will contain the date is then declared, followed by an associated variable of type *XmString*. Motif uses a more complex string representation than C, and provides an abstract data type called *XmString* to implement it. The details of the *XmString* data type will be explained in the following chapter.

The next declaration is a variable of type *XtAppContext* (*application context*) which is by convention called *context*. It is possible for a single application to have more than one toplevel widget and the corresponding windows may be on different servers; all the programs in this book will use a single toplevel widget.

The widget application hierarchy can be used to list the widgets which will be required to construct the application. The names of the widget program variables need not be the same as the names of the widgets from the hierarchy, but it prevents confusion if the same names are used. The next line of the program listing declares the two widget variables (*toplevel* and *date_label*) which will be required by this application.

The final declarations are an array of type *Arg* (*arguments*) and an associated

\\\

integer counter; these can best be considered as a single structure known as an *argument list*. The maximum number of arguments in the array is determined by a manifest value which has already been *#defined* in the program header. Argument lists are used to communicate resources to widgets as they are created.

The executable part of the listing commences with the creation of the *toplevel* widget using the intrinsics function *XtAppInitialize*. Prior to creating and returning the *toplevel* widget this function performs a large number of other housekeeping tasks concerned with initializing the intrinsics toolkit, creating the application context and opening a connection between the client and server machines. Should any of these operations fail, an error message will be output on *stderr* and the program will terminate. The prototype of *XtAppInitialize* is:

```
Widget XtAppInitialize(  XtAppContext *      context,
                         String              application_class,
                         XrmOrdinalDescList  options,            /*NULL*/
                         Cardinal            num_options,        /*zero*/
                         Cardinal    *       argc_in_out,        /*&argc*/
                         String      *       argv_in_out,        /*argv*/
                         String      *       fallback_resources,/*NULL*/
                         ArgList             args,
                         Cardinal            num_args );
```

The first two parameters, the *context* and the *application_class*, have already been described and provided for. The next two parameters, *options* and *num_options*, can be used to identify application specific command line options. For simple programs it is appropriate to specify the values NULL and ZERO (0), indicating that no specific command line options are supported.

The next two parameters are the command line parameters *argc* and *argv*, from the *main()* function. The initialization of the application will remove any standard X command line options, such as *-foreground blue*, from the *argv/ argc* structure. As the removal may change the number of parameters in the list, *argc* has to be passed by reference.

The next parameter, *fallback_resources*, can be used to specify an application class resource list which will be used if no application class resources can be located in the default resources files. It is appropriate to specify NULL here for simple programs.

The final parameters, *args* and *num_args*, are used to specify resource values which will be communicated to the *toplevel* shell as it is created. In this program the *toplevel* shell resource *XmNallowShellResize* has been specified *True* in the *args/ num_args* structure, immediately prior to the call to *XtAppInitialize*. This technique of intializing the *num_args* counter to zero and then setting subsequent values of the *ArgList* array using the macro *XtSetArg*, should be regarded as a cliché. The technique will be used repeatedly throughout the programs in this book to communicate resource values to widgets as they are created. It is also used to change the values of a widget's resources after it has been created or to retrieve resource values from a widget.

The major resources of the *ApplicationShell* widget class are listed in Table 2.1. The only resource which has an inappropriate default value is *allowShellResize* which has the value *False*. The default setting will prevent the shell widget from resizing itself should any of its children resize themselves. This default behaviour is less friendly than the alternative behaviour where the size of the shell changes in response to changes in the sizes of the shell's children, consequently it is set *True* by the program as the shell is created.

As mentioned above, *XtSetArg* is a macro, not a function. It requires three parameters. The first is an *Arg* structure where the *resource/ value* pair will be stored. The second parameter is the manifest name of the resource and the third is the value of the resource. The manifest name of a resource can be obtained from tables such as Table 2.1, by prepending *XmN* to the resource name.

The precise details of what tasks are carried out by *XtAppInitialize* and how they are carried out need not be understood in detail. The example given can be used unchanged to initialize an application and create the *toplevel* widget for all simple Motif clients.

The program listing continues with a call to the utility function *sdate*, to obtain

Table 2.1 *ApplicationShell* widget class major resources

inheritance hierarchy   core -> composite -> Shell -> WMShell -> VendorShell -> topLevelShell -> ApplicationShell

Resource name	type	(default) values	inherited from
mwmDecorations	manifest (unsigned char)	MWM_DECOR_ALL (default) MWM_DECOR_BORDER MWM_DECOR_RESIZEH MWM_DECOR_TITLE MWM_DECOR_SYSTEM MWM_DECOR_MINIMIZE MWM_DECOR_MAXIMIZE	VendorShell
controls the window manager decoration (values can be logically anded together)			
iconPixmap	Pixmap	NULL	WMShell
the pixmap to be used when the client is iconified, null specified default			
title	String	client instance name	WMShell
the string to be displayed in the window border title component			
allowShellResize	Boolean	False	Shell
if true shell will resize to accommodate its child widget when it resizes			
geometry	String	NULL	Shell
height	Dimension	0	Core
width	Dimension	0	Core
x	Position	0	Core
y	Position	0	Core
the position (on the display's root window) and size (not always in pixels)			

the system date in a suitable format. Subsequently, the date is converted from a C standard asciiz string to an *XmString*, using a conversion function provided by the Motif toolkit. More details of *XmStrings* will be given in the next chapter.

The *XmString* is then installed in the argument list as a *labelString* resource using the same *XtSetArg* technique described above. The *labelString* resource of a *label* widget specifies the string which is to be displayed within the widget's window. This resource is communicated to the *label* widget when it is created by the Motif convenience function *XmCreateLabel*. The prototype of the *XmCreateLabel* function is:

```
Widget XmCreateLabel (Widget     parent,
                      String     name,
                      ArgList    args,
                      Cardinal   num_args );
```

Every widget, with the exception of the *toplevel* widget, has one and only one parent widget. The identity of the parent widget is specified in the first parameter of the *XmCreate{widgetclass}* convenience functions, and can be determined from the application widget hierarchy diagram. The second parameter is the name of the widget which can also be determined from the application widget hierarchy diagram. It is the value of this parameter which is used by the resource mechanism to identify widgets and their resources. The program variable of type *Widget* need not have the same name, although it avoids a great deal of confusion if it does. The final parameters are the *args/ num_args* argument list which communicates programmer defined resource values to the widget as it is created.

The effect of the function is to create and return an instance of the *label* widget class, with the parent, name and resources as specified. The widget's resources are determined from the *arg/ num_arg* argument list, the resource file mechanism and the class default values, in that order of priority. Thus a resource value specified in the program code has precedence over any resource value specified by the user in their resource files. Consequently the only resources which should be specified in the program code are those which are essential to the application's functionality. All other resources should be specified in resource files in order to allow the user to tailor the application's non-functional aspects to their individual requirements. The major resources of the *Label* widget class are listed in Table 2.2.

A widget created by the *XmCreate{widgetclass}* convenience function is created in an *unmanaged* state; before the widget can become visible to the user it has to be managed. This is accomplished with the intrinsics function *XtManageChild*; the single parameter of this function is the identity of the widget to be *managed*. An explanation of precisely what *managing* a widget involves will be given later in this chapter.

Finally, before the main part of the application can commence, the *XmString* used to communicate the *labelString* resource to the *label* widget should be destroyed. The *label* widget has taken a copy of the string and consequently the value in the program is redundant. The destruction of the string is accomplished

\\\

Table 2.2 Label widget class, major resources

inheritance hierarchy   core -> primitive -> label

Resource name	type	(default) values
labelType	manifest	XmSTRING (default)
	(unsigned char)	XmPIXMAP
string or pixmap type label		
labelString	XmString	instance name of widget
fontList	XmFontList	"Fixed"
alignment	manifest	XmALIGNMENT_CENTRE (default)
	(unsigned char)	XmALIGNMENT_END
		XmALIGNMENT_BEGINNING
the label string, its fonts and its alignment within the widget		
labelInsensitivePixmap	Pixmap	default pixmap
labelPixmap	Pixmap	default pixmap
the pixmaps to use if the labelType is XmPIXMAP		
marginBottom	short	0
marginHeight	short	2
marginLeft	short	0
marginRight	short	0
marginTop	short	0
marginWidth	short	2
the amount of space around the label before the shadow, width and height are symmetrical		

with the *XmStringFree* function, as shown in the listing.

The main part of the application consists of two function calls. The first, to *XtRealizeWidget,* causes all managed widgets in the application widget hierarchy to become visible on the screen. The second call, to *XtAppMainLoop,* has the effect of transferring control from the program to the user's interactions with the widgets. As this program has no user interactions associated with it, this has little effect.

The outline of the code contained within this application can be used by all Motif programs:

> *Initialize the application and create the top level widget.*

> *Create all remaining widgets from the application hierarchy specifying their resources and behaviours.*

> *Realize the top level widget which will realize all other widgets and pass control over to the main event loop.*

The complexity of other clients is contained partly within their widget hierarchies, but particularly within the behaviours which are associated with their widgets. This is a simple application with no behaviour, and consequently has a simple implementation. A more complex version of this program which includes some behaviour will be introduced later in this chapter.

2.2 Protocols, intrinsics and widgets

The program presented in the previous section used various Motif facilities, which can be identified by the prefix *Xm*. The listing also used *intrinsics* facilities, which can be identified by the prefix *Xt*. The distinction between these two layers can initially be very confusing, Figure 2.3 is a diagram illustrating the different layers within the X/Motif programming environment which a Motif programmer has to be aware of.

The lowest layer of the diagram is the operating system and protocol layer and, as indicated, is invisible to the Motif programmer. X is an operating system independent windowing environment, consequently the facilities of a particular operating system should not be relied upon if operating system independent clients are to be produced. This hidden layer also contains the X protocol layer which contains the very low level networking and windowing facilities. The protocol layer is hidden underneath the X library layer (*Xlib*), which provides a one to one C binding of the protocol facilities. Thus every protocol facility in the protocol layer has an associated C function call in the X library layer.

The library level functions and facilities can be identified in program code by the prefix *X*. The library layer knows about windows on the server's display, but does not know about widgets. An interface which was developed using only

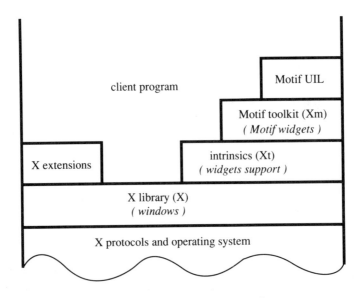

Figure 2.3   Motif from a programmer's point of view.

X library facilities would have to take responsibility for implementing all required functionality. In the *xdate* example program used in the previous section, the *label* widget 'knew' how to display its *labelString* resource. All that was required of the programmer was to inform the widget of the value of this resource, and it was automatically displayed within the widget's window. If the same program were to be developed using only *Xlib* facilities the programmer would have had to explicitly draw the *labelString* in the window after they had explicitly created the window with the required size.

One useful analogy of the differences between the library and the intrinsics layer is to think of the library layer as assembler code and to regard the intrinsics layer as a high level language. The advantages of using a high level language compared with assembler should be sufficiently obvious. There is one aspect of Motif programming where X library facilities are required; the library provides a set of low level graphics primitives which can be used to draw directly into a widget's window. The *Xlib* graphics primitives will be introduced later in this book.

The intrinsics layer mainly provides support for *widgets*, not exclusively those from the Motif toolkit. The intention is to provide a set of resources and facilities which provide a consistent platform upon which GUI functionality can be built, without dictating a particular *look and feel*. The *Xcalc* client, illustrated in Figure 1.3, is built from the Athena, not the Motif widget set. It is able to co-operate with the Motif window manager, as shown in Figures 1.2 and 1.3, as it relies upon the same conventions, intrinsics and *XLib* support as all other well behaved clients.

The intrinsics layer is able to manage any widget, without regard for the widget set which provides it and without regard for the particular class of widget within a widget set. It is able to do this as every widget is expected to supply a defined set of *methods*, including a creation method, a destruction method, a mapping method, a resize method etc. The intrinsics layer is not concerned with the details of how a widget implements these methods; all it is concerned with is providing the support for these methods to be called when required.

The Motif layer provides a set of widgets which have a consistent *look and feel*, allowing a complete GUI to be built with visual and behavioural consistency between the components. This consistency is in part provided by the toolkit and is supported by the *Motif Style Guide*, which suggests ways in which Motif widgets should be connected together. The intention is that if all Motif programmers comply with the style guide then the user will experience consistency between different applications.

There are other components which may be present in the Motif programmer's environment. Motif also supplies a *User Interface Language* (*UIL*); this allows Motif widgets, their resources and the application hierarchy to be expressed in a higher level abstract manner. Although this can simplify some aspects of Motif programming it does not offer any effective support for the definition of programmer supplied widget behaviours. The aspects of Motif programming which it does support are largely mechanistic and rather than involve explanation of a further layer in this book, the UIL will be omitted.

Also shown on Figure 2.3, are the conceptual location of any X extensions which may be available. Two such extensions are the *PHIGS* extension to X (*pex*) and the *UNIRAS* extension to X (*aux*). These are two different and complementary toolkits which provide a higher level of graphics functionality than that provided by *Xlib*. Other extensions which may be present include support for sound, support for video or support for manufacturer specific facilities. As these extensions are at the time of writing not a required part of an X or X/Motif distribution, it cannot be assumed that they are present in the environment and this book will not consider them further.

2.3 A whistle stop tour of Motif widgets

Figure 2.4 presents 'The Periodic Table of Motif Widgets', which attempts to classify most of the Motif widget classes. This section will briefly describe each of these classes and then introduce the Motif *widget class hierarchy*. The intention here is not to provide a complete description of all Motif widget classes, but to provide an overview from which a particular widget class can be considered for a particular requirement. Many, but not all, of the widget classes will be introduced at different stages, later in this book.

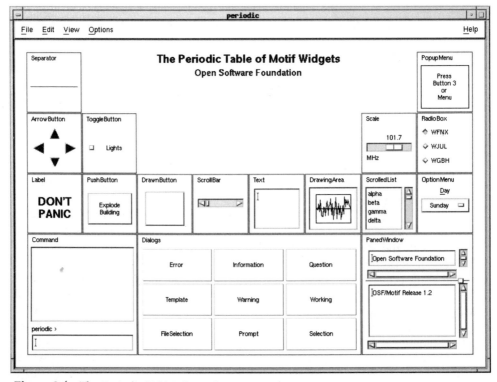

Figure 2.4   The Periodic Table of Motif Widgets.

The *XmSeparator* widget class is mostly used to draw a horizontal or vertical line between options on menus. Separators can be seen on the Motif window menu and root menu illustrated in Chapter 1. The *XmArrowButton* widget class can display its arrow in one of four orientations and can have programmer specified behaviour supplied for when it is pushed. The *XmLabel* widget class has already been introduced as a widget which is able to display a string or a pixmap. The *XmPushButton* widget class can be regarded as a *label* widget with push button behaviour added; it is usual for the programmer to specify application behaviour which is to be performed when the button is pressed.

An instance of the *XmToggleButton* widget class is usually used in combination with other instances of the same class to offer *n of many* choices to the user. In contrast the *XmRadioBox* widget contains a set of *toggleButtons* which offer *1 of many* choices to the user.

The *XmOptionMenu* widget also offers *1 of many* choices to the user. When the active component of the menu is pressed a menu is posted and one of the options of the menu can be chosen. The chosen option is then displayed as the active component. In contrast the *XmPulldownMenu* is used to offer choices of actions to the user. A *pull down* menu is used for the Motif window menus as described in Chapter 1. The *pop up* menu differs from a *pull down* or an *option* menu in not having a button from which it is activated. A *pop up* menu is used for the Motif root window menu as described in Chapter 1.

It is possible to attach further menus to the options which are offered by *pull down* or *pop up* menus. The extended *mwm* root menu from Chapter 1 provides an example of this facility. Such menus are known as *cascade menus*, and are not illustrated in the periodic table.

The *XmText* widget can be used to display or to edit, single line or multiple line asciiz strings. The Athena widget set version of the *text* widget was used to implement the main work area of the *xterm* and *xedit* clients introduced in Chapter 1. When only a single line of text is required the *XmTextField*, which is not shown, can be used.

The *XmScale* widget class allows a numeric value to be entered by interactively dragging a slider along a scale. The *composite* widget class *XmScrollBar* consists of a scale with arrow buttons at each end. A *composite* widget is one which contains instances of other widgets within itself. The *scrollBar* itself is a component part of another composite widget class, the *XmScrolledList* widget class, which hooks together a *scrollBar* and a *text* widget allowing single or multiple selections to be made from a list.

The *XmPanedWindow* provides a window *pane* which can be manipulated by the user to vary the amount of space accorded to each of its component parts. Window panes are present in the *xedit* client which was introduced in Chapter 1. The *XmDrawingArea* and *XmDrawButton* widget classes provide a *canvas* upon which the programmer can use *Xlib* graphics primitives to produce graphical output.

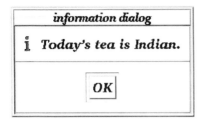
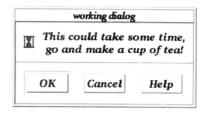

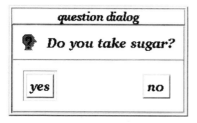
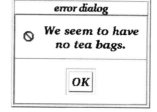

Figure 2.5   The *messageBox* dialogs.

Figure 2.6   The *prompt* dialog.

The series of dialog widgets in the top two rows of the middle of the periodic table are all instances of the *XmMessageBox* widget class, which provides a convenient means of implementing a short interaction with the user. Several of the *messageBox* dialogs are illustrated in Figure 2.5. The *prompt* dialog, shown in Figure 2.6, provides the capability to accept a short string from the user. The *selection* dialog, shown in Figure 2.7, provides a *prompt* dialog combined with a *scrolledList* and a number of *pushButtons*. The *command* widget, shown on the

Figure 2.7 The *selection* dialog.

periodic table, is similar to a *selectionBox* dialog maintaining a history of the commands which have been issued.

The most complex composite widget is the *fileSelectionBox* widget shown in Figure 2.8, which provides an interface to the underlying file system allowing the user to interactively navigate the directory structure and select or enter a filename.

Other useful widget classes which are not illustrated in the Periodic Table include the *XmFrame* widget class which provides a Motif standard border to its single child widget and the *XmCascadeButton* which is used to control pull down menus.

One complete set of widget classes is not illustrated at all in the table. The *shell* widget classes which allow interaction with the window manager, and whose windows are children of the display's root window are omitted. The dialogs shown in Figures 2.5 to 8 are instances of the appropriate widget contained within a *dialogShell*. The *dialogShell* widgets shown in Figures 2.5 to 8 can be distinguished from the *applicationShell* widgets shown in Figures 2.1 and 2.4 in not having *iconify* or *maximize* buttons. It is not possible for a dialog to be iconified or maximized independently from its parent shell, and thus it does not need these decorations.

Likewise the most useful members of the set of classes known as the *Constraint* widgets, which provide mechanisms for the placement of their multiple child widgets, are not illustrated. The relation of these classes to other classes can be illustrated in the Motif *widget class hierarchy,* shown in Figure 2.9.

This diagram may initially look rather intimidating but it greatly simplifies the understanding of the different classes of Motif widgets. To take an example: the *PushButton* widget class, which will be introduced later in this chapter, has a total of 61 different resources. It would seem that to have a complete understanding of

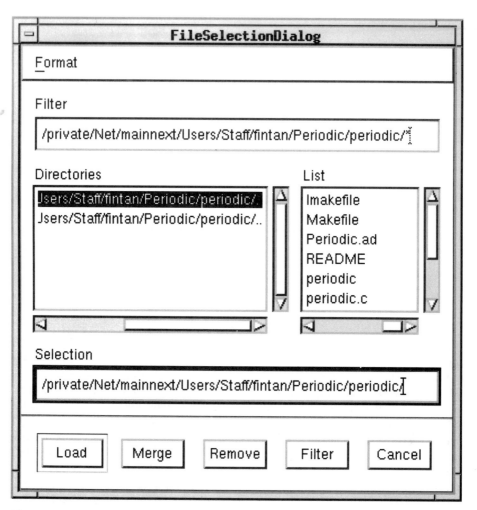

Figure 2.8 The *fileselection* dialog.

a *pushButton* all 61 resources would have to be understood. However the *pushButton* widget class itself only introduces 9 new resources; the remaining 52 resources are *inherited* from its parent class, the *Label* widget class.

The 9 new resources which the *pushButton* class introduces are all concerned with implementing and supporting push button behaviour. The 9 new resources are listed in Table 2.3. The relationship betwen the *label* and *pushButton* widget classes can be understood by considering a *pushButton* widget as a *label* widget which has had push button functionality added to it.

The sibling classes of the *PushButton* class, the *DrawButton*, *CascadeButton* and *ToggleButton* classes, each introduce some new resources, but each also inherits the 52 resources supplied by the *Label* widget class. Some of the resources which are introduced by the sibling classes are particular to their required functionality but

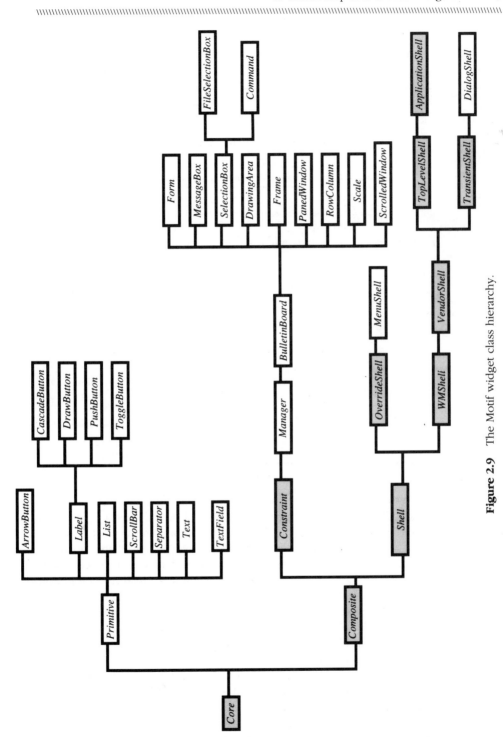

Figure 2.9 The Motif widget class hierarchy.

\\

Table 2.3   PushButton widget class resources

inheritance hierarchy   core -> primitive -> label -> pushButton

Resource name	type	(default) values
activateCallback	CallbackList	NULL
actions to be performed when the button is pressed and released		
armCallback	CallbackList	NULL
actions to be performed when the button is pressed		
armColor	Pixel	dynamic
color to use to show the button is armed		
armPixmap	Pixmap	unspecified
pixmap to use when the button is armed if labelType is XmPIXMAP		
defaultButton--ShadowThickness	Dimension	dynamic
determines the thickness of the shadow when the button is emphasized as the default		
disarmCallback	CallbackList	NULL
actions to be performed when the button is released		
fillOnArm	Boolean	True
allows color change upon arming		
multiClick	manifest (unsigned char)	XmMULTICLICK_DISCARD XmMULTICLICK_KEEP
determines if the button is sensitive to multiple clicks		
showAsDefault	short	0
shadow thickness when the button is emphasized as the default		

some are common to all buttons. For example, the *CascadeButton* class introduces a resource which identifies the menu which is to be pulled down when it is pressed; no other button requires this resource. The *ToggleButton* introduces a resource which identifies it as a *1 of many* or an *n of many* toggle button and no other button class requires this resource. All the button classes require a resource which can be used to identify the actions to be performed when it is pressed; each button class introduces this resource independently, but all buttons contain the resource.

Thus an understanding of the *Label* widget class resources will cause an understanding of most of the resources of any button and an understanding of the resources of any button class will contain some knowledge which can be generalized to other button classes.

The *Label* button class itself only introduces 18 of its 52 resources; the remaining 34 resources are inherited from its class parent the *Primitive* widget class. These 34 resources are inherited by all of *Primitive*'s child classes. To complete the picture of resource inheritance within the class hierarchy, the *Primitive* class introduces 15 resources and inherits the remaining 19 resources from the *Core* widget class. As the *Core* widget class is at the top of the class hierarchy these 19 resources are common to all widgets.

The resources which are supplied by the *Core* widget class are applicable to all Motif widgets; the most useful of them are listed in Table 2.4. The resources which are supplied by the *Primitive* widget class are applicable to all widget classes in the class hierarchy below the *Primitive* class. Such widgets are collectively known as *Primitive* widgets, and the most useful resources supplied by the *Primitive* class are listed in Table 2.5.

The major classes of all widgets are thus the *primitive* classes which are all single widgets with a specific function and the *composite* widget classes which are

Table 2.4 Core widget class major resources

inheritance hierarchy   core

Resource name	type	(default) values
background	Pixel	varies
determines the background color of the widget		
backgroundPixmap	Pixmap	XmUNSPECIFIED_PIXMAP
the background pattern of the widget		
borderColor	Pixel	XtDefaultForeground
determines the border color of the widget		
borderWidth	Dimension	1
determines the border width of the widget		
colormap	Colormap	varies
determines the relationship between pixel values and displayed colors		
depth	int	varies
determines the number of z planes used by the widget		
destroyCallback	CallbackList	NULL
actions to be performed before the widget is explicitly destroyed		
height	Dimension	varies
the height of the widget (not always in pixels)		
mappedWhenManaged	Boolean	True
if true the widget will be mapped (on the screen) whenever it is managed		
sensitive	Boolean	True
if false the widget will not respond to input events		
width	Dimension	varies
the width of the widget (not always in pixels)		
x	Position	0
the x location of the widget, relative to its parent		
y	Position	0
the y location of the widget, relative to its parent		

\\

Table 2.5   Primitive widget class major resources

inheritance hierarchy   core -> primitive

Resource name	type	(default) values
foreground	Pixel	varies
determines the foreground color of the widget		
helpCallback	CallbackList	NULL
actions to be performed when help is requested		
highlightOnEnter	Boolean	False
if true the widget will highlight when the mouse pointer enters its window		
highlightThickness	Dimension	2
determines the thickness of the highlight rectangle		
shadowThickness	Dimension	2
determines the thickness of the widget's shadow		
userData	XtPointer	NULL
allows user data to be attached to the widget		

containers for one or more children. The composite widgets divide into the *shell* widget classes and the *constraint* widget classes. The *shell* widget classes can only have a single child widget and contain the functionality to interact with the window manager. The *constraint* widget classes may have a number of children and take responsibility for the placement of those children.

As suggested by the title of this section, this is only a 'whistle stop' tour of the major Motif widget classes and their children. More detail will be added to some of these classes and to the widget class hierarchy in the chapters which follow.

Several points of potential confusion need to be emphasized before this tour can conclude. The first is that the *application widget hierarchy* and the *widget class hierarchy* are very distinct concepts. There is an *application widget hierarchy* for every application which is built: it describes the relationships between the widget *instances* within a particular application. There is only one *widget class hierarchy;* it describes the relationships between the widget *classes*.

The distinction between application and class hierarchies also subsumes a second point of potential confusion, between *classes* and *instances*. This distinction is analogous to the distinction between *types* and *variables* in high level programming languages. A class is analogous to a type; a type defines the range of values and the operations which can be performed on a variable of that type. An instance is analogous to a variable: a variable is defined by its own name and can only have the values or undergo the operations which are allowed for that type. Likewise a *class* defines the allowable nature of the *instances* of that class and defines the operations which can be performed upon the instances. The operations which can be performed are commonly known as *methods*.

The concepts of *classes, inheritance, instances* and *methods* are derived from *object oriented programming* (OOP) methodologies. There is not sufficient space in this book to give more than a brief overview of OOP techniques which are used to implement the Motif widgets, and which will also be used in a weaker form to implement the client programs which follow. Suggestions of other books which deal exclusively with OOP are given in Appendix A.

The final point of confusion is the relationship between the intrinsics and the Motif widgets. Many widget requirements are common to all widgets, not only those provided by Motif; these requirements are supplied by the intrinsic widget classes. In Figure 2.5 the widget classes at the top of the hierarchy, shown in shaded boxes, are supplied by the intrinsics. The widget classes at the bottom of the hierarchy, shown in normal boxes, are supplied by Motif. The intrinsic widgets are only used to supply resources common to all widgets, and consequently instances of these widgets are not normally created.

2.4 Adding behaviour to *xdate – xdtime*

In this section the client which was developed in Section 2.1, *xdate*, will be extended to add some user interface functionality. To introduce this process the *label* widget used in the first version of *xdate* will have to be replaced with a *pushButton* widget. As explained in the previous section the *PushButton* widget class is a child class of the *Label* class, consequently the *pushButton* instance will support all the resources of the *label* instance which it is replacing.

To change the *label* widget to a *pushButton* widget the Motif convenience function which creates the widget will have to be changed from *XmCreateLabel* to *XmCreatePushButton*. When this is effected the *#inclusion* of the <Xm/Label.h> header file will have to be replaced with the *#inclusion* of the <Xm/PushB.h> header file. Although it is not strictly required, the name of what was the *label* widget *date_label* should be changed to *dtime_button* and the application widget hierarchy as presented in Figure 2.2 similarly amended.

The revised version of the *xdate* program, known as *xdtime*, has an initial visual appearance which is identical to the previous version of the program. However, the *pushButton* widget supports user interaction in that it 'knows' how to be

Figure 2.10   *xdtime*, armed and disarmed.

\\

pushed. When the mouse pointer is positioned on the button and the first mouse button is pressed, the visual appearance of the widget changes to indicate that it has been pushed. Figure 2.10 shows the *xdtime* pushbutton widget in its normal and pushed appearances. The shadows surrounding the button have been exaggerated to make the differences between the visual appearance of an unpushed and pushed button more apparent.

The ability to be pushed is built into all instances of the *PushButton* widget class. A *pushButton* in its normal state is known as *disarmed;* a *pushButton* in its pushed state is known as *armed.* In order for a push button to achieve something useful when it is pushed there has to be some mechanism by which programmer defined behaviour can be added to the widget.

The mechanism to add application specific behaviour to a widget is supplied by the intrinsics and is known as the *callback* mechanism. The reasons why the term *callback* is used will be explained later in this chapter. A widget class which supports user interaction will provide *callback resources* which can be used to add behaviour. Table 2.3 indicates that the *PushButton* widget class supports three callback resources: the *activateCallback*, the *armCallback* and the *disarmCallback*. The application programmer can add behaviours to any or all of these *callback* resources. These behaviours are defined by the programmer in the form of *callback functions.* If the programmer were to provide a callback function which caused the terminal to bleep and installed this callback as a *pushButton*'s *armCallback* resource, then the terminal would bleep every time the *pushButton* was armed.

A callback function's prototype is strictly defined as:

```
void any_callback_function( Widget     widget,
                            XtPointer client_data,
                            XtPointer call_data);
```

The first parameter is of type *Widget* and when the function is executed will contain the identity of the widget which caused the callback function to be called. If a callback function was attached to the *dtime_button*'s *armCallback*, then when the mouse button was pressed the callback function would be called, and the identity of the Widget in the first parameter would be *dtime_button*.

The second and third parameters are of type *XtPointer*. This type can be considered largely equivalent to the C standard type *caddr_t* (C address type). C address type is an untyped pointer (*void**) which allows a pointer variable of that type to point to any C type. In the context of a callback function the *XtPointer* parameters can point to, or sometimes contain, a variable of any type. The second parameter, the *client_data* parameter, is available for the application programmer to use to supply data to the callback. The third parameter, the *call_data* parameter is used by the intrinsics to supply data to the callback.

To construct a callback function which will cause the terminal to bleep the *Xlib* function *XBell* can be used. The prototype for this function is:

```
void XBell( Display * display,
            int       loudness );
```

The *loudness* parameter determines the loudness of the bell in the range 0 to 100. The *display* parameter effectively identifies the server whose bell is to be rung. The identity of the display can be determined for any widget, by using the intrinsics function *XtDisplay*. The prototype for this function is:

```
Display * XtDisplay( Widget widget );
```

where the *widget* parameter is the identity of any widget whose window is being displayed by the server. Using these two functions the callback function can be defined as:

```
void bleep_callback( Widget       widget,
                     XtPointer  client_data,
                     XtPointer  call_data   ){
/* Utility callback to cause the server to bleep. *
 * Uses the Widget parameter only.                *
 */

   XBell( XtDisplay( widget), 100 );
} /* end fun bleep callback */
```

Assuming that the callback function has been declared and the *dtime_button* has been created, the callback can be added to the *dtime_button*'s *armCallback callbackList* resource using the intrinsics function *XtAddCallback*. The prototype for this function is:

```
void XtAddCallback( Widget         widget,
                    String         callback_name,
                    XtCallbackProc callback_function,
                    XtPointer      client_data );
```

where the *widget* parameter identifies the widget to add the callback to and the *callback_name* parameter is the name of the *callback* resource to which the callback is to be added. The *callback_function* parameter identifies the callback function to be added and the *client_data* parameter identifies any application data to be supplied. The appropriate call to *XtAddCallback* which will add the *bleep_callback* to the *date_button*'s *armCallback* resource is thus:

```
XtAddCallback( dtime_button,  XmNarmCallback,
               bleep_callback, (XtPointer) NULL );
```

As there is no *client_data* supplied to the *bleep_callback* when it is called, the last parameter has been specified as NULL. An explicit cast of this value to the *XtPointer* type has been employed as an example of good practice. C is quite happy to change the type of the value automatically; however, it is regarded as good programming style to ensure that all values are explicitly *cast* into the required type rather than to rely upon *promotion*. It is sometimes possible that C will automatically promote a value to a type which the programmer does not expect; with casting this can never happen.

The installation of the *bleep_callback* can take place at any time after the *dtime_button* has been created: the most suitable place would be immediately

\\\

following the creation and management of the *dtime_button*.

Having explored the construction, installation and use of callbacks, the mechanism can now be employed to do something more useful than cause the server to bleep when the *dtime_button* is pressed. It is useful to know the date; it is equally useful to know the time. The *xdate* client will be expanded so that when the button is pressed the time accurate to the nearest minute will be displayed. When the button is pressed a second time, the date will be redisplayed. If the button is double clicked when the date is displayed the application is to terminate. If the button is double clicked when the time is displayed the time will be updated. The visual appearance of the two states is shown in Figure 2.11.

The first stage in designing a client is to design the usability of the client using a *s*tate *t*ransition *d*iagram (STD). Although the usability of this client is simple enough for it to be clearly expressed in the English sentences above, this is not the case for more complex clients. By initially using state transition diagrams to describe the usability of simple clients the techniques will be understood when they are required for the design of more complex clients. The state transition diagram for the expanded *xdate* client, known as *xdtime*, is shown in Figure 2.12.

Full details of the notation, construction and use of state transition diagrams will be given in the next and subsequent chapters. For the moment all that is required is to note that the client undergoes an automatic transition into the *date display* state when it is launched. There are two transitions from this state. When the user presses the *dtime_button* the application moves to the *time display* state. A transition from the *time display* state back to the *date display* state occurs when the *dtime_button* is pressed in the time display state. As the application is now

Figure 2.11 *xdtime*, visual designs.

back in the *date display* state, pressing the *dtime_button* a third time will toggle to the *time_display* state, and so on.

When the application is in the *time display* state a double click on the button will cause a transition back to the same state with the time updated. When the application is in the *date display* state a double click will cause the application to terminate. This is not generally regarded as good practice as it is too easy for the user to accidentally *double click* the button and terminate the application without any possibility of confirming the action. The exit transition is included in this design only to illustrate the implementation of double click transitions in *pushButton* widgets.

The transitions are implemented in a Motif program by adding a callback function to the *dtime_button*'s *activate callback* resource. The implementation of this callback function will make use of a function called *stime*, provided by a module called *sdtime*; the construction and usage of *stime* is analogous to the function *sdate* used in the construction of *xdate*. The prototype of this function contained in *sdtime.h* is:

```
extern int stime( char * buffer );
/* function to return the clock time in the form  *
 * "hh:mm". hh is the clock hour in the range 00  *
 * to 23 and mm is the clock minutes in the range *
```

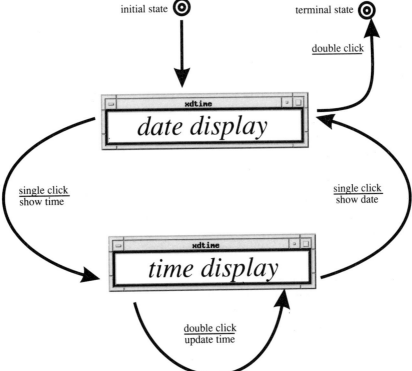

Figure 2.12   *xdtime*, state transition diagram.

\\\

```
 * 00 to 59.                                          *
 * buffer is a character string within which the      *
 * time string is to be placed.                       *
 * Returns true (1) if successful and the time in     *
 * the buffer, or false (0) if unsuccessful and a     *
 * null string in the buffer.                         *
 */
```

Using this function the callback function can be declared. The name of the function will be *date_time_transition_callback*. The function prototype will conform to the required prototype for a callback function given above. The function will make no use of the *client_data* parameter, but will have to examine the *call_data* parameter to determine if the callback function was called by a single or double click. The *call_data* parameter for callbacks attached to any *pushButton* widget is of type *XmPushButtonCallbackStruct*, whose structure is:

```
typedef struct {
           int       reason;
           XEvent * event;
           int       click_count;
      } XmPushButtonCallbackStruct;
```

The first of these parameters, *reason*, contains a manifest value indicating why the callback was called. For a callback attached to the *activateCallback* resource of a pushButton widget the value is *XmNactivateCallback*. All Motif *call_data* callback structures have a *reason* field as the first member of the structure. It is sometimes useful to examine this value when a callback function is attached to more than one resource, but in most cases it can be ignored. The second parameter, *event*, is a pointer to the X library *XEvent* data structure which was generated in the library layer and passed to the callback function by the intrinsics. It is often necessary to examine the contents of this structure and details of how to do so will be introduced in subsequent chapters. The final parameter, *click_count*, is only valid if the *pushButton* resource *multiClick* is set to *XmMULTICLICK_KEEP*.

The execution of the function will have to decide between the four possible transitions. If the button was double clicked in the date display state then the application should terminate, otherwise if the button was single clicked in the date display state the transition to the time display state should be implemented, otherwise the transition to the date display state should be implemented.

The exit transition is straightforward, calling the C standard *exit()* function. The other transitions can be implemented by obtaining the clock time or the date as an asciiz string, by converting the asciiz string to an *XmString*, and installing this string as the *labelString* resource of the *dtime_button*. The value of a widget's resource can be changed after it has been created using the intrinsics function *XtSetValues*. The prototype of this function is:

```
void XtSetValues( Widget    widget,
                  ArgList   args,
                  int       num_args);
```

Listing 2.2   xdtime application code

```
1    /* filename xdtime.c                                     *
2     *                                                       *
3     * Introductory X/Motif program to display the system date *
4     * within a push button widget, and toggle to the clock  *
5     * time when the button is pressed. A double click on the *
6     * date will exit the application, a double click on the *
7     * time will update the clock.                           *
8     *                                                       *
9     * Fintan Culwin June 93 v1.0                            *
10   */
11
12   #include "sdtime.h"
13
14   #include <Xm/Xm.h>
15   #include <X11/Shell.h>
16   #include <Xm/PushB.h>
17
18   #define MAX_ARGS      10
19
20   /* callback prototype declarations */
21   void date_time_transition_callback( Widget    widget,
22                                        XtPointer client_data,
23                                        XtPointer call_data);
24
25   void bleep_callback( Widget    widget,
26                        XtPointer client_data,
27                        XtPointer call_data);
28
29   void main ( int argc, char *argv[]){
30
31   char * application_class = "Xdtime";
32
33   char         the_date[ MAX_DTIME_LENGTH ];
34   XmString     x_the_date;
35
36   XtAppContext context;
37
38   Widget       toplevel, dtime_button;
39   Arg          args[ MAX_ARGS ];
40   int          num_args;
41
42      num_args = 0;
43      XtSetArg( args[num_args], XmNallowShellResize, True ); num_args++;
44      toplevel = XtAppInitialize( &context,
45                                  application_class,
46                                  NULL, 0,
47                                  &argc, argv,
48                                  NULL,
49                                  args, num_args );
50
51      /* get the date */
52      sdate( the_date );
53      /* convert to XmString */                          continued
```

continued

\\

Listing 2.2 *continued*

```
54    x_the_date = XmStringCreateLtoR( the_date,
55                       XmSTRING_DEFAULT_CHARSET);
56
57    /* create the push button */
58    num_args = 0;
59    XtSetArg( args[num_args], XmNmultiClick, XmMULTICLICK_KEEP);
60                                                 num_args++;
61    XtSetArg( args[num_args], XmNlabelString, x_the_date);
62                                                 num_args++;
63    dtime_button = XmCreatePushButton( toplevel, "dtime button",
64                                       args, num_args);
65    XtManageChild( dtime_button );
66
67    XtAddCallback( dtime_button, XmNarmCallback,
68                   bleep_callback, (XtPointer) NULL );
69    XtAddCallback( dtime_button, XmNactivateCallback,
70                   switch_date_time_callback, (XtPointer) NULL );
71    XtAddCallback( dtime_button, XmNdisarmCallback,
72                   bleep_callback, (XtPointer) NULL );
73    XtAddCallback( dtime_button, XmNdisarmCallback,
74                   bleep_callback, (XtPointer) NULL );
75    XmStringFree( x_the_date );
76
77    /* realize the widgets then get and dispatch events */
78    XtRealizeWidget( toplevel );
79    XtAppMainLoop( context );
80 } /* end fun main */
81
82
83 void date_time_transition_callback( Widget    widget,
84                                     XtPointer client_data,
85                                     XtPointer call_data){
86 /* callback function to install a time string or a date string  *
87  * in the widget paramater or to exit the application. Decision  *
88  * made on the click count field of the call data parameter or   *
89  * the value of a static variable.                               *
90  */
91
92  /* manifest state values */
93  #define DATE_DISPLAY 0
94  #define TIME_DISPLAY 1
95
96  /* set the initial value to date display */
97  static int client_state = DATE_DISPLAY;
98
99  char     time_or_date[ MAX_DTIME_LENGTH ];
100 XmString  x_time_or_date;
101
102 XmPushButtonCallbackStruct * push_call_data;
103
104 Arg      args[ MAX_ARGS ];
105 int      num_args;
106
107    /* recast the call data from XtPointer (for convenience) */
```

\\

Listing 2.2 *continued*

```
108    push_call_data = (XmPushButtonCallbackStruct *) call_data;
109
110    if ( (push_call_data->click_count == 2) &&
111        ( client_state == TIME_DISPLAY)     ) {
112      /* valid double click for exit transition */
113      exit(0);
114    } else {
115      if ( client_state == DATE_DISPLAY ) {
116        /* prepare for date to time transition */
117        stime( time_or_date );
118        client_state = TIME_DISPLAY;
119      } else {
120        /* prepare for time to date transition */
121        sdate( time_or_date );
122        client_state = DATE_DISPLAY;
123      } /* end if single click */
124      /* do the transition */
125      x_time_or_date = XmStringCreateLtoR( time_or_date,
126                             XmSTRING_DEFAULT_CHARSET);
127      num_args =0;
128      XtSetArg( args[ num_args ], XmNlabelString, x_time_or_date);
129                                        num_args++;
130      XtSetValues( widget, args, num_args );
131
132      XmStringFree( x_time_or_date );
133    } /* end if double click */
134 } /* end fun date_time_transition_callback */
135
136
137 void bleep_callback( Widget     widget,
138                      XtPointer client_data,
139                      XtPointer call_data){
140 /* Utility callback function to cause the server *
141  * to bleep. Uses the widget parameter only      *
142 */
143
144    XBell( XtDisplay( widget ), 100 );
145 } /* end fun bleep callback */
```

where the *widget* parameter identifies the widget whose resources are to be changed; *args* and *num_args* are an argument list constructed in the usual manner using *XtSetArg*. The callback function also has a requirement to maintain a record of the state of the application in order to decide between a date to time transition or a time to date transition. The definition of the function is given in Listing 2.2.

There is one inelegant feature in this callback function. The *pushButton* widget will process the first click of a double click sequence as if it were a single click. Thus when a double click action is performed by the user when the client is in the *date display* state, the application is already in the *time_display* state when the second click is processed. This is a consideration which the callback function has to be aware of. It also implies that the state transition design given in Figure 2.12 is not correctly implemented in this version of the program. The double click transition from the *date display* state goes via the *time display* state before transiting to the termination state. It is possible to implement the design in Figure 2.12 correctly, but the techniques to do so are too complex at this stage. It would be preferable for the *pushButton* widget to implement the double click user action as a distinct *callBack* resource.

Having declared and defined the two callback functions *bleep_callback* and *date_time_transition_callback* within a Motif program called *xdtime.c*, the callbacks can be installed into the *dtime_button* immediately after it has been created. The calls to *XtAddCallback* from *xdtime.c* are :

```
XtAddCallback( dtime_button, XmNarmCallback,
               bleep_callback, (XtPointer) NULL );
XtAddCallback( dtime_button, XmNdisarmCallback,
               bleep_callback, (XtPointer) NULL );
XtAddCallback( dtime_button, XmNdisarmCallback,
               bleep_callback, (XtPointer) NULL );
XtAddCallback( dtime_button, XmNactivateCallback,
               date_time_transition_callback,
               (XtPointer) NULL );
```

The behaviour of the widget is now defined. Arming the *dtime_button* by pressing the first mouse button when the mouse pointer is positioned on it will cause the arm callback *bleep_callback* to be executed and the terminal will bleep. Releasing the mouse button while the mouse pointer is positioned within the button will cause the activate callback *date_time_transition_callback* to be executed and the time will be displayed. Following this the disarm callbacks will be executed. CallBack resources are of type *CallbackList* and allow a number of callback functions to be stored within them. In this example the *bleep_callback* has been added twice to the *disarmCallback*'s *callbackList*, thus when the disarm callback is activated the terminal will bleep twice. Where there is more than one callback function in a *callbackList*, it cannot be assumed that they will be called in the sequence in which they were added to the list. Pressing and releasing the button a second time when it is within the button will cause a bleep, the date to be displayed and two bleeps. A double click in the *date display* state will cause an activation bleep, a transition to the *time display* state, two bleeps on deactivation and then another activation bleep before the application terminates. A double click in the *time display* state will be interpreted as two single clicks causing a transition to the *date display* state followed by a transition back to the *time display* state. This implements the required behaviour to update the time, albeit in a rather inelegant manner.

The distinction between *activation* and *disarming* can be made clear by activating the button, then sliding the mouse pointer off the button before releasing it. When this is done the terminal will bleep once when the button is armed and twice when the button is released indicating that it is disarmed. The activation behaviour of switching the date for the time, or vice versa, will not be called.

When the date is switched for the time, as a consequence of the *XtSetValues* call, the widget '*knows*' that it has to redraw itself. As the size of the time string is smaller than the size of the date string, the widget also resizes itself. As illustrated in Figure 2.11, the *applicationShell* will resize itself to accommodate the new size of its child and the window manager will resize the window's border. When the time string is switched for the date string, the original size will be restored. This behaviour could be prevented by setting the *applicationShell*'s *allowShellResize* resource to *False*.

The callback functions declared in the application program are never called explicitly from the main function. They are called indirectly from the application's *main event loop*. The call to *XtAppMainLoop* passes control to an event driven loop. This loop collects events such as keyboard key presses, mouse movements or mouse button presses, decides which widget the event should be associated with and calls the appropriate method within the widget. If the method has programmer supplied callbacks associated with it the callback functions will be called by the method. The callback function is called retrospectively, hence *call back*, from the event loop after it has been associated with a widget's callback resource.

2.5 The lifecycle of a widget

Figure 2.13 illustrates the lifecycle of a widget. The initial creation of a widget causes it to exist as a data structure in the client. At this stage, the widget does not have an associated window but it does contain within its data structure values for most of the resources which will determine the appearance of the window when it is created. One major set of window resources which does not have a value at this stage are the size and position of the window. The size and position values are collectively known as the widget's *geometry* resources.

The change from created widget to managed widget causes the widget's geometry resources to be initialized. At this stage the widget can take part in geometry negotiations but as it does not yet have an associated window on the server it cannot become visible to the user. Geometry negotiations take place between a widget and its parent. *Constraint* widgets, and widgets descended from *Constraint* in the class hierarchy, may have a number of children with which it has to negotiate.

In the example programs above, the managing of the *pushButton* or *label* widget caused it to work out how large it would have to be to display its *labelString*. This size is then communicated to its parent widget, the *applicationShell* widget, which will accept or modify the size and inform the child of its position. As an *applicationShell* widget can only have a single child, it would most probably accept the size and inform the child that its position would be top left relative to the *applicationShell* widget.

The change from managed widget to realized widget causes the widget's window to be created on the server. The geometry of the widget is already known if the widget has been managed, otherwise the realize process will first manage the widget. However, the window is not yet visible to the user on the screen as it has yet to be mapped.

The final change from managed widget to mapped widget usually occurs automatically and causes the widget to display itself within its window. All widgets inherit from the *Core* widget class a resource called *mappedWhenManaged*. The default value of this resource is *True* which ensures that the widget will be automatically mapped when it is managed. There are situations where it is advantageous to set this resource *False*, which will cause space for the widget to be allocated on the screen but the widget will not display itself within it.

The usual techniques for an application programmer to negotiate through these states are emphasized using bold arrows in Figure 2.13. The initial creation of an unmanaged widget using the Motif convenience function *XmCreate(widgetclass)*, is immediately followed by a call to *XtManageChild* causing the newly created widget to be managed.

The transition from managed to realized is occasioned by the realization of the *toplevel* widget. The *toplevel* widget cannot realize itself until all its managed children have been realized. Consequently the call to *XtRealizeWidget(toplevel)* is implemented by a recursive traversal of the application widget hierarchy realizing all managed widgets. As the *mapWhenManaged* resource is *True* by default, this will cause all the managed widgets in the application to become visible as well.

Figure 2.13 also shows some of the less common techniques which can be used by an application programmer to implement greater control over the processes

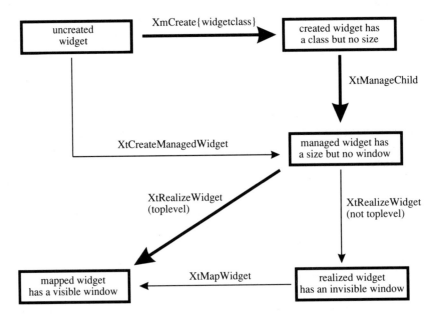

Figure 2.13   The lifecycle of a widget.

which cause a widget to become visible. The use of these techniques will be introduced later in the book.

A widget in a mapped and managed state has a set of behaviours available which it can use to implement its functionality. For example, the changing of the *labelString* resource of the *pushButton* widget caused it to redraw itself displaying the new string. The arming of the *pushButton* widget caused it to redraw its decorations indicating the armed state, and the activation of the *pushButton* widget caused it to call any functions installed in its *activate* callback resource. These *methods* are used to implement the widget's class functionality and are provided by Motif for its own use.

In addition there are other methods which are implemented by all widgets, allowing them to interact with the intrinsics. Some of these methods have already been met in the description of the widget's lifecycle above. All widgets support a *manage* method, a *realize* method, a *resize* method etc. For example, intrinsics functions such as *XtRealizeWidget,* make use of these methods to realize the widgets in the application hierarchy tree. The realize method of each widget in the tree will be called by *XtRealizeWidget* as the application hierarchy is recursively traversed. The precise details of how a widget realizes (or displays, or resizes, or activates) itself are not known by the intrinsics. All it knows is that the methods exist and how to call them.

The application programmer is in a similar position to the intrinsics. To program in Motif the precise details of how the widgets, from which the client is constructed, are implemented does not need to be known. All that is required is a knowledge of what facilities a widget provides and how to cause them to be triggered. As many of the facilities are supported by the intrinsics and are thus common to all widgets, the knowledge obtained from one widget class is applicable to all other widget classes.

Two final considerations of a widget's lifecycle deserve mention at this stage. At certain times the user interface functionality of a widget is not required. The widget could be removed from the visual display by unmanaging or unmapping it, but this can cause confusion to a user when parts of the interface disappear or reappear. A resource called *sensitive* is inherited from the *Core* widget class by all widgets and has the default value *True*. A widget which has this resource set *False* will take part in geometry negotiations and will be visible to the user; however its user interface functionality will be disabled. To make the user; aware that it is disabled the widget is presented in a '*greyed out*' state. Thus a *pushButton* can be made temporarily unavailable to the user by setting its sensitive resource *False*, and made available again by resetting its sensitive resource *True*. The restore option of the Motif window menu shown in Figure 1.4 is displayed in an insensitive state.

Finally, the initiation of a widget's lifecycle when it is created has been described. A widget can also have its lifecycle terminated by being destroyed. As widgets are automatically destroyed when the client is terminated, this part of a widget's lifecycle is usually omitted by application programmers. Should a

\\\

programmer require explicit destruction of a widget the intrinsics function *XtDestroyWidget* can be used.

2.6 Activities for Chapter 2

1. Implement the *xdtime* client without setting the value of the *allowShellResize* resource in the program code. Use the resource file mechanism to launch two instances of the client which have the value set to *False* and *True*. Investigate the differences between them when they are toggled and when the user resizes them.

2. Design and implement a client called *xpostit* which will provide the functionality of a *postit* sticker, allowing a short message to be displayed within a widget. For example the command line '*xpostit phone Mar at 4-30*' will produce the *xpostit* instance illustrated in Figure 2.14.

3. Add user functionality to the version of *xpostit* produced in 2. When the mouse button is double clicked anywhere within the postit window, the application should terminate.

Figure 2.14   *xpostit*, visual design.

CHAPTER THREE

\\

A design overview

Introduction

This chapter will introduce three aspects of application design. The first aspect, visual design, will only be given a superficial treatment. This is not to understate the importance of this topic but is in recognition of its complexity. For a large application developed by a team, a graphics designer would be involved in the design of icons, dialog layouts, default color selections, default fonts etc. In recognition of the importance and speciality of this aspect of design only general guidelines will be given. The emphasis in this section of the chapter will be the engineering techniques by which visual designs can be implemented, rather than detailed graphical design techniques.

The remaining two sections of the chapter deal with the two related topics of usability design and application design. The intention here is to give an initial insight into a technique for usability design, whose notation can subsequently be used as a guide to application design. The refinement and application of these techniques will continue throughout the remainder of the book. The examples introduced here are necessarily simple, but contain within them the essential detail of the techniques.

3.1 Visual design

The visual appearance of clients should not be neglected, or relegated to a post production phase of application development. The essence of a GUI is that it is graphical and part of its popularity and ease of use is conferred by this aspect. Humans are more able to assimilate information which is presented graphically than information presented textually. The truth of this assertion is contained in the folk wisdom cliché that a picture is worth a thousand words.

To be effective graphical communication has to be understated. The use of a large number of different fonts, the use of a large number of strident colors or the use of over complex graphical icons, will create an interface which the user will find uncomfortable to use. The converse of the above suggestions, a small number of fonts, discrete colors and simple icons, will create a more comfortable interface.

\\\

There is not sufficient space in this book for the details of effective graphical communication to be introduced. An excellent reference which deals with graphical communication in the context of Motif programming is given in Appendix A. This section will introduce the techniques by which graphical communication can be effected within Motif. The style guidelines which prescribe how the techniques should be applied will not be introduced in any detail.

3.1.1 Motif strings

The Motif widget set makes little use of the C standard ASCII coded zero terminated (*asciiz*) string type. The major exceptions to this are the *text* and *textField* widget classes. Most other widget classes use a string representation provided by Motif, known as an *XmString*. An *XmString* differs from an *asciiz* string largely by providing support for the use of different fonts in different segments of the string. It also provides support for extended character sets, and for linguistic environments where the text does not run from left to right. This book will only consider the simpler case where an English character set involving multiple fonts with the text running from left to right is being used.

An *XmString* consists of a number of *segments*, each of which can have a different font associated with it. *Xfonts* were introduced in Chapter 1 where it was noted that they have complicated names such as *-adobie-courier-bold-o-normal— 17-100-100-100-m-90-iso8859-1*. To facilitate the construction of *XmStrings* without using such unwieldy font identifiers, and to facilitate user configuration, an associated data structure known as an *XmFontList* is supplied. An *XmFontList* consists of a number of *Xfont* names each of which has a shorter programmer decided mnemonic name associated with it.

When an *XmString* is constructed, the font which is to be used when the string is displayed is specified using the mnemonic name. When the string is displayed the *Xfont* associated with the mnemonic name in the *XmFontList* structure is used. Thus by changing the contents of the *XmFontList* the visual appearance of the string can be changed. As *fontLists* can be specified in resource files, this mechanism allows the user to control the visual appearance of the application. Figure 3.1 illustrates the same *XmString* containing three segments, displayed with two different *fontList* specifications.

The string displayed in Figure 3.1 is illustrative of the type of string which is displayed as the version identification of an application. It uses three different fonts, one for the program name with the mnemonic *fancy,* one for the programmer's names with the mnemonic *italic* and one for the version details with the mnemonic *bold*. The construction of the *XmString* assuming the existence of a suitable *fontList* will be explained first, following which the construction of associated *fontLists* will be introduced.

XmStrings are constructed from asciiz strings using conversion functions supplied by Motif. For multiple segment strings each segment of the string is

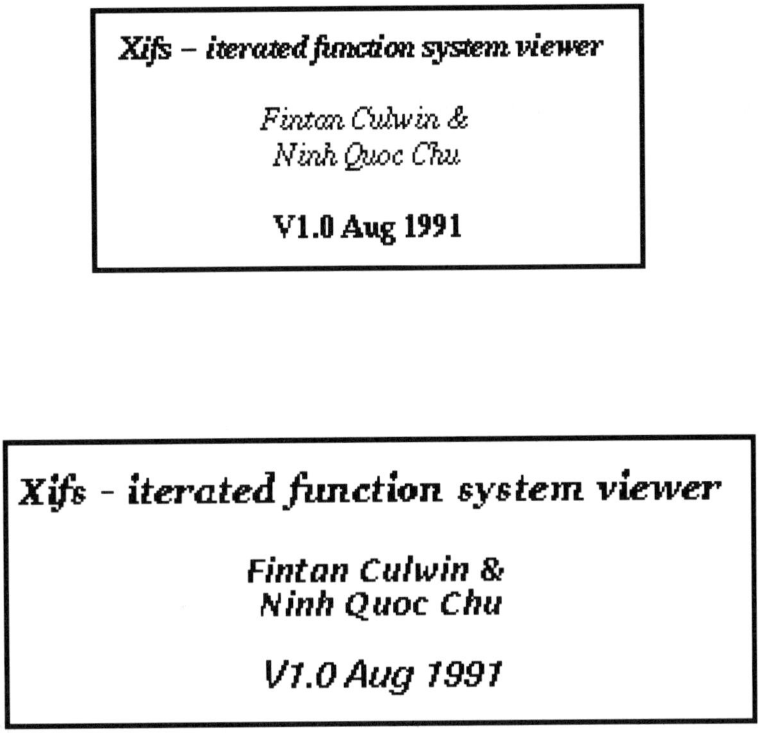

Figure 3.1   Version text illustrating alternative fonts.

individually constructed and subsequently catenated, using another Motif function to produce the composite string.

Unfortunately it is not possible for multiple segment *XmStrings* to be specified in a resource file and thus they have to be specified in the program code. To promote the internationalization of X/Motif clients, the text which will be used to construct *XmStrings* should be specified in a configuration header file. The relevant parts of a configuration header file for this example might be:

```
/* Fragment of an example application configuration header file. */
#define XIFS_TITLE       "Xifs - iterated function system viewer.\n\n"
#define XIFS_PROGRAMMERS "Fintan Culwin \n" \
                         "& Ninh Quoc Chu.\n\n"
#define XIFS_VERSION     "V1.0 Aug 1991."
```

Assuming that this header file has been *#included* to bring the string definitions into scope, a composite *XmString* using the font mnemonics introduced above can be constructed with the program fragment given in Listing 3.1. The individual components of the string are created using the utility function *XmStringCreate*; the prototype of this function is:

\\\

```
XmString XmStringCreate( char *          asciiz,
                         XmStringCharSet charset );
```

Listing 3.1   Code fragment illustrating the construction of XmStrings

```
 1  /* Fragment of an example application configuration header file. */
 2
 3  #define XIFS_TITLE        "Xifs - iterated function system viewer.\n\n"
 4  #define XIFS_PROGRAMMERS "Fintan Culwin \n" \
 5                           "& Ninh Quoc Chu.\n\n"
 6  #define XIFS_VERSION      "V1.0 Aug 1991."
 7
 8
 9  /* Fragment to construct a composite XmString    *
10   * using the #defined strings introduced above,  *
11   * and assuming a fontList structure containing *
12   * fancy, italic and bold is available.          *
13   */
14
15  XmString title_segment, name_segment,
16           version_segment, temp_string,
17           version_string;
18
19      title_segment   = XmStringCreate( XIFS_TITLE,  "fancy" );
20      name_segment    = XmStringCreate( XIFS_PROGRAMMERS, "italic" );
21      version_segment = XmStringCreate( XIFS_VERSION, "bold" );
22
23      temp_string     = XmStringConcat( title_segment, name_segment );
24      version_string  = XmStringConcat( temp_string ,version_segment );
25
26      XmStringFree(  title_segment );
27      XmStringFree(  name_segment );
28      XmStringFree(  version_segment );
29      XmStringFree(  temp_string );
30
31
32      /* omitted use of the XmString version_string as the *
33       * labelString resource during the creation of a     *
34       * label widget.                                    */
35
36      XmStringFree( version_string  );
```

The effect of the function is to create and return an *XmString* containing the asciiz text supplied and using the charset mnemonic identifier which is also represented as an asciiz string. If the identity of the mnemonics in the *fontList* is not known by the programmer, the literal XmSTRING_DEFAULT_CHARSET can be used, which will cause the first character set in the *fontList* to be used. Release 1.2 of Motif has specified that the literal XmSTRING_DEFAULT_TAG should be used for this purpose, but the obsolete XmSTRING_DEFAULT_CHARSET can still be used.

Having created two *XmStrings* they can be catenated together to produce a third string using the function *XmStringConcat*; the prototype of this function is:

\\

```
XmString XmStringConcat( XmString first_string,
                         XmString second_string );
```

XmStrings take up client resources which should be released as soon as the string is no longer required. This can be accomplished by using the function *XmStringFree*, whose prototype is:

```
void XmStringFree( XmString no_longer_required );
```

In the example fragment above the strings which are constructed in order to catenate the complete string are freed as soon as the complete string is constructed. The complete string is itself freed after it has been used to specify the *labelString* resource of a label widget, as the label widget maintains its own copy of the *XmString* and it is no longer required once the *Label* widget has been created.

The example used in Figure 3.1 was implemented using the code fragment above to construct a *label* widget called *version label*. The widget is contained within an application called *version_demo*, whose construction will be introduced below. If the application class name of this client is *Version_demo* and the instance name *version_demo*, the simplest way by which a *fontList* can be associated with the label widget is within a resource file. The *fontList* specification used for the first image in Figure 3.1 was:

```
Version_demo*FontList:    "*times*medium-i*12*"="italic",\
                          "*times*bold-i*12*"="fancy",\
                          "*times*bold-r*12*"="bold"
```

The inclusion of a more particular specification in the resource files, caused the appearance of the client to change to that shown in the second image in Figure 3.1:

```
version_demo*fontList    "*lucidabright*-i*12*"="italic",\
                         "*lucida-medium*12*"="fancy",\
                         "*lucida-bold-r*12*"="bold"
```

It is also possible for a *fontList* structure to be created and associated with a widget within an application. However if this facility is used it would not be possible for the user to change the fonts used via the resource mechanism, and consequently the advice is not to use this facility.

The creation of an *XmString* using *XmStringCreate*, as introduced above, is suitable for creating simple strings which contain no new line characters and specifying explicitly a mnemonic fontname. If the default character set would have been acceptable then the simpler function *XmStringCreateLocalized* could have been used. If the string being created contains new line characters, then the function *XmStringCreateLtoR* should be used. Details of these two functions and other utility functions for manipulating *XmString*s can be located in Appendix B.

3.1.2 Pixmaps

Graphical communication is enhanced by the use of iconic symbols in place of
text. Iconic symbols also have the advantages of taking up less screen space, and
have more potential to be understood by users from other linguistic environments.
The visual design of the symbol should make use of any widely understood
conventions; for example a triangle is widely understood from international road
signs to indicate a warning, likewise an octagon indicates stop. Where no widely
understood convention exists, the design of the symbol should embody the
essence of the concept and not attempt to be a realistic representation. Again there
is no space for the full complexity of symbolic communication to be explored;
only the techniques by which it can be implemented within Motif programs will be
presented.

Chapter 1 introduced the use of the *bitmap* standard client and the format of the
output which it produces. If the bitmap client were used to produce a bitmap
header file called *fractree.h*, the (edited) contents of the file might be:

```
/* Filename fractree.h ( fractal tree header file)      *
 * Contains 64 by 64 fractal tree bitmap image          *
 * Produced by bitmap standard client                   *
 */

int    fractree_width   = 64;
int    fractree_height  = 64;
char   fractree_bits[ ] = { 0x?? 0x?? ...... };
```

This file can be *#included* by a client program, and the information which it
contains converted into a format which a client can display. To do this, the
information has first has to be converted into a *pixmap*. A *bitmap* is a sequence of
bits which can be considered to be a displayable rectangular area; each *pixel* of
the displayed area would correspond to one bit of the bitmap. Assuming a black
and white display, each set bit from the bitmap would be displayed as a black
pixel and each unset bit as a white *pixel*. With a greyscale or a color display,
more than one bit is required to define the color of each pixel, and the sequence
of bits analogous to a bitmap to define the colors is known as a *pixmap*. It is more
usual to consider a *bitmap* as a special instance of a *pixmap* which has only one
bit per pixel.

The bitmap data can be converted into a value of the *Xlib Pixmap* data type using
the function *XCreatePixmapFromBitmapData*; the prototype of this function is:

```
Pixmap XCreatePixmapFromBitmapData( Display * display,
                                    Drawable  drawable,
                                    char *    bitmap_data,
                                    int       bitmap_width,
                                    int       bitmap_height,
                                    Pixel     foreground_color,
                                    Pixel     background_color,
                                    int       depth );
```

This is an intimidating number of parameters with a bewildering set of considerations; a more detailed explanation of many of the considerations will be given in the latter part of this book. For the time being the discussion will be limited to the construction of a black and white pixmap.

The first parameter identifies the display upon which the *pixmap* is to be displayed; the intrinsics function *XtDisplay* can be used to determine the value from any created widget. The prototype of *XtDisplay* is:

```
Display * XtDisplay( Widget widget );
```

The second parameter identifies a *Drawable*, another *Xlib* data type which includes the *Xlib* type *Window*. The *Drawable* is a program object within which the *pixmap* could be imaged. In this situation the most obvious type of object is a window on the display. The *Window* which is supplied is not necessarily the window within which the *Pixmap* will be displayed. Consequently the most convenient window to specify is the root window of the display. The identity of the root window can be determined using the *Xlib* macro *DefaultRootWindow*, using as its single parameter the display pointer already obtained:

```
Window DefaultRootWindow( Display * display);
```

The next three parameters define the bitmap information which has already been *#included* within the bitmap header file. The *Pixel* value for the black color to be used as the foreground and the *Pixel* value for the white color to be used as the background, can be obtained using a pair of macros *BlackPixel* and *WhitePixel*. Each of these macros requires two parameters, the display pointer and the screen number. The value of the screen number can be obtained from the display pointer using the *DefaultScreen* macro:

```
Window DefaultScreen( Display * display);
Pixel  WhitePixel(    Display * display, int screen_number);
Pixel  BlackPixel(    Display * display, int screen_number);
int    DefaultDepth(  Display * display, int screen_number);
```

Finally the last parameter can also be obtained using the macro *DefaultDepth*, which has an identical profile to the *BlackPixel* and *WhitePixel* macros described above. Putting all this together produces a program fragment which will convert the information from the *bitmap* header file into a *Pixmap* value, as shown in Listing 3.2.

The *Pixmap* variable is declared with the safe default value NULL, which will cause the *Xlib* toolkit to raise an error message if it is ever used before a valid pixmap has been created. The function *XCreatePixmapFromBitmapData* will return NULL if it is not possible for a pixmap to be created. Having created the *Pixmap*, it can be used to specify the *labelPixmap* resource of a label widget, which has had its *labelType* resource set to XmPIXMAP, as also shown in Listing 3.2.

When the widget is mapped the image defined by the bitmap information will be displayed within the label. The widget does not maintain its own copy of the

\\\

Listing 3.2   Fragment to create a Pixmap from a bitmap header file produced by the bitmap standard client

```
1   /* Filename fractree.h ( fractal tree header file)      *
2    * Contains 64 by 64 fractal tree bitmap image          *
3    * Produced by bitmap standard client                   *
4    */
5
6   int    fractree_width   = 64;
7   int    fractree_height  = 64;
8   char   fractree_bits[ ] = { 0x?? 0x?? ...... };
```

```
1   /* Fragment to create a pixmap from bitmap information    *
2    * from the Bitmap client, #included into the program.    *
3    * Assuming that the identity of any_widget is available. *
4    */
5
6   static Pixmap    fract_pix = (Pixmap) NULL;
7   /* static as the label widget does not take a copy */
8
9   Display *        display;
10  Widget           version_pixmap;
11
12  Arg              args[ MAX_ARGS ];
13  int              num_args;
14
15     display = XtDisplay( any_realized_widget );
16     fract_pix = XCreatePixmapFromBitmapData( display,
17                      DefaultRootWindow( display ),
18                      fractree_bits,
19                      fractree_width,
20                      fractree_height,
21                      BlackPixel(  display, DefaultScreen( display )),
22                      WhitePixel(  display, DefaultScreen( display )),
23                      DefaultDepth( display, DefaultScreen( display )));
24
25     num_args = 0;
26     XtSetArg( args[num_args], XmNlabelType,    XmPIXMAP ); num_args++;
27     XtSetArg( args[num_args], XmNlabelPixmap,  fract_pix); num_args++;
28     version_pixmap = XmCreateLabel(version_form,
29                                "version pixmap",
30                                args, num_args );
```

pixmap, only a copy of the pixmap's identity. Consequently the Pixmap identity used to specify the resource should be retained in order that the resources used by the *Pixmap* can be released when the pixmap is no longer required. The resources used by the pixmap can be released using the *Xlib XFreePixmap* function:

```
XFreePixmap( fract_pix );
fract_pix = ( Pixmap ) NULL;
```

An example of a label widget configured to display a pixmap is given in Figure 3.2. Further consideration of bitmaps, pixmaps, colors and other aspects of graphics programming in X/Motif will be deferred until Chapters 6 and 7.

3.1.3 The form widget

All interfaces comprise more than one widget, thus an important aspect of visual design is the spatial relationship between widgets. These considerations should not only take into account the initial positioning of the widgets, but also the repositioning of the widgets as the interface is resized. Chapter 2 introduced a set of widget classes whose major function is to control the positioning of their children. All these widget classes are child classes of the intrinsics *Constraint* widget class and are collectively known as *constraint* widgets, since they impose constraints upon the positions of their children.

This section will introduce the most powerful Motif constraint widget, the *Form* widget. To explore the construction and use of *Form* widgets, a simple version dialog using the two widgets described in the previous sections will be constructed. The default visual appearance of the *version demo* dialog is illustrated in Figure 3.3. In addition to the two label widgets a third *PushButton* widget has been added, which when pushed will close the dialog removing it from the screen. The application widget hierarchy for the client is illustrated in Figure 3.4.

Any widget in an application widget hierarchy which is a direct child of a *form* widget inherits from the *form* widget a number of resources which control its positioning within the form. This is an example of inheritance via the application hierarchy and should not be confused with inheritance via the class hierarchy. For example: the *pushButton* widget *version button* in the application hierarchy shown

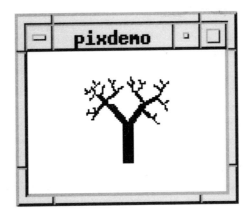

Figure 3.2   Label widget displaying a pixmap.

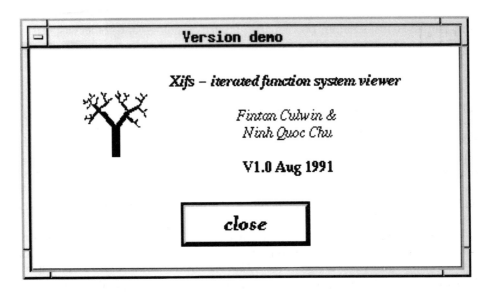

Figure 3.3   *Version_demo* visual design.

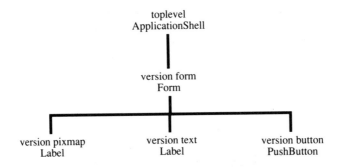

Figure 3.4   *Version_demo* application widget hierarchy.

in Figure 3.4 is a child of a *form* widget, and by virtue of this relationship it inherits a resource called *topAttachment* which controls the positioning of the top of the widget. The Motif class hierarchy, shown in Figure 2.5, indicates that the *PushButton* widget class is not a direct or indirect child class of the *Form* widget class, and thus cannot inherit this resource via the usual inheritance mechanism. The inheritance of resources from the *Form* widget class, and other constraint widget classes, is the only common example of application hierarchy inheritance.

As suggested above every child of a *form* widget inherits four resources called *topAttachment, rightAttachment, bottomAttachment* and *leftAttachment*, which control the positioning of the four sides of the child widget within the form. The default value for these resources is ATTACH_NONE, which will cause all widgets to be positioned in the top left-hand corner of the form overlaying each other. The other possible values for these resources are ATTACH_FORM and ATTACH_OPPOSITE_FORM which causes the side of the widget to be attached to the side of the form, ATTACH_WIDGET and ATTACH_OPPOSITE_WIDGET, which causes the side to be attached to another widget, ATTACH_POSITION which causes the side to be attached to an imaginary line aligned along the proportional height or width of the form, and finally ATTACH_SELF which causes the widget to retain its original proportional position when the form is resized.

To implement the visual design of a form widget the required positioning of the children has first to be decided and then the appropriate values for the *attachment resources* specified. Figure 3.5 illustrates one possible spatial relationship of the three widgets which will comprise the version dialog; Figure 3.6 illustrates an alternative visual design. It should be obvious that the favoured design in this case is given in Figure 3.5 but for other dialogs designs such as that in Figure 3.6 might be more appropriate so both designs will be explored.

In Figure 3.5, the majority of the resources are specified as ATTACH_POSITION,

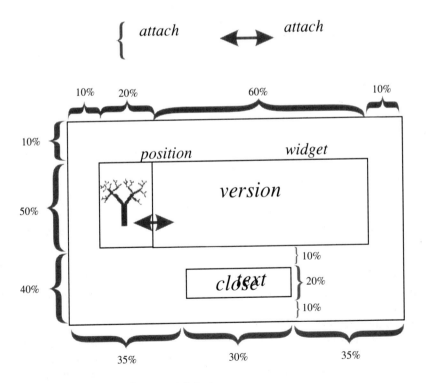

Figure 3.5   *Version_demo* spatial design.

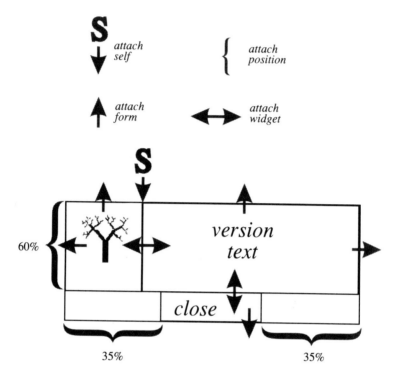

Figure 3.6   *Version_demo* alternative spatial design.

with the positional value specified in another resource called *topPosition*, *rightPosition*, *bottomPosition* or *leftPosition*. For example the *rightAttachment* resource of the *version pixmap* widget is specified as ATTACH_POSITION, requiring a resource called *rightPosition* to be set to 30, which will cause the right-hand edge of the pixmap to be positioned 30% along the width of the enclosing form widget.

By default the value used to specify the position is expressed as a percentage, although if this is inconvenient a resource of the *form* widget called *fractionBase* can be set to indicate a different convention. Thus if the value of *fractionBase* were specified as 256 then the positional resources would be interpreted as expressing the position in two hundred and fifty-sixths of the height or width of the form.

The only attachment resource in Figure 3.5 which is not specified as ATTACH_POSITION is the *leftAttachment* resource of the *version text* widget. The value of this resource is specified as ATTACH_WIDGET, and the widget to which it is to be attached is specified in another resource called *leftWidget*. In this example the value of this resource would be the *version pixmap* widget. As the

\\\

rightAttachment resource of this widget is already set to ATTACH_POSITION and the *rightPosition* value to 30(%) this will ensure that the left side of *version text* will remain at its designed position of 30%. The alternative possibility, of simply specifying the *leftAttachment* of the *version text* as ATTACH_POSITION and the associated value of *leftPosition* as 30(%), is not favoured as a change to relative positions of the pixmap and label would require two changes in the resource settings. The favoured method would only require the *rightAttachment* of the pixmap widget to be changed.

A summary of the attachment resources of the form's children which would produce the visual design in Figure 3.5 is given in Table 3.1. As all but one of these resources are positional and as explained above the remaining resource is effectively positional, resizing the form will cause the relative sizes of the components of the dialog to remain constant. Figure 3.7 illustrates the appearance of the dialog as the widget is resized.

The settings of the attachment resources which implement the visual design given in Figure 3.6 are a little more complex. The intention here is that the width of the *version pixmap* will be set when the form is realized and will not change thereafter. The appropriate setting of *rightAttachment* is thus ATTACH_SELF. The top and left sides of the pixmap are to remain attached to the form, thus the appropriate setting for *topAttachment* and *leftAttachment* is ATTACH_FORM. The bottom of the pixmap is set to 60% of the height of the form, using ATTACH_POSITION for the *topAttachment* resource and 60 for the *bottomAttachment* resource.

A similar set of considerations applies to the *version text* widget. Its *topAttachment* and *rightAttachment* will be specified as ATTACH_FORM, its *leftAttachment* as ATTACH_WIDGET with the *leftWidget* value set to *version pixmap* and its *bottomAttachment* set to ATTACH_WIDGET with the *bottomWidget* value set to *version button.*

The *version button's* *topAttachment* will be set to ATTACH_SELF so that it always retains its initial height, its *bottomAttachment* to ATTACH_FORM, and its *leftAttachment* and *rightAttachment* both set to ATTACH_POSITION with the values of *leftPosition* and *rightPosition* both set as specified in the design.

A summary of the attachment resources of the form's children which would produce the visual design in Figure 3.6 is given in Table 3.2. Figure 3.8 illustrates the appearance of the dialog as the widget is resized.

The remaining settings of the attachment resource are ATTACH_OPPOSITE_WIDGET and ATTACH_OPPOSITE_FORM. When the *leftAttachment* resource of a widget is set to ATTACH_WIDGET and a widget identity is specified in the *leftWidget* resource, the understanding is that the left side of the widget being attached will be positioned along a line defined by the right side of the widget to which it is being attached. When the ATTACH_OPPOSITE_WIDGET value is specified for a *leftAttachment,* the understanding is that the left side of the widget being attached will be positioned along a line defined by the left (opposite) side of the widget to which it is

\\\

Table 3.1   Version demo attachment resources

widget	parent	class
version bitmap	version form	Label

resource	value
leftAttachment	XmATTACH_POSITION
leftPosition	10
topAttachment	XmATTACH_POSITION
topPosition	10
rightAttachment	XmATTACH_POSITION
rightPosition	30
bottomAttachment	XmATTACH_POSITION
bottomPosition	60

widget	parent	class
version text	version form	Label

resource	value
leftAttachment	XmATTACH_WIDGET
leftWidget	version bitmap
topAttachment	XmATTACH_POSITION
topPosition	10
rightAttachment	XmATTACH_POSITION
rightPosition	90
bottomAttachment	XmATTACH_POSITION
bottomPosition	60

widget	parent	class
version button	version form	Label

resource	value
leftAttachment	XmATTACH_POSITION
leftPosition	35
topAttachment	XmATTACH_POSITION
topPosition	70
rightAttachment	XmATTACH_POSITION
rightPosition	65
bottomAttachment	XmATTACH_POSITION
bottomPosition	90

attached. This will ensure that the left-hand sides of a series of widgets are attached in a single line, if the *leftAttachment* resource of all but the first widget is specified as ATTACH_OPPOSITE_WIDGET and the identity of the first widget is specified for the *leftAttachment* resources.

ATTACH_OPPOSITE_FORM has a similar meaning: the side of the widget will be attached to the opposite side of the form. If the *leftAttachment* of a widget is specified as ATTACH_OPPOSITE_FORM then the left side of the widget being attached will be positioned along the right-hand side of the form. This seems to

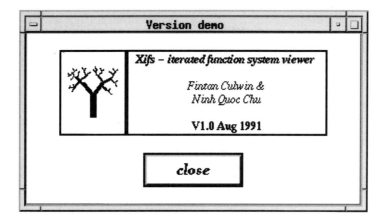

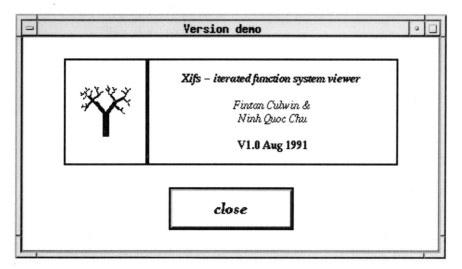

Figure 3.7   *Version_demo* resizing.

imply that the widget would be positioned entirely outside the form's window and thus invisible. However a further set of *offset* resources can be used which could be used to re-position the widget within the window. The use of *offset* resources is relatively rare and will not be considered further.

A summary of the *form* attachment resources is given in Table 3.3. The setting of attachment resources implements the spatial design of a dialog, which underpins part of the communication of the dialog's functionality and usability. Thus in general, these settings should be made in the application code to ensure that the user cannot override them and destroy the usability of the dialog. Prior to Motif release 1.2, when an attachment is being made to another widget it is not

\\\

Table 3.2   Version demo alternative attachment resources

widget	parent	class
version bitmap	version form	Label

resource	value
leftAttachment	XmATTACH_FORM
topAttachment	XmATTACH_FORM
rightAttachment	XmATTACH_SELF
bottomAttachment	XmATTACH_POSITION
bottomPosition	60

widget	parent	class
version text	version form	Label

resource	value
leftAttachment	XmATTACH_WIDGET
leftWidget	version bitmap
topAttachment	XmATTACH_FORM
rightAttachment	XmATTACH_FORM
bottomAttachment	XmATTACH_WIDGET
bottomWidget	version button

widget	parent	class
version button	version form	Label

resource	value
leftAttachment	XmATTACH_POSITION
leftPosition	35
topAttachment	XmATTACH_SELF
rightAttachment	XmATTACH_POSITION
rightPosition	65
bottomAttachment	XmATTACH_FORM

possible for the attachment settings to be specified in a resource file, as the identity of the widget being attached to cannot be deduced by the resource mechanism. When *attachWidget* or *attachOppositeWidget* is specified the attachment resources must therefore be made in the application code. The general advice is to develop the application with the attachment resources specified as far as possible in a resource file, as this will allow experimentation and tuning to be rapidly performed. When the spatial design is finalized then the attachment specifications should be moved to the application code.

The *form* widget provides a very powerful, and once understood, elegant mechanism for the spatial positioning of a number of widgets. The initial complexity of the considerations is best resolved by investigation and experimentation. A suitable exercise is suggested in the end of chapter activities. For some situations the use of one of the other *constraint* widgets may be more appropriate than the use of a *form* widget. There is not space in this book to give a description of the resources and to illustrate the use of these widgets.

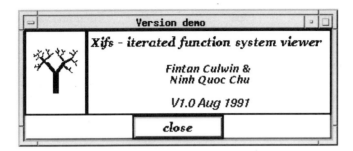

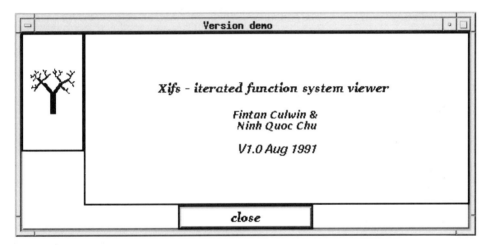

Figure 3.8   *Version_demo* alternative resizing.

3.1.4 Visual control from resource files

The presentation of the *version dialog* can be further improved by the setting of resources in application resource files. Figure 3.10 illustrates the version dialog as shown in Figure 3.3, with one structural and a number of resource changes. The most obvious change has been to enclose the *pixmap* and *text* components of the dialog within *frames*. This is accomplished by changing the application widget hierarchy to make the *pixmap* and *text* widgets children of *frame* widgets. The expanded application widget hierarchy is illustrated in Figure 3.9.

A *frame* widget has a single child widget which it encloses exactly and is used to provide a frame for widgets which do not themselves have a frame. The major resources of the *frame* widget class are given in Table 3.5. *PushButton* widgets have their own frame and thus do not require a *frame* parent. Having supplied a frame to all the visual components, the appearance of the frames can be manipulated for all components by setting the value of the *shadowThickness*

Table 3.3 Form widget class attachment resources

Resource name	type	(default) values
leftAttachment	manifest (unsigned char)	ATTACH_NONE
the widget's left side will be positioned to the left of the form		
leftAttachment	manifest (unsigned char)	ATTACH_SELF
the widget's left side will retain its original positioning (even when resized)		
leftAttachment	manifest (unsigned char)	ATTACH_FORM
		ATTACH_OPPOSITE_FORM
the widget's left side will be attached to the left (opposite right) side of the form		
fractionBase	int	100
leftAttachment	manifest (unsigned char)	ATTACH_POSITION
leftPosition	int	undefined
the widget's left side will be positioned leftPosition/fractionBase from the left		
leftAttachment	manifest (unsigned char)	ATTACH _WIDGET
		ATTACH_OPPOSITE_WIDGET
leftWidget	widget	undefined
the widget's left side will be positioned along a line defined by the right (opposite left) side of the leftWidget		
leftOffset	int	0
defines an offset which will be applied after the attachments above have been applied (does not have any effect for ATTACH_POSITION)		

a similar set of resources is available for the top, right and bottom attachments

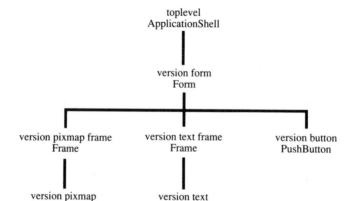

Figure 3.9 *Version_demo* expanded application widget hierarchy.

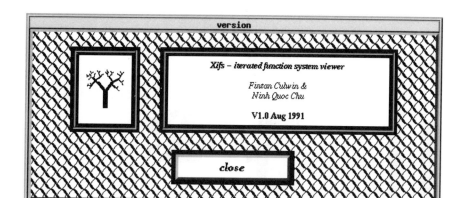

Figure 3.10   *Version_demo* alternative visual design.

resource. In addition to setting the *shadowThickness* resource of the three components in Figure 3.10, the *borderWidth* and *borderColor* resources have also been set to produce the solid border which surrounds the frames.

The *shadowWidth, borderWidth* and *borderColor* resource of all the components in the dialog, including the frame which is an integral part of the *pushButton,* can and should be set with wildcard specifications in the application resource file. This will ensure that the appearance of the three components is consistent, leading to an harmonious appearance.

The spatial resource settings of the *pushButton* widget class are complex, comprising *border, margin, shadow* and *highlight* resources. Taken together these resources define the sizes of the various regions between the edge of the window and the start of the string or pixmap. Figure 3.11 illustrates the relative location of these areas defined by these resources in the horizontal direction for the bottom left of a *pushButton.* As many of these resources are introduced into the widget hierarchy by the *core* and *primitive* classes, the understanding of the use of these resources in a *pushButton* widget can be applied to other widgets.

The other resource which has been changed is to specify a *backgroundPixmap* resource for the *version form* widget. The advantages of setting this resource are not only aesthetic. When a number of applications are running on a single display, setting a unique pixmap resource for all the dialog backgrounds in an application will allow the user to easily identify which dialogs are associated with which application. The bitmap used in Figure 3.10 is an *X* standard bitmap called *xlogo16.* A list of the *X* standard bitmaps is given in Appendix B.

The identification of which dialogs belong to which application can also be assisted by setting a consistent color for all dialog backgrounds, using the background resources of the dialog *form* widgets. The color specification can be made using one of the recognized color names given in Appendix B. The color

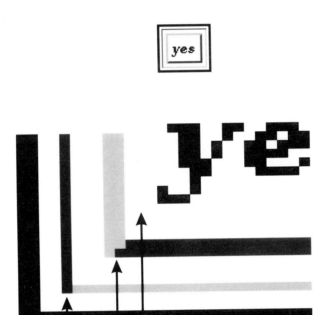

Figure 3.11   The spatial resources of the pushButton widget class.

used for *backgrounds* should be a pale color, in order to allow the contents of the dialogs to have a high contrast with it. The use of colors within Motif applications will be considered in detail in the later chapters of this book.

The final change is made to the window manager components of the dialog shell. By default the *motif window manager* will provide all the components shown in Figure 3.3 to *dialogShells*. These are all possible components with the exception of the *iconify* and *maximize* buttons, which are not required as a dialog cannot be iconified or maximized independently of the application. For the dialog shown in Figure 3.10 the *resize* handles are not required, and as the dialog will be removed by pressing the *close* button the window manager *menu* button has been removed as well.

The removal of the unwanted window manager components is effected by setting the value of a *shell* resource called *XmNmwmDecorations*. The possible values of this resource are:

```
MWM_DECOR_ALL          MWM_DECOR_BORDER  ·
MWM_DECOR_RESIZEH      MWM_DECOR_TITLE
MWM_DECOR_MENU         MWM_DECOR_MINIMIZE
MWM_DECOR_MAXIMIZE
```

To obtain the required components the individual manifest values are *ored* together. Thus for Figure 3.10 only the *border* and *title* components were required giving the value MWM_DECOR_BORDER | MWM_DECOR_TITLE. The resource settings used for Figure 3.10 are given in Table 3.4. If the Motif decoration resources are to be set from a program then the header file *MwmUtils.h* has to be *#included*.

3.2 Designing an interface using state transition diagrams

A **s**tate **t**ransition **d**iagram (std) can initially be used to model an existing interface and subsequently as a design tool to assist in the construction of interfaces. The intention of a state transition diagram is to provide a graphical model of the options which are available to the user and the consequences of selecting one of these options.

To introduce state transition diagrams an electronic stopwatch will be modelled. The stopwatch is shown in Figure 3.12. It consists of a display which shows the number of minutes, seconds and hundredths of seconds which have elapsed and two buttons. One button is known as the *start/stop* button and the other as the *zero* button.

Assuming the stopwatch is in an initial state where it is not running and the

Table 3.4   Presentation resources for *version demo*

widget	parent	class
version_shell		ApplicationShell

resource	value	
mwmDecorations	XM_DECOR_BORDER | XM_DECOR_TITLE	
title	version	

widget	parent	class
version form	toplevel	Form

resource	value	
background	white	
foreground	grey20	
backgroundPixmap	cross_weave	

widget	parent	class
version pixmap frame	version_form	Frame
version text frame		
version button		pushButton

resource	value	
shadowThickness	8	
borderWidth	4	
borderColor	grey80	

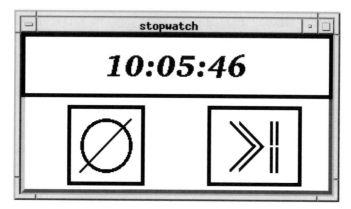

Figure 3.12 Stopwatch visual design.

display is zeroed; pressing the *start/stop* button will start the stopwatch running. Pressing the *start/stop* button a second time will stop the stopwatch running. Pressing the *zero* button at this stage will reset the stopwatch to its initial state. Pressing the *zero* button while the stopwatch is running will reset the stopwatch to zero and continue running.

This description of the stopwatch's operation can be represented in the state transition diagram shown in Figure 3.13. On state transition diagrams a double circle indicates an initiation or a termination of the interface. This interface does not have a termination and has an automatic transition from the initiation state to the initial state where the display is zeroed and the watch is stopped.

From the stopped state there are two possible transitions. Pressing the *zero* button will zero the display and return to the same stopped state. Pressing the *start/stop* button will cause a transition to the running state. From the running state there are two possible transitions. Pressing the *zero* button will reset the display to zero and return to the same running state. Pressing the *start/stop* button will cause a transition to the stopped state.

A state on a state transition diagram is represented by a rectangular box. For GUI based interfaces the box can best be used to illustrate the display which the user will see when the interface is realized. A state is defined as a place in the interface which is visually or functionally distinct from the rest of the interface.

A transition on a state transition diagram is represented by an arrow which may have two labels. The upper label represents the event which will cause the transition to take place. The event is most commonly caused by a user's action, such as the pressing of a button. Some transitions are automatic and consequently have no event labels. The lower label on a transition arrow represents the actions which the application takes in response to the event.

The production of a state transition diagram makes the interface designer's

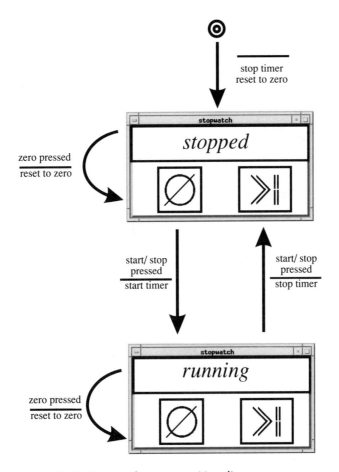

Figure 3.13 Stopwatch, state transition diagram.

cognitive model of the interaction explicit. The interface shown in Figure 3.13 is not the only one which could have been produced to control the stopwatch. If the interface had been developed by a designer whose cognitive model is based on a mechanical stopwatch, it might have been implemented as shown in Figure 3.14.

In this interface the only method of zeroing a stopwatch is to use the *zero* button when the watch is stopped; pressing the *zero* button on a running stopwatch will have no effect. To reset and restart a running stopwatch it first has to be stopped, then zeroed and then restarted. This is congruent with the manner in which a mechanical stopwatch may be operated but does not make best use of an electronic stopwatch.

The designer's cognitive model of a proposed interface is an implicit informal model. As an informal model it is idiosyncratic and may contain inconsistencies or

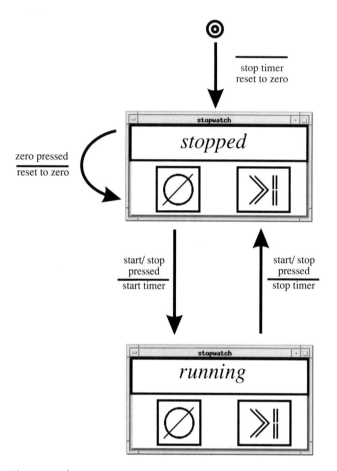

Figure 3.14   Stopwatch, alternative state transition diagram.

ambiguities. It is based upon the designer's personal experience which as illustrated above may not make best use of the facilities available.

A state transition diagram is an explicit formal model. As a formal model it is communicable and can be shown not to contain inconsistencies or ambiguities. There are a number of patterns which can be looked for in state transition diagrams which if present will indicate potential problems with usability in the implemented interface. These patterns will be introduced throughout the rest of this book.

The formal model of the interface can also be considered as the model which the interface designer hopes to establish as the user's cognitive model of the dialog. Thus the production of a state transition diagram is initially a process by which the interface designer can refine his or her personal model into a formal model, and consequently the model which they hope to communicate to the user via the implemented interface.

For this communication to be effective the message has to be complete but as simple as possible. This simplicity can be effected by a number of design heuristics which include minimizing the number of states in the interface, ensuring consistency in the actions which are used to move between states, providing a distinct visual indication of the different states and attempting to make the dialogs which comprise an interface consistent with each other and with dialogs in other applications. All of these heuristics will assist a user in constructing a cognitive model which reflects the formal model, and will thus allow them to use the interface effectively with minimal effort.

3.3 Designing an interface, application design

The common basis of most software design methods is the division of the software into modularized components. These components exist at different scales of analysis, programs, packages, subprograms, blocks, etc. The design and implementation of a windowing program can be effected by the separation of the *presentation layers* from the *application layers*. This has the major advantage of allowing the application modules from the application layer to be easily reused, possibly with a different user interface toolkit. It also allows the possibility of pre-existing application modules being repackaged with a windows based user interface. This division of the software can best be effected by using a third intermediate layer, called a *translation layer*, which implements communication between the application and presentation layers. This is shown diagrammatically in Figure 3.15.

To provide an example of this design approach the design and implementation of a *click counter* will be presented. A mechanical click counter has a *reset* button, a *counting* button and a numeric display. Pressing the *reset* button will cause the display to reset to zero; pressing the *counting* button will increment the displayed value by 1. Mechanical click counters are commonly used to count people or vehicles and are operated by pressing the counting button once every time a person or vehicle passes.

The *click counter* application developed in this chapter will improve the functionality of a mechanical click counter by including a *decrement* button which will decrement the count by 1. The visual design of the click counter is presented in Figure 3.16. The value displayed is limited to three digits and it should be noted that incrementing from 999 will yield 000 and likewise decrementing from 000 will yield 999.

The state transition diagram for the interactive use of the *click counter* is presented in Figure 3.17. This diagram indicates a single state to which all three possible transitions return and that each transition is associated with a single push button control. This simplicity of design indicates that the click counter will be easy for a user to learn and operate.

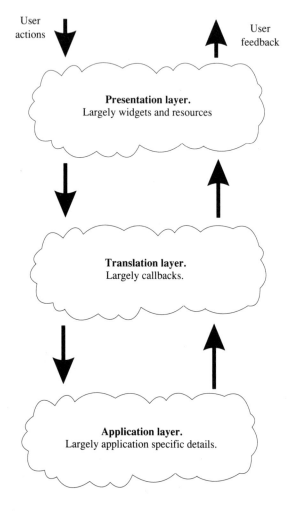

Figure 3.15 GUI application design.

Using the visual design as a guide the application widget hierarchy can be produced, as shown in Figure 3.18. The only non-obvious implementation decision is to make all the control buttons children of a *Form* widget called *control form*, which is itself a child of the *main form Form* widget. This decision was taken to allow the *click counter* to be rapidly re-engineered should the manual controls not be required. For example, the counter functionality could be used to automatically record the number of input/output errors which have been detected by a software package, or as a Geiger counter recording the total number of radioactive particles detected. In these situations the manual controls would not be required and can be easily removed from the counter by

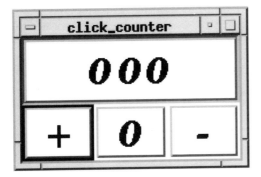

Figure 3.16   Click counter, visual design.

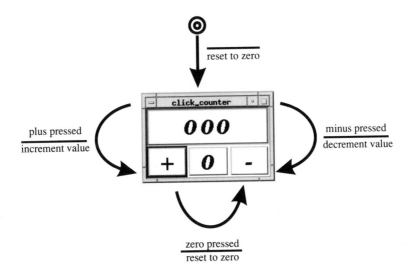

Figure 3.17   Click counter, state transition diagram.

unmanaging the *control form* widget.

The implementation of the presentation layer which creates the widgets can be accomplished using a main program file based upon the main program files presented in the previous chapter. The widget resources which should be set in the program code and the values to which they should be set are presented in Table 3.5.

The *click counter* application layer can be designed from a consideration of the required functionality of a click counter. The design decisions in the construction

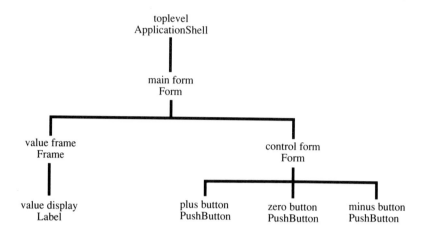

Figure 3.18 Click counter, application widget hierarchy.

of this module should be made independently from any considerations of the use to which the click counter is to be put in any particular application, in order to increase its potential reusability.

The design of the module is presented in Figure 3.19 and the implementation as a header file in Listing 3.3. The associated program file is in Listing 3.4. The application module can be constructed and subjected to formal testing from a text based interactive or an automatic test harness before being incorporated into the windows application.

Figure 3.19 is an object diagram illustrating that the *click_counter module* will contain an encapsulated variable called *click_value*. As the variable is encapsulated it cannot be accessed directly from outside the module. The only way in which it can be accessed is by the functions which are exported from the module. For any encapsulated variable the most common access functions are those which set the variable's value and those which retrieve the variable's value. These are shown in this design as the two functions *set_click_value* which requires a parameter indicating the value to which it is to be set, and the *get_click_value* function which will return the value of the encapsulated variable. A module would also provide functions which are specific to the application requirements which the module supports. In this example two functions called *increment_click_value* and *decrement_click_value* are supplied.

The encapsulation of the *click_value* variable within the module indicates that it is *private* to the module, and its existence is 'unknown' outside the module. The use of a round edged box indicates that a component of the module is a variable or type. A private function of the module would be represented by a square edged

Table 3.5   Resource settings for the click counter presentation module

widget	parent	class
toplevel		ApplicationShell

resource	value
XmNallowShellResize	True

widget	parent	class
main form	toplevel	Form

widget	parent	class
value_frame	main_form	Frame

resource	value
XmNtopAttachment	XmATTACH_FORM
XmNleftAttachment	XmATTACH_FORM
XmNrightAttachment	XmATTACH_FORM
XmNbottomAttachment	XmATTACH_POSITION
XmNbottomPosition	55

widget	parent	class
value_display	value_frame	Label

widget	parent	class
control_form	main_form	Form

resource	value
XmNleftAttachment	XmATTACH_FORM
XmNrightAttachment	XmATTACH_FORM
XmNtopAttachment	XmATTACH_WIDGET
XmNbottomAttachment	XmATTACH_FORM
XmNtopWidget	value_frame

widget	parent	class
plus_button	control_form	PushButton

resource	value
XmNleftAttachment	XmATTACH_FORM
XmNrightAttachment	XmATTACH_POSITION
XmNtopAttachment	XmATTACH_FORM
XmNbottomAttachment	XmATTACH_FORM
XmNrightPosition	33

widget	parent	class
zero_button	control_form	PushButton

resource	value
XmNleftAttachment	XmATTACH_WIDGET
XmNrightAttachment	XmATTACH_POSITION
XmNtopAttachment	XmATTACH_FORM
XmNbottomAttachment	XmATTACH_FORM
XmNleftWidget	plus button
XmNrightPosition	67

continued

Table 3.5 *continued*

widget	parent	class
minus_button	control_form	PushButton

resource	value
XmNleftAttachment	XmATTACH_WIDGET
XmNrightAttachment	XmATTACH_FORM
XmNtopAttachment	XmATTACH_FORM
XmNbottomAttachment	XmATTACH_FORM
XmNleftWidget	zero_button

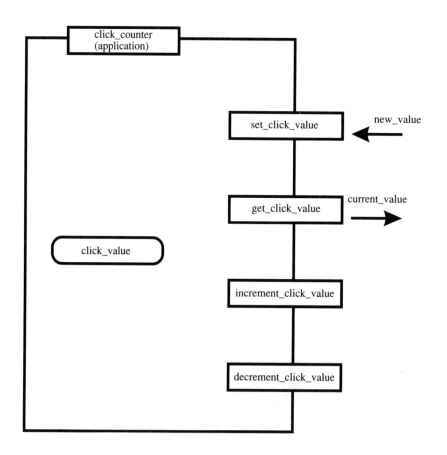

Figure 3.19   Click counter, application design.

Listing 3.3   Click counter application module header file

```
1   /* filename click_counter_application.h (cl_cnt_a.h)    *
2    *                                                       *
3    * Header file for the click counter application module. *
4    * Written for Motif book Chapter 3.                     *
5    *                                                       *
6    * Fintan Culwin version 1.0 Feb 1992, checked Jan 94    *
7   */
8
9   #ifndef CLICK_COUNTER_A
10  #define  CLICK_COUNTER_A
11
12  #define MIN_CLICK_VALUE 0
13  #define MAX_CLICK_VALUE 999
14
15  extern int get_click_value( void );
16  /* function to return the current value of the click counter */
17
18  extern int set_click_value( int set_to );
19  /* function to set the value of the click counter to set_to. *
20   * If the value of set_to is less than the value of          *
21   * MIN_CLICK_VALUE the counter is set to MIN_CLICK_VALUE. If  *
22   * value is greater than MAX_CLICK_VALUE the counter is set   *
23   * to MAX_CLICK_VALUE                                         */
24
25  extern increment_click_counter( void );
26  /* function to increment the value of the click counter. If  *
27   * the value of the counter is equal to MAX_CLICK_VALUE the   *
28   * result of the incrementation will be MIN_CLICK_VALUE.      */
29
30  extern decrement_click_counter( void );
31  /* function to decrement the value of the click counter. If  *
32   * the value of the counter is equal to MIN_CLICK_VALUE the   *
33   * result of the incrementation will be MAX_CLICK_VALUE.      */
34
35  #endif /* #ifndef CLICK_COUNTER_A */
```

Listing 3.4   Click counter application module code file

```
1   /* filename click_counter_application.c (cl_cnt_a.c)    *
2    *                                                       *
3    * Code file for the click counter application module.   *
4    * Written for Motif book Chapter 3.                     *
5    *                                                       *
6    * Fintan Culwin version 1.0 Feb 1992, checked Jan 94.   *
7   */
8
9   #include "c_c_a.h"
10
11  static int click_value = 0;
12  /* Declaring the click_value outside any function causes it to  *
13   * be created and initialized during program initialization, and *
```

continued

\\

Listing 3.4 *continued*

```
14   * to exist for the lifetime of the program. Declaring it static *
15   * limits its visibility to this file only.                     */
16
17   extern int get_click_value( void ){
18          return( click_value );
19   } /* end fun get click value */
20
21
22   extern int set_click_value( int set_to ){
23
24       if ( set_to > MAX_CLICK_VALUE ) {
25           click_value = MAX_CLICK_VALUE;
26       } else {
27         if ( set_to < MIN_CLICK_VALUE ) {
28           click_value = MIN_CLICK_VALUE;
29         } else {
30           click_value = set_to;
31         } /* end if */
32       } /* end if */
33   } /* end fun set click value */
34
35
36   extern increment_click_counter( void ){
37
38       if ( click_value < MAX_CLICK_VALUE ) {
39           click_value++;
40       } else {
41           click_value = MIN_CLICK_VALUE;
42       } /* end if */
43   } /* end fun increment click value */
44
45   extern decrement_click_counter( void ){
46
47       if ( click_value > MIN_CLICK_VALUE ) {
48           click_value--;
49       } else {
50           click_value = MAX_CLICK_VALUE;
51       } /* end if */
52   } /* end fun decrement click value */
```

box, as with the functions which are made *public* by the module in this example. Public components of the module are represented by components which cross the boundary of the module box.

The encapsulation of *private* variables, types and functions within a module and the exporting of *public* facilities from the module is a form of *object based* programming. The advantages of this approach, which ensures that data objects and the operations which act upon them are inseparable, are increased reliability, maintainability and reuse. In C the implementation of the public aspects is made within header (*.h*) files, that of the private aspects within the associated code (*.c*) files. The details of how the various C type definition (*typedef*), visibility specifiers (*extern/ static*) and lifetime specifiers (*auto/ static*) are used in support of *object based* implementation are outside the scope of this book. Suggestions of suitable books which explore these ideas more thoroughly are given in Appendix A.

Having designed and implemented the presentation and application layers, the translation layer to link them together can be produced. Each of the transitions identified on the state transition diagram is associated with the user pressing one of the three *pushButton* controls. This suggests that each of the transitions will be implemented as a callback function, which will be exported from the translation module to the presentation module. The prototypes of these three callbacks in the translation module are:

```
extern void zero_callback(      Widget    widget,
                                XtPointer client_data,
                                XtPointer call_data );
extern void increment_callback( Widget    widget,
                                XtPointer client_data,
                                XtPointer call_data );
extern void decrement_callback( Widget    widget,
                                XtPointer client_data,
                                XtPointer call_data );
```

Each callback function will be associated with the *activateCallback* resource of the relevant *pushButton*; this can be accomplished using the *XtAddCallback* intrinsics function. When the callback function is called as a consequence of the user's action, the first parameter contains the identity of the widget which caused the callback to be called. For this application this will be the identity of the *pushButton* widget, which is of little use to the callback function.

Each of the callbacks will be required to change the value displayed in the *value display* widget; consequently they will require the identity of this widget to be passed to the callback function in the *client_data* parameter. As there is no other information which needs to be passed from the presentation layer to the translation layer, the *client_data* parameter will only be required to identify the *value display* widget. This can be effected by casting the widget identity to the required type (*XtPointer*), and providing this as the *client_data* parameter of the *XtAddCallback* function calls. Thus the format of the *XtAddCallback* function calls for the three callbacks would be:

```
XtAddCallback( zero_widget, zero_callback,
               activate_callback,
               (XtPointer) value_display);
XtAddCallback( increment_widget, increment_callback,
               activate_callback,
               (XtPointer) value_display);
XtAddCallback( decrement_widget, decrement_callback,
               activate_callback,
               (XtPointer) value_display);
```

The implementation of each of these callback functions will be similar. It will call one of the functions from the application layer to change the state of the click counter object, then retrieve the value of the click counter using the enquiry function and finally update the value in the *value_display* widget. This last activity is common to all three callbacks and can be factored out of their design. This gives the design of the translation layer as illustrated in Figure 3.20.

The header file for the translation layer is shown in Listing 3.5 and the implementation of the callback functions and the *show_value* function is shown in Listing 3.6. The operation of the *increment* callback function is illustrated in Figure 3.21. The implementations of the *zero* and *decrement* callback functions will be similar to the implementation of the *increment* function and are left as an end of chapter activity.

The *click counter* presentation layer in addition to creating the widget hierarchy and installing the callbacks also has a responsibility to ensure that the counter is in a defined state when it is first realized. This is shown on the state transition diagram as the action component of the automatic transition from the initiation state to the initial state. The initialization of the click counter application and

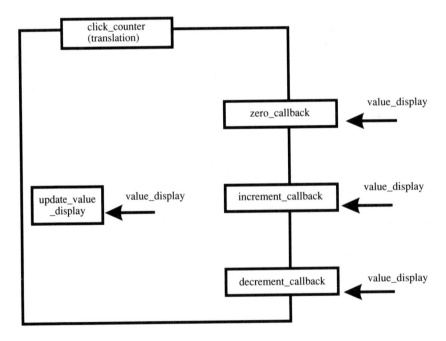

Figure 3.20   Click counter, translation design.

Listing 3.5 Click counter translation module header file

```
1   /* filename click_counter_translation.h (cl_cnt_t.h)    *
2    *                                                        *
3    * Header file for the click counter translation module. *
4    * Written for Motif book Chapter 3.                      *
5    *                                                        *
6    * Fintan Culwin version 1.0 Feb 1992, checked Jan 94    *
7   */
8
9   #ifndef CLICK_COUNTER_T
10  #define  CLICK_COUNTER_T
11
12  #include <Xm/Xm.h>
13
14  #define MAX_STRING_LEN 20
15  #define MAX_ARGS       10
16  #define ZERO           0
17
18  extern void increment_callback( Widget    widget,
19                                  XtPointer client_data,
20                                  XtPointer call_data );
21  /* callback function to implement the increment behaviour  *
22   * requires the label widget for the value to be displayed *
23   * in, to be passed in the client data parameter.          */
24
25  extern void decrement_callback( Widget    widget,
26                                  XtPointer client_data,
27                                  XtPointer call_data );
28  /* callback function to implement the decrement behaviour  *
29   * requires the label widget for the value to be displayed *
30   * in, to be passed in the client data parameter.          */
31
32  extern void    zero_callback( Widget    widget,
33                                  XtPointer client_data,
34                                  XtPointer call_data );
35  /* callback function to implement the zero behaviour       *
36   * requires the label widget for the value to be displayed *
37   * in, to be passed in the client data parameter.          */
38
39  #endif
```

Listing 3.6 Click counter translation module code file

```
1   /* filename click_counter_translation.c (cl_cnt_t.c)    *
2    *                                                        *
3    * Code file for the click counter translation module.   *
4    * Written for Motif book Chapter 3.                      *
5    *                                                        *
6    * Fintan Culwin version 1.0 Feb 1992, checked Jan 94    *
7   */
8
9   #include "c_c_t.h"
10
```

continued

|||||||||||||||||||||||||||||||||||||||||||||||||||||||||||||||||||||||||||||||||||||||||||||||||||||||||||||||||||||||||||||||||||||||||||

Listing 3.6 *continued*

```
11   static void display_value( Widget widget );
12   /* prototype for common hidden function to change the    *
13    * value display. The widget paramater will have its     *
14    * value resource set to the value of the click counter. */
15
16
17   extern void increment_callback( Widget  widget,
18                                     caddr_t client_data,
19                                     caddr_t call_data ){
20       increment_click_counter( );
21       display_value( (Widget) client_data);
22   } /* end fun increment callback */
23
24
25   extern void decrement_callback( Widget  widget,
26                                     caddr_t client_data,
27                                     caddr_t call_data ){
28       decrement_click_counter( );
29       display_value( (Widget) client_data);
30   } /* end fun decrement callback */
31
32
33   extern void     zero_callback( Widget  widget,
34                                    caddr_t client_data,
35                                    caddr_t call_data ){
36       set_click_value( ZERO );
37       display_value( (Widget) client_data);
38   } /* end fun zero  callback */
39
40
41   static void display_value( Widget widget ){
42
43   int        the_value;
44   char *     ascii_value[ MAX_STRING_LEN ];
45   XmString   X_value_string;
46
47   Arg        args[ MAX_ARGS ];
48   int        num_args;
49
50       /* get the value and convert to Xm string */
51       the_value = get_click_value();
52       sprintf( ascii_value, "%u", the_value );
53       X_value_string = XmStringCreate( ascii_value,
54                                        XmSTRING_DEFAULT_CHARSET);
55
56       /* install as the label widget's resource */
57       num_args = 0;
58       XtSetArg( args[num_args], XmNlabelString, X_value_string );
59                                                 num_args++;
60       XtSetValues( widget, args, num_args );
61
62       /* release resources used by the Xm string */
63       XmStringFree( X_value_string );
64   } /* end fun display value */
```

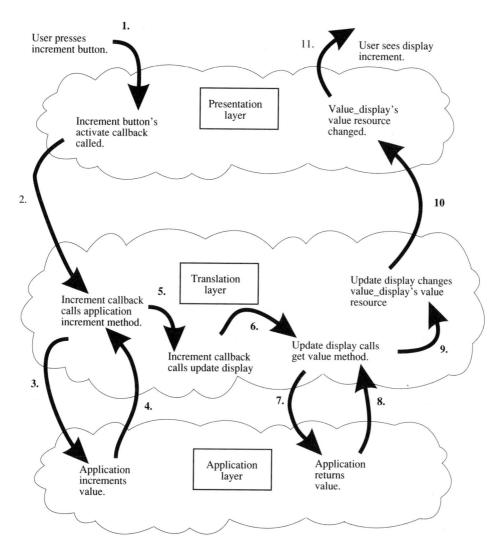

Figure 3.21 Operation of the increment action.

presentation layers can be accomplished by an explicit call of the translation layer *zero* callback function. This call will take the form:

```
zero_callback( (Widget)    NULL,
               (XtPointer) value_display,
               (XtPointer) NULL);
```

and can be included in the source code after the widgets have been created but

\\\

before they are realized. The first and third parameters can be safely set to NULL values, as the callback makes no use of these parameters.

The construction of the *click counter* is now complete. It comprises the presentation layer file which is also the main program and is contained in *click_counter.c (cl_cnt_a.c)*. The translation layer is contained in the files *click_counter_t.h* and *click_counter_t.c (cl_cnt_t.h* and *cl_cnt_t.c)*; the application module is contained in the files *click_counter_a.h* and *click_counter_a.c (cl_cnt_a.h* and *cl_cnt_a.c)*.

The presentation module only *#includes* the translation module, thus it has no direct knowledge of the application module. Likewise the translation module only *#includes* the application module and has no direct knowledge of the presentation module. The application module has no *#includes* and thus has no direct knowledge of either of the other two modules. This implements the application using the three modules described above and maximizes the possibility of the application and translation modules being successfully reused.

3.4 Activities for Chapter 3

1. To investigate the usage of *XmStrings*, *pixmaps*, attachment resources and visual resources construct an application which consists of four *label* widgets within a *form* widget. Two of the widgets should contain multi-segment *XmStrings* and the other two *pixmaps*. Use the resource mechanism to explore the different possible visual appearances.

2. The electronic stopwatch used as an example in this section can be expanded to include a lap function by the provision of a *lap button*. When the *lap button* is pressed for a first time the display will freeze but the stopwatch will continue running. When the *lap button* is pressed a second time the display will unfreeze and continue displaying the current elapsed time. While the lap display is active the *start/stop* and *zero* buttons are not effective. Construct a state transition diagram for this stopwatch.

3. If you have a video recorder, or other programmable electronic device, such as a microwave, construct a state transition diagram for a part of its functionality.

4. If you have a bank card which allows you to withdraw cash from an electronic teller machine, use your memory of the teller's interface to construct a state transition diagram of the actions involved with withdrawing an amount of cash. Validate your personal cognitive model next time you use the teller.

5. Figure 3.22 illustrates an application called *Base converter*. The intention of the application is to allow the user to enter a literal value in the format of the currently selected base in the input area at the top of the interface. (You may assume that the user will always enter a suitable literal value.) Pressing any of the base toggle buttons will cause the value to be displayed in the format of the selected base. Construct a state transition

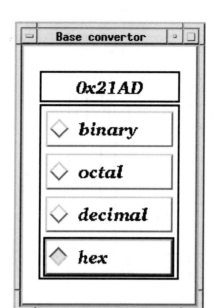

Figure 3.22   Base converter, visual design.

diagram and an application module for this application.

6. Figure 3.23 illustrates an application called *Currency .converter.* The intention of the application is that if the value of the *pound*, exchange *rate* or *dollar* fields are changed by moving the slider, the values of the other two components will change as appropriate. Construct a state transition diagram and an application module for this application.

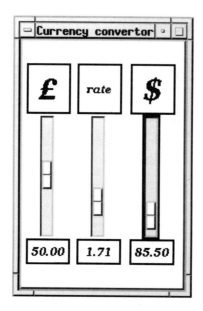

Figure 3.23   Currency converter, visual design.

\\

CHAPTER FOUR

Motif application menus

Introduction

The application level *main pull down menu* has become instantly recognizable to all users of standard GUIs. This chapter will introduce the contents and construction of a Motif application *main pull down menu*, and one standard option, an *exit dialog*, which can be obtained from it. The Motif style guide suggests the minimal components of the *main menu* bar and some of the options on the *pull down* menus which are accessed from it. The application menu developed in this chapter, where appropriate, will comply with the recommendations of the Motif style guide.

The menu system which is developed in this chapter is incomplete in that it is an application menu without an application. The remaining chapters of this book will provide an example application and illustrate techniques by which it can be attached to the application *main menu*. The system constructed in this chapter can be used as the basis upon which application *main menus* for other applications can be built.

The style guide suggests that the first (leftmost) *pull down* menu should be the *file* menu, and that its last option should be one to *exit* the application. The style guide also suggests that the last *pull down* menu should be the *help* menu, and that the button for this menu should be attached to the right-hand side of the application *main menu* bar.

The precise details of the *exit* and other interfaces are not mandated by the style guide. This chapter will implement a minimal *exit* interface which will be attached to the *exit* button of the *file* pull down menu. The next chapter will implement a combined *save/ save as* interface which will also be attached to the *file* menu, and a *help system* which will be attached to the *help* button of the *main menu*. One of the design objectives of these systems and interfaces is to provide a design and implementation which is easily reusable in other applications.

4.1 The application main menu

The visual appearance of the Motif standard application *main menu* is illustrated in Figure 4.1. Although it is not obligatory for an application to conform with the

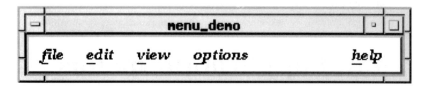

Figure 4.1   The application level main menu.

style guide, there are two major advantages for the construction of interfaces which do. The first advantage is that the user will recognize the application *main menu* and will be able to transfer their knowledge of operating *main menus* from other applications. The second advantage of using a standard *main menu* is that the Motif toolkit provides some support to the programmer for its construction, and once a standard application *main menu* has been constructed it is possible for it to be reused in other applications.

Figure 4.2 illustrates the contents of the *pull down* menus which will be implemented in this section. Only the implementation of the *file*, *option* and *help* menus will be presented in detail in this chapter. The implementation of the *edit* and *view* menus should be obvious, once the construction of the other menus has been considered.

There is a style guide convention that options on a *pull down* menu, which lead to a further menu when they are activated, are followed by an arrow. The *option 3 button* in Figure 4.2 offers a further menu and, as shown, is followed by an arrow. A menu which is accessed from another menu is known as a *cascade menu*. A further convention is that menu options which lead to a further interaction with the user before their functionality can be effected are followed by two dots. The *open*, *save as* and *exit* options from the file menu in Figure 4.2 provide examples of this convention.

Several options on the menu system are also accessible via *accelerators*. An *accelerator* is a combination of key presses which can be used to activate the actions of a menu button, without first having to post the menu. For example, the *exit* option of the *file* menu has the accelerator CTRL+E associated with it. This indicates that pressing the control key simultaneously with the 'E' key, whenever the application has keyboard focus, will activate the actions of the *exit* button.

The menu system also offers *mnemonics*. A *mnemonic* is a single key press which can be used to activate the actions of a menu button, once the menu has been posted. For example the *exit* button on the *file* menu has the x of e$x$it underlined to indicate that the mnemonic x is associated with the button. Pressing the x key whenever the *file* menu is posted will activate the actions of the *exit* button.

The *file* and *edit* menus in Figure 4.2 are implemented as *tear off* menus, which are only availabe in Motif release 1.2. This is indicated by the *tear off control* button at the top of the menus. When the mouse pointer is over the

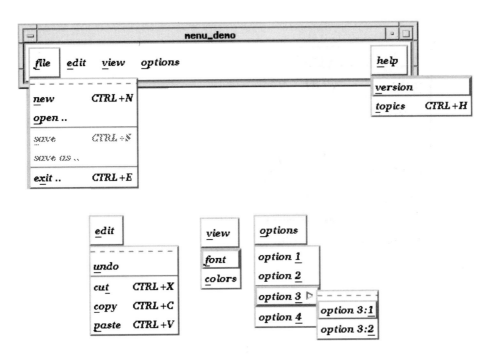

Figure 4.2   The application level pull down menus.

tear off control button the menu can be dragged away from the menu bar allowing it to remain permanently available to the user, without first having to post it. A torn off menu can be reattached to the menu bar by pressing its control button on the bar. The appearance of the *torn off file* menu is illustrated in Figure 4.3.

Figure 4.4 illustrates a partial application widget hierarchy for the application main menu illustrated in Figure 4.2. Only the hierarchies of the *file* and *help* menus have been completed; the remaining parts of the hierarchy will be given later in this section or suggested as an end of chapter activity.

For a complete application hierarchy, the *main menu* widget would have at least one sibling which would be used as the *work space* of the application. For the purposes of this example no *work space* will be provided. The *main menu* is implemented as an instance of the *RowColumn* widget class, configured to behave as a *menu bar*. The *RowColumn* widget class is a *Composite* widget class which provides geometry management for its children. One of the most common uses for a *RowColumn* widget is to provide a *pane* upon which menus of various types are mounted.

The children of the *main menu* are the *cascadeButton* widgets which implement the buttons of the menu, and also the *menuShell* widgets which are the parents of the *menu panes* upon which the menu buttons will be mounted. The *CascadeButton* widget class is a sibling class of the *PushButton* class, which was

Figure 4.3 The file menu when torn off.

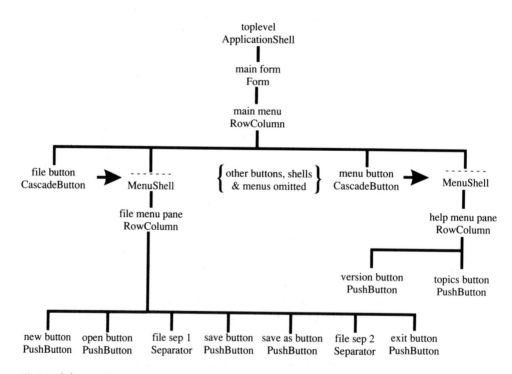

Figure 4.4 Application main menu, partial widget hierarchy.

introduced in previous chapters. The *CascadeButton* class differs from the *PushButton* class largely in not having *arming* and *disarming* callbacks; but it does have a resource called *subMenuId* which identifies the menu pane which is to be *posted* when the cascade button is pressed. The resources introduced by the *CascadeButton* widget class are listed in Table 4.1.

It might be expected that the widgets which implement a *pull down* menu would all be children of the *cascade* button which control them. Figure 4.4 shows that the highest level of a *pull down* menu hierarchy is a *menuShell* instance, which is a sibling of the *cascadeButton* which controls the menu. The reason for this is that the *cascadeButton* is a *primitive* widget which does not have the capability to control any children. The *rowColumn* widget which provides the *menu pane* upon which the *cascadeButton* is mounted does have this capability, and thus can be used as the parent of the *menuShell*. The relationship between the *cascadeButton* and its associated menu is illustrated by an arrow on the application widget hierarchy, as shown in Figure 4.4.

A *pull down* menu widget hierarchy is comprised of a *menuShell*, which is the parent of a *rowColumn menu pane* upon which the *cascadeButtons, pushButtons* and *separators* which make up the menu are mounted. A *menuShell* is a sub-class of the *overrideShell* widget class. *OverrideShells* have the capability to bypass the window manager and will thus be mapped quickly, without any window decorations. Because the window manager is unaware of the existence of such shells, *menuShells* should only be used as the shell for a *pull down, option* or *pop up* menus which are intended to be visible upon the display for only a short period of time. The reasons why the *menuShells* in the *pull down* widget hierarchies do not have names will be made clear shortly.

The *RowColumn* widget which is the child of the *menuShell* is configured to act as a *pull down* menu. One difference between the application *main menu rowColumn* and the *pull down* menu *rowColumn* widgets is immediately obvious.

Table 4.1 The major resources of the *CascadeButton* widget class

inheritance hierarchy   core -> primitive -> label -> cascadeButton

Resource name	type	(default) values
activateCallback	CallbackList	NULL
actions to be performed when the button is pressed and released		
cascadingCallback	CallbackList	NULL
actions to be performed before the pull down menu is posted		
cascadePixmap	Pixmap	dynamic
pixmap to be displayed when a submenu is attached		
mappingDelay	int	180
time taken to display the submenu after activation		
subMenuId	Widget	NULL
identity of the pulldown menu pane to be posted when the button is activated		

Application menus are laid out horizontally, *pull down* menus are laid out vertically. This difference is achieved by setting the value of a *rowColumn* resource. The setting of this resource is facilitated by using Motif convenience functions to create *main menu* and *pull down* menus; these utility functions will be introduced shortly.

4.2 Constructing the main menu

The design of an application *main menu* widget hierarchy can be accomplished from the visual design of the menu system, as shown in Figures 4.2 and 4.4. The design should include the *menu panes* and *menu shells,* and the required relationships between them, as discussed above.

The construction of an application *main menu* can be implemented in a modular manner, in the same source code file as the *main()* function of the application. In order to prevent the *main()* function from becoming too complex, the creation of the application menu and the pull down menus can be accomplished in subsidiary functions. Figure 4.5 is a JSP data flow diagram for the construction of the application menu.

A single function called *create_main_menu* will be called from *main()* requiring the identity of the *main form* widget to be passed to it. This function will create the menu system by calling a number of sub-functions. The first sub-function is required to create and return the *main menu* widget as a child of the *main form* widget. A suitable function called *XmCreateMenuBar* is provided by the Motif toolkit. The prototype for this function is:

```
Widget XmCreateMenuBar( Widget   parent,
                        char *   name,
                        Arg      args[],
                        Cardinal num_args );
```

The parameters identify the *parent* widget of the menu bar, the *name* of the menu bar and the resources to be set for the menu bar as it is created. The effect of the

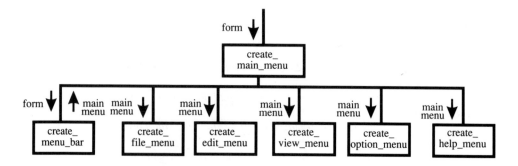

Figure 4.5   Application main menu creation, JSP design.

function is to create an instance of the *rowColumn* widget, with its resources automatically configured to implement a *menu bar*. The resources of the *rowColumn* widget class are complex. The use of an *Xm* convenience function, which automatically sets these resources to the required values, greatly simplifies program construction and ensures that the relevant resources are set to the required values. The major resources of the *rowColumn* widget class are given in Table 4.2.

Table 4.2   The major resources of the **RowColumn** widget class

inheritance hierarchy	core -> composite -> constraint -> manager
	->bulletinBoard -> rowColumn

Resource name	type	(default) values
adjustLast	Boolean	True
if true forces last row (or column) of children to be flush		
with the edge of the rowColumn widget		
adjustMargin	Boolean	True
if true forces button labels to align vertically or horizontally		
entryAlignment	manifest (unsigned char)	XmALIGNMENT_BEGINNING
		XmALIGNMENT_CENTRE
		XmALIGNMENT_END
determines allignment, if isAligned resource is true		
entryClass	WidgetClass	XmToggleButtonGadgetClass
		XmCascadeButtonWidgetClass
determines allowed widgets, if isHomogeneous is true		
isAligned	Boolean	True
enables the setting of entryAlignment		
isHomogeneous	Boolean	dynamic
if true forces all child widgets to be of the class specified in entryClass		
menuAccelerator	String	dynamic
identifies accelerator key for pop up or menu bar activation		
menuHelpWidget	Widget	NULL
identifies the help button on menu bars		
menuHistory	Widget	NULL
identifies the last option or toggle child selected		
mnemonic	KeySym	NULL
identifies the mnemonic key for option menu entries		
numColumns	short	1
determines the number of columns (or rows)		
orientation	manifest (unsigned char)	XmVERTICAL
		XmHORIZONTAL
determines the orientation of the children		

continued

\\

Table 4.2 *continued*

Resource name	type	(default) values
packing	manifest (unsigned char)	XmPACK_TIGHT
		XmPACK_COLUMN
		XmPACK_NONE
	determines the spacing of the children	
radioAlwaysOne	Boolean	True
	if true enforces one-of-many behaviour on toggle button children	
radioBehaviour	Boolean	False
	if true enforces radio box behaviour	
rowColumnType	manifest (unsigned char)	XmWORK_AREA
		XmMENU_BAR
		XmMENU_POPUP
		XmMENU_PULLDOWN
		XmMENU_OPTION
	determines the type of rowColumn to create	
subMenuId	Widget	null
	specifies the menu pane for an option menu RowColumn	
tearOffModel	manifest (unsigned char)	XmTEAR_OFF_ENABLED
		XmTEAR_OFF_DISABLED (default)
	when enabled allows pull down or pop up menus to be torn off (Motif 1.2 only)	

The parent of the menu bar widget is a *form* widget, thus the menu bar instance will inherit attachment resources. The top, left and right attachments will have to be set to *attachForm;* the bottom attachment will have to be specified as *attachSelf.* With these attachments the menu will resize itself appropriately as the *applicationShell* is resized. As these attachments are essential to preserve the visual integrity of the *main menu* they should be set from the application code, not from resource files.

The second sub-function, *create_file_menu*, will create the *file pull down* menu before creating the *cascadeButton* which controls it. The reason for this is that the *cascadeButton* has to be made aware of the identity of the *menu pane* which it is controlling. The simplest manner of achieving this is to inform the *cascadeButton* as it is created and in order to do this the *menu pane* has to be created before the *cascadeButton.* The menu pane can be created by using the convenience function *XmCreatePullDownMenu.* The prototype for this function is:

```
Widget XmCreatePullDownMenu( Widget    parent,
                             char *    name,
                             Arg       args[],
                             Cardinal  num_args );
```

The interpretation of the parameters of this function is identical to the interpretation of the parameters of the *XmCreateMenuBar* function given above. The effect of the function is to create an unnamed instance of the *MenuShell* widget class as a child of the *parent* widget supplied. Subsequently the function will create an instance of the *rowColumn* widget class configured as a *pull down menu pane* with the *name* supplied, as a child of the *menuShell*. As the *menuShell* instance is created in this manner, and as it is never required to be accessed by the program or by the resource file mechanism, it is appropriate for it to be unnamed. Thus the application widget hierarchy in Figure 4.4 specifies no name for the *menuShells*.

If Motif 1.2 is being used and the menu is intended to be used as a *tear off* menu, the *RowColumn* resource *tearOffModel* should be set to the value XmTEAR_OFF_ENABLED as the *menu pane* is created. Although it is possible for this resource to be set following the creation of a menu, this may cause the user to become unsure if the menu can or cannot be torn off. Consequently it should be set only as the menu is created. It is possible for the resource to be set from resource files, allowing the user to determine for themselves which menus should be capable of being torn off. However this facility is not as straightforward as using other resource file specification techniques and is not covered in this book.

The *menu pane* is managed automatically as a consequence of the activation of the *cascadeButton* which controls it, thus the *menu pane* should not be explicitly managed by the application code following its creation.

Having created the *menu pane*, the buttons and separators which populate it are created. If the components of the menu are created in the same order in which they appear on the *pull down* menu, then the *menu pane* will display them in the required sequence. The *cascadeButtons* on the *pull down* menu can be created using the utility function *XmCreateCascadeButton*, the *pushButtons* with the utility function *XmCreatePushButton* and the *separators* with the utility function *XmCreateSeparator*.

The prototypes of these functions and the interpretation of their parameters is essentially identical to the interpretation of the other *XmCreate{whatever}* functions given above. The effect of the functions is to create and return an instance of the specified widget class with the parent, name and resources as specified. Despite the non-management of the *menu pane*, the components of the menu are themselves managed following their creation. The additional resources of the *CascadeButton* class have already been given in Table 4.1. The resources of the *PushButton* class were given in Chapter 2. The major resources of the *Separator* widget class are presented in Table 4.3.

Having created the *menu pane* as a child of the *menuShell* and populated it with the components of the *pull down* menu, the *cascadeButton* which controls the *pull down* menu can be created using the *XmCreateCascadeButton* utility function. As this widget is created the *cascadeButton* resource *subMenuId* should be set to the identity of the *menu pane* which it is to control. The effect of this resource specification is to cause the *menu pane* to be managed whenever the *cascadeButton* is pressed. Management of the *menu pane* causes it to become mapped and as it has a *shellWidget* as a parent this causes it, and its children, to become visible upon the screen. The activation method of the *cascadeButton* also ensures that the menu is correctly positioned relative to the *cascadeButton* itself.

Listing 4.1 presents the text of the functions *create_main_menu* and

\\\

Table 4.3 The new resources of the *Separator* widget class

inheritance hierarchy   core -> primitive -> separator

Resource name	type	(default) values
margin	Dimension	0
determines the spacing on each end of the separator		
orientation	manifest (unsigned char)	XmVERTICAL
		XmHORIZONTAL
determines the orientation of the separator		
separatorType	manifest (unsigned char)	XmNO_LINE
		XmSINGLE_LINE
		XmDOUBLE_LINE
		XmSINGLE_DASHED_LINE
		XmDOUBLE_DASHED_LINE
		XmSHADOW_ETCHED_IN (default)
		XmSHADOW_ETCHED_OUT
determines the appearance of the separator		

create_file_menu. The function *main()* from which *create_main_menu* is called would be largely identical to the other *main()* functions presented in previous chapters. After creating the *toplevel* widget, the *main()* function would create a *form* widget as its child and pass the identity of the *form* widget to *create_main_menu.* Following the creation of the *main menu*, *main()* can conclude with the realization of the *toplevel* widget and the main loop of the application.

The creation of the other *pull down* menus is comparable to the creation of

Listing 4.1   Create_main_menu and create_file_menu

```
 1  /* functions to create the main menu and the file menu. Contained in *
 2   * a main() program file which has #included exit_d.h for the exit    *
 3   * dialog components attached to the file menu exit button.           *
 4   */
 5
 6  void create_main_menu( Widget parent ){
 7  /* function called from main() to create the entire main menu bar and      *
 8   * all the pull dowm menus which are attached to it. The parent parameter *
 9   * is assumed to be a form widget and the main menu bar will attach        *
10   * itself to the top of the form.                                          *
11   */
12
13  Widget main_menu;
14  Arg args[ MAX_ARGS ];
15  int num_args;
16
17      /* create the main menu bar */
18      num_args = 0;
```

continued

\\

Listing 4.1 *continued*

```
19        XtSetArg( args[num_args], XmNleftAttachment, XmATTACH_FORM ); num_args++;
20        XtSetArg( args[num_args], XmNtopAttachment, XmATTACH_FORM ); num_args++;
21        XtSetArg( args[num_args], XmNrightAttachment, XmATTACH_FORM ); num_args++;
22        XtSetArg( args[num_args], XmNbottomAttachment, XmATTACH_SELF); num_args++;
23        main_menu = XmCreateMenuBar( parent, "main menu", args, num_args );
24        XtManageChild( main_menu );
25
26        /* and attach the sub menus to it */
27        create_file_menu( main_menu );
28        create_edit_menu( main_menu );
29        create_view_menu( main_menu );
30        create_option_menu( main_menu );
31        create_help_menu( main_menu );
32
33  } /* end fun create main menu */
34
35
36  void create_file_menu( Widget parent ){
37  /* function to create and attach the file menu to the menu bar which  *
38   * it assumes has been passed as the parent parameter.                 *
39   */
40
41  Widget file_menu_pane, file_menu_button,
42         new_button, open_button, file_sep_1,
43         save_button, save_as_button, file_sep_2,
44         exit_button;
45
46  Arg args[ MAX_ARGS ];
47  int num_args;
48
49        /* create the menu pane for the menu */
50        num_args = 0;
51        file_menu_pane = XmCreatePulldownMenu( parent, "file menu pane",
52                                               args, num_args );
53        /* note this widget is not managed by the client */
54
55        /* populate the menu pane */
56        num_args = 0;
57        new_button = XmCreatePushButton( file_menu_pane, "new button",
58                                         args, num_args);
59        XtManageChild( new_button );
60
61        num_args = 0;
62        open_button = XmCreatePushButton( file_menu_pane, "open button",
63                                          args, num_args);
64        XtManageChild( open_button );
65
66        num_args = 0;
67        file_sep_1 = XmCreateSeparator( file_menu_pane, "file sep 1",
68                                        args, num_args);
69        XtManageChild( file_sep_1 );
70
71        num_args = 0;
```

continued

\\\

Listing 4.1 *continued*

```
72      save_button = XmCreatePushButton( file_menu_pane, "save button",
73                                      args, num_args);
74      XtManageChild( save_button );
75
76      num_args = 0;
77      save_as_button = XmCreatePushButton( file_menu_pane, "save as button",
78                                      args, num_args);
79      XtManageChild( save_as_button );
80
81      num_args = 0;
82      file_sep_2 = XmCreateSeparator( file_menu_pane, "file sep 2",
83                                      args, num_args);
84      XtManageChild( file_sep_2 );
85
86      num_args = 0;
87      exit_button = XmCreatePushButton( file_menu_pane,"exit button",
88                                      args, num_args);
89      XtManageChild( exit_button );
90
91      /* create the exit dialog and add the activation function as the *
92       * exit button's activate callback.                              */
93      create_exit_dialog( parent );
94      XtAddCallback( exit_button, XmNactivateCallback,
95                      activate_exit_dialog, (XtPointer) NULL );
96
97      /* create the file cascade button on the menu bar and attach the *
98       * file menu pane to it.                                         */
99      num_args = 0;
100     XtSetArg( args[num_args], XmNsubMenuId, file_menu_pane); num_args++;
101     file_menu_button = XmCreateCascadeButton( parent, "file menu button",
102                                      args, num_args );
103     XtManageChild( file_menu_button );
104 } /* end fun create file menu */
```

the *file* menu described above. Only the *option* menu and the *help* menu require some additional consideration. The *option* menu itself has a *sub menu* attached to its third button. The creation of this *cascading* menu is identical in its considerations to the creation of the first level *pull down* menu to which it is attached. The detailed application widget hierarchy of this *pull down, cascade* menu system is presented in Figure 4.6. The implementation of this design as program code can be found in the function *create_option_menu* in Listing 4.2.

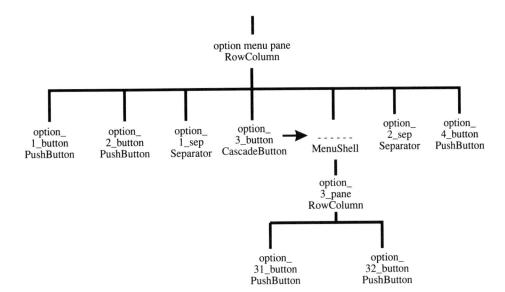

Figure 4.6 Option menu, application widget hierarchy.

Listing 4.2 Create_option_menu

```
1   void create_option_menu( Widget parent ){
2   /* function to create the option menu and the cascade menu attached to *
3    * it, attaching the option menu to the option button on the menu bar   *
4    * which the function assumes has been passed as the parent parameter    *
5   */
6
7   Widget option_menu_pane, option_menu_button,
8          option_1_button, option_2_button, option_sep_1,
9          option_3_button, option_sep_2, option_4_button,
10         option_3_pane, option_31_button, option_32_button;
11
12  Arg args[ MAX_ARGS ];
13  int num_args;
14
15   /* create the menu pane for the menu */
16   num_args = 0;
17   option_menu_pane = XmCreatePulldownMenu( parent, "option menu pane",
18                                        args, num_args );
19   /* note this widget is not managed by the client */
20
21   /* populate the menu pane */
22   num_args = 0;
23   option_1_button = XmCreatePushButton( option_menu_pane,"option 1 button",
24                                      args, num_args);
25   XtManageChild( option_1_button );
26
27   num_args = 0;
28   option_2_button = XmCreatePushButton( option_menu_pane,"option 2 button",
```

continued

\\

Listing 4.2 *continued*

```
29                                              args, num_args);
30    XtManageChild( option_2_button );
31
32    num_args = 0;
33    option_sep_1 = XmCreateSeparator( option_menu_pane,"option sep 1",
34                                      args, num_args);
35    XtManageChild( option_sep_1 );
36
37    /* create the cascade menu before creating the button *
38     * on the pull down menu which controls it             */
39
40    /* create the menu pane for the menu */
41    num_args = 0;
42    option_3_pane = XmCreatePulldownMenu( option_menu_pane,"option 3 pane",
43                                          args, num_args );
44    /* note this widget is not managed by the client */
45
46    /* populate the cascade menu pane */
47    num_args = 0;
48    option_31_button = XmCreatePushButton( option_3_pane,"option 31 button",
49                                           args, num_args);
50    XtManageChild( option_31_button );
51
52    num_args = 0;
53    option_32_button = XmCreatePushButton( option_3_pane,"option 32 button",
54                                           args, num_args);
55    XtManageChild( option_32_button );
56
57
58    /* inform the option 3 cascade button of the identity *
59     * of its cascading menu pane                         */
60    num_args = 0;
61    XtSetArg( args[num_args], XmNsubMenuId, option_3_pane);num_args++;
62    option_3_button = XmCreateCascadeButton( option_menu_pane,"option 3 button",
63                                             args, num_args);
64    XtManageChild( option_3_button );
65
66    num_args = 0;
67    option_sep_2 = XmCreateSeparator( option_menu_pane,"option sep 2",
68                                      args, num_args);
69    XtManageChild( option_sep_2 );
70
71    num_args = 0;
72    option_4_button = XmCreatePushButton( option_menu_pane,"option 4 button",
73                                          args, num_args);
74    XtManageChild( option_4_button );
75
76    /* create the option cascade button on the menu bar and attach the *
77     * option menu pane to it.                                          */
78    num_args = 0;
79    XtSetArg( args[num_args], XmNsubMenuId, option_menu_pane);num_args++;
80    option_menu_button = XmCreateCascadeButton( parent, "option menu button",
81                                                args, num_args );
82    XtManageChild( option_menu_button );
83    } /* end fun create option menu */
```

The implementation of the *help* menu requires one further consideration. The visual design in Figure 4.1 conforms with the style guide requirement to place the *help* button at the extreme right-hand side of the main menu. This is accomplished by setting a resource called *menuHelpWidget* of the *rowColumn* application *main menu pane* to the identity of the *help cascadeButton*. This is implemented within the function *create_help_menu* after the help button has been created, using the intrinsics function *XtSetValues*. The text of the function *create_help_menu* is given in Listing 4.3.

Listing 4.3   Create_help_menu

```
1   void create_help_menu( Widget parent ){
2   /* function to create and attach the help menu to the menu bar which *
3    * it assumes has been passed in the parent parameter                 *
4   */
5
6   Widget help_menu_pane, help_menu_button,
7          version_button, topics_button;
8
9   Arg args[ MAX_ARGS ];
10  int num_args;
11
12      /* create the menu pane for the menu */
13      num_args = 0;
14      help_menu_pane = XmCreatePulldownMenu( parent, "help menu pane",
15                                      args, num_args );
16      /* note this widget is not managed by the client */
17
18      /* populate the menu pane */
19      num_args = 0;
20      version_button = XmCreatePushButton( help_menu_pane,"version button",
21                                      args, num_args);
22      XtManageChild( version_button );
23
24      num_args = 0;
25      topics_button = XmCreateCPushButton( help_menu_pane, "topics button",
26                                      args, num_args);
27      XtManageChild( topics_button );
28
29      /* create the help cascade button on the menu bar, attach the *
30       * file menu pane to it and inform the menu_bar of the help id */
31      num_args = 0;
32      XtSetArg( args[num_args], XmNsubMenuId, help_menu_pane);num_args++;
33      help_menu_button = XmCreateCascadeButton( parent, "help menu button",
34                                      args, num_args );
35      XtManageChild( help_menu_button );
36
37      /* inform the main menu pane of the identity of its help button */
38      num_args =0;
39      XtSetArg( args[num_args], XmNmenuHelpWidget, help_menu_button); num_args++;
40      XtSetValues( parent, args, num_args );
41  } /* end create help menu */
42
```

\\

4.3   Resource settings for the main menu

A partial list of the resource values for *menu demo*, which should be set from the application code, is given in Table 4.4. Listing 4.4 is part of the resource file for the application, detailing the resources which should be set by the application developer. The major contents of this file are the setting of a *labelString* and *mnemonic* resource for all the buttons in the application and the setting of an *acceleratorText* and *acceleratorKey* resources for some.

The specification of a *labelString* resource for the buttons concludes with a double dot, if the button is intended to cause a further interaction with the user. As explained above this is a style guide requirement. The *labelString* value setting of the third button of the option menu does not however specify that it concludes with an arrow. Motif is able to recognize when a *cascadeButton* on a *pull down* or *cascade* menu controls a further *cascade* menu, and will append the arrow itself.

The specification of a *mnemonic* value provides a key which can be used to activate a *pull down* menu option, when the menu is posted. As shown in Figures 4.1 and 4.2, when a mnemonic value is specified the associated letter in the *labelString* is underlined as a visual indication of the existence of the mnemonic. The underlining is effected by Motif and requires no action from the programmer.

Table 4.4   Partial application code resource settings for *menu_demo*

widget	parent	class
toplevel		ApplicationShell

resource	value	
allowShellResize	True	

widget	parent	class
main menu	main form	RowColumn (menuBar)

resource	value	
leftAttachment	XmATTACH_FORM	
topAttachment	XmATTACH_FORM	
rightAttachment	XmATTACH_FORM	
bottomAttachment	XmATTACH_SELF	
menuHelpWidget	help_menu_button	

widget	parent	class
file menu button	main menu	CascadeButton

resource	value	
subMenuId	file_menu_pane	

widget	parent	class
file menu pane	main menu	RowColumn

resource	value	
tearOffModel	XmTEAR_OFF_ENABLED	

\\

Listing 4.4   Menu_demo partial resource file

```
! filename Menu_demo
! located in the home directory or in the $APPRESDIR directory
!
! Written for Motif book Chapter 4
! Fintan Culwin v1.0 July 92

*FontList:                                 *charter-bold*19*

! resource settings for the main menu
*file menu button.labelString:             file
*file menu button.mnemonic:                f
*edit menu button.labelString:             edit
*edit menu button.mnemonic:                e
*view menu button.labelString:             view
*view menu button.mnemonic:                v
*option menu button.labelString:           options
*option menu button.mnemonic:              o
*help menu button.labelString:             help
*help menu button.mnemonic:                h

! resource settings for the file menu
*new button.labelString:                   new
*new button.mnemonic:                      n
*new button.accelerator:                   Ctrl<Key>N
*new button.acceleratorText:               CTRL+N
*open button.labelString:                  open ..
*open button.mnemonic:                     o
*save button.labelString:                  save
*save button.mnemonic:                     s
*save button.accelerator:                  Ctrl<Key>S
*save button.acceleratorText:              CTRL+S
*save as button.labelString:               save as ..
*save as button.mnemonic:                  a
*exit button.labelString:                  exit ..
*exit button.mnemonic:                     x
*exit button.accelerator:                  Ctrl<Key>E
*exit button.acceleratorText:              CTRL+E

! remaining resource settings omitted
```

When a menu has been posted, the user can select an option from the menu by pressing the mnemonic key on the keyboard. The mnemonics to activate the *pull down* menus from the *main menu* bar are effected by pressing a key combination (usually control plus the mnemonic key), and will cause the *pull down* menu to be posted.

Accelerators are similar to mnemonics but do not require the menu to be posted before the option can be activated. When a menu option has an accelerator associated with it, pressing the accelerator combination on the keyboard will cause the activation callbacks associated with the option to be called, without requiring the menu to be posted. The style guide suggests that when an accelerator is available, the accelerator key combination should be indicated alongside the name of the option.

The accelerator keys are specified in resource files as strings of the form *modifier<key>character*. Where *modifier* indicates the modifier key to be used (usually the *control, meta* or *alternate* key), *<key>* indicates that the specification of a normal key follows and *character* indicates the key to be pressed in association with the modifier to activate the accelerator. Thus the specification "*Ctrl<key>N*" as the accelerator for the *new* option indicates that pressing the control and N keys simultaneously is to cause the *new* button's activate callbacks to be called. The *acceleratorText* resource is specified separately from the *labelString* resource in order to make it more comprehensible to the user. When an accelerator text resource is specified for a button on a *pull down* menu, Motif will ensure that the accelerator text is displayed right justified within the button.

4.4 The file menu exit interface

The style guide suggests that the last option of the *file* menu should be the *exit* option. This alone is a suitable justification for the standardization of application interfaces. Anyone who has had the experience when using a command line interface of successively using the commands *exit, quit, system, terminate*, etc.,[1] or anyone who has hunted through a non-standard GUI looking for the exit option, will fully appreciate this standardization.

Figure 4.7 presents a state transition diagram of a minimal *exit* interface. There is one transition leading into the interface which leads to the *exit confirm dialog*, and one transition leaving the interface from the *cancel* button of the dialog. The transition from the *quit* button of the dialog leads to the termination state of the application. A more realistic *exit* interface would include a dialog upon the *exit confirm dialog exit* transition which would ensure that should there be unsaved changes in the application's state; the user could not quit without a warning. This section will introduce the design and construction of the minimal implementation.

The entire collection of components and transitions is known as an *interface*. Each component of the interface is known as a *dialog*, and is represented on a STD as a minimal visualization emphasizing the usable components of the dialog. The transitions on the interface can be identified by appending the name of the component which activates the transition to the name of the dialog from which the transition originates. Thus the *exit confirm dialog exit* transition referred to above identifies the transition from the *exit confirm dialog*, which is activated when the *exit* button is pressed.

---

1 My favourite example is an application (which shall be unidentified), which gives the error message '*use quit to terminate the application*' when the command *exit* is attempted.

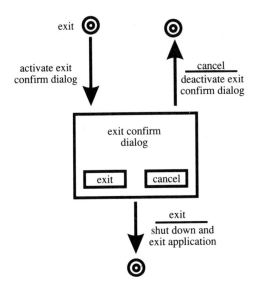

Figure 4.7 Exit confirm interface, state transition diagram.

4.5 Motif *messageBox* based dialogs

The appearance of the *exit confirm dialog* is illustrated in Figure 4.8. From its appearance it should by now be clear that it probably consists of a *shell* widget, a *constraint* widget, a *label* widget to display the pixmap, a *label* widget to display the text message, a *separator* widget and two *pushButton* widgets, one for the *exit* button and one for the *cancel* button.

It would be possible for a Motif programmer to construct the required dialog, by producing an application widget hierarchy design, detailed visual design, resource setting specifications, etc. As many different applications and different parts of the same application have a similar requirement for a dialog which asks the user a question, or gives the user a message, or gives the user a warning, the Motif toolkit provides a facility which will create an entire dialog as if it were a single widget.

The different *messageBox* configurations were presented in Figure 2.5, as part of the periodic table of Motif widgets. The standard dialogs are presented by Motif to the programmer as if they were a single widget of the *MessageBox* widget class. To use a *messageBox* instance as a dialog, it requires a suitable shell, the most appropriate being a *dialogShell*. The most convenient method for a Motif programmer to use a standard *messageBox* dialog, is to create the dialog using one of the Motif convenience functions. The most suitable configuration of a *messageBox* for the exit confirmation dialog is as a *question dialog*. The appropriate utility function is *XmCreateQuestionDialog*, whose prototype is:

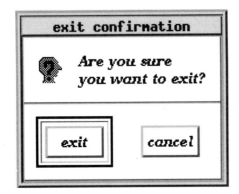

Figure 4.8   The exit confirm interface visual design.

```
Widget XmCreateQuestionDialog( Widget   Parent,
                               char *   name,
                               Arg      args,
                               int      num_args );
```

The interpretation of the parameters of this function is identical to the interpretation of other *XmCreate(whatever)* functions described in the previous section. The effect of the function is to create a named instance of the *messageBox* widget class configured as a question dialog, as a child of an unnamed *dialogShell* instance. The other *Xm* utility functions which can be used to create *messageBox* based dialogs include:

```
XmCreateErrorDialog         XmCreateInformationDialog
XmCreateWarningDialog       XmCreateWorkingDialog
(XmCreateQuestionDialog)    XmCreateMessageDialog
```

These functions have identical prototypes and similar effects to *XmCreateQuestionDialog,* differing only in the pixmap which is displayed. The last function, *XmCreateMessageDialog,* creates a dialog which has a null (invisible) pixmap symbol. The major resources of the *messageBox* widget class are given in Table 4.5.

The visual appearance of the exit confirm question dialog required by this application does not include a *help* button. However a *help* button is provided by default as part of the *messageBox*. The *help* button can be removed from the dialog by obtaining its identity, using the Motif function *XmMessageBoxGetChild* and subsequently unmanaging it. The prototype for *XmMessageBoxGetChild* is:

```
Widget XmMessageBoxGetChild( Widget   parent,
                             manifest required_child);
```

where the parent parameter is the messageBox widget whose child is required and the manifest value identifies which child is required. The possible manifest values include:

\\\

Table 4.5 The new resources of the *MessageBox* widget class

inheritance hierarchy   core -> composite -> constraint -> manager
-> bulletinBoard -> messageBox

Resource name	type	(default) values
cancelCallback	CallbackList	NULL
actions to be performed when the cancel button is pressed		
cancelLabelString	XmString	"Cancel"
label string to be displayed in the cancel button		
defaultButtonType	manifest (unsigned char)	XmDIALOG_CANCEL_BUTTON
		XmDIALOG_OK_BUTTON
		XmDIALOG_HELP_BUTTON
identifies the default button		
dialogType	manifest (unsigned char)	XmDIALOG_ERROR
		XmDIALOG_INFORMATION
		XmDIALOG_MESSAGE
		XmDIALOG_QUESTION
		XmDIALOG_WARNING
		XmDIALOG_WORKING
determines the type of dialog (the pixmap displayed)		
helpLabelString	XmString	"Help"
label string to be displayed in the help button		
messageAlignment	manifest (unsigned char)	XmALIGNMENT_BEGINNING (default)
		XmALIGNMENT_CENTRE
		XmALIGNMENT_END
determines the alignment of the message label		
messageString	XmString	null string
determines the message to be displayed		
minimizeButtons	Boolean	False
if false forces all buttons to be the same width		
okCallback	CallbackList	NULL
actions to be performed when the ok button is pressed		
okLabelString	XmString	"OK"
label string to be displayed in the ok button		
symbolPixmap	Pixmap	dynamic
identifies the pixmap to be displayed		

```
XmDIALOG_CANCEL_BUTTON          XmDIALOG_DEFAULT_BUTTON
XmDIALOG_HELP_BUTTON            XmDIALOG_MESSAGE_LABEL
XmDIALOG_OK_BUTTON             XmDIALOG_SEPARATOR
XmDIALOG_SYMBOL_LABEL
```

The help widget once obtained can be unmanaged using the intrinsics function *XtUnmanageChild*, whose prototype is:

```
void XtUnmanageChild( Widget to_be_unmanaged);
```

The effect of this function is to unmanage the widget supplied, causing it to become invisible. Should the identity of the *dialogShell* widget which is the parent of the *messageBox* ever be required, it can be obtained using the intrinsics function *XtParent*, whose prototype is:

```
Widget XtParent( Widget whose_parent_required );
```

As every widget in an application, apart from the *toplevel* shell, has one and only one parent, there is no ambiguity in the effects of this function. One reason for an application to obtain the identity of the *dialog shell* widget may be to set the shell's *title* resource to an appropriate value. Figure 4.8 indicates that the value of the exit confirm dialog's shell title resource has been set to "exit confirmation", although this is best accomplished using the resource file mechanism.

4.6 Exit interface, implementation

All of these considerations are best implemented within a function called *create_exit_dialog*, contained within a module called *exit_dialog*. The module would also export a complementary function *destroy_exit_dialog*, and two functions to activate and deactivate the dialog, called *activate_exit_dialog* and *deactivate_exit_dialog* respectively.

The encapsulation of the *exit dialog* within a code module is best designed using an object diagram. The object diagram for the *exit_dialog* module is given in Figure 4.9. The C header file which is obtained from this object diagram is given in Listing 4.5.

To include the *exit dialog* within the application *main menu*, which was introduced in the previous section, it would first be necessary to *#include* the *exit dialog* header file into the main code file. The exit dialog creation function can then be called from the *create_file_menu* function and the *activate_exit_dialog* callback function installed as the *exit* button's activate callback resource. Thus the action by the user of pressing the *exit* button will cause the *exit_dialog* to be activated and presented to the user.

The activation of the dialog is effected by managing the *messageBox* widget using the intrinsics function *XtManageChild*. The *exit_dialog* module defines private callback functions to be attached to the *quit* and *cancel* buttons. The quit callback in this implementation is straightforward, implemented simply as a call to the standard C function *exit()*. As discussed above this would not be appropriate for a realistic application as unsaved changes might be lost. An extension to the dialog to accommodate this requirement is suggested as an end of chapter activity.

The required actions of the *cancel* callback function are to deactivate the dialog. As the *exit_dialog* was activated by being managed it might be expected that it would be deactivated by being unmanaged, using the intrinsics function *XtUnManageChild*. However as by default a *messageBox* is automatically unmanaged whenever any of its *pushButtons*, apart from the *help* button, are activated, an explicit call to *XtUnManageChild* is not required.

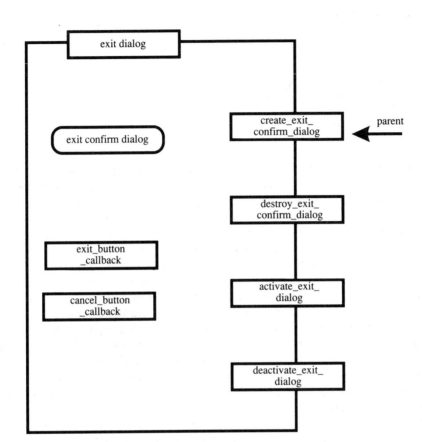

Figure 4.9 Exit confirm dialog object diagram.

Listing 4.5 Exit confirm dialog, header file

```
1  /* filename exit_dialog.h (exit_d.h)                          *
2   * file to illustrate X/Motif application main menu construction  *
3   * Written for Motif book chapter 4                           *
4   *                                                            *
5   * fintan culwin v1.0 July 92                                 *
6   */
7
8  #ifndef EXIT_D
9  #define  EXIT_D
10
11 #include <Xm/Xm.h>
12 #include <Xm/MessageB.h>
13
14 void create_exit_dialog( Widget parent );
15
16 void destroy_exit_dialog( void );
```

continued

\\

Listing 4.5 *continued*

```
17
18   void activate_exit_dialog( Widget    widget,
19                              XtPointer client_data,
20                              XtPointer call_data );
21
22   void deactivate_exit_dialog( void );
23
24   #endif /* ifndef EXIT_D */
```

It might be decided that as the deactivate function has no requirement explicitly to unmanage the dialog and as it has no other actions to perform, it might be omitted from the implementation. The advice given here is to implement the function as a null function and to call it explicitly from the *cancel* button's activate callback. There are two reasons for this: first, although there are no explicit actions required by cancellation in this version of the program, maintenance changes during the lifespan of the application may create some requirements. If the function is defined and installed at this stage it will facilitate such maintenance changes. The second reason for the inclusion of a null function is to make the design consistent. If every dialog module provides *creation, destruction, activation* and *deactivation* facilities and installs callbacks into all its active components it is easier to validate the implementation. With this design and implementation rationale there is no reason to determine during validation why this dialog is exceptional in not having callbacks attached to all its active components.

The implementation of the body of this module as a C code file is given in Listing 4.6. As discussed above the incorporation of the interface into the application can be accomplished by very minor changes in the construction of the standard *main menu*. The *#inclusion* of the same module into any other main application module, will allow the same dialog to be used by different applications. This will allow *exit interfaces* to be standardized between different applications and will reduce the amount of programmer effort required to construct an application.

Listing 4.6   Exit confirm dialog, code file

```
1    /* filename exit_dialog.c (exit_d.c)                    *
2     * Written for Motif book Chapter 4                     *
3     *                                                      *
4     * fintan culwin v1.0 July 92                           *
5     */
6
7    #include "exit_d.h"
8
9    #define MAX_ARGS    10
10
11   static Widget exit_dialog = (Widget) NULL;
```

continued

\\

Listing 4.6 *continued*

```
12
13   /* local prototypes */
14   void exit_button_callback( Widget    widget,
15                              XtPointer client_data,
16                              XtPointer call_data);
17
18   void cancel_button_callback( Widget    widget,
19                                XtPointer client_data,
20                                XtPointer call_data);
21
22   void create_exit_dialog( Widget parent ){
23
24   Widget temp_widget = parent;
25
26   Arg args[ MAX_ARGS ];
27   int num_args;
28
29     /* ensure the parent of the dialog is a shell widget */
30     while( ! XtIsShell( temp_widget )) {
31          temp_widget = XtParent( temp_widget );
32     } /* end while */
33
34     num_args = 0;
35     exit_dialog = XmCreateQuestionDialog( temp_widget,
36                                           "exit dialog",
37                                           args, num_args );
38
39     /* remove the help button from the dialog */
40     temp_widget = XmMessageBoxGetChild( exit_dialog,
41                                         XmDIALOG_HELP_BUTTON );
42     XtUnmanageChild( temp_widget );
43
44     /* add the actions to the buttons */
45     XtAddCallback( exit_dialog, XmNokCallback,
46                    exit_button_callback, (XtPointer) NULL );
47     XtAddCallback( exit_dialog, XmNcancelCallback,
48                    exit_button_callback, (XtPointer) NULL );
49
50   } /* end fun create exit dialog */
51
52   void destroy_exit_dialog( void ){
53     XtDestroyWidget( XtParent(exit_dialog));
54   } /* end fun destroy exit dialog */
55
56
57   void activate_exit_dialog( void ){
58     XtManageChild( exit_dialog );
59   } /* end fun activate exit dialog */
60
61
62   void deactivate_exit_dialog( void ){
63
64       /* null - no actions at present dialog is auto unmanaged *
```

continued

\\

Listing 4.6 *continued*

```
65        * whenever any of its buttons are pressed. */
66   } /* end fun deactivate exit dialog */
67
68
69   void exit_button_callback( Widget    widget,
70                              XtPointer client_data,
71                              XtPointer call_data){
72        /* standard C function to terminate the application */
73        exit(0);
74   } /* end fun exit button callback */
75
76   void cancel_button_callback( Widget    widget,
77                                XtPointer client_data,
78                                XtPointer call_data){
79        deactivate_exit_dialog();
80   } /* end fun exit button callback */
```

4.7 Gadgets and widgets

The numerous *cascadeButtons*, *pushButtons* and *separators* which are used in the menu system introduced in this chapter all consume server and client resources. Each individual button requires its own window, consuming memory resources on the server. Each window also has to be created and maintained, consuming processor time on the client. A possible optimization is to use *gadgets* instead of *widgets* where possible.

A *gadget* can be described as windowless *widget*, sharing the window resources of its parent and relying on the parent to dispatch events to it. Not all widget instances can be replaced with equivalent gadget instances; only a limited set of *primitive* widget classes have gadget counterpart classes. Specifically the *ArrowButton*, *Label*, *CascadeButton*, *PushButton*, *ToggleButton* and *Separator* classes have equivalent gadget classes.

A *gadget* instance has all the resources, including behaviours, as its counterpart *widget* instance with the exception of color resources and translation resources. Thus a *widget* can only be replaced with a *gadget* if the default translations are to be used and the gadget is to have the same foreground and background colors as its parent. The gadget does not have its own window, but it contains geometry resources which its parent uses to position it within its own window.

To replace a widget with a gadget the #*inclusion* of the widget class header file has to be replaced with the #*inclusion* of the corresponding gadget class header file. The name of the gadget class header file is the same as the widget class header file with a 'G' appended. Thus the gadget equivalent of the *pushButton* header file *PushB.h* is *PushBG.h*. Likewise, the utility function to create a *pushButton* widget instance, *XmCreatePushButton*, has an equivalent, *XmCreatePushButtonGadget*, to create a *pushButton* gadget instance. There are gadget equivalents for all the widget facilities appropriate to the other classes listed above. Once a gadget instance has been created and installed into an application it can be treated in exactly the same way as its widget equivalent, apart from the restrictions noted above.

For most applications the effects of replacing widgets with gadgets are minimal, and on the basis of only being able to optimize a program once it is working, the use of gadgets will not be pursued in this book.

4.8 Activities for Chapter 4

1. The implementation of the *exit interface* does not make any check to ensure that there are no unsaved changes in the application's state before the application is terminated. Redesign the *exit interface* to provide a suitable dialog if there are any unsaved changes.

2. Assume that a separate module supplies to the main module a Boolean function called *any_unsaved_changes* :

   ```
   int any_unsaved_changes( void );
   ```

   Redesign the prototype of the creation function to accept a Boolean function as a parameter. Reimplement the interface to call this function during the *exit confirm dialog exit* transition and indirect to a suitable dialog if there are unsaved changes. Test the reimplementation by providing a dummy Boolean function which always returns the value true (and subsequently the value false).

3. A partial application widget hierarchy for the main menu demonstration application has been given in the text of the chapter. Complete the application widget hierarchy and consider the number of widgets used in the light of the X slogan 'windows are cheap!'

4. Implement the *version_dialog* from Chapter 3 as a separate module providing *creation*, *destruction*, *activation* and *deactivation* functions. Attach this dialog to the *version* button of the *help* menu.

\\

CHAPTER FIVE

Standard interfaces

5.1 Standard interfaces

The previous chapter has introduced the construction of the application level *main menu*. This chapter will continue the development of an application interface by introducing two of the standard interfaces which are expected to be provided by all applications, a combined *save/ save as* interface and a *help* interface.

The primary design intention is to produce interfaces which have usability engineered into them from the outset, rather than being added as an afterthought. The secondary intention is to produce interfaces which have a high degree of potential reusability. Although the interfaces developed in this chapter will be integrated with the application *main menu* which was presented in the previous chapter, they will be constructed in such a way that they can be rapidly reused with other application level *main menus* or even reused with non-standard application level interfaces. In addition the *help* interface will be engineered in order that it can be rapidly reconfigured to present help for different applications.

The entire collection of interactive objects and the transitions which interconnect them will be referred to as an *interface*. The individual objects which form the visual parts of the interface will be referred to as *dialogs*. The action of a user when operating the interface will be referred to as an *interaction*. The act of moving from one state to another in an interface will be known as a *transition*. Where two separate interfaces are coupled very closely together they will be referred to as a *system*. The interface attached to the *help* button in this chapter is an example of a system.

5.2 A file menu *save/ save as* interface

5.2.1 The *save/ save as* interface, usability design

The Motif style guide gives detailed guidance concerning most of the options which should be offered on the application level menus. It gives fewer details of the interactions which should ensue when any of the options are selected. There is no detailed guidance given in the style guide for the precise interface which is to

\\\

be presented to a user when any of the prescribed options are selected from the application level **main menu**. However a number of standard interactions have evolved. An initial state transition diagram for a possible combined *save/ save as* interface is presented in Figure 5.1.

This state transition diagram introduces some new conventions. First it is possible for an interface to arrive at a certain state from a number of different paths. Where this occurs the different lines from the different paths can be joined. In Figure 5.1 an example of this occurs immediately prior to the transition to the termination state. The other new convention is to allow for the possibility of different transitions to be taken in response to some decision outside the scope of

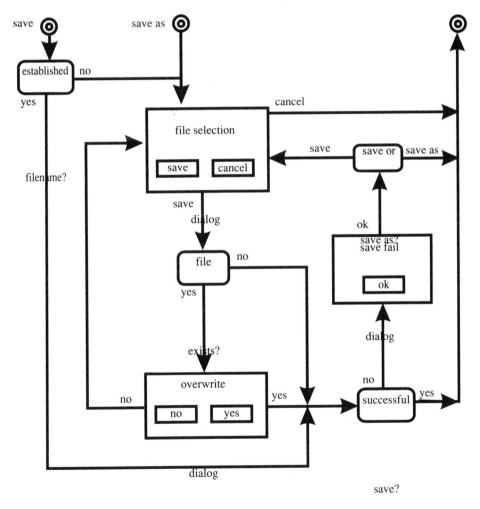

Figure 5.1 Initial *save/ save as* state transition diagram.

the user's actions. Where this occurs the decision is represented as a question in a round edged box, with two or more transitions originating from the box. Each transition originating from the box is labelled with the answer to the question which will cause the transition to be taken. In Figure 5.1 an example of this occurs where a filename entered by the user is tested to ensure that a file with the same name does or does not exist.

The distinction between a *save* and a *save as* interaction is dependent upon a filename being established prior to the *save* option being selected by the user. If *save as* is selected, the user is indicating that they wish to explicitly enter a filename by which the application state is to be saved. If *save* is selected the user is indicating that they wish the application to be saved using a filename which is already established. One way of enforcing this distinction is to make the *save* file menu option unavailable until a filename has been established. A second, possibly more friendly, method is to allow the user to select the *save* option at any stage and to indirect to the *save as* transition if a filename has not been established. This second solution is implemented in the interface presented here, as shown in the indirection from the *save* to the *save as* transition on the initial *save* transition.

The first action of both interactions should be to make the *save* and *save as* options unavailable to the user. This will allow the combined *save/ save as* interface to be operated in *non-modal* manner. Thus if the user discovers at some stage within the interaction that the application is not yet ready to be saved, all the other functionality of the application can still be used and the *save/ save as* interface returned to when the application is ready to be saved. To accomplish this the style guide suggests that the *save* and *save as* buttons should be made insensitive while the *save/ save as* interface is active, preventing a second save interaction being activated whilst the first has yet to complete. The availability of the buttons is restored as the last action of the interface.

An alternative design decision would have been to make the entire *save/ save as* interface *modal*. This would prevent a second save operation being attempted whilst the first has yet to complete but it would not allow any other interactions to be made with the application while a save operation was active. A design heuristic is to make as few interfaces and dialogs as possible modal, allowing the user to use as much of the application as possible in all situations, consequently simplifying the user's cognitive model of the interface.

The *save as* transition and the indirected *save* transition lead initially to a *file selection dialog*. This is constructed from a Motif *FileSelectionBox* widget illustrated in Figure 2.8. The *FileSelectionBox* widget will be explained in detail later in this chapter. The dialog in this interface offers two major options to the user, *save* and *cancel*. Pressing the *cancel* button has the effect of terminating the entire *save/ save as* interface without attempting to save the application state. Pressing the *save* button has the effect of attempting to save the application's state, using the filename which is entered in the filename box of the dialog.

The filename which the user has selected via the *file selection dialog* may identify a file which already exists. In this situation the application could automatically overwrite any existing file but this would have the effect of making a permanent, possibly irreversible, change to the user's environment. Such a change should not be made without an explicit confirmation from the user.

A *question dialog*, named *overwrite dialog*, is used in this interface to obtain permission from the user to overwrite any existing file. The *question dialog* is a standard Motif *messageBox* dialog illustrated in Figure 2.5. If the user refuses permission to overwrite the file, the *overwrite dialog* is removed and the application returns to the *file selection dialog* state. If the user grants permission the interface is now in the state where a writeable filename has been established; this is the same state which would have been reached if the file did not already exist. The two possible paths from the *file selection dialog* rejoin at this stage, immediately prior to the actual save operation.

The situation where the *save* button has been pressed by the user and a filename is already established also joins at this point. This will allow the *save* functionality to overwrite an existing file without an explicit confirmation from the user. To be totally secure the *save* transition could join the *save as* path immediately prior to the *file exists* decision. With the interaction as shown in Figure 5.1 there is a possibility that a file could be accidentally overwritten by a user selecting *save*, instead of *save as* from the *file* menu. The advantage of this design is an increased ease of use, which allows a skilled user to accomplish a save operation with a single menu selection. If the design was amended so that the transitions join prior to the *file exists?* decision, then a file could not be overwritten in any circumstance without an explicit confirmation from the user. The disadvantage of this amendment is that it could be cumbersome for an experienced user.

Once the actual save operation has been reached by whatever route, there is the possibility that the save will not be successful. The user should be made aware of this failure; in this design this is accomplished by a *warning dialog*, named *save fail*, which occurs on the failure transition of the file save operation. The warning dialog is another Motif *messageBox* standard dialog illustrated in Figure 2.5. This dialog has to be modal in order to prevent any other interaction with the application until the user has responded to the warning. The user indicates that they have attended to the warning by pressing the single *OK* button which appears on the dialog. If the interaction was occasioned by the user pressing the *save as* button or the *save* button when no filename was established, the state reverts to the *file selection dialog* state; otherwise the entire *save/ save as* interface will terminate.

Upon a successful save operation the filename which was used when the file was saved will be stored as the established filename for future save operations, and the entire *save/ save as* interface can terminate.

A review of the entire interface at this stage will reveal two possible problems with its usability in addition to the overwrite problem described above. The first potential problem concerns a successful save from the *save* button where a filename which does not exist is already established. A review of the complete path indicates that this is accomplished without any user interface components being presented to the user. Thus the user has no feedback that the operation is taking place, nor that it has completed successfully. This need not be considered a problem for a skilled user, who would be aware that no confirmation of a successful save is to be expected, but might be confusing to a novice user, who might press the *save* button several times looking for such a confirmation. A possible solution to this might be to use an *information dialog* to inform the user that the save operation has been completed successfully.

The second potential problem with the interface is not so obvious; if the save operation can always be performed with a minimal delay the user will need no confirmation while it is happening. However this can rarely be guaranteed; consequently a *working dialog* should be used to inform the user that the save operation is taking place. The *working dialog* is another Motif *messageBox* dialog, illustrated in Figure 2.5. If a *working dialog* is used then the first potential problem is also solved, as the disappearance of the *working dialog* from the interface together with the non-appearance of the failure *warning dialog* can be used by the user as a confirmation that the save was successful.

The revised *save/ save as* state transition diagram is presented in Figure 5.2; it is this design which will be implemented in the remaining sections of this chapter.

5.2.2 The Motif *FileSelectionBox* widget class

The *file selection dialog* used in the *save/ save as* interface is constructed from a Motif *FileSelectionBox* widget. The appearance and the components of this widget have already been presented in Figure 2.8. The major resources of the *FileSelectionBox* widget class are listed in Table 5.1.

The selection of files which is presented in the *file list* component is determined by the file filter string shown in the *filter* component. The currently selected file is shown in the *selection* component. The list of files which match the filter may be longer than can be fitted into the *list* component, in which case the user can scroll the list using the file list *scrollBar*s component. The user can navigate the underlying operating system's directory hierarchy by selecting directories from the *directories* component.

The Motif toolkit provides a convenience function to simplify the creation of a *dialogShell* which contains a *fileSelectionBox* widget. The prototype of this function is:

```
Widget XmCreateFileSelectionDialog( Widget parent,
                                    char * name,
                                    Arg  * args,
                                    int    num_args );
```

which will create and return a *dialogShell* containing a *fileSelectionBox* widget with the name and resources as specified. As with the *messageBox* based dialogs a convenience function is provided to obtain the identity of the widgets

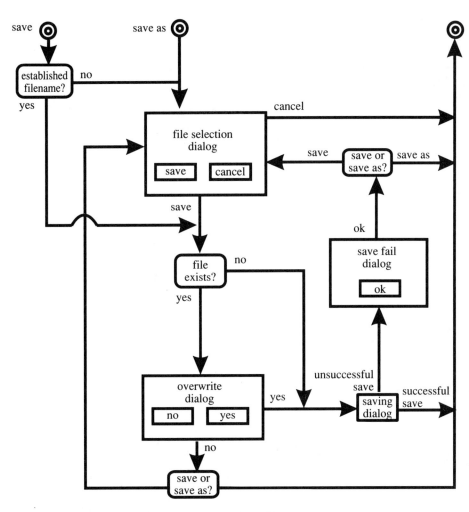

Figure 5.2   Revised *save/save as* state transition diagram.

which comprise the composite *fileSelectionBox* widget. The prototype of this function is:

```
Widget XmFileSelectionBoxGetChild( Widget    file_select_box,
                            manifest  child_required);
```

where *file_select_box* identifies the *fileSelectionBox* whose child is required and *child_required* identifies the widget whose identity is required and can take one of the values:

Table 5.1   The major resources of the *FileSelectionBox* widget class
inheritance hierarchy   Core -> Composite -> Constraint -> Manager -> BulletinBoard
-> SelectionBox -> FileSelectionBox

Resource name	type	values
directory	XmString	varies
the base directory for searches		
directoryValid	Boolean	varies
read only directory valid flag		
dirListItems	XmStringTable	varies
read only list of available directories		
dirListItemCount	int	varies
*read only number of entries in **dirListItems***		
dirListLabelString		"Directories"
the label displayed for the directory list component		
dirMask	XmString	varies
the combined directory and file mask		
dirSpec	XmString	varies
the contents of the file selection text component		
fileListItems	XmStringTable	
read only list of available files		
fileListItemCount	int	varies
*read only number of entries in **fileListItems***		
fileListLabelString	XmString	"Files"
the label displayed for the file list component		
filterTypeMask	manifest	
	(unsigned char)	XmFILE_REGULAR *(default)*
		XmFILE_DIRECTORY
		XmFILE_ANY_TYPE
determines the type of files listed in the file list		
filterLabelString	XmString	"Filter"
the label displayed for the file filter component		
noMatchString		"[ ]"
string to be displayed in the file list if no matching files are located		
pattern	XmString	varies
*the search pattern used in conjunction with **directory** for searches*		

Note. The FileSelectionBox inherits from the *SelectionBox*, *BulletinBoard*, *Manager*, *Constraint*, *Composite* and *Core* widget classes. The *SelectionBox* resources in particular should be consulted for additional relevant resources.

```
XmDIALOG_APPLY_BUTTON          XmDIALOG_CANCEL_BUTTON
XmDIALOG_DEFAULT_BUTTON        XmDIALOG_DIR_LIST
XmDIALOG_DIR_LIST_LABEL        XmDIALOG_FILTER_LABEL
XmDIALOG_FILTER_TEXT           XmDIALOG_HELP_BUTTON
XmDIALOG_LIST                  XmDIALOG_LIST_LABEL
XmDIALOG_OK_BUTTON             XmDIALOG_SELECTION_LABEL
```

\\

```
XmDIALOG_SEPARATOR                  XmDIALOG_TEXT
XmDIALOG_WORK_AREA
```

The list of files is updated by the widget automatically whenever a new directory is selected, whenever the filter text is changed and whenever the filter button is pressed. It is also possible to cause the list to be updated under program control using the convenience function *XmFileSelectionDoSearch*:

```
Widget XmFileSelectionDoSearch( Widget   file_selection_widget,
                        XmString new_filter );
```

The effect of this function is to install the *new_filter* string into the widget and then cause the file list to be updated. If the *new_filter* string is null then the existing filter string is used.

The user can select a file by clicking upon its name in the file list, or by typing a filename into the selection component. The name of the selected file can be extracted as an *XmString* from the *call_data* structure passed with the *okCallback* which is called whenever the *ok* button is pressed. The type name of this structure is *XmFileSelectionBoxCallbackStruct* and it contains, amongst other parts, a component called *value* of type *XmString* which contains the currently selected filename.

The use of a *fileSelectionBox* widget to implement the requirements of the combined *save/ save as* interface will be given below, where the implementation of the *save/ save as* interface is described in detail.

5.2.3 The *save/ save as* interface, detailed design

The overall design approach used in the construction of event driven GUI applications has already been introduced in Chapter 3. The application is implemented in three layers. The highest layer is the application level presentation layer which provides the application level *main menu*. The lowest layer, the application layer, contains the functionality of the application as opposed to the functionality of the user interface. Connecting these two layers is a translation layer which consists of a number of largely independent modules. The *save/ save as* interface which is being developed in this chapter is an example of such a module.

The application translation layer interface modules are themselves divided into three sub-modules, in a similar manner to the division of the whole application into three layers. Each translation layer module may consist of a presentation sub-module which contains the visual interface components, a translations sub-module which contains the behaviour of the interface and a support sub-module which contains state variables and other objects which are required by the translation sub-module.

The application layer will be shared with other parts of the program. The only method of the application layer which is of concern to the *save/ save as* interface is the function to save the application workspace. The object diagram for this part of the application layer is shown in Figure 5.3 and the corresponding part of the header file in Listing 5.1. This is the only place in the *save/ save as* interface where the application layer functionality is required. If an existing application is being redeveloped with an X Motif interface, a 'skin' function may have to be placed around an existing save function to provide the required prototype.

The public aspects of the *save/ save as* translation module can in part be derived from the state transition diagram in Figure 5.2. From this diagram it is clear that two callback functions, the *save_callback* and the *save_as_callback*, will have to be provided. In addition to these functions, a function to *create* the interface and a function to *destroy* the interface will also be required.

As explained above, while the *save/ save as* interface is active it should not be possible to activate a second instance of the interface. This is a responsibility of the application presentation layer which should not allow the *save/ save as* interface to be offered to the user while an instance of the interface is active. To provide support for this the *save/ save as* translation layer provides a public Boolean enquiry function called *is_save_available*. The object diagram for the public aspects of the *save/ save as* interface translation layer is presented in Figure 5.4 and the corresponding header file in Listing 5.2.

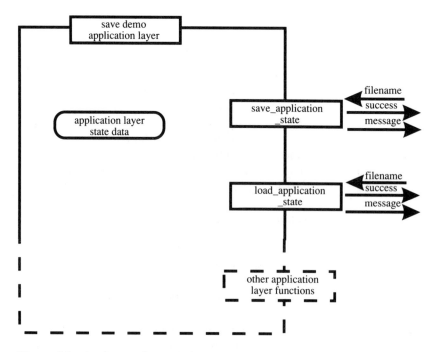

Figure 5.3 Application layer i/o functions object diagram.

Listing 5.1   Save/ save as application layer i/o functions header file

```
1   /* filename save demonstration application layer header    *
2    * file (sv_dmo_a.h). Supplies demonstration application save *
3    * function for the save/ save as interface.                *
4    *. See Motif book Chapter 5.                               *
5    * fintan culwin v1.0 March 92  revised Jan 94.             *
6    */
7
8   #ifndef SV_DMO_A
9   #define  SV_DMO_A
10
11  #include <stdio.h>
12
13  extern int save_app_workspace( char *  filename,
14                                 char ** message);
15  /* function to save the application workspace data in a file *
16   *  with the filename provided. Returns true (1) if the save  *
17   *  is successful and false (0) otherwise with a suitable     *
18   *  message explaining why.                                   *
19   */
20
21  extern int load_app_workspace( char *  filename ,
22                                 char ** message);
23  /* function to load the application workspace data from a    *
24   *  file with the filename provided. Returns true (1) if the  *
25   *  load is successful and false (0) otherwise with a suitable*
26   *  message explaining why.                                   *
27   */
28
29  #endif /* ifndef SV_DMO_A */
```

Listing 5.2   Save/ save as dialog translations public functions header file

```
1   /* filename save_demo_translation.h (s_d_t.h)         *
2    * standard custom dialog save/ save as translation   *
3    * layer.                                             *
4    *                                                    *
5   .* fintan culwin v1.0 March 92                        *
6    */
7
8   #ifndef S_D_T
9   #define  S_D_T
10
11  #include <X11/Shell.h>
12  #include <Xm/MessageB.h>
13  #include <Xm/FileSB.h>
14
15  #include "s_d_a.h"
16  #include "s_d_t_p.h"
17  #include "s_d_t_s.h"
18
19
```

continued

\\

Listing 5.2 *continued*

```
20   extern void create_save_as_interface( Widget parent );
21   /* function to create the save/ save as dialog widgets, to be called *
22    * once before any other function from this layer is called          */
23
24   extern void destroy_save_as_interface( void );
25   /* function to destroy the save/ save as dialog widgets, to be called *
26    * when the dialog is no longer required.                             */
27
28   extern int is_save_available( void );
29   /* enquiry function to determine if a save is currently active, to   *
30    * be used to prevent a re-entry into the dialog.                     */
31
32   extern void save_callback( Widget    widget,
33                              XtPointer client_data,
34                              XtPointer call_data );
35   /* the call back to be attached to the save button */
36
37   extern void save_as_callback( Widget    widget,
38                                 XtPointer client_data,
39                                 XtPointer call_data );
40   /* the call back to be attached to the save as button */
41
42   #endif /* ifndef S_D_T */
```

The *save/ save as* interface *translation* module is supported by a *sub-presentation* module and a *support* module. The sub-presentation module contains the dialogs which are identified from the state transition diagram in Figure 5.2. The four dialogs required are the *file_selection_dialog*, the *overwrite_dialog*, the *saving_dialog* and the *save_fail_dialog*.

These dialogs can be modelled from their life cycle considerations. Each of the dialogs will have to be created before it is required, and will have to be destroyed when it is no longer required. While the dialog exists it can either be visible to the user (active) or invisible to the user (inactive). To support the transitions between these two states two functions, one to activate the dialog and one to inactivate the dialog, will be required.

The object diagram for the *file_selection_dialog* is presented in Figure 5.5 and the corresponding header file in Listing 5.3. The other three dialogs will have a similar object diagram and a similar set of methods. The only significant difference in that the *save fail* dialog will require the failure message to be passed to it as it is activated. An implementation decision has been taken to include all four dialogs in the same code module. This decision was taken to simplify the source code file management associated with the *save/ save as* interface. An alternative implementation would have required each of the four dialogs to be separately implemented in its own code module.

The *save/ save as* interface also has a requirement to support several non-widget objects. The state of the interface needs to be modelled by a state variable with appropriate access and enquiry functions. Likewise the established filename

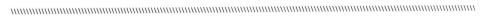

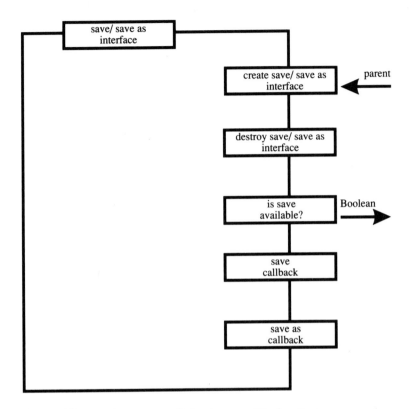

Figure 5.4 *save/ save as* translation layer, public functions.

Listing 5.3   Save/ save as presentation layer functions header file

```
1   /* filename save_demo_translation_presentation.h (s_d_t_p.h)   *
2    * standard custom dialog save/ save as translation             *
3    * layer presentation objects and functions                     *
4    *                                                               *
5    * fintan culwin v1.0 March 92                                   *
6   */
7
8   #ifndef S_D_T_P
9   #define  S_D_T_P
10
11  #include <Xm/Xm.h>
12  #include <X11/Shell.h>
13  #include <Xm/MessageB.h>
14  #include <Xm/FileSB.h>
15
16  #include "s_d_t_s.h"
17
```

continued

\\\

Listing 5.3 *continued*

```
18   #define MAX_BUFFER_SIZE 300
19
20   /* creation, destruction, activation and deactivation, standard *
21    * functions for the file selection dialog.                     *
22   */
23   extern Widget create_file_select_dialog( Widget           parent,
24                                    XtCallbackProc cancel_callback,
25                                    XtCallbackProc save_callback );
26   extern void activate_file_select( void );
27   extern void deactivate_file_select( void );
28   extern void destroy_file_select_dialog( void );
29
30
31   /* creation, destruction, activation and deactivation, standard *
32    * functions for the overwrite dialog.                          *
33   */
34
35   extern Widget create_overwrite_dialog( Widget           parent,
36                                    XtCallbackProc yes_callback,
37                                    XtCallbackProc no_callback );
38   extern void activate_overwrite_dialog( void );
39   extern void deactivate_overwrite_dialog( void );
40   extern void destroy_overwrite_dialog( void );
41
42                        other dialog function prototypes omitted.
43
44   #endif /* ifndef S_D_T_P */
```

and a temporary filename also need to be supported. The object diagram for the *save state* encapsulated variable is shown in Figure 5.6 and the object diagram for the filenames in Figure 5.7. Again in order to simply source code file management these two objects have been implemented in a single source code module, whose header file is presented in Listing 5.4.

With the application layer access functions, the four dialogs and the support objects public function prototypes designed in detail, the translation module itself can now be designed.

The state transition diagram can be used to identify the private functions which will be required by this module. The initiation transitions have already been used to identify the public callback functions which will be exported from the *save/ save as* interface. The remaining transitions which originate from dialogs can be used to identify the private callbacks which will be required. This will provide the following list of private callbacks:

```
file_select_cancel_callback
file_select_save_callback
overwrite_yes_callback
overwrite_no_callback
save_fail_ok_callback
```

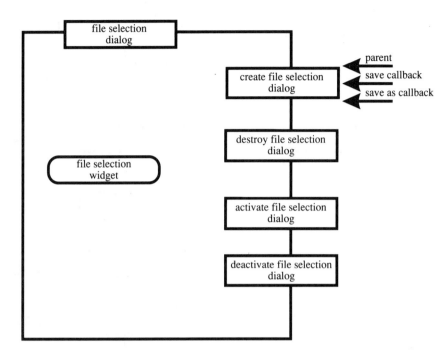

Figure 5.5   File selection dialog, object diagram.

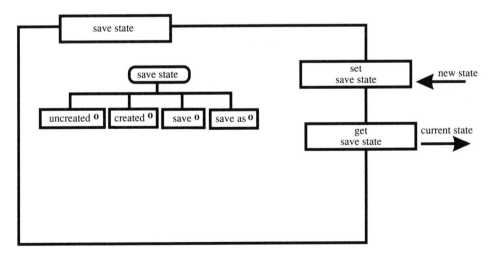

Figure 5.6   Save state object diagram.

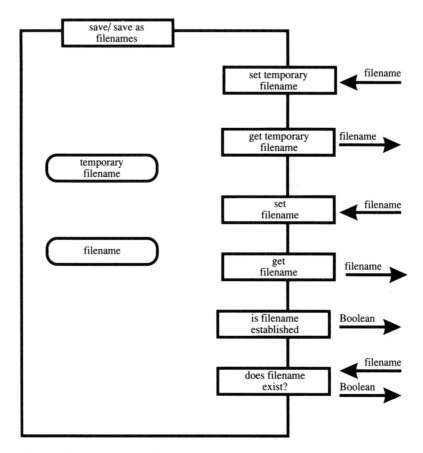

Figure 5.7   *save/ save as* filename object diagram.

Listing 5.4   Save/ save as dialog translations support functions header file

```
 1  /* filename save_demo_translation_support.h (s_d_t_s.h)   *
 2   * standard custom dialog save/ save as translation        *
 3   * layer support objects and functions                     *
 4   *                                                          *
 5   * fintan culwin v1.0 March 92                              *
 6   */
 7
 8
 9  #ifndef S_D_T_S
10  #define  S_D_T_S
11
12
13  /* interface states */
14  #define S_D_UNCREATED 0
```

continued

\\\

Listing 5.4 *continued*

```
15  #define S_D_AVAILABLE 1
16  #define S_D_SAVE       2
17  #define S_D_SAVE_AS    3
18
19  /* get value and set value interface state functions */
20  extern void set_save_state( int new_state );
21  extern int  get_save_state( void );
22
23  /* set value and get value filename functions */
24  #define MAX_FILE_NAME_SIZE 40
25
26  extern char * set_temp_filename( char * new_filename );
27  extern char * get_temp_filename( void );
28
29  extern char * set_filename( char * new_filename );
30  extern char * get_filename( void );
31
32  /* utility file & filename functions */
33  extern int is_filename_established( void );
34  extern int does_file_exist( char * filename );
35
36  #endif /* ifndef S_D_T_S */
```

The decisions which are identified on the state transition diagram will require consideration. The *established filename?* and *file exists?* decisions can be implemented as enquiry functions of the *save/save as* filenames module, as shown in Figure 5.7. The *save or save as?* decision can be implemented by using the dialog state enquiry function which has already been constructed.

A review of the state transition diagram will now indicate that only the *saving_dialog* remains to be considered. This yields a further required function which will be called *do_save*. Finally a heuristic design strategy is to provide a common exit function through which all possible exit paths will indirect. This function will be called *exit_save_as_dialog*.

The first cut of the detailed design of the combined *save/save as* dialog is now complete. The major components of the design implementation are shown in Figure 5.8. A one sentence description of this diagram would be that the application *main menu* in the application presentation layer passes control to the *save/save as* translation interface, which uses its own translation, presentation and support modules and may call the save functionality of the application layer.

5.2.4 The *save/save as* interface, implementation

The construction of the state variable part of the translation support objects module is comparable with the implementation of the *click counter* object from Chapter 3. The construction of the filenames part is a little more complicated involving the use of standard C string and file handling facilities. The

\\

Figure 5.8   *save/ save as* interface design overview.

implementation of this module is not considered in detail in this chapter. The code for the module can be found in the save interface translations support files (*save_i_t.h* and *save_i_t.c*) in Appendix C.

For the purposes of this demonstration the application save function will be implemented as a dummy function, which merely displays on the standard error stream (*stderr*) that the function has been called and the filename which has been passed to it as a parameter. The function will always return *True* indicating the success of the save operation, although for testing purposes this would at some stage have to be amended to *False* and a suitable message returned. The implementation of this module is also not considered in detail in this chapter; the code for the module can be found in the save demo application files (*save_d_a.h* and *save_d_a.c*) in Appendix C.

Once constructed the interface can be attached to the application *main menu* developed in Chapter 4. To accomplish this the *save/ save as* translations header file will have to be *#included* into the module which creates the *file* menu, and the *save/save as* interface creation function called from this module. A suitable place would be from within the function which creates the *file* menu.

The *save callback* function and the *save as callback* functions exported from the translation module would have to be installed as the *save* button's and the *save as* button's *activateCallback* resource using the *XtAddCallback* function:

```
XtAddCallback( save_button,   XmNactivateCallback,
               save_callback, (XtPointer) NULL );

XtAddCallback( save_as_button,   XmNactivateCallback,
               save_as_callback, (XtPointer) NULL );
```

The application level presentation layer should take responsibility for ensuring that the *save* and *save as* buttons are unavailable to the user while the *save/save as* interface is active. The most appropriate manner of accomplishing this is to attach callbacks to the main menu's *file* button's *cascadingCallback* resource. These callbacks will be called when the *file cascadeButton* is pressed but before the *menu pane* containing the *save* and *save as* buttons is managed. The callbacks themselves will call the translation layer enquiry function to determine if the *save/save as* interface is active and set the sensitivity of the *save* and *save as* buttons appropriately. The identity of the buttons can be passed to the callback in the *client_data* parameter, which implies that the same callback can be attached twice to the *file* cascade button with different actual *client_data* parameters.

The text of the callback function called *save_pulldown_callback* is given in Listing 5.5. The implementation of this function makes use of the intrinsics function *XtSetSensitive*, whose prototype is:

```
XtSetSensitive( Widget  widget,
                Boolean sensitivity );
```

The effect of the function is to set the sensitivity of the widget specified according to the value of the sensitivity parameter. A widget whose sensitivity is set to *False* has its user interface functionality disabled and, as shown in Figure 4.3, is presented to the user in a 'greyed out' state to indicate that it cannot be used.

This callback function will have to be added to the main menu's *file cascadeButton*'s *cascadingCallback* resource twice, once specifying the *save* button as the *client_data* parameter and once specifying the *save as* button as the *client_data* parameter. Assuming the *file* menu *cascadeButton* widget is called *file_menu_button*, the *save cascadeButton* is called *save_button* and the *save as cascadeButton* is called *save_as_button*. The installation of the callbacks could be accomplished with:

```
XtAddCallback( file_menu_button,      XmNcascadingCallback,
               save_pulldown_callback, (XtPointer) save_button );
XtAddCallback( file_menu_button,      XmNcascadingCallback,
               save_pulldown_callback, (XtPointer) save_as_button );
```

once all three widgets have been created.

\\

Listing 5.5   Save pull down callback function (part of save_demo.c)

```
1   /* save pulldown callback, part of save demo main file. Callback    *
2    * function to be attached to the main menu file cascadeButton's     *
3    * cascading callback twice. Once with the save button as the        *
4    * client_data parameter, once with the save_as as the client_data   *
5    * parameter. The function uses the save/ save as interface's        *
6    * state enquiry function to determine the sensitivity of the save   *
7    * and save as buttons.                                              *
8    */
9
10  void save_pulldown_callback( Widget    widget,
11                               XtPointer client_data,
12                               XtPointer call_data){
13
14  /* callback to determine if the save/save as interface is currently  *
15   * available, and set the sensitivity of the widget passed in the    *
16   * client_data parameter as appropriate.                             *
17   */
18
19  Widget the_button;
20
21      /* recast the client_data parameter back into *
22       * a widget (for convenience).                */
23      the_button = ( Widget)  client_data;
24      if ( is_save_available()){
25          XtSetSensitive( the_button, True );
26      } else {
27          XtSetSensitive( the_button, False );
28      } /* end if */
29  } /* end save pulldown callback */
```

Before considering the construction of the translation module the translation
layer's presentation module will have to be described. As explained above, this
module contains the four dialogs which are required to implement the
presentation aspects of the *save/ save as* dialog. Only two of these dialogs will be
considered in detail here, the *overwrite_dialog* and the *file_selection_dialog*. The
remaining dialogs, the *saving_dialog* and the *save_fail_dialog*, are very similar in
their construction. The complete code for this module can be found in the save
demo translations presentation files (*s_d_t_p.h* and *s_d_t_p.c*) in Appendix C.

The parent of the *file selection dialog* widget is required to be the *toplevel
applicationShell* widget. This will ensure that when the *file selection dialog* is
activated it will by default be presented to the user centred within the
applicationShell. The three remaining dialogs are each children of the
file selection dialog, which will in a similar manner ensure that by default they are
presented centred within the *file selection dialog* when they are activated. The
application widget hierarchy for the presentation layer is presented in Figure 5.9,
although it should be noted that the responsibility for effecting this hierarchy
resides with the translation layer function *create_save_as_interface*.

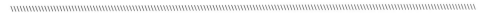

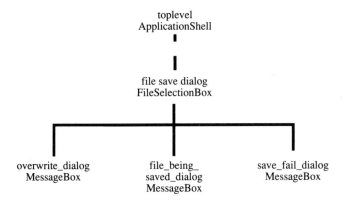

Figure 5.9   *save/ save* as interface, application widget hierarchy.

Each of the four presentation objects has a creation function, a destruction function and two state transition functions, one to cause a transition from the inactive to the active state and one to cause a transition from the active to the inactive state. The complete code for the four functions associated with the *overwrite_dialog* is presented in Listing 5.6.

Listing 5.6   Overwrite dialog functions

```
1   extern Widget create_overwrite_dialog( Widget          parent,
2                                          XtCallbackProc  yes_callback,
3                                          XtCallbackProc  no_callback ){
4
5   Widget   temp;
6   Arg      args[ MAX_ARGS ];
7   int      num_args;
8
9      num_args = 0;
10     XtSetArg( args[num_args], XmNmwmDecorations,
11                     XM_DECOR_BORDER | XM_DECOR_TITLE);
12                                          num_args++;
13     overwrite_dialog = XmCreateQuestionDialog( parent,
14                                         "overwrite dialog",
15                                         args, num_args );
16
17     temp = XmMessageBoxGetChild( overwrite_dialog,
18                     XmDIALOG_HELP_BUTTON);
19     XtUnmanageChild( temp );
20
21     XtAddCallback( overwrite_dialog, XmNokCallback,
22                 yes_callback,    (XtPointer) NULL );
23     XtAddCallback( overwrite_dialog, XmNcancelCallback,
24                 no_callback,    (XtPointer) NULL  );
25     return overwrite_dialog;
```

continued

\\\

Listing 5.6 *continued*

```
26  } /* end fun create overwrite dialog */
27
28
29  extern void activate_overwrite_dialog( void ){
30
31  char        buffer[ MAX_BUFFER_SIZE ];
32  XmString    question;
33  Arg         args[ MAX_ARGS ];
34  int         num_args;
35
36     strcpy( buffer, "Overwrite the file \n" );
37     strcat( buffer, get_temp_filename());
38     strcat( buffer, " ?");
39     question = XmStringCreateLtoR( buffer, XmSTRING_DEFAULT_CHARSET );
40
41     num_args = 0;
42     XtSetArg( args[ num_args ], XmNmessageString, question ); num_args++;
43     XtSetValues( overwrite_dialog, args, num_args );
44
45     XmStringFree( question );
46     XtManageChild( overwrite_dialog );
47  } /* end fun activate overwrite */
48
49
50  extern void deactivate_overwrite_dialog( void ){
51     /* null - currently autounmanage */
52  } /* end fun deactivate overwrite dialog */
53
54
55  extern void destroy_overwrite_dialog( void ){
56        XtDestroyWidget( XtParent(overwrite_dialog));
57        overwrite_dialog = NULL;
58  } /* end fun destroy overwrite dialog */
```

The creation function *create_overwrite_dialog* is straightforward using the convenience function *XmCreateQuestionDialog* to create a *messageBox* widget, together with a *dialogShell*, configured as a *question dialog*. Following its creation the unwanted *help* button is unmanaged and the two callback procedures passed as parameters to *create_overwrite_dialog* are attached to the appropriate callback resources of the *overwrite_dialog*.

The destruction function *destroy_overwrite_dialog* is equally straightforward, destroying the widget using the intrinsics *XtDestroyWidget* function to release any resources which are allocated to the widget and then assigning the overwrite dialog widget an explicitly safe (null) value. The widget which is explicitly destroyed is the *dialogShell* parent of the *messageBox* widget. Destruction of a widget results in the destruction of all child widgets; however, destruction of a child widget does not result in destruction of its parent. As a *dialogShell* is created as a parent of the *overwrite_dialog* widget when it is created, this widget should also be destroyed when the *overwrite_dialog* widget is destroyed.

The deactivate function *deactivate_overwrite_dialog* is in this implementation a null function. All *messageBox* dialogs are by default automatically unmanaged when any of their buttons, apart from the *help* button, is pressed. This implementation takes advantage of this default behaviour but recognizes that maintenance changes at some stage in the application's lifecycle may require explicit operations to be performed as the dialog is deactivated. The provision of null function and the calling of the function at the appropriate places by the translations module will facilitate such maintenance.

The activate function *activate_overwrite_dialog* is the most complex. It uses the support layer function *get_temp_filename* to obtain the filename which has been selected by the user, and catenates this as a C string to phrase the appropriate question. The C string is then converted into an *XmString*, before being installed into the widget as its *messageString* resource. Once the *XmString* has been installed it is no longer required and the resources it occupies are released using the *XmStringFree* function. The dialog can then be managed causing it to become visible to the user.

The support functions for the other two *messageBox* based dialogs, the *saving_dialog* and *save_fail_dialog*, are very similar to the support functions for the *overwrite_dialog* described above. The only significant difference is that the *saving_dialog* has all its buttons disabled and consequently has to be explicitly unmanaged using *XtUnmanageChild* within its deactivate function. The *save_fail_dialog* has to be modal to the application to ensure that it is attended to before any other application actions are attempted. This is accomplished by setting its *dialogStyle* resource to XmDIALOG_APPLICATION_MODAL as it is created. The code for these functions is not presented in this chapter. It can be found in the save demo translations presentation code file (*s_d_t_p.c*) in Appendix C.

The support functions for the *file_selection_dialog* are also very similar. The activate function has a requirement to update the file list which is accomplished with a call to *XmFileSelectionDoSearch* before the dialog is managed. The other significant change is that this dialog is not unmanaged by default when any of its buttons are pressed, consequently it has to be unmanaged explicitly as it is deactivated. The source code for the *file_selection_dialog* functions can also be found in the save demo translations presentation code file (*s_d_t_p.c*) in Appendix C. The visual appearance of the *file selection dialog* used in this demonstration does not offer to the user all the possible components shown in Figure 2.8. A simpler dialog is presented to the user as shown in Figure 5.10. The non-required components are removed by obtaining their widget identities using *XmFileSelectionBoxGetChild*, and subsequently the widgets are unmanaged using *XtUnmanageChild*. The appearance of the other dialogs in the interface is shown in Figure 5.11.

Finally the public and private functions of the translation module itself can be constructed, making use of the support functions which have already been implemented. It is these functions which will determine the behaviour of the interface. They are constructed making use of the facilities of the sub-presentation and support modules which have already been implemented.

Figure 5.10   *save/ save as* interface, file selection dialog appearance.

The first function to be considered is the creation function *create_save_as_interface*. The major part of this function consists of a sequence of four calls to create the four individual dialogs of the presentation module. The *file_selection_dialog* is created first and the identity of this widget, which is returned by the function, is used as the parent of the three remaining dialogs. This implements the application widget hierarchy shown in Figure 5.9. This hierarchy also indicates that the parent of the *file selection dialog* should be the application *toplevel* widget. It is expected but not guaranteed that this is the parent widget which will be supplied to *create_save_as_dialog*. The creation function enforces the required parentage by a simple loop involving the intrinsics functions *XtIsTopLevelShell* and *XtParent*, ascending the widget hierarchy until a *shell* widget is found. The code for this loop is:

Figure 5.11 *save/ save as* interface, other dialogs appearance.

```
/* derive the parent shell from the supplied widget */
parent_shell = parent;
while ( ! XtIsTopLevelShell( parent_shell )){
      parent_shell = XtParent( parent_shell);
} /* end while */
```

where *parent_shell* is a locally declared Widget variable and *parent* is the *parent* widget parameter supplied to the function.

\\\

The destruction function *destroy_save_as_interface* is more straightforward consisting solely of four calls to the four destroy dialog functions supplied by the presentation module.

The public *save_as_callback* function is relatively straightforward to implement. It should never be called before the *save/ save as* interface has been created or while the interface is already active. It is implemented defensively using the state enquiry function and calls the interface creation function or abends as appropriate. Once it is satisfied that the interface has been created and that it is not already in use, its actions are to set the interface state to *save as* and to call the *activate_file_selection_dialog* function, which causes the interface to be presented to the user.

The public *save_callback* function is a little more complex. It has the same defensive code as the *save_as_callback* function and once this is established its first action, as shown on the state transition diagram in Figure 5.2, is to indirect to the *save_as_callback* if there is no established filename. If this is not the case, the interface state is set to *save*, the established filename is copied to the temporary filename and a check is made to determine if the filename already exists. Should the filename exist, the function activates the presentation layer *overwrite_dialog*, otherwise it passes control to the *do_save* function before it terminates. These actions can be verified as being in accord with the relevant parts of the state transition diagram shown in Figure 5.2. The code for these two public callback functions is presented in Listing 5.7.

Listing 5.7   Save and save_as callback functions

```
 1  extern void save_as_callback( Widget    widget,
 2                                XtPointer client_data,
 3                                XtPointer call_data ){
 4
 5      /* create the dialog if it is uncreated */
 6      if ( get_save_state() == S_D_UNCREATED ) {
 7         create_save_as_dialog( widget );
 8      } /* end if */
 9
10      /* abend if the dialog is already active */
11      if ( get_save_state() != S_D_AVAILABLE ( {
12         return;
13      } /* end if */
14
15      set_save_state(S_D_SAVE_AS);
16      activate_file_select();
17  } /* end save as callback */
18
19
20  extern void save_callback( Widget    widget,
21                             XtPointer client_data,
22                             XtPointer call_data ){
23
24      if ( get_save_state() == S_D_UNCREATED ){
```

continued

Listing 5.7 *continued*

```
25          create_save_as_dialog( widget );
26      } /* end if */
27
28      if ( get_save_state() != S_D_AVAILABLE ) {
29          return;
30      } /* end if */
31
32      if ( !is_filename_established() ){
33          save_as_callback( widget, client_data, call_data );
34      }else{
35          set_save_state( S_D_SAVE );
36          set_temp_filename( get_filename());
37          if( does_file_exist( get_temp_filename())){
38              activate_overwrite_dialog();
39          } else {
40              do_save();
41          } /* end if file exists */
42      } /* end if filename established */
43  } /* end fun save callback */
```

The remaining functions from the design can now be considered. The *file selection dialog* has possibly been activated by the *save_as_callback* or by the *save_callback*. The *cancel_callback* which originates from this dialog *file_selection_cancel_callback* can be implemented simply as a call to the *exit_save_as_dialog* function. The *file_select_ok_callback* is more complicated. When this callback is activated the user has indicated that an attempt is to be made to save the application state using the filename in the *selection* component of the file selection dialog. This information is made available to the callback as a component of the *call_data* structure in the form of an *XmString* with the component name *value*. The function needs to extract this component from the *call_data* structure, convert it to a C string and install the C string as the temporary filename. Once all this has been done the function then has an identical requirement to the save callback, either to activate the *overwrite_dialog* or to call the *do_save* function depending upon the result of the *does_file_exist* function. The code for the two functions *file_select_cancel_callback* and *file_select_ok_callback* is presented in Listing 5.8.

The overwrite dialog has two callback functions, *overwrite_dialog_yes_callback* and *overwrite_dialog_no_callback* to be provided. The *overwrite_dialog_yes_callback* first calls the *overwrite_dialog_deactive* function and then calls the *do_save* function. The *overwrite_dialog_no_callback* also commences by calling the *overwrite_dialog_deactive* function, and then has to decide if the entire dialog was called as a *save* dialog or as a *save as* dialog. It does this using the state enquiry function. If it indicates a save interaction it passes control to the *exit_save_as_dialog* function. If it indicates a *save as* interaction it simply exits, as the *file_selection_dialog* has not yet been deactivated and is still available to the user.

\\\

Listing 5.8   File select callback functions

```
1   static void file_select_cancel_callback( Widget    widget,
2                                             XtPointer client_data,
3                                             XtPointer call_data ){
4       exit_save_as_dialog();
5   } /* end fun file select cancel callback */
6
7
8   static void file_select_ok_callback( Widget    widget,
9                                        XtPointer client_data,
10                                       XtPointer call_data ){
11
12  XmString x_filename;
13  char     * filename;
14
15  XmFileSelectionBoxCallbackStruct * c_data;
16
17      /* extract the filename from the call_data structure and  *
18       * convert to an asciiz string                            */
19      c_data = ( XmFileSelectionBoxCallbackStruct *) call_data;
20      x_filename = c_data->value;
21      XmStringGetLtoR( x_filename, XmSTRING_DEFAULT_CHARSET,
22                      &filename );
23
24      /* install as the temporary filename */
25      set_temp_filename( filename );
26      XtFree( filename );
27
28      /* indirect as appropriate */
29      if( does_file_exist( get_temp_filename())) {
30        activate_overwrite_dialog();
31      } else {
32        do_save();
33      } /* end if file exists */
34  } /* end fun select ok callback */
```

The *do_save* function commences by activating the *saving dialog* and then calling the application layer save application workspace function. The application layer returns a Boolean value indicating the success or otherwise of the save operation and if the save is not successful a message explaining why not. If the save operation was successful, the *saving dialog* is deactivated, the temporary filename is installed as the established filename and the *exit_save_as_dialog* function is called. If the save operation is unsuccessful the working dialog is deactivated and the *save_fail_dialog* is activated, using the message returned from the application as a part of its *labelString* resource.

Two final functions are required: the *save_fail_dialog* has possibly been activated by a failure transition from the *do_save* function and the *exit_save_as_dialog* may have been called from several places. The callback function attached to the *save_fail* ok button, the *save_fail_ok_callback,* has a

\\\

Listing 5.9 *continued*

```
37                                    &failure_message) {
38         /* save was successful, store temp filename as *
39          * established filename.                        */
40         set_filename( get_temp_filename());
41         deactivate_working_dialog();
42         exit_save_as_dialog();
43      } else {
44         deactivate_working_dialog();
45         activate_save_fail_dialog( failure_message);
46      } /* end if */
47  } /* end fun do save */
48
49
50  static void exit_save_as_dialog( void ){
51
52      if (get_save_state() == S_D_SAVE_AS ){
53          deactivate_file_select();
54      } /* end if */
55      set_save_state( S_D_AVAILABLE );
56  } /* end exit save(as) dialog */
```

Finally, to complete the visual design of the interface the string resources of various *pushButtons* need to be overridden. The appropriate entries for resource file specifications are presented in Listing 5.10.

Listing 5.10   Partial resource file for the save demo application

```
 1   ! Filename Save_demo - resource settings for the save_demo app.
 2   ! Written for Motif book Chapter 5.
 3   ! Fintan Culwin March 92
 4   ! located in the home directory or in the $APPRESDIR directory
 5
 6   *FontList:                          *charter-bold*12*.
 7   *foreground:                        black
 8   *background:                        white
 9
10   *save button*labelString:           save
11   *save as button*labelString:        save as ..
12   *exit button*labelString:           exit ..
13   *exit button*accelerator:           Ctrl<key>E
14   *exit button*acceleratorText:       CTRL+E
15
16   *file selection dialog*dirListlabelString:     ""
17   *file selection dialog*applyLabelString:       OK
18   *file selection dialog*filterLabelString:      Filter
19   *file selection dialog*cancelLabelString:      Cancel
20
21   *overwrite dialog*okLabelString:        OK
22   *overwrite dialog*cancelLabelString:    Cancel
23
```

5.3 The *help* system

An essential style guide requirement is the provision of a *help* system accessible from the *topics* button on the *help* pull down menu. As with the *save/ save as* interface the style guide gives no detailed guidance concerning the precise construction of this system. It does however provide an additional requirement that *context sensitive* help be available from any part of the application when the *help* button on a dialog, or when the *help* key on the keyboard, is pressed.

The *help system* presented in this section has been designed to be rapidly reconfigurable by the application developer, system manager or end user, for reuse in different Motif applications. It achieves this by the use of a configuration file which informs the *help system* of the names of the topics for which help is available and the names of the text files which contain the help text for each topic. The help provision in this system is limited to a single list of topics, each of which has an associated help text. For a complex application this may not be a suitable help format; the style guide suggests that a hierarchy of help lists should be provided. The intention here is to provide a minimal help system which could be extended if the application merits it.

5.3.1 The *help* system, usability design

The state transition diagram for the *help system* is presented in Figure 5.12. This diagram has two input transitions, one labelled *topics* and one labelled *help*. The *topics* transition is intended to be attached to the *topics* button on the *help menu*. This transition leads initially to a *topic select dialog*, where the user can choose to *view* a help text from a list of available topic headings, or can *close* the dialog and exit the *help interface*. When a topic is selected from the list by pressing the *view* button and help on that topic is available, a separate *topic view* interface is entered.

The help system consists of two interfaces, the *help interface* and the *topic view interface*. Because the interaction described in the state transition diagram consists of two independent interfaces it is described as a *system* rather than an *interface*.

The *topic view interface* is independent of the *help interface* for two reasons. The first is that the user may wish a *topic view dialog* to remain visible after the *topic select dialog* has been closed. If the *topic view dialog* were a part of the *help interface* then closing the *topic select dialog* would imply that the *topic view dialog* would close as well.

The second reason for having a separate *topic view interface* is so that the user can use several *topic viewers* simultaneously. Each topic which is selected from the *topic select dialog* will cause a separate *topic view dialog* to be created, allowing help on a number of topics to be viewed simultaneously. The possibility of multiple instantiations is indicated in the state transition diagram by the double arrow on the input transition.

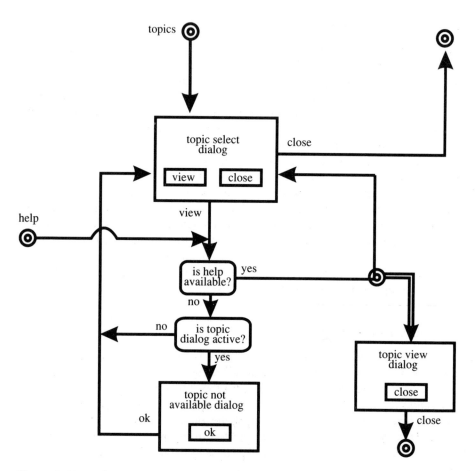

Figure 5.12   Help system, state transition diagram.

The transition between the *topic select dialog* and the *topic view interface* is implemented defensively, with a check made to ensure that help for the topic is available. If no help is available for a particular topic then an information dialog called *topic not available dialog* is used to inform the user.

The *help interface* has an second input transition, labelled *help*, which is intended to be used for *context sensitive* help. All the Motif standard dialogs include a *help* button and all Motif widget classes which are descendants of the *Manager* widget class include a help callback, called *helpCallback*, which is automatically called when the *help key* on the keyboard is pressed and the dialog has keyboard focus. The intention of the *help* transition into the *help interface* is that it can be attached to a widget's *helpCallback* in order to provide *context sensitive* help. The calling widget will use the *client_data* parameter to provide a topic name, for which help is requested.

The help transition leads to the *is help available?* decision. If help on the requested topic is available then the *topic view interface* is entered with help on the topic being displayed to the user. If help on the requested topic is not available and the *topic select dialog* is active, the *topic not available dialog* is used to inform the user. In these situations the interface returns to the *topic select dialog* state allowing it to select another topic or to *close* the help interface. If the *help* input transition is used specifying a topic for which no help is available, the interface indirects directly to the *topic select dialog* bypassing the *topic not available dialog*.

The physical appearance of the *help interface* is illustrated in Figures 5.13, 5.14 and 5.15. The *topic select dialog* is constructed from a Motif *scrollBox* widget. The *topic view dialog* is constructed from a Motif *ScrolledWindow* widget containing a *Text* widget. These new widget classes will be explained in detail shortly. The remaining part of the interface, the *topic not available* dialog, is constructed from a *messageBox* widget which has already been introduced.

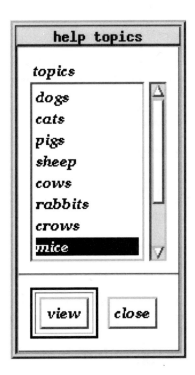

Figure 5.13   Help interface, topic select dialog.

Figure 5.14   Help interface, help not available dialog.

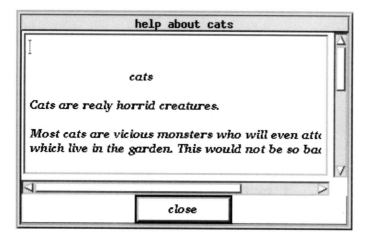

Figure 5.15   Topic interface, topic view dialogs.

5.3.2 The *help* system, detailed design

The design of the *help interface* will divide the help translation layer into a translation module, a sub-presentation module and a support module. This is the same approach which was used for the design of the *save/ save as* interface in the previous section of this chapter.

The state transition diagram indicates that there are two input transitions into the *help interface*, which will have to be exported as callback functions from the translation module. In addition the translation module will have to provide functions to create and destroy the interface. The header file can be constructed these considerations and is presented in Listing 5.11.

Listing 5.11   Help interface translations module header file

```
1   /* filename help_system_translations.h (help_i_t.h) *
2    * help system public aspects                        *
3    *
4    * fintan culwin July 1992 for Motif book Chapter 4 *
5   */
6
7   #ifndef HELP_I_T
8   #define  HELP_I_T
9
10  #include <Xm/Xm.h>
11
12  extern void create_help_system( Widget parent );
13
14  extern void destroy_help_stystem( void );
15
16  extern void topics_callback( Widget    widget,
17                               XtPointer client_data,
18                               XtPointer call_data );
19
20  extern void help_callback(   Widget    widget,
21                               XtPointer client_data,
22                               XtPointer call_data );
23
24
25  #endif /* ifndef HELP_I_T */
```

The *help interface* sub-presentation layer public aspects can likewise be easily produced from a consideration of the interface objects which will be required. As shown in Figure 5.12, the *help interface* comprises two screen objects, the *topic select dialog* and the *topic not available dialog*. The *topic view dialog* is not considered a part of the *help interface* for reasons explained above. Both of these interface components will require a creation function, a destruction function, an activation function and a deactivation function, for reasons which were explained in the discussion of the *save/ save as* presentation module above. The header file for the help interface presentation module is given in Listing 5.12.

\\

Listing 5.12   Help interface presentation header file

```
 1   /* filename help_interface_presentation.h (help_i_p.h)  *
 2    *                                                        *
 3    * fintan culwin July 1992                                *
 4    */
 5
 6   #ifndef HELP_I_P
 7   #define  HELP_I_P
 8
 9   #include <Xm/Xm.h>
10   #include <Xm/SelectionB.h>
11   #include <Xm/MessageB.h>
12
13   #include "help_i_s.h"
14
15   extern void create_topic_select_dialog( Widget   parent,
16                                   XtCallbackProc  view_callback,
17                                   XtCallbackProc  close_callback);
18   /* function to create the topic select dialog and install  *
19    * the relevant callback functions to be activated when a   *
20    * topic is selected by the user                            *
21    */
22
23   extern void destroy_topic_select_dialog(    void );
24   extern void activate_topic_select_dialog(   void );
25   extern void deactivate_topic_select_dialog( void );
26   /* functions to destroy activate and deactivate the topic *
27    * selection dialog                                        *
28    */
29
30   extern void create_topic_not_available_dialog( Widget parent,
31                                   XtCallbackProc ok_callback);
32   extern void destroy_topic_not_available_dialog(    void );
33   extern void activate_topic_not_available_dialog(   void );
34   extern void deactivate_topic_not_available_dialog( void );
35
36   #endif /* ifndef HELP_I_P */
```

The *help interface* support layer is considerably different from the support layer
provided for the *save/ save as* interface. The major support provided is a list, each
element of which comprises the name of a topic and the help text associated with
the topic. The functions which are provided to manipulate the list are a creation
function which will create the list, a destruction function which will release any
resources used by the list, an access function called *get_topic_list*, which will
return a list comprising the topic names only, and an access function called
get_topic_info which will accept a topic name and return the associated help text.
The object diagram for this module is presented in Figure 5.16, and the header file
which is obtained from it is given in Listing 5.13. This module also contains a state
variable recording the availability of the *topic select* dialog, details of which are
contained in the listing.

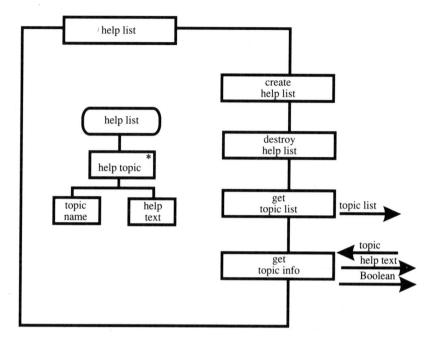

Figure 5.16   Help interface, list object diagram.

Listing 5.13   Help interface support module header file

```
1   /* filename help_interface_support.h (help_i_s.h)        *
2    *                                                        *
3    * fintan culwin v1.0 July 92 *
4   */
5
6   #ifndef HELP_I_S
7   #define  HELP_I_S
8
9   #include <string.h>
10
11  #define TOPIC_VIEW_ACTIVE       0
12  #define TOPIC_VIEW_INACTIVE     1
13
14  #define MAX_TOPICS 20
15
16  extern int create_help_list( void );
17  /* function to initialize the list of topics and help files    *
18   * returns the number of topics if successful and 0 otherwise *
19  */
20
21  extern void destroy_help_list( void );
22  /* function to destroy the list, releasing resources */
23
```

continued

\\\

Listing 5.13 *continued*

```
24   extern int get_topic_list( char * topics[] );
25   /* function to return a list of the topics as an array of pointers   *
26    * to asciiz strings.                                                 *
27    */
28
29   extern int get_topic_info( char * topic, char ** info );
30   /* function to accept a topic name, look up the file name in the      *
31    * help list, read the text from the file returning it in the info    *
32    * parameter. Returns true if successful and false otherwise          *
33    */
34
35   /* get value and set value functions for the *
36    * topic select dialog state variable         */
37   extern void set_topic_view_state( int new_state );
38   extern int is_topic_view_active( void );
39
40   #endif /* ifndef HELP_I_S */
```

The internal workings of the support module are of no concern to the other modules which comprise the *help interface*. The list could be implemented as a static or dynamic structure (for simplicity this example interface uses a static list). The module obtains its topics and help text from a number of configuration files, which can be manipulated by the application developer to revise the help interface for a different application. The configuration files could also be amended by the system manager to configure the help system for local customizations.

The major configuration file is an ascii text file called *"help.index"*, containing an iteration of pairs of lines, each pair consisting of the name of a topic and the pathname of the file which contains the associated help text. In order to reconfigure the contents of the help system, a new *help.index* file and associated text files can be provided. The configuration file is consulted by the creation functions as the interface is created and the topic list contained is presented to the user in the *topic select dialog*. When a topic is selected by the user the help text is retrieved from the identified help file, if it is available, and presented to the user in a *topic viewer*.

The translation layer for the *help interface* differs from the *save/ save as* interface in two respects. The first difference is that the help functionality does not change the application's state and consequently does not have any interaction with the application layer. The second difference is that the *help_callback* can be called from places in the application other than the *application main menu*. Consequently the help system translations header file may be *#included* in modules other than the application main menu.

The *topic view interface* is completely contained within the *help interface*. The state transition diagram indicates that it has a single input transition which will create an instance of the *topic view dialog*. As this is a very simple interface

\\

comprising a single dialog it can be constructed from a single module whose public aspects comprise a creation function called *create_topic_viewer*. The header file for this module is given in Listing 5.14.

Listing 5.14   Topic view interface module header file

```
1   /* filename topic_view_interface.h ( topic_v.h)        *
2    * single header file for the topic view interface, an  *
3    * embedded interface of the help interface.            *
4    * fintan culwin v1.0 July 92                           *
5    */
6   #ifndef TOPIC_V_I
7   #define  TOPIC_V_I
8
9   #include <Xm/Xm.h>
10  #include <Xm/Text.h>
11  #include <Xm/PushB.h>
12  #include <Xm/Form.h>
13  #include <Xm/DialogS.h>
14
15  extern void create_topic_viewer( Widget    parent,
16                                    char *    topic_name,
17                                    char *    information );
18
19  #endif /* ifndef TOPIC_V_I */
```

The complete high level design of the *help interface*, showing the application main presentation layer, the application layer, other translation modules and the two interfaces which comprise the *help system,* is given in Figure 5.17.

5.3.3 The Motif *SelectionBox, ScrolledWindow* and *Text* widget class

The implementation of the *help system* will require the introduction of three new widget classes. The *topic select dialog* is implemented using a *SelectionBox* widget; the *topic view dialog* is implemented using a *text* widget contained within a *scrolledWindow* widget. Before the detailed implementation of the help system can be explained these three widget classes will have to be introduced.

The *SelectionBox* composite widget is illustrated in Figure 2.7 and its major resources are listed in Table 5.2. An instance of a *SelectionBox* widget contained within a *dialogShell* can be created using the *XmCreateSelectionBoxDialog* convenience function. The prototype of this function and their interpretation are identical to the other *XmCreate(whatever)Dialog* functions which have already been introduced. As shown in Figure 5.13 the *selectionBox* used in this interface does not require all possible components. In the default configuration the *help* button and the *text* component are supplied. The identities of these widgets are obtained using the convenience function *XmSelectionBoxGetChild*, before being

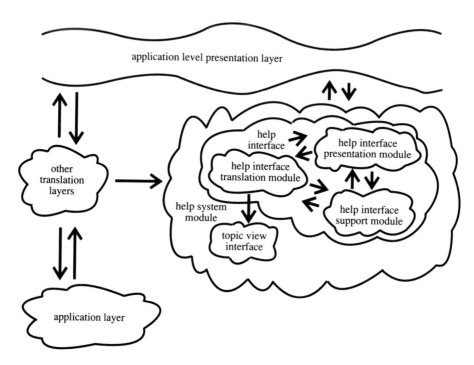

Figure 5.17   Help system, high level architecture.

unmanaged using the *XtUnmanageChild* function. The prototype of *XmSelectionBoxGetChild* is:

```
Widget XmSelectionBoxGetChild( Widget     selection_box,
                               manifest   child_required );
```

where the *selection_box* parameter identifies the *selectionBox* whose child is required and the *child_required* parameter identifies which component of the *selectionBox* is required. Possible values of the *child_required* parameter are:

```
XmDIALOG_APPLY_BUTTON            XmDIALOG_CANCEL_BUTTON
XmDIALOG_DEFAULT_BUTTON            XmDIALOG_HELP_BUTTON
XmDIALOG_LIST                     XmDIALOG_LIST_LABEL
XmDIALOG_OK_BUTTON                XmDIALOG_WORK_AREA
XmDIALOG_SELECTION_LABEL          XmDIALOG_TEXT
XmDIALOG_SEPARATOR
```

The user can select an item from the *list* by clicking upon an item and can activate the selection by pressing the *OK* button. When the *text* component is present the user can also enter a selection directly into the text field. If the value entered in the *text* field does not match one of the items in the list and the resource *mustMatch* is True, then the *noMatchCallback* is called when the *OK* button is

Table 5.2   The major resources of the *SelectionBox* widget class

inheritance hierarchy   Core -> Composite -> Constraint -> Manager
-> BulletinBoard -> SelectionBox

Resource name	type	(default) values
applyCallback	CallbackList	NULL
actions to be performed when the apply button is clicked		
applyLabelString	XmString	"Apply"
label string to be displayed in the apply button		
cancelCallback	CallbackList	NULL
actions to be performed when the cancel button is clicked		
cancelLabelString	XmString	"Cancel"
label string to be displayed in the cancel button		
dialogType	manifest (unsigned char)	XmDIALOG_COMMAND
		XmDIALOG_PROMPT
		XmDIALOG_SELECTION (default)
		XmDIALOG_WORK_AREA
determines the number of managed children		
helpLabelString	XmString	"Help"
label string to be displayed in the help button		
listItems	StringTable	NULL
the items of the list (as an array of XmStrings)		
listItemCount	int	0
the number of items in the list		
listLabelString	XmString	"Items"
the label to be displayed above the list		
listVisibleItemCount	int	8
the number of items visible in the list		
minimizeButtons	Boolean	False
if False forces all buttons to be the same size		
mustMatch	Boolean	False
*if True forces a call to **noMatchCallback** on activation if the string in the text component does not match one of the strings in the list*		
noMatchCallback	CallbackList	NULL
*actions to be performed when the ok button is clicked if **mustMatch** is True and the string in the text component does not match one of the strings in the list*		
okCallback	CallbackList	NULL
actions to be performed when the ok button is clicked		
okLabelString	XmString	"OK"
label string to be displayed in the OK button		
selectionLabelString	XmString	"Selection"
the label displayed above the selection input area		
textString	XmString	""
the text in the selection input area		

pressed instead of the *okCallback*. If there are more items in the list than can be shown in the list component the *selectionBox* automatically supplies a *scrollBar*, which the user can use to scroll the list.

The *Text*, and the related *TextField*, are the only common Motif widgets which manipulate C standard asciiz strings. As shown in the *selectionBox* widget above the *TextField* widget is capable of being used as a single line text entry field. The *Text* widget is used for multiple line text entry, where it automatically implements most of the functionality of a text editor. The Athena version of the *text* widget is used to implement the text areas of the *xedit* and *xterm* clients which were introduced in Chapter 1. Both *Text* and *TextField* widgets are capable of being set for the display of text only. Motif supplies a large number of resources and convenience functions which can be used to manipulate the text within a text widget, when it is being used for editing. The major resources of the *Text* widget are listed in Table 5.3. The *TextField* widget class has a very similar set of resources and convenience functions.

Table 5.3   The major resources of the *Text* widget class

inheritance hierarchy   Core -> Primitive -> Text

Resource name	type	(default) values
cursorPosition	TextPosition	0
the location of the insert cursor in characters, with the start of the text being 0		
columns	short	varies
the number of text columns displayed		
editable	Boolean	True
if true allows the contents of the widget to be edited		
entryMode	manifest (unsigned char)	XmMULTI_LINE_EDIT
		XmSINGLE_LINE_EDIT
determines single or multiple line configuration		
maxLength	int	largest integer
determines the maximum number of characters in the text		
rows	short	varies
the number of text rows displayed		
resizeHeight	Boolean	False
if true the widget will attempt to expand vertically to display all the text		
resizeWidth	Boolean	False
if true the widget will attempt to expand horizontally to display all the text		
topCharacter	TextPosition	0
the location of the first character visible to the user		
value	char *	""
the contents of the widget		
valueChangedCallback	CallbackList	NULL
actions to be performed when a character is entered		
wordWrap	Boolean	False
if true will break lines in a multiple line widget at word breaks		

The *text* widget in *text view* interface is implemented within a *scrolledWindow* widget, as shown in Figure 5.15. With this configuration the user is able to use the *scrollBars* provided by the *scrolledWindow* to view a large body of text within a smaller window. In the default configuration the scrolling of the text is handled automatically by the *scrolledWindow* without any programmer intervention. The major resources of the *ScrolledWindow* widget class are listed in Table 5.4.

The convenience function *XmCreateScrolledText* will create a suitable configuration and return the identity of the *text* widget contained within the *scrolledWindow*. The prototype of this function and the interpretation of the parameters is identical to that of the other *XmCreate{whatever}* functions which have already been introduced. Should the identity of the *scrolledWindow* be required, for example, should its attachment resources require setting, it can be obtained using the *XtParent* function.

5.3.4 The *help* system, implementation

The implementation of the support module is not of direct concern to the implementation of the user interface. The code file for the header file presented in Listing 5.13 is given in Appendix C.

Table 5.4   The major resources of the *ScrolledWindow* widget class

inheritance hierarchy   Core -> Composite -> Constraint -> Manager
-> BulletinBoard -> ScrolledWindow

Resource name	type	(default) values
clipWindow	Window	NULL
window identity when the work area's window is clipped		
horizontalScrollBar	Widget	NULL
identity of the horizontal scroll bar widget		
scrollBarDisplayPolicy	manifest (unsigned char)	XmSTATIC
		XmAS_NEEDED
*if **as needed** scroll bars will only be displayed if the work area is larger than the **clipWindow***		
scrollBarPlacement	manifest (unsigned char)	XmTOP_LEFT
		XmBOTTOM_RIGHT (default)
		XmTOP_RIGHT
		XmBOTTOM_LEFT
determines the positioning of the scroll bars		
scrollingPolicy	manifest (unsigned char)	XmAUTOMATIC
		XmAPPLICATION_DEFINED
determines if the scrolledWindow or the programmer will control scrolling		
verticalScrollBar	Widget	NULL
identity of the vertical scrollBar widget		
workWindow	Widget	NULL
identity of the work area widget		

\\\

The *create_topic_select_dialog* function of the presentation module obtains the topic list from the *get_topic_list* support module function. The list is returned from the support module as an array of asciiz strings, which is converted into an array of *XmStrings* before being installed as the *listItems* resource of the *selectionBox* widget as it is created. The *listItemsCount* resource is set to the number of topics in the list and the *autoUnmanage* resource is set *False*. Following its creation the identities of the *text* and *help* widgets are obtained and the widgets unmanaged. Finally the two callbacks supplied to the function from the translation layer are installed into the *selectionBox's okCallback* and *closeCallback* resources. The text of the *create_topic_select* dialog is given in Listing 5.15.

Listing 5.15   Help interface presentation module code file

```
 1   /* filename help_interface_presentation.c (help_i_p.c)    *
 2    *                                                         *
 3    * fintan culwin v1.0 July 92                              *
 4    */
 5
 6   #include "help_i_p.h"
 7   #include "help_i_s.h"
 8
 9   #include <string.h>
10
11   #define MAX_ARGS         10
12   #define MAX_BUFFER_SIZE  255
13
14   static Widget topic_select = NULL;
15
16
17   extern void create_topic_select_dialog( Widget     parent,
18                                   XtCallbackProc  view_callback,
19                                   XtCallbackProc  close_callback){
20   /* function to create the topic select dialog and install  *
21    * the relevant callback function to be activated when a    *
22    * topic is selected by the user                            *
23    */
24
25   Widget temp = parent;
26   Arg    args[ MAX_ARGS ];
27   int    num_args;
28
29   char    * topic_list[ MAX_TOPICS ];
30   XmString x_topic_list[ MAX_TOPICS ];
31   int      num_topics;
32   int      index;
33
34      /* obtain the topic list from the support module and *
35       * convert to XmStrings.                             */
36      num_topics = get_topic_list( topic_list );
37      for ( index = 0; index < num_topics; index++ ){
38          x_topic_list[ index ] = XmStringCreateLtoR( topic_list[ index],
```
continued

Listing 5.15 *continued*

```
39                                           XmSTRING_DEFAULT_CHARSET );
40     } /* end for */
41
42     /* find the toplevel shell*/
43     while( ! XtIsTopLevelShell( temp )) {
44        temp = XtParent( temp );
45     } /* end while */
46
47     num_args = 0;
48     XtSetArg( args[num_args], XmNmwmDecorations,
49                          XM_DECOR_BORDER | XM_DECOR_TITLE);
50                                              num_args++;
51     XtSetArg( args[ num_args ], XmNlistItems, x_topic_list);
52                                              num_args++;
53     XtSetArg( args[ num_args ], XmNlistItemCount,num_topics);
54                                              num_args++;
55     XtSetArg( args[ num_args ], XmNautoUnmanage, False);
56                                              num_args++;
57     topic_select = XmCreateSelectionDialog( temp,
58                                  "topic select dialog",
59                                  args, num_args );
60
61     /* remove the unwanted components */
62     temp = XmSelectionBoxGetChild( topic_select, XmDIALOG_HELP_BUTTON);
63     XtUnmanageChild( temp );
64     temp = XmSelectionBoxGetChild( topic_select, XmDIALOG_TEXT);
65     XtUnmanageChild( temp );
66     temp = XmSelectionBoxGetChild(topic_select,
67                                  XmDIALOG_SELECTION_LABEL);
68     XtUnmanageChild( temp );
69
70     /* add behaviours to the remaining buttons */
71     XtAddCallback( topic_select, XmNokCallback,
72                   view_callback, (XtPointer) NULL );
73     XtAddCallback( topic_select, XmNcancelCallback,
74                   close_callback, (XtPointer) NULL );
75   } /* end fun create topic select dialog */
76
77
78   extern void destroy_topic_select_dialog( void ){
79      XtDestroy( XtParent(topic_select));
80   } /* end fun destroy topic selection dialog */
81
82
83   extern void activate_topic_select_dialog( void ){
84      XtManageChild( topic_select );
85      set_topic_view_state( TOPIC_VIEW_ACTIVE);
86   } /* end fun activate topic select dialog */
87
88   extern void deactivate_topic_select_dialog( void ){
89      XtUnmanageChild( topic_select );
90      set_topic_view_state( TOPIC_VIEW_INACTIVE);
91   } /* end fun deactivate topic select dialog */
```

continued

Listing 5.15 *continued*

```
92
93
94   /*  topic not available dialog */
95    static Widget topic_not_available = NULL;
96
97   extern void create_topic_not_available_dialog( Widget   parent,
98                                          XtCallbackProc  ok_callback){
99
100  Widget temp = parent;
101  Arg    args[ MAX_ARGS ];
102  int    num_args;
103
104     num_args = 0;
105     XtSetArg( args[ num_args ], XmNautoUnmanage, False); num_args++;
106     topic_not_available=XmCreateErrorDialog(temp,
107                                          "topic not available",
108                                          args, num_args );
109
110     temp = XmMessageBoxGetChild( topic_not_available,
111                            XmDIALOG_HELP_BUTTON);
112     XtUnmanageChild( temp );
113     temp = XmMessageBoxGetChild( topic_not_available,
114                            XmDIALOG_CANCEL_BUTTON);
115     XtUnmanageChild( temp );
116
117     XtAddCallback( topic_not_available, XmNokCallback,
118               ok_callback, (XtPointer) NULL );
119  } /* end fun create topic dialog */
120
121
122  extern void destroy_topic_not_available_dialog( /* void */){
123     XtDestroyWidget( XtParent(topic_not_available));
124  } /* end fun destroy topic not available dialog */
125
126
127  extern void activate_topic_not_available_dialog( char * topic_name ){
128
129  Arg    args[ MAX_ARGS ];
130  int    num_args;
131
132  XmString  topic_string;
133  char      buffer[ MAX_BUFFER_SIZE ];
134
135     /* create the message string */
136     strcpy( buffer, "There is no help available \n");
137     strcat( buffer, "for the topic ");
138     strcat( buffer, topic_name );
139     strcat( buffer, ".");
140     topic_string = XmStringCreateLtoR( buffer,
141                                    XmSTRING_DEFAULT_CHARSET );
142
143     /* install the string and activate the dialog */
144     num_args = 0;
```

continued

Listing 5.15 *continued*

```
145    XtSetArg(args[num_args], XmNmessageString, topic_string);
146                                          num_args++;
147    XtSetValues( topic_not_available, args, num_args );
148
149    XmStringFree( topic_string );
150    XtManageChild( topic_not_available );
151  } /* end fun activate topic dialog */
152
153
154  extern void deactivate_topic_not_available_dialog( /* void */ ){
155      XtUnmanageChild( topic_not_available );
156  } /* end fun deactivate topic not available dialog */
```

The destruction, activation and unmanaging functions are simply implemented using the *XtDestroy, XtManageChild* and *XtUnmanageChild* functions respectively. The creation, destruction, activation, and deactivation functions for the *topic_not_available* dialog are not significantly different from the *MessageBox* dialogs used in the *save/save as* dialog presented earlier in this chapter.

Before considering the *help interface* translation module in detail the *topic viewer* interface needs to be considered. The construction of this interface differs from the construction of the interfaces presented so far not only because it is a simple interface implemented in one code module, but also because it is capable of multiple instantiations.

The *topic view dialog* is created and activated in a single function. Likewise it is destroyed and deactivated in a single function. The activation function is a public function, whose prototype is declared in the *topic view interface*'s header file. The deactivate function is private to the body of the module. For this dialog the deactivate function is a callback function attached to the dialog's single *close* button. The *topic view dialog* is a specialized dialog, which requires a widget hierarchy design. A suitable widget hierarchy design is given in Figure 5.18.

The creation function receives as parameters a parent widget, the topic name and the help text. The actions of the function are to obtain the identity of the *toplevel* shell by ascending the widget hierarchy. The *dialogShell* is created as a child of the *toplevel* shell in order that the *topic viewer* appears centred within the main application window when it is presented to the user. The *title* resource of the dialog shell is set to a suitable value as it is created.

Once a *form* widget has been created as a child of the *dialogShell*, the function creates the *text* widget as child of an unnamed *scrolledWindow* widget which itself is a child of the *form*. The help text supplied as a parameter is installed as the *value* resource of the *text* widget which also has its *editable* resource set *False*, and is set to multiple line mode using its *editMode* resource. The *text* widget takes a copy of the help text as it is installed into the widget, consequently the resources used by the help text are released as soon as they are not required.

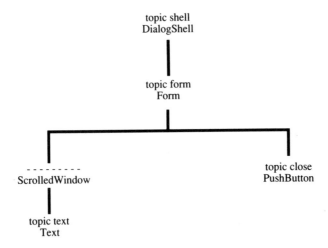

Figure 5.18   Topic viewer, application widget hierarchy.

Subsequently a *pushButton* widget is created as a child of the *form*. The attachment resources of the *pushButton* are set upon its creation and the deactivate function is attached to its *activateCallback* resource.

The application widget hierarchy indicates that the sibling of the *pushButton* widget is the unnamed *scrolledWindow* widget. The attachment resources of this widget are set following the creation of the *pushButton* widget in order that the *pushButton* widget can be conveniently specified as the *scrollWindow*'s *bottomAttachment* resource. The identity of the *scrolledWindow* widget is obtained from the identity of the *text* widget returned by the *XmCreateScrolledText*, using the *XtParent* function.

Having created and managed the widgets which comprise the *topic view dialog* the function terminates. Unlike the other dialogs which have been introduced there is no static widget variable which holds the identity of the widget for the program. Should the function be called again, another instance of the dialog will be created. It is this aspect of the implementation which allows multiple *topic viewers* to be made available to the user.

The deactivation callback function obtains the identity of the *pushButton* widget which caused it to be called from the widget parameter. It then ascends the widget hierarchy to the *dialogShell* and calls *XtDestroyWidget* using the *dialogShell* widget as a parameter. The *XtDestroyWidget* function not only destroys the widget supplied as a parameter but also all of its offspring. Consequently destroying the *dialogShell* explicitly causes the entire dialog to be destroyed. The body of the topic view module is given in Listing 5.16.

Having implemented the *help interface* support module, presentation module and the *topic view interface*, the transition module can be implemented using the facilities provided by these modules.

\\

Listing 5.16   Topic view interface code file

```
1   /* filename topic_view_interface.h ( topic_v.h)          *
2    * single code file for the topic view interface, an     *
3    * embedded interface of the help interface.             *
4    */
5
6   #include "topic_v.h"
7
8   /* local prototype */
9   static void text_view_close_callback( Widget     parent,
10                                         XtPointer  client_data,
11                                         XtPointer  call_data);
12
13  extern void create_topic_viewer( Widget   parent,
14                                    char *  topic_name,
15                                    char *  information ){
16
17  Widget  temp = parent;
18  Widget  help_shell, help_form, help_text,
19          help_scroll, help_close;
20  char    shell_name[ MAX_BUFFER_SIZE ];
21
22  Arg    args[ MAX_ARGS ];
23  int    num_args;
24
25     /* find the top level shell */
26     while( ! XtIsTopLevelShell( temp )){
27        temp = XtParent( temp );
28     } /* end while */
29
30     /* create the dialog shell */
31     strcpy( shell_name, "help about ");
32     strcat( shell_name, topic_name);
33     num_args = 0;
34     XtSetArg( args[num_args], XmNmwmDecorations,
35                               XM_DECOR_BORDER |
36                               XM_DECOR_TITLE  | XM_DECOR_RESIZEH);
37                                               num_args++;
38     XtSetArg( args[num_args] , XmNtitle, shell_name); num_args++;
39     help_shell = XmCreateDialogShell( temp, "help shell",
40                                       args, num_args );
41     XtManageChild( help_shell);
42
43     /* create the form */
44     num_args = 0;
45     help_form = XmCreateForm( help_shell, "help form",
46                               args, num_args );
47     XtManageChild( help_form);
48
49    /* create the text widget within (an unnamed) scrolledWindow *
50     * widget                                                    */
51     num_args = 0;
52     XtSetArg( args[num_args] , XmNeditMode, XmMULTI_LINE_EDIT);
```

continued

\\

Listing 5.16 *continued*

```
53                                                      num_args++;
54     XtSetArg( args[num_args] , XmNeditable, False);    num_args++;
55     XtSetArg( args[num_args] , XmNvalue, information); num_args++;
56     help_text = XmCreateScrolledText( help_form, "help text",
57                                     args, num_args );
58     XtManageChild( help_text);
59     free( information );
60
61
62     /* create the pushButton to close the topic viewer */
63     num_args = 0;
64     XtSetArg( args[num_args] ,XmNleftAttachment, XmATTACH_POSITION);
65                                                      num_args++;
66     XtSetArg( args[num_args] ,XmNleftPosition,   35);     num_args++;
67     XtSetArg( args[num_args] ,XmNrightAttachment, XmATTACH_POSITION);
68                                                      num_args++;
69     XtSetArg( args[num_args] ,XmNrightPosition,   65);    num_args++;
70     XtSetArg( args[num_args] ,XmNbottomAttachment, XmATTACH_FORM);
71                                                      num_args++;
72     XtSetArg( args[num_args], XmNtopAttachment, XmATTACH_SELF);
73                                                      num_args++;
74     XtSetArg( args[num_args] , XmNtopOffset, -30);        num_args++;
75     help_close = XmCreatePushButton( help_form, "help close",
76                                     args, num_args );
77     XtManageChild( help_close)
78     XtAddCallback( help_close, XmNactivateCallback,
79                   text_view_close_callback, (XtPointer) NULL );
80
81     /* find the identity of the scrolledWindow and set its *
82      * attachment resources                           */
83     help_scroll = XtParent( help_text );
84     num_args = 0;
85     XtSetArg( args[num_args],XmNleftAttachment, XmATTACH_FORM);
86                                                      num_args++;
87     XtSetArg( args[num_args],XmNrightAttachment, XmATTACH_FORM);
88                                                      num_args++;
89     XtSetArg( args[num_args],XmNtopAttachment,   XmATTACH_FORM);
90                                                      num_args++;
91     XtSetArg( args[num_args],XmNbottomAttachment , XmATTACH_WIDGET);
92                                                      num_args++;
93     XtSetArg( args[num_args],XmNbottomWidget, help_close);
94                                                      num_args++;
95     XtSetValues( help_scroll, args, num_args );
96  } /* end fun create topic viewer */
97
98
99  static void text_view_close_callback( Widget      parent,
100                                     XtPointer  client_data,
101                                     XtPointer  call_data);
102
103  Widget temp = parent;
104
105    while( ! XtIsShell( temp )) {
```

continued

Listing 5.16 *continued*

```
106          temp = XtParent( temp );
107      } /* end while */
108      XtDestroyWidget( temp );
109  } /* end fun text view close callback */
```

The state transition diagram identifies two input callback transitions which along with the interface creation and destruction functions have already been declared in the transition module's header file. The state transition diagram, shown in Figure 5.12, identifies the other functions which will be required. There are three callback functions, the *topic_select_view_callback*, *topic_select_close_callback* and the *topic_not_available_ok_callback*. In addition there are two decision functions to be implemented, the *is_help_available* decision and the *is_topic_select_dialog_active* decision.

The interface creation function is implemented by calling the creation functions supplied by the support and presentation modules. Likewise the interface destruction function is implemented by calling the appropriate destruction functions.

The *topics_callback* input transition is implemented as a call to the activation function of the *topic_select_dialog*. The *topic_select_view_callback* is attached to the *activateCallback* resource of a *selectionBox* composite widget. The *call_data* parameter of this callback is a pointer to a structure which contains a field called *value*, which contains the selection chosen by the user as an *XmString*. This string is converted to a standard asciiz string before control is passed to the *is_topic_available_decision* function.

The other input transition, the *help_callback* has a similar structure. When the *help_callback* is installed into a widget, the *client_data* parameter is set as an asciiz string identifying the topic required. The *help_callback* function extracts this string from the *client_data* parameter and then passes control to the *is_topic_available_decision*.

The two functions pass control to the *is_topic_available_decision*, rather than call the function and implement the requisite actions themselves, in order to avoid having a single part of the interface duplicated within the transition module.

The *is_topic_available_decision* receives the topic name as a parameter and calls the support module *get_topic_info* function to obtain the help text for the topic. If the help text can be obtained it is passed to the *create_topic_view* function, which will display the text within a *text view dialog*. If the help text is not available and the *topic_select_dialog* is active then the *topic_not_available_dialog* is activated passing the topic name onward to it as a parameter. Otherwise the *topic_select_dialog* is activated to present the user with the list of topics when a non-available topic is requested by the context sensitive input transition.

The implementation of the *topic view* interface has already been sufficiently described. The *topic_not_available_dialog* has a single output transition, the

\\\

topic_not_available_dialog_ok_callback, which has the tasks of deactivating the *topic_not_available_dialog* and then activating the *topic_select_dialog*. The state transition diagram and a review of the code indicates that the *topic_select_dialog* may already be active; however as activating an already active dialog has no effect this is an acceptable implementation. The complete text of the translations module code file is given in Listing 5.17.

Listing 5.17   Help interface translation code file

```
 1  /* filename help_interface_translations.c (help_i_t.c) *
 2   * help interface public aspects                        *
 3   *                                                      *
 4   * fintan culwin July 1992                              *
 5   */
 6
 7  #include "help_i_t.h"
 8  #include "help_i_s.h"
 9  #include "help_i_p.h"
10  #include "topic_v.h"
11
12  /* local prototypes */
13  static void topic_select_view_callback( Widget    widget,
14                                          XtPointer client_data,
15                                          XtPointer call_data);
16  static void topic_select_close_callback( Widget    widget,
17                                           XtPointer client_data,
18                                           XtPointer call_data);
19  static void topic_not_available_ok_callback( Widget    widget,
20                                               XtPointer client_data,
21                                               XtPointer call_data);
22
23  static void is_topic_available_decision(Widget widget, char * topic );
24
25
26  extern void create_help_system( Widget parent ){
27
28     create_help_list();
29     create_topic_select_dialog( parent,
30                                 topic_select_view_callback,
31                                 topic_select_close_callback);
32     create_topic_not_available_dialog( parent,
33                                 topic_not_available_ok_callback );
34  } /* end fun create help system */
35
36
37  extern void destroy_help_system( void ){
38
39     destroy_help_list();
40     destroy_topic_select_dialog();
41     destroy_topic_not_available_dialog();
42  } /* end fun destroy help system */
43
44
```

continued

Listing 5.17 *continued*

```
45  extern void topics_callback( Widget    widget,
46                               XtPointer client_data,
47                               XtPointer call_data ){
48
49      activate_topic_select_dialog();
50  } /* end fun topics callback */
51
52
53
54  extern void help_callback(  Widget    widget,
55                              XtPointer client_data,
56                              XtPointer call_data ){
57  char * topic;
58
59      topic = (char *) client_data;
60      is_topic_available_decision( widget, topic );
61  } /* end fun help callback */
62
63  static void topic_select_view_callback( Widget    widget,
64                                          XtPointer client_data,
65                                          XtPointer call_data){
66  XmString x_topic;
67  char *   topic;
68
69      /* extract the selected topic from the call_data structure */
70      x_topic = ((XmSelectionBoxCallbackStruct *) call_data)->value;
71      XmStringGetLtoR( x_topic, XmSTRING_DEFAULT_CHARSET, &topic );
72      /* and indirect to decision */
73      is_topic_available_decision( widget, topic );
74  } /* end fun topic select view callback */
75
76
77  static void is_topic_available_decision(Widget widget, char * topic ){
78
79  char * information;
80  int    is_available;
81
82      is_available = get_topic_info( topic, &information );
83      if ( is_available ){
84          create_topic_viewer( widget, topic, information );
85      } else {
86          if ( !is_topic_view_active()){
87              activate_topic_select_dialog();
88          } else {
89              activate_topic_not_available_dialog( topic );
90          } /* end if */
91      } /* end if */
92  } /* end fun is topic available decision */
93
94
95  static void topic_select_close_callback( Widget    widget,
96                                           XtPointer client_data,
97                                           XtPointer call_data){
```

continued

\\

Listing 5.17 *continued*

```
 98
 99    deactivate_topic_select_dialog();
100 } /* end fun topic select close callback */
101
102
103 static void topic_not_available_ok_callback( Widget      widget,
104                                              XtPointer client_data,
105                                              XtPointer call_data){
106
107    deactivate_topic_not_available_dialog();
108    activate_topic_select_dialog();
109 } /* end fun topic not available ok callback  */
```

5.3.5 Integrating the *help* system with other parts of the application

Before concluding this description of the *help system*, the integration of help callbacks into other parts of the interface will be considered. In order to integrate the help system into the *save/ save as* interface, the *save/ save as* interface translations header file will have to be amended to *#include* the *help interface* translations header file. The creation functions of the dialogs which are to support *help* buttons will have to have their prototypes amended to accept a *help_callback* parameter. The call of the creation function when the interface is created, will specify the *help_callback* exported from the *help interface* translations as the actual parameter.

The creation of the dialogs will also have to be amended, in order that the *help* button component will not be unmanaged and the *help_callback* parameter installed as the dialog's *helpCallback* resource. As described above the *help_callback* within the *help interface* expects the *client_data* parameter to contain an asciiz string which identifies the topic upon which help is requested. To support this a static string within the dialog's creation function should be initialized to the topic, and this string specified as the *client_data* parameter to the *XtAddCallback* function. Listing 5.18 illustrates an amended *create_overwrite_dialog* function, which supports a *help* button.

The state transition diagram of the *save/ save as* interface will also have to be amended. Each component of the dialog which is to support a *help* button will have to have the *help* button illustrated on its representation. However the diagram would become far too confusing if each of these buttons were individually connected to the input transition of the *help interface*. This can be avoided by the use of hierarchical transitions, where the entire dialog is bounded and an identified transition into the *help interface* is illustrated. Figure 5.19 contains an amended *save/ save as* state transition diagram.

Listing 5.18   Amended create overwrite dialog

```
1   /* amended overwrite dialog from the save/save as interface  *
2    * presentation module, illustrating the inclusion of a help *
3    * button and callback to the help system.                   *
4    */
5
6   extern Widget create_overwrite_dialog( Widget          parent,
7                                           XtCallbackProc  yes_callback,
8                                           XtCallbackProc  no_callback,
9                                           XtCallbackProc  help_callback ){
10
11  Arg     args[ MAX_ARGS ];
12  int     num_args;
13  Widget temp;
14
15  static const char * topic = "overwrite";
16
17          num_args = 0;
18          overwrite_dialog = XmCreateQuestionDialog( parent,
19                            "overwrite_dialog",  args, num_args );
20
21      XtAddCallback( overwrite_dialog, XmNokCallback,
22                      yes_callback,     (XtPointer) NULL );
23      XtAddCallback( overwrite_dialog, XmNcancelCallback,
24                      no_callback,      (XtPointer) NULL  );
25      XtAddCallback( overwrite_dialog, XmNhelpCallback,
26                      help_callback,    (XtPointer) topic  );
27      return overwrite_dialog;
28  } /* end fun create overwrite dialog */
```

5.4 STDs, usability design and GUI engineering

This chapter has expanded and consolidated the use of state transition diagrams (STDs), as a tool which can be used in the construction of GUIs. This section will summarize the various ways in which STDs can be used.

The initial use of STDs is a design tool to make an explicit model of the visual and usability aspects of an interface and its dialogs. As an explicit model it is considerably more consistent and precise than a written description of the dialog. Thus at this stage it can be used as a specification of the interface which is to be produced. During this process of establishing the specification for the interface it can be used during peer review or management review meetings, as a vehicle for discussing the proposed interface.

There are a number of heuristic and formal checks which can be made upon the interface at this stage. The interface can be evaluated for complexity by using a count of the number of distinct states and transitions which it contains. Initially this measure can be used as a relative complexity index to compare two or more proposed dialogs. With further experience it can be used to estimate the complexity of a dialog when user training, learnability and ease of use issues are

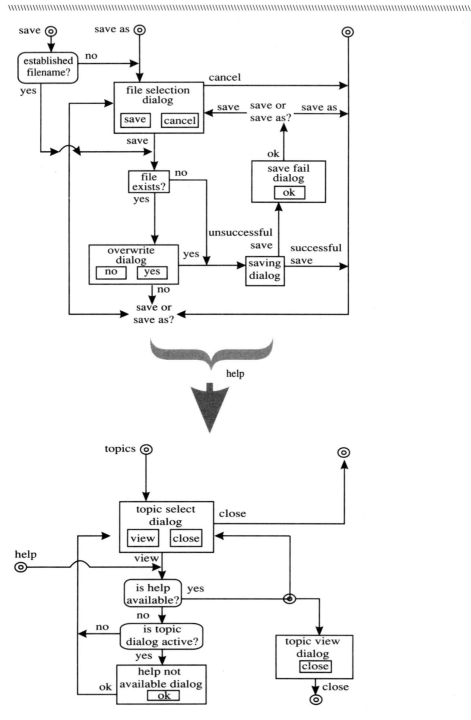

Figure 5.19 State transition diagram illustrating context sensitive help being called from the *save/ save as* interface.

being considered. The final state transition dialog can also be used as a training and support aid when the application is complete.

A second check which can be applied at this stage is to ensure that each of the proposed states is sufficiently distinct. Two states differ if they offer different functionality to the user and should be visually distinct in order to allow the user to differentiate between them. The number of transitions from a state should be related to the number of active components which it has. If a state has three active components (e.g. *pushButtons*), then at least three transitions should originate from it. If there are fewer transitions than active components then one or more of the components does not have function and may require removal or desensitization. If there are more transitions than components then a component may be overloaded, or a transition may not be available to the user, or the transition may be a shortcut intended for a skilled user.

The interface as a whole can be checked at this stage. The number of independent paths through the interface can be used as a further measure of complexity and the possibility of paths which lead to a dead end or which have no visible indication can be checked for. The consistency of the interface can also be checked, e.g. ensuring that all positive and negative responses from the user have a similar semantic meaning.

Most of the above possibilities for the use of a state transition diagram could also be accomplished by construction of a prototype. However the process of constructing a prototype is more expensive than the construction of STD. An STD can be employed to design the prototype, ensuring that an effective prototype is constructed. An STD may even make a usability prototype superfluous. If the sponsor of an application is sufficiently committed to the project they may be willing to explore the STD with the usability designer and avoid the time and expense of prototype construction.

Once the STD is finalized it can be regarded as a specification of the interface which is to be constructed. It can now be used as an engineering design tool during construction of the interface. Each of the individual dialogs from which the interface is constructed can be individually constructed using the create/ activate/ deactivate/ destroy lifecycle model, and implemented within the presentation module. The decisions which are used for the hidden transitions of the interface can be implemented by enquiry functions of the support module. The translation module itself can be constructed from the transitions identified upon the STD, using the facilities provided by the other two modules.

As these dialogs, state variables and callbacks can be easily enumerated from the STD they can be used to manage the production process. The extent of construction of the interface can be estimated from the number of the identified components which have been completed and the number yet to be completed.

After the interface has been constructed the state transition diagram can be used to audit the code. Each transition line through the diagram represents a path of execution through the code. By relating the code to the transition paths, any parts of the interface which have not been implemented and any parts of the interface which have been duplicated can be identified. Any duplication of parts of the interface should be avoided as it can lead to maintenance problems.

The STD can be used to validate the test effectiveness. An effective test set should cause all parts of the interface and all possible transitions to be traversed, although this in itself may not be sufficient to ensure that the interface has been adequately tested. By tracing the paths through the interface which have been traversed while the module is under test, the coverage of the test set can be monitored.

Finally, the STD can be used as a training resource. It can be presented to the users as part of the training resources, in order to ensure that the user's cognitive model of the interface is congruent with the formal model. The STD can also be used to ensure that the training program has resources which cover all parts of the interface.

5.5 Activities for Chapter 5

1. The next time you are using a commercial wimps package, pay particular attention to the *save/ save as* dialogs. Consider in what ways they are similar to and different from the dialog presented in this chapter.

2. The *save/ save as* dialog is obvious complemented by a combined *new/ open* dialog. Design and implement a combined *new/ open* dialog.

3. Many clients decorate their main application window frame with the name of the currently active filename or '*untitled*' if no name has been established. This responsibility could be made part of the presentation layer's responsibilities or part of the *save/ save as* interface's responsibilities. Produce a design rationale for both of these solutions, evaluate both designs and implement one of them.

4. The presentation of the filenames in this chapter is not appropriate; ideally only the filenames should be shown in the *messageBox* dialogs. Amend the *file_selection_dialog_save_callback* so that it removes the pathname from the filename stored as the temporary filename.

5. A number of other standard dialogs which are supported by Motif are not included in this chapter. The dialogs include *XmPromptDialog*, *XmSelectionDialog* and *XmCommand*. Familiarize yourself with the visual appearance of these dialogs and their functionality, in order that you will be able to consider them for use where they are appropriate.

6. Reimplement the *save/ save as* and *new/ open* interfaces to offer transitions to the help system to the user.

7. The save *pushButton* on the *file_selection_dialog* can be double clicked by experienced users to cause a transition to the *saving* state, avoiding the *file exists?* decision. Amend the state transition diagram given in Figure 5.4 to show this possibility and the implementation of the interface to effect it.

\\\

CHAPTER SIX

The *graphplot* application

Introduction

This chapter will introduce an application work area to accompany the application *main menu* and standard interfaces which were introduced in previous chapters. The usual caveat must be stated: the application presented in this chapter is not a complete or realistic example; any realistic example would be much larger than the length of this book could accommodate. However, the design and construction of this example application employs techniques which are scaleable to larger applications. If the design considerations and techniques used for this application are understood, they can be applied to larger, more realistic, examples. The application introduced in this chapter is called *graphplot*, and is intended to be used for the drawing of simple scatter plot graphs.

Two important widget classes are introduced in some detail in this chapter, the *Text* widget class and the *DrawingArea* widget class. This is the only place in the book where the use of the *Text* widget class is considered in any detail. A complete introduction to the workings of this class is beyond the scope of this book, but a start is made here.

The inclusion of the two standard interfaces, the *save/ save as* and *help* interfaces, which were introduced in the previous chapter, is described at the end of that chapter. In the next chapter two specialized interfaces will be introduced and their inclusion into the *graphplot* application will also be described. These activities illustrate the reusability of interfaces which are designed and implemented using the techniques described in this book.

6.1 *Graphplot* application, usability design

The visual appearance of *graphplot* is illustrated in Figure 6.1. The application work area consists of a graphics area, called *points graph*, where points on a graph are plotted; and a text input area, called *text points,* where values for the graph can be entered. The user can interact with the application by clicking with the mouse on the *points graph* area, or by entering integer co-ordinate values in the *text points* area. Either of these methods will result in a point being added to the graph and the co-ordinates being added to the list in the text area.

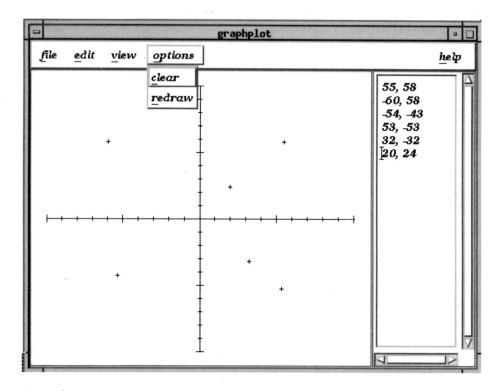

Figure 6.1   *Graphplot* application, visual design.

The allowed x and y co-ordinate values range from -100 to $+100$. If the user enters co-ordinates outside this range, or if the text entered by the user cannot be understood as a co-ordinate pair, the input will be removed from the text area and no point will be plotted. The usable area of the graph is indicated by the axes and does not extend to the limits of the *points graph* area. If the user clicks the mouse outside the limits of the axes no point will be recorded, neither as a point on the graph nor as an entry in the list.

Figure 6.1 also illustrates that the *options* menu offers two possibilities, to *clear* the application work area or to *redraw* the entire graph. The usability design of this application work area is given in Figure 6.2. This usability design differs from the usability designs which have been presented so far because it is a design for the application's main work area, not an interface accessed from the *main menu*. Central to the design is the *application main state*, which is a non-modal state to which the application returns after every interaction. There are two possible transitions from the *application main state*, one caused by a mouse click on the *points graph* component and one by the entry of text into the *text points* component.

The *redraw* and *clear* transitions for the *options* menu are illustrated at the top of the design as simple transitions which pass through the conceptual space of the

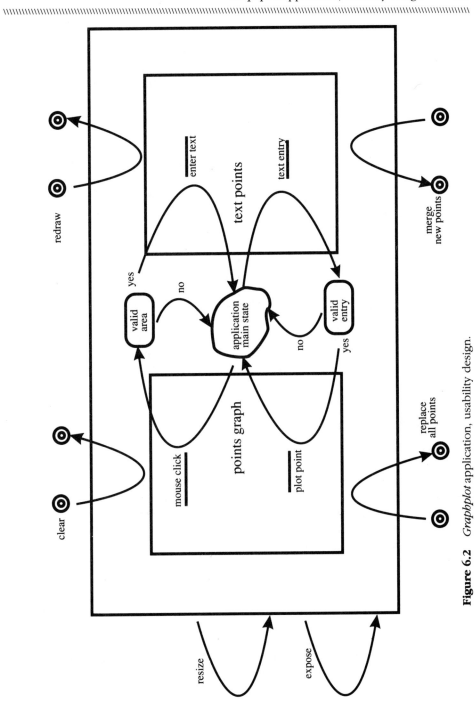

Figure 6.2 *Graphplot* application, usability design.

\\\

application, but have no direct interaction with the *mouse click* and *text entry* transitions. At the bottom of the design are two transitions known as the *replace all points* and *merge new points*. These transitions will have the effect of deleting all existing points and replacing them with a new set, or adding a set of points to the existing points. It is intended that these transitions will be connected to the *file* menu options when the application is constructed.

At the side of the usability design are *resize* and *expose* transitions. It is possible that at any instant the user will resize the application, using the resize handles provided by the window manager. When resized the most appropriate behaviour for this application is to maintain the width of the *text points* area constant but to expand or contract its height. The height of the command bar should remain constant but the width of the bar should expand or contract. The remaining space will be occupied by the *graph points* area, which will clear the existing graph, redraw its axes and replot all points using the new scale.

An expose transition is required for situations where all or part of the application becomes visible after it has been hidden by another window. For the programs which have been presented so far, this consideration has been automatically taken care of by the widgets which comprise the application interface. All widgets used so far have been able to redraw themselves when resized or exposed. Not all widget classes, in particular the class which will be used to implement the *graph points* area, are capable of supporting such behaviour and require the programmer to define appropriate behaviour for resizing and exposure.

6.2 *Graphplot* application, high level design

The application widget hierarchy for the main work area and its relation to the *main menu* is given in Figure 6.3. Details of the widget hierarchy for a *main menu* were given in Figure 4.4 and are omitted from this figure. The work area consists of a *ScrolledText* widget used for the *text points* area, and a *DrawingArea* widget used for the *points graph* area. Each of these widgets is a child of a *Frame* widget, which are themselves children of the *main form.*

The *ScrolledText* widget class was introduced in Chapter 5, where it was used to implement the *help* viewer. The *Frame* widget class was introduced in Chapter 3 where it was used, as it is here, to provide a consistent visual surround to the components of an interface.

The *DrawingArea* widget class provides an area which the application can draw upon and is thus a suitable class for the *points graph*. The major resources of the *DrawingArea* widget class are given in Table 6.1. The widget class hierarchy indicates that the *DrawingArea* class is a subclass of the *Manager* class and thus inherits the ability to manage children. Drawing area widgets are rarely used as manager widgets and are mostly used as a drawing canvas. The major support for drawing is provided by the *inputCallback* resource, which can be used to determine where on the drawing area the user is pointing when they press or release one of the mouse buttons.

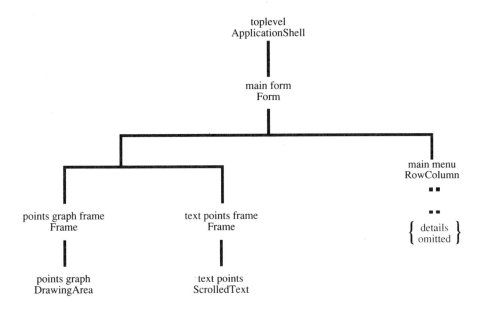

Figure 6.3   *Graphplot* application, application widget hierarchy.

Table 6.1   The major resources of the *DrawingArea* widget class

inheritance hierarchy   Core -> Composite -> Constraint -> Manager ->
BulletinBoard -> DrawingArea

Resource name	type	(default) values
exposeCallback	CallbackList	NULL
actions to be performed when the widget is exposed		
inputCallback	CallbackList	NULL
actions to be performed when the widget receives mouse or keyboard input		
marginHeight	Dimension	10
marginWidth	Dimension	10
the spacing between the edge of the widget and any children		
resizeCallback	CallbackList	NULL
actions to be performed when the widget is resized		
resizePolicy	manifest(unsigned char)	XmRESIZE_NONE
		XmRESIZE_GROW
		XmRESIZE_ANY (default)
determines the response of the widget in response to resize requests from its children		

The design approach used for the application work area is identical to the design approach used for other applications. The visual components of the interface are implemented in a presentation layer module. The behaviour of the interface is implemented in a translations module which uses the facilities of the presentation module. The support module in previous examples has been used to maintain state data for the interface. The state of this design is the state of the application, consequently, the support module for the application workspace interface is the application layer itself. An overview of the components of the high level design is illustrated in Figure 6.4.

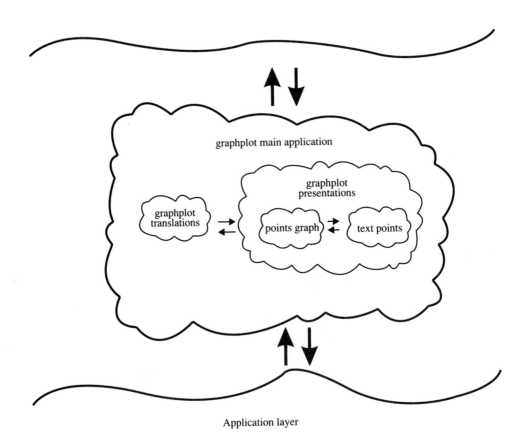

Figure 6.4   *Graphplot* high level design components.

6.3 *Graphplot* main application, presentation module

The presentation module is divided into two components, implementing the *text points* and *points graph* parts of the interface. Each of these components requires a creation and a destruction function, but neither of them require an activation or deactivation function. The components are permanently presented to the user, and are thus created in an active state.

Each component will also provide a set of functions which implement its essential behaviour. The *text points* component provides functions to add a text point, clear all the text points and to get all the text points. The *points graph* component provides functions to plot a new point and to clear the graph. The object diagrams for these components are given in Figures 6.5 and 6.6. The implementation of the public aspects of these diagrams as a C header file, called *graphplot_application_presentation.h* (gplot_ap.h), is given in Listing 6.1.

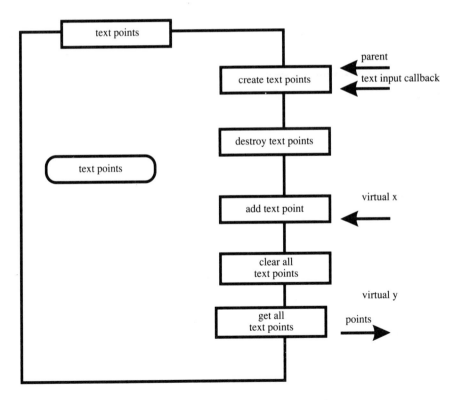

Figure 6.5   The *text points* presentation component, object diagram.

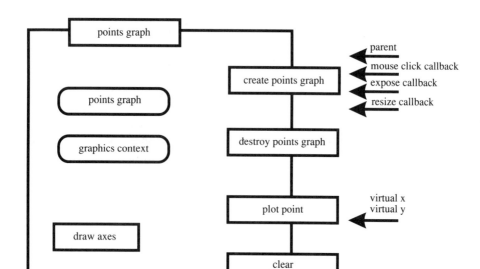

Figure 6.6   The *points graph* presentation component, object diagram.

Listing 6.1   Graphplot application presentation module header file

```
 1   /* filename graphplot application presentation.header.  *
 2    * (gplot_ap.h). File to introduce X/Motif graphics      *
 3    *                                                        *
 4    * Written for Motif book Chapter 6.                      *
 5    *                                                        *
 6    * fintan culwin v1.0 Oct 92  revised Jan 94              *
 7    */
 8
 9   #ifndef GPLOT_AP
10   #define  GPLOT_AP
11
12   #include <Xm/Xm.h>
13   #include <Xm/DrawingA.h>
14   #include <Xm/Text.h>
15   #include <Xm/Frame.h>
16
17   /* text points component */
18   extern Widget create_text_points( Widget parent,
19                           XtCallbackProc text_input_callback );
20   extern void   destroy_text_points( void );
21   extern void   add_text_point( int new_virtual_x, int new_virtual_y );
22   extern void   clear_all_text_points( void );
```

continued

\\\

Listing 6.1 *continued*

```
23   extern char * get_all_text_points( void );
24
25   /* points graph component */
26   extern Widget create_points_graph( Widget parent,
27                              XtCallbackProc mouse_click_callback,
28                              XtCallbackProc expose_callback,
29                              XtCallbackProc resize_callback );
30   extern void destroy_points_graph( void );
31   extern void plot_point( int virtual_x, int virtual_y );
32   extern void clear_points_graph( void );
33
34   #endif /* ifndef GPLOT_AP */
```

6.3.1 The *text points* presentation component

The creation of the *text points* component is straightforward, creating a *Text* widget instance called *text points* within a *ScrolledWindow* instance, using the convenience function *XmCreateScrolledText*. The parent parameter for the *XmCreateScrolledText* function is a *Frame* widget called *text_points_frame*, which is created as a child of the parent parameter supplied. The callback parameter supplied to *create_text_points*, with the formal name *text_input_callback,* is installed as the *text* widget's *modifyVerifyCallback* resource. This callback will be activated whenever the *text point*'s text is changed.

The resource settings of the *text points* widget which should be set by the application are listed in Table 6.2. The attachment resources of the *text_points_frame* are not set within the *create_text_points* function, as this would limit its potential reusability. Instead the identity of the *text_points_frame* is returned from the function and the responsibility for setting the attachment resources transferred to the function which creates the *text points* component.

The only resource which has not been previously explained is the *userData* resource. This resource is inherited from the *Manager* widget class and is provided for programmer use. The *userData* resource is of type *XtPointer* so it can be used to point to a data structure. Alternatively it can be guaranteed that the *Xtpointer* data type is large enough to contain an integer value. The *userData* resource is also introduced by the Motif *Primitive* widget class and thus is available to all its descendent widget classes.

In this application the *userData* resource of the *text points* text widget is used to maintain a count of the number of points that are stored in the list. This is a major design decision; the alternative possibility would have been to maintain the count in the application layer. This decision was consequential upon a more fundamental decision to use the text contained within the text widget as the only place in the application where the list of valid points would be stored. The justification for this decision was to guarantee the integrity of the list of points which might be compromised if two distinct lists, one in the text widget and one

\\

Table 6.2   Resource settings for the text points components

Widget	parent	class
text_points_frame	main_form	Frame

resource		value
bottomAttachment		XmATTACH_FORM
rightAttachment		XmATTACH_FORM
topAttachment		XmATTACH_WIDGET
topWidget		main_menu

Widget	parent	class
text_points	text_points_frame	ScrolledText

resource		value
columns		10
editMode		XmMULTI_LINE_EDIT
scrollBarDisplayPolicy		XmAS_NEEDED
scrollingPolicy		XmAUTOMATIC
userData		0

in the application layer were maintained. With this decision taken, the decision to use the *userData* resource to maintain a count of the points followed. As the list is empty when the widget is created, the value of the *userData* resource must initially be set to zero.

The *clear_all_text_points* and *get_all_text_points* functions thus use both the *value* and *userData* resources of the text widget. The *clear_all_points* function is implemented using a call to the Motif convenience function *XmTextReplace* function with the parameters set to replace the entire text with a null string. The prototype of the *XmTextReplace* function is:

```
void XmTextReplace( Widget          widget,
                    XmTextPosition  fromPos,
                    XmTextPosition  toPos,
                    char            * newString );
```

where *widget* is the text widget whose text is to be replaced, *fromPos* is the place where the replacement is to start, *toPos* is the place where replacement is to finish and *newString* is the replacement text. The *XmTextPosition* data type is used to specify character positions within a *text* widget's text, the unit of measurement being character positions with the first position having the value 0. To replace all the text *fromPos* has to be specified as zero and *toPos* has to specify the extent of the text. The number of characters in a text widget can be determined using the convenience function *XmTextGetLastPosition*, whose prototype is:

```
XmTextPosition XmTextGetLastPosition( Widget widget );
```

The implementation of the function *clear_all_points* can be found in Listing 6.2.

Listing 6.2   The clear_all_text_points function

```
 1  /* Part of the graphplot application presentation module, *
 2   * text points_component.                                  */
 3
 4
 5  extern void clear_all_text_points( void ){
 6
 7  Arg args[ MAX_ARGS ];
 8  int num_args;
 9
10      XmTextReplace( text_points, (XmTextPosition) 0,
11                     XmTextGetLastPosition(text_points),
12                     "" );
13      num_args = 0;
14      XtSetArg( args[num_args], XmNuserData,
15                               0); num_args++;
16      XtSetValues( text_points, args, num_args );
17  } /* end fun clear all text points */
```

The function *get_all_text_points* returns a string containing a series of lines separated by new line characters. The first line contains the count of the number of points in the list, and each succeeding line a co-ordinate pair comprising two integer values in the range −100 to +100, separated by comma. The implementation of the function obtains the value of the *userData* resource using *XtGetValues* and obtains the text from the text widget using *XmTextGetString*. The prototype of *XmTextGetString* is:

```
char * XmTextGetString( Widget widget );
```

The function returns a pointer to a copy of the *value* resource of the text widget supplied as a parameter. The calling environment is responsible for releasing the resources used by the string using the *XtFree* function.

Having obtained the number of items in the list, C standard facilities can be used to convert the integer count to a string and catenate it with the text obtained from the widget, returning the combined string. The implementation of the function *get_all_text_points* is given in Listing 6.3.

The *add_text_point* function is implemented by converting the virtual *x* and *y* co-ordinate values, supplied as parameters, into a formatted string and then calling *XmTextReplace* to append the string to the end of the text contained in the *text points* text widget. This will cause the text widget's *modifyVerifyCallback* resource to be activated, in a similar manner to the activation that would occur if the user had typed the string in at the keyboard. The callback function attached to this resource will cause the point to be plotted on the graph, as will be explained shortly. The implementation of *add_text_point* is given in Listing 6.4.

\\\

Listing 6.3   The get_all_text_points function

```
1   /* Part of the graphplot application presentation module, *
2    * text points_component.                                 */
3
4
5   extern char * get_all_text_points( void ){
6
7   char * all_points, *all_points_plus_count;
8   int    num_points;
9   int    total_length;
10  char   buffer[ MAX_BUFF_SIZE ];
11
12  Arg args[ MAX_ARGS ];
13  int num_args;
14
15      /* get the number of data points from the widget */
16      num_args = 0;
17      XtSetArg( args[num_args], XmNuserData,
18                              &num_points); num_args++;
19      XtGetValues( text_points, args, num_args );
20      sprintf( buffer, "%i \n", num_points );
21
22      /* and the points themselves */
23      all_points = XmTextGetString( text_points );
24
25      /* catenate strings to one structure */
26      total_length = strlen(buffer) +strlen(all_points) +1;
27      all_points_plus_count = (char *)malloc( total_length,
28                                  sizeof( char ));
29      strcpy( all_points_plus_count, buffer );
30      strcat( all_points_plus_count, all_points );
31
32      XtFree( all_points );
33      return( all_points_plus_count );
34  } /* end fun get all text points */
```

Listing 6.4   The add_text_point function

```
1   /* Part of the graphplot application presentation module, *
2    * text points_component.                                 */
3
4
5   extern void add_text_point( int new_virtual_x, int new_virtual_y ){
6
7   char buffer[ MAX_BUFF_SIZE ];
8   XmTextPosition last_place;
9
10      /* format the integer co-ordinates as strings *
11       * separated by commas                        */
12      sprintf( buffer, "%d, %d \n", new_virtual_x, new_virtual_y );
13
14      /* and append to the existing list of points, which will *
```

continued

\\\

Listing 6.4 *continued*

```
15          * indirectly cause a (valid)  point to be plotted        */
16       last_place = XmTextGetLastPosition( text_points );
17       XmTextReplace( text_points, last_place, last_place, buffer );
18    }/* end fun add point */
```

6.3.2 The *points graph* presentation component

The creation of the *points graph* component is again straightforward creating an instance of the *DrawingArea* widget class, called *points graph*, using the Motif convenience function *XmCreateDrawingArea*. The *XmCreateDrawingArea* function has a prototype which is essentially identical to the other *XmCreate(whatever)* functions already introduced. The *drawingArea* widget is created as a child of a *frame* widget called *points_graph_frame*, which itself is a child of the parent widget supplied to the function.

The only resources which require setting from the application code are the attachment resources of the *points_graph_frame* widget. These resources are given in Table 6.3 and as with the attachment resources of the *text_points_frame* they are not set by the *points graph* creation function. Instead the creation function returns the identity of the *points_graph_frame* widget and requires the calling environment to set the attachment resources.

Three callbacks are installed into the *drawingArea* widget as it is created. The callback function supplied as a parameter to the creation function, with the formal name *mouse_click_callback*, is installed as the *drawingArea*'s *inputCallback* resource. This callback will be activated whenever an input event, either from the mouse or from the keyboard, occurs within the widget. The *expose_callback* function parameter is installed as the *drawingArea*'s *exposeCallback*; this function will be called whenever the widget is exposed. Likewise the *resize_callback* function parameter is installed as the *drawingArea*'s *resizeCallback*; this function will be called whenever the widget is resized.

The *points graph* component also maintains a static *graphics context* variable. Graphics contexts will be explained in detail in the following chapter. For the time

Table 6.3   Resource settings for the points graph components

Widget	parent	class
points_graph_frame	main_form	Frame

resource	value
bottomAttachment	XmATTACH_FORM
leftAttachment	XmATTACH_FORM
rightAttachment	XmATTACH_WIDGET
rightWidget	text_points_frame
topAttachment	XmATTACH_WIDGET
topWidget	main_menu

\\

being graphics contexts will be introduced as a required parameter of all *X library* drawing function calls. A simple graphics context, supporting black and white drawing, can be created using the code contained within the *create_points_graph* function in Listing 6.5.

Listing 6.5   The create_points_graph function

```
1   /* Part of the graphplot application presentation module,*
2    * points_graph component.                              */
3
4   /* static objects required for the plot graph module */
5   static Widget points_graph;
6   static GC gc;
7
8   /* prototype for private function */
9   static void draw_axes( void );
10
11  extern Widget create_points_graph( Widget   parent,
12                            XtCallbackProc mouse_click_callback,
13                            XtCallbackProc expose_callback,
14                            XtCallbackProc resize_callback ){
15
16  Widget points_graph_frame;
17
18  Arg args[ MAX_ARGS ];
19  int num_args;
20
21     num_args = 0;
22     points_graph_frame = XmCreateFrame( parent, "points graph frame",
23                                   args,    num_args );
24     XtManageChild( points_graph_frame );
25
26     num_args =0;
27     points_graph = XmCreateDrawingArea( points_graph_frame,
28                                   "points graph",
29                                   args, num_args );
30     XtManageChild( points_graph );
31
32     XtAddCallback( points_graph, XmNexposeCallback,
33                   expose_callback,
34                   (XtPointer) NULL );
35     XtAddCallback( points_graph, XmNresizeCallback,
36                   resize_callback,
37                   (XtPointer) NULL );
38     XtAddCallback( points_graph, XmNinputCallback,
39                   mouse_click_callback,
40                   (XtPointer) NULL );
41
42     /* creation of a graphics context for black & white drawing *
43      * temporary kludge only - see later revision.              */
44     gc = XCreateGC( XtDisplay( parent),
45                       RootWindowOfScreen( XtScreen( parent)),
46                       0, NULL );
```

continued

Listing 6.5 *continued*

```
47      XSetForeground( XtDisplay( parent), gc,
48                      BlackPixelOfScreen( XtScreen( parent)));
49      XSetBackground( XtDisplay( parent), gc,
50                      WhitePixelOfScreen( XtScreen( parent)));
51
52      return points_graph_frame;
53  } /* end fun create_points_graph */
```

The *draw_axes* private function will illustrate the use of the graphics context. As was explained in the usability design section above, the axes indicate the usable area of the *drawingArea*'s window and do not extend to the limits of the window. The detailed visual design of the *points graph* decided that the axes would extend to within 5% of the width or height of the window's dimensions, rather than to within a constant number of pixels. This decision was taken to ensure a consistent visual appearance as the window is resized.

To accomplish this the first action of the *draw_axes* function is to determine the dimensions of the window, using the *XtGetvalues* function to retrieve the current values of the *width* and *height* resources. These values are of type *Dimension*, but inconveniently the *X library* graphics functions require values of type *int*. The *x* and *y* midpoints of the window and the horizontal axis offset, all of type *int*, are obtained from the width and height using C's type conversion facility. The horizontal axis is then drawn using the library function *XDrawLine*, whose prototype is:

```
void XDrawLine( Display * display,
                Window    window,
                GC        gc,
                int       startX, startY,
                int       endX,   endY );
```

The first two parameters identify the display and window upon which the line is to be drawn and can be obtained using the *XtDisplay* and *XtWindow* functions respectively. The third parameter identifies the graphics context to be used, and the final four parameters identify the starting and ending points of the line. The *x* and *y* co-ordinates are specified relative to the top left-hand corner of the window which has the co-ordinate value (0, 0), with *x* values increasing to the right and *y* values increasing downwards. The prototypes of the *XtDisplay* and *XtWindow* functions are:

```
Display * XtDisplay( Widget widget );
Window    XtWindow( Widget widget );
```

The use of these functions can be determined from their use in the function *draw_axes*, which is given in Listing 6.6.

\\

Listing 6.6   The draw_axes function

```
 1  /* Part of the graphplot application presentation module, *
 2   * points_graph component.                                */
 3
 4  static void draw_axes( void ){
 5
 6  Arg args[ MAX_ARGS ];
 7  int num_args;
 8
 9  Dimension width, height;
10  int        mid_x, mid_y,
11             horizontal_offset, vertical_offset, tick_index;
12  float      tick_interval;
13
14     num_args = 0;
15     XtSetArg( args[num_args], XmNwidth,
16                              &width ); num_args++;
17     XtSetArg( args[num_args], XmNheight,
18                              &height ); num_args++;
19     XtGetValues( points_graph, args, num_args );
20
21     mid_x   =  ((int) width)  / 2;
22     mid_y   =  ((int) height) / 2;
23
24     /* draw the horizontal axis */
25     horizontal_offset  =  ((int) width) / 20;
26     XDrawLine( XtDisplay( points_graph ), XtWindow( points_graph),
27               gc, horizontal_offset, mid_y,
28               ((int)width) - horizontal_offset, mid_y );
29
30     /* add the tick marks */
31     tick_interval = (((float) width)-(horizontal_offset * 2.0))/ 20.0;
32     for ( tick_index = 1; tick_index <= 10; tick_index++ ){
33     int offset = 2;
34        if ( (tick_index % 5) == 0 ){
35            offset *= 2;
36        } /* end if */
37        XDrawLine( XtDisplay( points_graph ), XtWindow( points_graph),
38            gc,
39            (mid_x - ((int)((float)tick_index)* tick_interval)),
40            mid_y-offset,
41            (mid_x - ((int)((float)tick_index) * tick_interval)),
42            mid_y+offset );
43        XDrawLine( XtDisplay( points_graph ), XtWindow( points_graph),
44            gc,
45            (mid_x + ((int)((float)tick_index) * tick_interval)),
46            mid_y-offset,
47            (mid_x + ((int)((float)tick_index) * tick_interval)),
48            mid_y+offset );
49     } /* end for */
50
51     /* draw the vertical axis omitted as it essentially *
52     /* repeats drawing the horizontal axis.             */
53  } /* end fun draw axes   */
```

Having drawn the horizontal axis the tick marks can be added. The tick interval has already been calculated and stored in a float variable, with a value equal to one twentieth of the length of the axis. The tick interval is stored as a float value to avoid integer approximation introducing errors when the position of the tick marks is calculated.

Ten tick marks are placed on each side of the axis with the fifth and tenth being twice the size of the others. The drawing of the tick marks is implemented as a loop which draws two tick marks, one on each side of the axis, on each iteration. The tick marks themselves are drawn using the *XDrawLine* function introduced above, with some rather complicated type conversion used to maintain accuracy.

The drawing of the vertical axis is substantively similar to the drawing of the horizontal axis, and has been omitted from the listing of the function *draw_axes* presented in Listing 6.6. The *draw_axes* private function is only called from the public *clear_points_graph* function. It has been extracted into a separate function in order to simplify the *clear_points_graph* implementation, which is given in Listing 6.7.

Listing 6.7   The clear_points_graph function

```
1  /* Part of the graphplot application presentation module, *
2   * points_graph component.                               */
3
4  extern void clear_points_graph( void ){
5
6  Dimension width, height;
7
8  Arg args[ MAX_ARGS ];
9  int num_args;
10
11     if (XtIsRealized(points_graph)){
12         num_args = 0;
13         XtSetArg( args[num_args], XmNwidth,
14                                   &width ); num_args++;
15         XtSetArg( args[num_args], XmNheight,
16                                   &height ); num_args++;
17         XtGetValues( points_graph, args, num_args );
18
19         /* clear the window by filling with the background color  *
20          * (white), remembering to restore the graphics context  *
21          * to its initial state.                                 */
22         XSetForeground( XtDisplay( points_graph), gc,
23                         WhitePixelOfScreen( XtScreen( points_graph)));
24         XFillRectangle( XtDisplay( points_graph),
25                         XtWindow( points_graph),
26                         gc, 0, 0,
27                         (unsigned int) width,
28                         (unsigned int) height);
29         XSetForeground( XtDisplay( points_graph), gc,
30                         BlackPixelOfScreen( XtScreen( points_graph)));
31
32         draw_axes();
33     } /* end if */
34  } /* end fun clear points graph */
```

\\

This function determines the dimensions of the window in an identical manner to *draw_axes* above. Having determined the size of the window the window is cleared by being filled with the background color. To accomplish this the foreground color of the graphics context is set to white, the window is cleared using the *X library XFillRectangle* function and the foreground color of the graphics context reset to black. The prototype of *XFillRectangle* is:

```
void XFillRectangle( Display * display,
                     Window    window,
                     GC        gc,
                     int    topLeftX,      topLeftY,
            unsigned int  rectangleWidth, rectangleHeight);
```

The effect of the function is to fill the specified rectangle with the foreground color specified in the graphics context. The entire action routine of the *clear_points_graph* function is protected by a test to ensure that the widget has been realized. It is possible for the *clear_points_graph* function to be called as part of a callback function, the event which triggered the callback occurring before the window has been created. The test for realization prevents this function from attempting to draw onto a non-existing window.

The final public function provided by the *points graph* component of the application presentation module is *plot_point*. This function will accept a *virtual* x, y co-ordinate pair and plot a cross on the graph at the corresponding *actual* x, y co-ordinates. This is a common strategy for graphics programming when resizable windows are being used. The application's view of the drawing area is as a virtual space, in this case a space with co-ordinates extending from (−100,−100) to (+100,+100). All storage and manipulation of information is performed using this virtual view. Only at the last stage, as the information is imaged, are the *virtual* co-ordinates transformed to *actual* co-ordinates.

The virtual y axis is oriented with co-ordinate values increasing up the image. The y axis of an *Xwindow* has increasing values defining points down the image. Thus the first action of any transformation is to invert the y co-ordinate by multiplying it by −1.

The implementation of the *plot_point* function thus determines the size of the window and from this the actual dimensions of the usable area allowing for the unused border. The conversion factors are then calculated as the ratios of the usable dimensions to the virtual dimensions. The virtual co-ordinates can then be transformed into actual co-ordinates before the cross is drawn on the screen using *XDrawLine*. The implementation of *plot_point* is given in Listing 6.8.

Listing 6.8   The plot_point function

```
1   /* Part of the graphplot application presentation module,*
2    * points_graph component.                               */
3
4   extern void plot_point( int virtual_x, int virtual_y ){
5
6   Dimension width, height;
7   int       x_offset, y_offset,
8             usable_width, usable_height,
9             actual_x, actual_y;
10
11  float     x_factor, y_factor;
12
13  Arg args[ MAX_ARGS ];
14  int num_args;
15
16      virtual_y *= -1;
17      num_args = 0;
18      XtSetArg( args[num_args], XmNwidth,
19                              &width ); num_args++;
20      XtSetArg( args[num_args], XmNheight,
21                              &height ); num_args++;
22      XtGetValues( points_graph, args, num_args );
23
24      x_offset      = ((int) width)  / 20;
25      y_offset      = ((int) height) / 20;
26      usable_width  = ((int) width)  - x_offset *2;
27      usable_height = ((int) height) - y_offset *2;
28      x_factor      = ((float) usable_width) / 200.0;
29      y_factor      = ((float) usable_height) / 200.0;
30
31      actual_x = (x_offset + (int) ( (float) (virtual_x ) * x_factor))
32                   + ((int)width)/2 - x_offset;
33      actual_y = (y_offset + (int) ( (float) (virtual_y ) * y_factor))
34                   + ((int)height)/2- y_offset;
35
36      XDrawLine( XtDisplay( points_graph),
37                 XtWindow( points_graph), gc,
38                 actual_x - 2, actual_y,
39                 actual_x + 2, actual_y );
40      XDrawLine( XtDisplay( points_graph ),
41                 XtWindow( points_graph), gc,
42                 actual_x, actual_y -2,
43                 actual_x, actual_y +2);
44  } /* end fun plot point */
```

6.4 *Graphplot* main application, translation module

Having constructed the presentation module which provides the visual
components of the application workspace and the behaviours which are
appropriate for those components, the translation module which implements the
behaviour of the application workspace as defined by the usability design can be

constructed. The usability design indicates that eight behaviours are defined, four of which are to be exported from the module. The four exported behaviours are to clear the graph, to redraw the graph, to replace all points in the graph and to merge new points into the graph. The first two of these behaviours are to be implemented as callback functions as they are intended to be attached directly to user controls. The remaining two are implemented as normal functions as they are intended to be called from the application data layer. In addition to these four public behaviours, a creation and a destruction function will also have to be made public. The object diagram for the translation module is given in Figure 6.7 and the C header file for the public aspects is given in Listing 6.9.

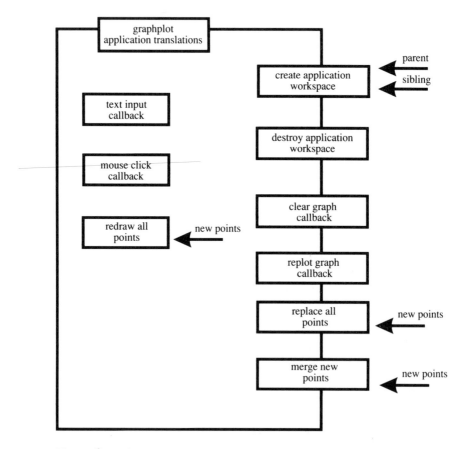

Figure 6.7   The translation module object diagram.

\\

Listing 6.9   Graphplot application translation module header file

```
1   /* Filename graphplot_application_transitions.h (gplot_at.h). *
2    * File to illustrate X/Motif graphics introduction.          *
3    * Written for Motif book Chapter 6.                          *
4    *                                                            *
5    * fintan culwin v1.0 Oct 92                                  *
6   */
7
8   #ifndef GPLOT_AT
9   #define  GPLOT_AT
10
11  #include <Xm/Xm.h>
12
13
14  extern void create_application_workspace( Widget parent,
15                                             Widget sibling);
16
17  extern void destroy_application_workspace( void );
18
19  extern void clear_graph_callback( Widget    widget,
20                                    XtPointer client_data,
21                                    XtPointer call_data);
22
23  extern void replot_graph_callback( Widget    widget,
24                                     XtPointer client_data,
25                                     XtPointer call_data);
26
27  extern void replace_all_points( char * new_points );
28
29  extern void merge_new_points( char * new_points );
30
31  #endif /* ifndef GPLOT_AT */
```

The remaining behaviours from the design, to respond to a text entry in the *text point* component, to respond to a mouse click in the *points graph* component, and behaviours to respond to *expose* and *resize* events, are implemented as private functions of the translation module. As mentioned above this implementation only needs to supply resize and expose behaviours to the *points graph* component. The repositioning of the components as the application is resized is taken care of with the attachment resource settings which have been given in Tables 6.2 and 6.3. The redrawing of all components, apart from the *points graph*, when exposed or resized is implemented by the widgets themselves. When exposed or resized the *points graph* will use the same programmer defined behaviour; it will clear the existing graph and replot all the points which are contained within the *text points* list.

The declaration of these private functions at the start of the translations implementation file is given in Listing 6.10. This listing indicates that an additional private function called *redraw_all_points* is declared. The discussion of the various behaviours above has identified three functions: *replace_all_points, replot_graph_callback* and *expose_and_resize_callback*, all of which have a requirement to redraw all the points. The design has factored out this common requirement into a single function.

The creation function, *create_application_workspace* is intended to be passed the identity of the *main_form* widget in its *parent* parameter and the identity of the *main_menu* widget in its *sibling* parameter, when it is called from the *main()* program function. It is implemented as calls to the two creation functions supplied by the presentation module, following which the attachment resources of the *frame* widgets returned by those functions are set. The destruction function is simply implemented as a call to the destruction functions supplied by the presentation module. These functions are omitted from the program listings presented in this chapter, but can be found in Appendix C.

Listing 6.10   Graphplot translations, private declarations

```
 1   /* filename graphplot_application_transitions.c (gplot_at.c). *
 2    * file to illustrate X/Motif graphics introduction.          *
 3    * Written for Motif book Chapter 6.                           *
 4    *                                                             *
 5    * fintan culwin v1.0 Oct 92                                   *
 6    */           .
 7
 8   #include "gplot_at.h"
 9   #include "gplot_ap.h"
10
11   #define MAX_ARGS    10
12
13   /* private prototypes */
14
15   static void mouse_click_callback( Widget     widget,
16                                     XtPointer client_data,
17                                     XtPointer call_data);
18
19   static void text_input_callback( Widget     widget,
20                                     XtPointer client_data,
21                                     XtPointer call_data);
22
23   static void redraw_all_points( char * all_points );
```

6.4.1 Translation module, *text_input_callback* function

The major function of the translation module is the *text_input_callback* function. As shall be explained below, the *mouse_input_callback* function does not draw directly on the graph but causes the *text_input_callback* function callback to be activated and as a consequence causes the cross to be plotted. The *text_input_callback* function is attached to the *text* widget's *modifyVerifyCallback* resource as the *text* widget is created. The *modifyVerifyCallback* functions will be called every time the text within the widget is changed, by either the addition or deletion of text. The callback function can allow or deny the proposed change by manipulating the *call_data* structure which is passed to the function by the intrinsics.

The structure pointed to by the *call_data* parameter when the *text* widget's *modifyVerifyCallback* callback function is called, is a structure of type *XmTextVerifyCallbackStruct* which has the following declaration:

```
typedef struct {
        int                 reason;
        Xevent          *   event;
        Boolean             doit;
        XmTextPosition      currentInsert;
        XmTextPosition      newInsert;
        XmTextPosition      startPos;
        XmTextPosition      endPos;
        XmTextBlock         text;
} XmTextVerifyCallbackStruct, *XmTextVerifyPtr;
```

The first two fields are common to all *call_data* structures; the *reason* passed for this callback is XmCR_MODIFYING_TEXT_VALUE. The *event* structure does not contain any useful information for this application. The *doit* field is passed into the callback function with the value *True* indicating that the proposed action should be carried out. The callback function can change the value of *doit* to *False* to prevent the action being carried out. The *currentInsert* and *newInsert* fields are not relevant for a *modifyVerifyCallback* callback. The *startPos* and *endPos* delineate the text to be deleted or replaced. When text is to be inserted these two fields will have the same value. The final field is itself a structure which has the declaration:

```
typedef struct {
        char            *   ptr;
        int                 length;
        XmTextFormat        format;
} XmTextBlockRec,* XmTextBlock;
```

The *ptr* field is the text to be inserted and the *length* field is the number of characters it contains. If text is to be deleted the length of the text to be inserted is 0. The final field, *format*, identifies eight bit or sixteen bit text format. For simple applications, such as this one, it can be assumed to be eight bit text format.

The *text_input_callback* in this application may be called when text is deleted from the *points list* and as shall be explained all such requests should be allowed. It may also be called each time the user enters a single character, or it may be called when a co-ordinate pair is posted into the text by the application.

The implementation is consequently structured into three parts to deal with deletions, single character insertions and single line insertions. It is possible that the user may cause multiple line insertions to be posted by *pasting* or *dragging* text; this implementation assumes that this will never happen. The implementation of the *text_input_callback* function is given in Listing 6.11. The first part of the

\\

function is an early return when a deletion is requested, allowing the deletion to take place.

Listing 6.11   The text_input_callback function

```
1   /* Part of the graphplot application translation module. */
2
3   static void text_input_callback( Widget     widget,
4                                    XtPointer client_data,
5                                    XtPointer call_data){
6
7   XmTextVerifyCallbackStruct * text_data;
8
9   char    * the_string,
10  char    new_line[ MAX_BUFFER_SIZE ];
11  int     string_lenf;
12  char    *start_of_line, *end_of_line;
13  int     text_x, text_y;
14  int     good_pair;
15  int     num_points;
16
17  Arg args[ MAX_ARGS ];
18  int num_args;
19
20     /* recast the call data into its actual type */
21     text_data = ( XmTextVerifyCallbackStruct *) call_data;
22
23     /* return early if this is a deletion */
24     if ( text_data->text->length == 0 ){
25        return;
26     } /* end if */
27
28     /* deal with single and multiple character insertions separately */
29     if (text_data->text->length == 1){
30
31        /* only deal with C/R characters */
32        if( *(text_data->text->ptr) == '\n') {
33           the_string = XmTextGetString( widget );
34           /* locate the line within the text */
35           end_of_line = start_of_line = the_string + startPos;
36           while( ( *start_of_line  != '\n'      ) &&
37                  (  start_of_line  != the_string) ){
38                 start_of_line--;
39           } /* end while */
40           if ( *start_of_line == '\n'){
41              start_of_line++;
42           } /* end if */
43           /* determine if it contains a valid co-ordinate pair */
44           if ( (sscanf( start_of_line,
45                 " %i , %i " &text_x,&text_y) == 2)      &&
46                 ((text_x >= -100) && (text_x <= 100))   &&
47                 ((text_y >= -100) && (text_y <= 100))  ){
48              sprintf( new_line, "%i , %i \n", text_x, text_y);
49           }else {
50              XBell(XtDisplay(widget), 100);
```

continued

Listing 6.11 *continued*

```
51                        strcpy( new_line, "");
52                    } /* end if */
53
54                    /* replace the line entered by the user with an *
55                     * integer pair only, or a dummy string        */
56                    XmTextReplace( widget,
57                                    XmTextPosition( start_of_line - the_string),
58                                    XmTextPosition( end_of_line - the_string), ,
59                                    new_line);
60                    /* cancel the insertion of the C/R & tidy up */
61                    text_data->doit = False;
62                    XtFree( the_string );
63                } /* end if C/R only */
64
65      }else { /* multiple character insertions  */
66
67          /* decide if string format and values are acceptable */
68          good_pair = ( (sscanf( text_data->text->ptr,
69                          , " %i , %i ", &text_x, &text_y) == 2)  &&
70                          (( text_x >= -100) && (text_x <= 100 )) &&
71                          (( text_y >= -100) && (text_y <= 100 )) );
72
73          if( good_pair ){
74              /* ensure insertion point is visible */
75              XmTextSetInsertionPosition( widget,text_data->endPos);
76              plot_point( text_x, text_y);
77              /* count the point */
78              num_args = 0;
79              XtSetArg( args[num_args], XmNuserData,
80                                  &num_points ); num_args++;
81              XtGetValues( widget, args, num_args );
82              num_points++;
83              num_args = 0;
84              XtSetArg( args[num_args], XmNuserData,
85                                  num_points ); num_args++;
86              XtSetValues( widget, args, num_args );
87          } else {
88              /* bleep for feedback */
89              XBell(XtDisplay(widget), 100);
90              /* deny the insertion */
91              text_data->doit = False;
92          }/* end if good string */
93
94      } /* end if one or multiple characters */
95  }/* end fun text input callback */
```

Single character input is also allowed unless the character is a carriage return which indicates that the user has completed a line of text which may contain a co-ordinate pair. When a carriage return is detected a copy of the text contained within the *text* widget is obtained using the utility function *XmTextGetString* and the line which the user entered is located within the text. Once the line is located it is tested for the presence of two integers, with appropriate values, separated by a comma. If a valid co-ordinate pair is found it is reformatted into a text buffer, otherwise the buffer is set to a null string. This buffer is then used to replace the line which the user has just entered, using the *XmTextReplace* function. This will cause the *text_input_callback* function to be called recursively, with either a multiple character replacement request or a zero length replacement string. The final action of the single character part of the function is to deny the insertion of the carriage return character into the text widget and to release the resources occupied by the copy of the text.

The effect of the single character entry part of the function is thus to await a carriage return and to pass valid co-ordinate pairs onwards to the multiple character entry part of the function or to delete invalid entries.

The multiple character entry part of the function validates the new entry. If a valid virtual co-ordinate pair is detected, the co-ordinates are passed onto the *points graph plot_point* function which will produce the cross on the graph. The value of the *userData* resource, which as explained above maintains a count of the number of points, is then incremented. As co-ordinate pairs may be inserted into the *text* widget by the program, without the user using the keyboard, the text widget's insertion cursor is moved to ensure that inserted text is always visible to the user. This is accomplished with the utility function *XmTextSetInsertionPosition*.

Should the multiple character text inserted into the widget not represent a valid virtual co-ordinate pair, the user is informed by a bleeping from the terminal and the entry of the new text is denied.

6.4.2 Translation module, *mouse_click_callback* function

The other major function of the translation module is the *mouse_click_callback* function. This function is attached to the *drawingArea*'s widget's *inputCallback* resource as the *points graph* widget is created. The *inputCallback* functions will be called every time a mouse button is pressed down or released and every time a key on the keyboard is pressed down or released.

The *mouse_click_callback* is only concerned with mouse button releases. The *Xevent* data structure which is passed as part of all *call_data* parameters can be used to determine precisely what type of event caused the callback function to be called. The *Xevent* data type is declared as a C union, with a variety of variant parts depending upon precisely which type of event it is reporting. The simplest variant is *xany* containing a field called *type* which indicates the type of event. Button releases are indicated by the manifest value *ButtonRelease*. Once a *ButtonRelease* event has been confirmed the *xbutton* variant of the event union can be used. This variant contains x and y fields indicating the position of the mouse pointer in window co-ordinates when the mouse button was released.

Having obtained the *actual* co-ordinates of the button release they are transformed into *virtual* co-ordinates, using a process similar to the transformation of virtual co-ordinates to actual co-ordinates explained in the *plot points* function of the *points graph* component above. The *mouse_click_callback* does not plot the cross on the graph itself nor does it call the *plot_point* function directly. Instead it calls the public *add_text_point* function of the *text points* component, passing the virtual co-ordinates as parameters. This function formats the integer virtual co-ordinates into a text line which is appended to the list of points in the *text* widget. This will cause the *text* widget's *modifyVerifyCallback* function to be called passing the text line to it in the *call_data* parameter. This has the effect of updating the points list, incrementing the count of the number of points, and plotting the cross on the graph. The *mouse_click_callback* function is given in Listing 6.12.

Listing 6.12   The mouse_click_callback function

```
1   /* Part of the graphplot application translation module. */
2
3   static void mouse_click_callback( Widget      widget,
4                                     XtPointer client_data,
5                                     XtPointer call_data){
6
7   XmDrawingAreaCallbackStruct * call_details;
8   XEvent *event;
9
10  int         mouse_x, mouse_y, x_offset, y_offset,
11              usable_width, usable_height;
12  Dimension   width, height;
13  int         virtual_x, virtual_y;
14  float       x_factor, y_factor;
15
16  Arg args[ MAX_ARGS ];
17  int num_args;
18
19     /* recast the call_data and extract the event */
20     call_details = (XmDrawingAreaCallbackStruct *) call_data;
21     event = call_details->event;
22
23     /* only bother with button releases */
24     if ( event->xany.type == ButtonRelease){
25        /* get actual co-ordinates of the mouse */
26        mouse_x = event->xbutton.x;
27        mouse_y = event->xbutton.y;
28
29        /* convert to virtual co-ordinates */
30        num_args = 0;
31        XtSetArg( args[num_args], XmNwidth,
32                                  &width ); num_args++;
33        XtSetArg( args[num_args], XmNheight,
34                                  &height ); num_args++;
35        XtGetValues( widget, args, num_args );
36
37        x_offset      = ((int) width)  / 20;
38        y_offset      = ((int) height) / 20;
```

continued

\\\

Listing 6.12 *continued*

```
39        usable_width  = ((int) width)    - x_offset *2;
40        usable_height = ((Position) height) - y_offset *2;
41        x_factor      = 200 / ((float) usable_width)  ;
42        y_factor      = 200 / ((float) usable_height) ;
43
44        virtual_x =  (int)((((float)( mouse_x -((int) width)/2))) *
45                         x_factor);
46        virtual_y =  (int)((((float)( mouse_y -((int) height)/2))) *
47                         y_factor);
48        virtual_y *= -1;
49
50     /* add the virtual point to the text list */
51        add_point( virtual_x,  virtual_y);
52     } /* end if */
53  } /* end fun mouse_click_callback */
```

Should the user click the mouse outside the limits of the axes, the virtual co-ordinates generated will be outside the allowed range of (–100, –100) to (+100, +100). This will be detected by the *text_input_callback* function as it validates the string. No point will be plotted nor will an invalid point be added to the text widget; instead the terminal will bleep giving the user an indication that the point has not been plotted.

This apparently convoluted method of producing the cross on the graph was used in order to assure the integrity of the list of points in the text widget and its relationship to the points which are displayed on the graph. The multiple character entry part of the *text_input_callback* function is the only place in the application where calls to *plot_point* are made, and then only when a validated co-ordinate string has been inserted into the text widget and the count of the number of points incremented.

6.4.3 Translation module, other functions

The implementation of *replot_graph_callback* is much more straightforward. It operates by obtaining a copy of the points list from the *text points* component using its public *get_all_points* function. It can then clear the *text points* and *points graph* components using the public functions *clear_all_text_points* and *clear_points_graph* respectively. The points list is then passed onwards to the private function *redraw_all_points* which will cause all the points to be redrawn. Before the function can safely terminate the resources utilized by the copy of the points list have to be released using the C standard *free* function.

The *redraw_all_points* function obtains the number of points from the first line of the points list which is passed to it. It then iterates through the list extracting the virtual co-ordinates and passing them to the *add_text_point* function which, as explained above, will add them to the text list and plot them on the graph. The

\\\

implementation of the functions *replot_graph_callback* and *redraw_all_points* is given in Listing 6.13.

The remaining functions, *replace_all_points* and *merge_new_points*, are simple to implement. The *replace_all_points* function is virtually identical to the *replot_graph_callback* described above. The *merge_new_points* function is very similar, using *redraw_all_points* without first clearing the existing points list. The implementation of these functions can be found in Appendix C.

All that remains are the actual function parameters to be passed to the *create_points_graph* function, to be installed as the *exposeCallback* and *resizeCallback* resources. As described above the actions of both these callback functions is identical to redraw the graph completely. A callback function which accomplishes exactly this has already been constructed, *replot_graph_callback*. Consequently it is this function which is used as the actual parameter for both of the formal function parameters.

Listing 6.13   The replot_graph_callback and redraw_all_points functions

```
 1   /* Part of the graphplot application translation module,*/
 2
 3   extern void replot_graph_callback( Widget     widget,
 4                                      XtPointer client_data,
 5                                      XtPointer call_data ){
 6
 7   char * all_points;
 8
 9       all_points = get_all_points( );
10       clear_points_graph( );
11       clear_all_text_points( );
12       redraw_all_points( all_points );
13       free( all_points );
14   } /* end fun replot graph callback */
15
16
17   static void redraw_all_points( char * all_points ){
18
19   int    num_points, this_point;
20   int    virtual_x, virtual_y;
21   char * this_line;
22   int    all_ok;
23
24       this_line = all_points;
25       all_ok = True;
26       /* extract the number of points in the list */
27       all_ok = (sscanf( this_line, " %i ", &num_points)) == 1;
28       /* traverse the list processing all points */
29       while ( (all_ok) && (num_points-- > 0)){
30          /* find the start of the next line */
31          while( *this_line != '\n' ){
32             this_line ++;
33          } /* end while */
```

continued

\\

Listing 6.13 *continued*

```
34          this_line ++;
35          /* extract the co-ordinate pair */
36          all_ok = (sscanf( this_line, " %i , %i ",
37                          &virtual_x, &virtual_y)) == 2;
38          if ( all_ok) {
39              /* add the point to the list */
40              add_text_point( virtual_x, virtual_y );
41          } /* end if */
42      } /* end while */
43  } /* redraw all points */
```

6.5 An alternative expose and resize strategy

The expose and resize strategy used in this chapter, redrawing the entire image whenever an *expose* or *resize* event occurs, is not the only strategy which could be used. The strategy used here is probably the most appropriate one for this application, as the amount of effort required to redraw the entire image is not excessive. For situations where the effort involved in redrawing the entire image is considerable an alternative strategy should be used.

One possible strategy, suitable only for exposures, is to request that the *server* maintain a *save-under* copy of the entire screen. The server can respond to all exposures by copying from the *save-under* copy to the screen window. However it is not guaranteed that all *servers* will always be able to honour this request and as it does not provide any support for resizing it cannot be used for most applications.

A more suitable alternative solution is for the application to maintain a copy of the contents of the *drawingArea*'s window and to copy from this *off-screen* copy to the screen window when an exposure occurs. This strategy can also cope with resizing by changing the size of the *off-screen* copy in response to the resizing of the *on-screen* window.

When using this solution the application must maintain a copy of everything which is drawn to the screen window on a *pixmap*, whose dimensions are identical to those of the screen window. *Pixmaps* were introduced in Chapter 3, where an image produced by the *bitmap* standard application was loaded into a *pixmap* and subsequently used as the *labelPixmap* resource of a *label* widget.

In order to use an *off-screen pixmap* in the *graphplot* application a *static* variable of type *pixmap* would have to be maintained in parallel with the *static* widget *graph_plot* variable. The declaration of this variable should initialize its value to NULL to indicate that it does not yet contain a valid *pixmap*.

```
/* amended static variable declarations from the graphplot *
 * presentation module, graph_plot component.             */
static Widget  graph_plot;
static Pixmap  graph_plot_pixmap = (Pixmap) NULL;
```

\\

Listing 6.14   The graph_plot_resize_callback function

```
1  /* Implemented as a private callback function of the presentation  *
2   * module graph points component.                                  *
3   */
4  static void graph_plot_resize_callback( Widget    widget,
5                                          XtPointer client_data,
6                                          XtPointer call_data){
7
8  Dimension width, height;
9  int       depth;
10
11 Arg args[ MAX_ARGS ];
12 int num_args;
13
14    if ( XtIsRealized( widget)){
15       /* destroy any existing pixmap */
16       if ( points_graph_pixmap != (Pixmap) NULL ){
17          XFreePixmap( XtDisplay( widget), points_graph_pixmap );
18          points_graph_pixmap = (Pixmap) NULL;
19       } /* end if */
20
21       /* get size (and depth) of the resized new window */
22       num_args = 0;
23       XtSetArg( args[num_args], XmNwidth,
24                                 &width ); num_args++;
25       XtSetArg( args[num_args], XmNheight,
26                                 &height ); num_args++;
27       XtSetArg( args[num_args], XmNdepth,
28                                 &depth ); num_args++;
29       XtGetValues( points_graph, args, num_args );
30
31       /* create the new pixmap if the window is sized */
32       if (( width != 0) && ( height != 0)) {
33          points_graph_pixmap = XCreatePixmap( XtDisplay( widget ),
34                                               XtWindow( widget ),
35                                               (unsigned int) width,
36                                               (unsigned int) height,
37                                               depth );
38
39          /* redraw the image by explicitly calling *
40           * the replot callback                    */
41          replot_graph_callback( widget,
42                                 (XtPointer) NULL,
43                                 (XtPointer) NULL);
44       } /* end if window is sized */
45    } /* end if widget is realized */
46 } /* end fun graph plot resize callback */
```

\\

```
/* Amended plot_point function from translation presentation  *
 * module. Duplicating the drawing of a cross on the screen    *
 * window, with a cross on the off-screen pixmap               *
 */
    XDrawLine( XtDisplay( points_graph), XtWindow( points_graph), gc,
                actual_x - 2, actual_y,
                actual_x + 2, actual_y );
    XDrawLine( XtDisplay( points_graph ), XtWindow( points_graph), gc,
                actual_x, actual_y -2,
                actual_x, actual_y +2);
    XDrawLine( XtDisplay( points_graph), points_graph_pixmap, gc,
                actual_x - 2, actual_y,
                actual_x + 2, actual_y );
    XDrawLine( XtDisplay( points_graph ), points_graph_pixmap, gc,
                actual_x, actual_y -2,
                actual_x, actual_y +2);
```

The only change required in the *XDraw[whatever]* functions is to replace the second parameter, which identifies the screen window in the original call, with the identity of the *pixmap* to be drawn into. Because program objects of type *Window* and of type *Pixmap* can both be used as the destination of *X library* drawing function calls, they are collectively known as *drawables*. The other *graphplot* function which contains drawing requests, *draw_axes* and *clear_points_graph*, will require similar amendments.

The changes outlined above will ensure that an identical copy of whatever is displayed on the screen is maintained on an *off-screen pixmap*. The purpose of this copy is to allow the hidden parts of the screen to be refreshed from the *pixmap* whenever they are exposed. Figure 6.8 illustrates a typical situation where expose events will be generated. The *graphplot* application window is occluded in two places by overlapping windows. When the user moves keyboard focus to the *graphplot* window, possibly by clicking upon its title bar, the window manager will move it to the top of the window hierarchy. The *graphplot* will now be totally visible and the *Xserver* will generate at least two expose events, one for each of the previously occluded areas.

The simplest strategy for an *expose* callback function is to copy the entire *off-screen pixmap* to the *on-screen* window. If this strategy is implemented then in the example above the window will be redrawn at least twice in quick succession in response to the user's action, one redraw occurring in response to each expose event. There are two possible solutions to this problem. The first is to respond only to the last exposure event in the event queue. When the server generates events, it will give each of the events a serial number. The last event of a series will have a serial number of zero. Thus the first solution ignores all expose events, except the event with serial number zero. The application responds to the zeroth event by redrawing the entire window.

The second solution uses the information in each expose event structure to determine the precise area which has been exposed. It then only copies the

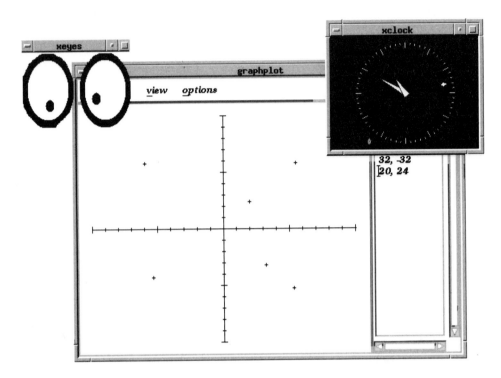

Figure 6.8   Generation of multiple *expose* events.

affected area from the off-screen pixmap to the on screen window. In the example above when the window is raised there will most probably be only two expose events, one of which will indicate that the top left of the window has been exposed and one that the top right has been. The expose callback will be called twice, copying the top left and top right of the off-screen pixmap respectively.

There is little difference in the performance of the two possible solutions, and apart from situations where a very large screen window is being used, the first solution should be favoured in terms of simplicity. Both solutions require the application programmer to manipulate the *call_data* structure passed to the *expose* callback function. The structure passed is of type *XmDrawingAreacallbackStruct*, whose declaration is:

```
typedef struct {
        int      reason;
        Xevent * event;
        Window   window;
    } XmDrawingAreacallbackStruct;
```

The only field which is of interest for an *expose* callback function is the *event* field. As explained above this field is present in all *call_data* structures and is a 'C'

\\

union. The *event* structure for an *expose* event is of type *XExposeEvent*. The *XExposeEvent* structure contains a field called *count* of type int containing the serial number of the event; fields called *x* and *y*, of type *int* indicating the top left of the exposed area relative to the exposed window; and fields called *width* and *height* of type *int* defining the area exposed.

Using these considerations the *points_graph_expose_callback* function can be produced, and is presented in Listing 6.15. The alternative solution, to respond to each event in the queue, will be introduced as an end of chapter exercise.

Listing 6.15   The graph_plot_expose_callback function

```
1   /* Implemented as a private callback function of the presentation  *
2    * module graph points component.                                  *
3    */
4   static void graph_plot_expose_callback( Widget      widget,
5                                            XtPointer client_data,
6                                            XtPointer call_data){
7
8   XEvent  * expose_event;
9   Dimension width, height;
10
11  Arg args[ MAX_ARGS ];
12  int num_args;
13
14     if (XtIsRealized( widget )) {
15        if ( points_graph_pixmap == (pixmap) NULL ){
16           /* call the resize callback explicitly */
17           graph_plot_resize_callback( widget,
18                                     (XtPointer) NULL,
19                                     (XtPointer) NULL );
20        } else {
21           expose_event = ((XmDrawingAreaCallbackStruct*)
22                          call_data)->event;
23           /* only respond to the zeroth event in the queue */
24           if ( expose_event->xexpose.count == 0) {
25              /* get the size of the window */
26              num_args = 0;
27              XtSetArg( args[num_args], XmNwidth,
28                                        &width ); num_args++;
29              XtSetArg( args[num_args], XmNheight,
30                                        &height ); num_args++;
31              XtGetValues( plot_graph, args, num_args );
32              /* copy everything from the pixmap to the window */
33              XCopyArea( XtDisplay( widget), points_graph_pixmap,
34                         XtWindow( widget), gc,
35                         0, 0,
36                         (unsigned int)width, (unsigned int)height,
37                         0, 0);
38           } /* end if count == 0 */
39        } /* end if pixmap == NULL */
40     } /* end if IsRealized */
41  } /* end fun graph_plot_expose_callback */
```

6.6 An alternative *points graph* implementation

There is an alternative implementation of the *points graph* module which will avoid the *resize* and *expose* considerations described above. This implementation is probably not suitable for the *graphplot* application, but may be appropriate for other applications which use a *drawingArea* widget. In this second alternative implementation the *drawingArea* widget is a child of a *scrolledWindow* widget. The *drawingArea* widget maintains a fixed size and a portion of it is visible through a variably sized *scrolledWindow*. Figure 6.9 illustrates the visual appearance of this implementation, Figure 6.10 the required application widget hierarchy and Figure 6.11 the relationship between the *drawingArea* and the *scrolledWindow*.

The *scrolledWindow* widget was first introduced in Chapter 5, where it was used to provide a viewing window onto the text of a *text* widget. The *Motif* toolkit

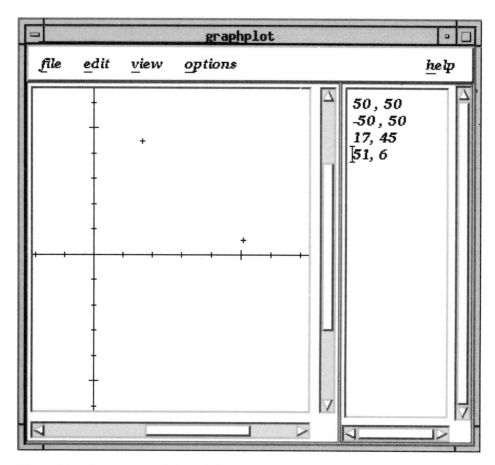

Figure 6.9   Alternative *graphplot* visual design.

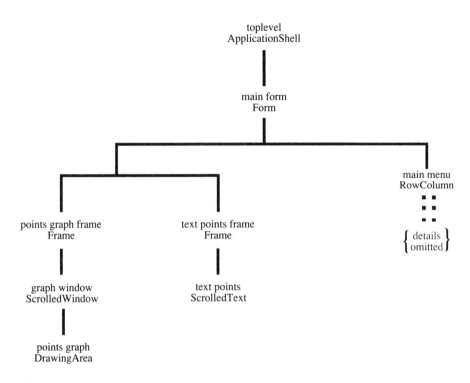

Figure 6.10   Alternative *graphplot* application widget hierarchy.

provides a utility function, *XmCreateScrolledText*, to support this configuration, but does not provide a corresponding function to support the configuration of a *scrolledWindow* and *drawingArea*. To create such a configuration the application first creates a *scrolledWindow* and subsequently a *drawingArea* widget as a child of the *scrolledWindow*. If the *scrollingPolicy* resource of the *scrolledWindow* is set to *XmAUTOMATIC* this is all that is required. The *scrolledWindow* will create the required *scrollBar* widgets, recognize the *drawingArea* as its *work* window and install the necessary callbacks to react to the resizing of the scrolled window, the operation of the *scrollBars* by the user and the exposure of the window. The *expose* and *resize* callbacks used by previous implementations are no longer required.

The revised *points_graph* creation function is given in Listing 6.16. The identity of the *scrolledWindow* is not retained as a *static* variable as the identity, should it ever be required, can be obtained from the *points_graph* widget using the *XtParent* function. There are two potential pitfalls with using this implementation. The first is that it is possible for the *scrolledWindow* to be resized larger than the size of the drawing area widget, causing the *drawingArea* to be positioned by default in the top left-hand corner of the visible area. The second potential

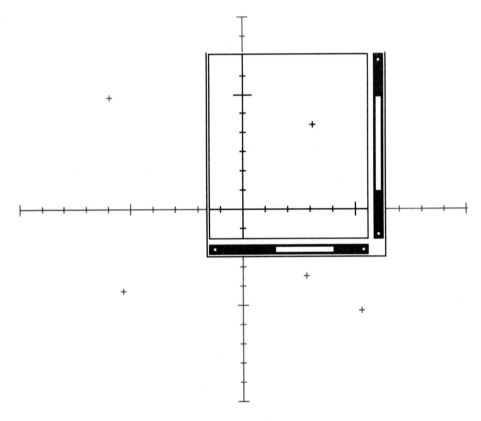

Figure 6.11   Relationship between the *scrolledWindow* and the *drawingArea*.

problem concerns performance; if the *drawingArea* is large the storage requirements of the image may be excessive for the server and speed of operation of the *scrolledWindow* may be inadequate. Solutions to these pitfalls are outside the scope of this book.

Listing 6.16   Alternative points_graph creation function

```
1   extern Widget create_points_graph( Widget parent,
2                           XtCallbackProc mouse_click_callback ){
3
4   Widget graph_frame, graph_window;
5
6   Arg args[ MAX_ARGS ];
7   int num_args;
8
9       num_args = 0;
10      graph_frame = XmCreateFrame( parent, "graph frame",
```

continued

Listing 6.16 *continued*

```
11                                       args, num_args );
12       XtManageChild( graph_frame );
13
14       num_args=0;
15       XtSetArg( args[num_args], XmNscrollingPolicy,
16                               XmAUTOMATIC ); num_args++;
17       XtSetArg( args[num_args], XmNscrollBarDisplayPolicy,
18                               XmSTATIC ); num_args++;
19       graph_window = XmCreateScrolledWindow( graph_frame,
20                                             "graph window",
21                                             args, num_args );
22       XtManageChild( graph_window );
23
24       num_args =0;
25       plot_graph = XmCreateDrawingArea( graph_window,
26                                         "plot graph",
27                                         args, num_args );
28       XtManageChild( plot_graph );
29
30       XtAddCallback( plot_graph, XmNinputCallback,
31                     mouse_click_callback,
32                     (XtPointer) NULL );
33
34       /* creation of a graphics context for black & white drawing *
35        * temporary kludge only - see later revision.              */
36       gc = XCreateGC( XtDisplay( parent),
37                       RootWindowOfScreen( XtScreen( parent)),
38                       0, NULL );
39       XSetForeground( XtDisplay( parent), gc,
40                       BlackPixelOfScreen( XtScreen( parent)));
41       XSetBackground( XtDisplay( parent), gc,
42                       WhitePixelOfScreen( XtScreen( parent)));
43
44       return graph_frame;
45  } /* end fun create_points_graph */
```

6.7 Activities for Chapter 6

1. Adapt the *main menu* program from Chapter 4 to make it suitable for this application and connect it to the *graphplot* from this chapter.

2. Install a *help* system for this application using the help system from Chapter 5. Include appropriate help information for the *text points* and *points graph* components. The help callback can be connected to the *text* and *drawingArea*'s help callbacks, and activated by the user pressing the *help* key on the keyboard when these parts of the application have keyboard focus.

3. Install the *save/ save as* interface from Chapter 5 into this application. To make it functional an application layer will have to be provided. A call from the *save/ save as* interface to save the application state should be

implemented as a call to the public *get_all_text_points* function of the *points graph* module and the subsequent transfer of the points list to an external file.

4. Using the *new/ open* interface from activity 2 of Chapter 5, implement a functional *new/ open/ merge* interface for the *points graph* application.

5. The *plot graph* component of this application will plot a point in response to a click of any mouse button. Amend the implementation to respond only to one of the buttons.

6. Extend the functionality of the application by providing a method which will plot a *'best fit'* straight line of the data on the graph.

7. Revise the implementation of the expose callback introduced in this chapter, to combine the exposed areas from each expose event in the event queue into a single area. Upon receipt of the zeroth expose event only the merged area should be copied from the *pixmap* to the screen.

\\\

CHAPTER SEVEN

The color selection and font selection interfaces

Introduction

The *graphplot* application developed in the last chapter suffered from one potential limitation: it would only display black and white graphs. Although a monochrome image is suitable for the *graphplot* application, many applications require the user to interactively select colors for the application from the palette of available colors. The first section of this chapter will illustrate the development of a reusable *color selection interface* and its installation into the *graphplot* application.

A related requirement for graphical applications is the interactive selection of a font from the collection of available fonts. The second part of the chapter will illustrate the development of a reusable *font selection and text entry interface* and its subsequent inclusion into the *graphplot* application.

It is assumed that by now the philosophy and pragmatics of the development methodology have been sufficiently understood, consequently the details of many aspects of the construction of the interfaces will be omitted. Only the most salient points of and the techniques used in the construction of the interfaces will be explained in detail. Details of the code used in this chapter can be found in Appendix C. Following the construction of each of the interfaces, the mechanisms by which they can be installed into the *graphplot* application introduced in the last chapter, will be described.

7.1 X and colors

The use of colors in X applications was introduced in Chapters 1 and 3, where the use of the command line and resource file *foreground* and *background* color options was explained. This mechanism makes use of the ascii text interface to X color capabilities. Ascii text provides a device independent mechanism by which colors can be specified; the mechanism will accept color specifications such as 'sky blue' and will translate them into the closest available color on the display in use.

The ascii text mechanism is suitable for applications where the use of color is incidental to the purpose of the application, and is used solely to differentiate separate parts of the application's interface. The colors used for these purposes should be specified in resource files in order that users can customize them to their own preferences.

Other applications may have a requirement for more sophisticated use of color. For example, an application which displays photorealistic images requires a very precise control over the colors used. Between these two extremes there are a range of applications which have a requirement to allow the user to interactively select a color from the range of available colors. An example of such an application is the *graphplot* application, where a color selection dialog can be offered to the user allowing them to interactively choose different colors for different sets of points.

Any X application which uses color should take into account the possibility that it will be used in environments which have differing color capabilities. The simplest environment is where there are only two colors available – a monochrome environment. In this environment each *pixel* on the screen is encoded by a single *bit* in the computer's memory. If the bit is set the pixel will display in the foreground color, otherwise the bit is clear and the pixel will display in the background color.

Perhaps the next simplest environment is where each *pixel* on the screen is encoded by a number of bits and there is a fixed relationship between the pattern of bits and the displayed color. For example a pixel might be encoded by two bits; the bit pattern 00 always encodes a black pixel, 01 a light grey pixel, 10 a dark grey pixel and 11 a white pixel. Such an environment can be considered as two bitmaps, one behind the other, which are placed on top of each other to provide the display. Thus the environment is described as having a *depth* of two (bitmaps), or as having two *z planes*.

An environment which has two z planes and four fixed colors is not very common or useful. An environment with eight z planes and 256 fixed colors is a little more useful and common. Environments with 24 z planes and approximately sixteen million fixed colors are the most useful. The relationship between the z planes and the color displayed is illustrated in Figure 7.1. An environment which has a fixed relationship between bit patterns and displayed colors is known as a *DirectColor* or *StaticColor* display.

The most complex, and currently the most common, environment uses different numbers of bits to encode each pixel and to encode each color. There is then no fixed relationship between the bit pattern in the z plane and the color displayed. Using the two bit z plane introduced above each pixel is encoded in two bits, but the displayed color may be defined by four bits. The pixel pattern from the z plane is used as an index into a color lookup table, the contents of which determine the displayed color. Thus there are 16 different possible colors, only four of which can be displayed at any one time. As it is possible to change the contents of the color lookup table, it is possible to select any four colors from the 16 available colors. The relationship between a two bit z plane and a four bit color definition is illustrated in Figure 7.2.

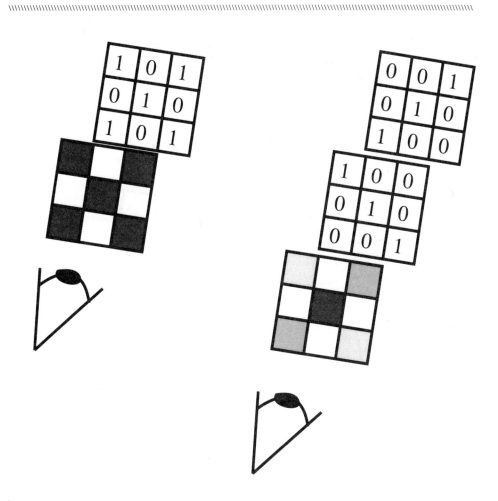

Figure 7.1   The display of colors using a fixed relationship.

A two bit z plane and a four bit color definition is not a common environment. A more typical environment is an eight bit color plane with a 24 bit color definition. This environment allows 256 different colors selected from a gamut of sixteen million colors. An environment which has a variable relationship between bit patterns and displayed colors is known as a *PseudoColor* display.

The simplest encoding of color definitions uses an *rgb* (**r**ed, **g**reen, **b**lue) system. In this system, assuming a 24 bit color definition, eight bits are used to encode the red intensity, eight to encode the green intensity and eight to encode the blue intensity. If none of the 24 bits are set the color displayed will be black; if all bits are set the color displayed will be white. If all the red bits are set and none of the other bits, the color displayed will be an intense red; likewise an intense green or blue can be displayed by setting all the green or blue bits and not setting

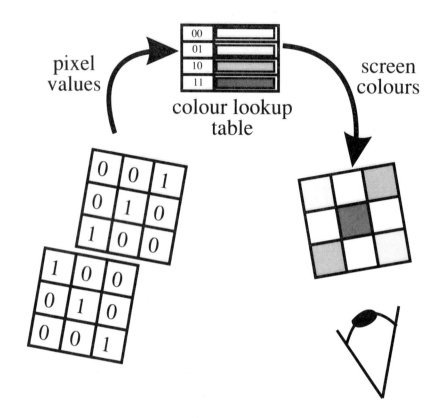

Figure 7.2   The display of colors using a color look up table.

any other bits. By setting different combinations of red, green and blue bits sixteen million different colors can be encoded.

The X Window system always uses 16 bits to encode the red, green or blue component of a color, giving a 48 bit color definition. As this encoding will give more than 2,800 million colors, which is far more colors than can possibly be differentiated by the human eye, it is unlikely that it will ever become inadequate. The X server is responsible for mapping the 48 bit standard encoding to the actual number of bits required by the hardware.

In the X Window system the color lookup table which relates z plane patterns to a color definition is known as a *Colormap*. Motif implements this as a resource introduced into the widget hierarchy by the *Core* widget class, with the resource name *ColorMap*. By default this resource is copied from the widget instance's parent, and in the case of a *toplevel* shell is effectively copied from the default colormap of the X server's root window. The *Colormap* consists of a list of *color cells*, each of type *XColor*, which contains the rgb color definition for the pixel value which indexes the cell. Thus the pixel value 0 indexes the first color cell of the *Colormap*, 1 the second, and so on. The number of entries in the *Colormap* is equal to the number of colors which can be encoded in the z plane.

This Colormap structure is maintained by the server even for *DirectColor* and *StaticColor* displays. A *PseudoColor* system will maintain a read–write *Colormap*, allowing the application to change the mapping between the *Pixel* value and the color displayed. A *DirectColor* or *StaticColor* display's *Colormap* is read-only and as such cannot be changed by the application.

A read–write *Colormap* must be treated with extreme care. Many displays will only allow one *Colormap* to be active at any one time. If all applications are content to inherit the *Colormap* from the root window and to use the color definitions contained within it, there will be few problems. However if an application, or a part of an application, insists on creating and installing its own *Colormap,* problems can occur. As only one colormap can be active at any one time, when input focus changes from application to application all the colors on the display may change.

For example the default colormap may define the pixel value 1 as red and an application installed colormap may define the pixel value 1 as green. Thus when the input focus changes from the root window to the application, all pixels on the display which were displayed as red will change to green. A photorealistic imaging application has a definite requirement to control its colormap and if the default is unsatisfactory would request the window manager to install a different colormap. The changing of colors on the entire display as the photorealistic imaging application receives and releases input focus would be acceptable to the user because they require the functionality it provides to the application they are using. However if the application does not require the functionality, the changing of colors would be unacceptable to the user.

The *X library* provides mechanisms by which an application can request a private editable *colorcell* or *colorcells* from the *Colormap;* obtain colors from the Colormap using rgb or ascii colorname specifications; translate between ascii colornames and rgb values and vice versa; create, install and remove private colormaps, etc. A list of the most useful *X library* functions concerned with colors is given in Table 7.1. Details of these functions can be located in Appendix C.

A drawing color is specified to an *X library* drawing function by setting the *foreground* and *background* components of the *graphics context* specified in the drawing function call. The *graphics context* contains a large number of components which are used to define the manner in which drawing function calls are effected. For example besides the color to be used when drawing a line, the *graphics context* also defines the thickness of the line, the pattern of the line (solid or dashed) and the manner in which two lines join together. Rather than send all this information from the client to the server every time a drawing function is used, the information is *cached* at the server within a *graphics context,* and the *graphics context* to be used is specified as a parameter to the call. The components of the *graphics context* structure are listed in Table 7.2 and the functions to manipulate a *graphics context* are listed in Table 7.3.

\\

Table 7.1   The X library color functions

Colorcell Functions	
BlackPixel	Macro to obtain the black pixel value.
WhitePixel	Macro to obtain the white pixel value
XAllocColor	Allocate closest color using rgb color definition.
XAllocColorCells	Allocate closest colors using rgb color definition.
XAllocColorPlanes	Allocate color planes from the colormap.
XAllocNamedColor	Allocate closest color using ascii color definition.
XFreeColors	Releases colorcells previously allocated.
XLookupColor	Converts rgb color definition to ascii definition.
XParseColor	Converts ascii color definition to rgb definition.
XQueryColor	Converts pixel value to rgb definition.
XQueryColors	Converts pixel values to rgb definitions.
XStoreColor	Redefine a read/ write colormap colorcell, using rgb definition.
XStoreColors	Redefines read/ write colormap colorcells using rgb definitions.
XStoreNamedColor	Redefines a read/ write colormap colorcell, using ascii definition.

Colormap Functions	
DefaultColormap	Macro to obtain the default colormap of a screen.
DisplayCells	Macro to obtain the maximum number of cells on a screen. (This is not to be relied upon!).
XCopyColormapAndFree	Copies a colormap and frees cells in the colormap being copied from.
XCreateColormap	Creates a new colormap.
XFreeColormap	Restores default colormap and destroys installed colormap previously created.
XGetStandardColormap	Obtains information concerning the standard colormap installed in a window.
XInstallColormap	Installs colormap into the display, for window manager use only.
XListInstalledColormap	Returns a list of the colormaps installed into the display.
XSetWindowColormap	Sets the colormap resource of a window.
XUninstallColormap	Removes colormap from the display, for window manager use only.

Table 7.2   The components of the graphics context

structure name symbolic name	type default value	notes
arc_mode GCArcMode	int ArcPieSlice	The filling of a solid chord. Values *ArcPieSlice, ArcChord*
background GCBackground	unsigned long 0	Determines the background pixel used when drawing
cap_style GCCapStyle	int CapButt	The end of an unjoined line. Values *CapNotLast, CapButt, CapRound, CapProjecting*

continued

Table 7.2 *continued*

structure name	type	
symbolic name	**default value**	**notes**
clip_mask	Pixmap	Bitmap which defines the area to be used
GCClipMask	null	during clipping operations
clip_x_origin	int	X origin for clipping
GCClipXOrigin	0	
clip_y_origin	int	Y origin for clipping
GCClipYOrigin	0	
dash_offset	int	Offset from start of line to start of dash
GCDashOffset	0	pattern
dash_list	char	Dashed line information
GCDashes	4	(i.e. 4 pixels on, 4 pixels off)
fill_style	int	The filling of solid areas. Values *FillSolid*,
GCFillStyle	FillSolid	*FillTiled, FillStippled*
fill_rule	int	The fill algorithm to be used. Values
GCFillRule	EvenOddRule	*EvenOddRule, WindingRule*
font	Font	Font to be used in text operations
GCFont	(varies)	
foreground	unsigned long	Determines the foreground pixel used
GCForeground	0	when drawing
function	int	Determines the logical operation applied to
GCFunction	GXcopy	the new and existing pixels when drawing
graphics_exposures	Boolean	Generate exposure evenly on copy area and
GCGraphicsExposures	True	copy plane operations
join_style	int	The joining of two lines. Values *JoinMitre*,
GCJoinStyle	JoinMitre	*JoinBevel, JoinRound*
line_style	int	Continuity of the line. Values *LineSolid*
GCLineStyle	LineSolid	*LineOnOffDash, LineDoubleDash*
line_width	int	Determines the width of the line in pixels
GCLineWidth	0	
plane mask	unsigned long	Determines which *z* planes are changed
GCPlaneMask	all 1's	when drawing
stipple	Pixmap	The one plane pixmap (bitmap) used for
GCStipple	solid bitmap	stippling operations.
subwindow_mode	int	Draw through or clip around subwindows.
GCSubwindowMode	ClipByChildren	Values *ClipByChildren, IncludeInferiors*
tile	Pixmap	Pixmap to be used for tiling operations
GCTile	solid foreground	

continued

Table 7.2 *continued*

structure name	type	
symbolic name	**default value**	**notes**
ts_x_origin	int	X offset for tiling or stippling operations
GCTileStipXOrigin	0	
ts_y_origin	int	Y offset for tiling or stippling operations
GCTileStipYOrigin	0	

Table 7.3   The X library graphics context functions

Function	
DefaultGC	Macro to obtain the default gc of a screen.
XChangeGC	Changes any or all of a graphics context's components.
XCopyGC	Copies any or all of a graphics context's components.
XCreateGC	Creates a new graphics context.
XFreeGC	Destroys a graphics context.
XSetArcMode	Sets the *arc_mode* component of a graphics context.
XSetBackground	Sets the *background* component of a graphics context.
XSetClipMask	Sets the *clip_mask* component of a graphics context.
XSetClipOrigin	Sets the *clip_x_origin* and *clip_y_origin* components of a graphics context.
XSetClipRectangles	Sets the *clip_mask* component of a graphics context to the union of a list of rectangles supplied.
XSetDashes	Sets the *dash_offset* and *dash_list* components of a graphics context.
XSetFillRule	Sets the *fill_rule* component of a graphics context.
XSetFillStyle	Sets the *fill_style* component of a graphics context.
XSetForeground	Sets the *foreground* component of a graphics context.
XSetFunction	Sets the *function* component of a graphics context.
XSetGraphicsExposures	Sets the *graphics_exposures* component of a graphics context.
XSetLineAttributes	Sets the *line_width*, *line_style*, *cap_style* and *join_style* components of a graphics context.
XSetPlaneMask	Sets the *plane_mask* component of a graphics context.
XSetStipple	Sets the *stipple* component of a graphics context.
XSetState	Sets the *foreground*, *background*, *function* and *plane_mask* components of a graphics context.
XSetSubWindowMode	Sets the *subwindow_mode* component of a graphics context.
XSetTile	Sets the *tile* component of a graphics context.
XSetTSOrigin	Sets the *ts_x_origin* and *ts_y_origin* components of a graphics context.

7.2 The color selection interface

The design of a *color selection interface* must take into account the display characteristics of the environment within which it is to be used. Figures 7.3, 7.4 and 7.5 illustrate three different color selection dialogs which are suitable for *one bit*, *two to eight bit* and *more than eight bit* z plane displays respectively. The

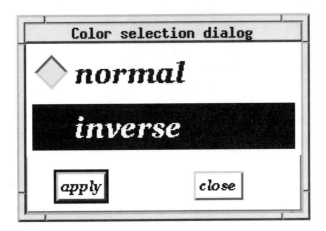

Figure 7.3 The one bit color selection dialog.

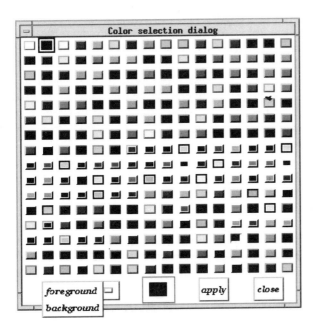

Figure 7.4 The two to eight bit color selection dialog.

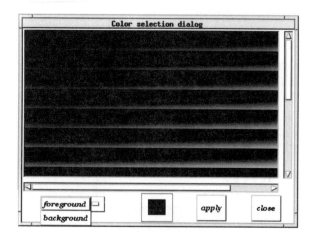

Figure 7.5   The more than eight bit color selection dialog.

one bit dialog provides the user with an opportunity to select between a normal and an inverse color scheme by use of a *radioBox* dialog. The *two to eight bit* dialog provides the user with an array of *pushButtons* which can be used to select a color from the palette. The *more than eight bit* dialog provides the user with a color *swathe* from which the user can indicate the required color. All of these dialogs offer choices from the colors found in the *ColorMap* when the application is launched. Techniques and interfaces which allow the user to define a color are beyond the scope of this book.

The latter two of the three dialogs also provide an *option menu* to choose between *foreground* and *background* color selection and a *feedback area* illustrating the appearance of the currently selected colors. All dialogs provide an *apply* button which commits the current selection, and a *close* button which will remove the dialog from the display.

An overview of the modules which will be required to construct this interface is presented in Figure 7.6. The major difference between this design and the designs in previous chapters is that the *color selection interface* presentation module contains three presentation components, one for each of the three possible dialogs. The translation module will determine the appropriate dialog type, store this information in the support module and call the appropriate creation function of the presentation module. Likewise the interface translation functions will at times have to take different actions, depending upon the environment the application is operating within.

The interface to the *application layer* consists of functions to set and get the *foreground* and *background* pixel values to be used by the application. Other parts of the application can use the enquiry functions of the application layer to

Application main menu

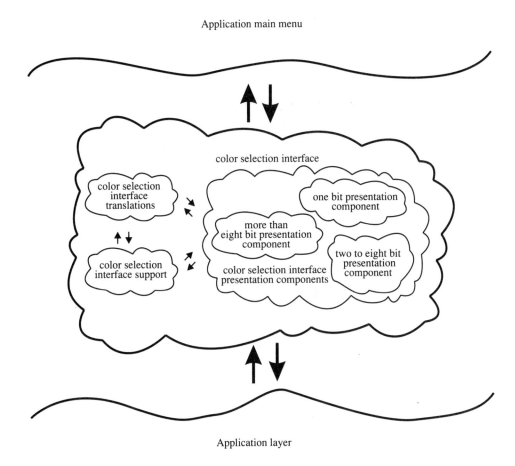

Application layer

Figure 7.6   The color selection interface, design overview.

obtain the foreground and background values which have been set by the color selection interface.

This section of the chapter will only consider in detail the *two to eight bit* dialog. The significant considerations of the other two dialogs will be mentioned in the following section. Details of all the code for all dialogs can be found in Appendix C.

7.2.1 The color selection interface, two to eight bit presentation module

The usability design for the *two to eight bit* color selection dialog is presented in Figure 7.7, its object diagram in Figure 7.8, and the application widget hierarchy in Figure 7.9. A section of the creation function is presented in Listing 7.1. The

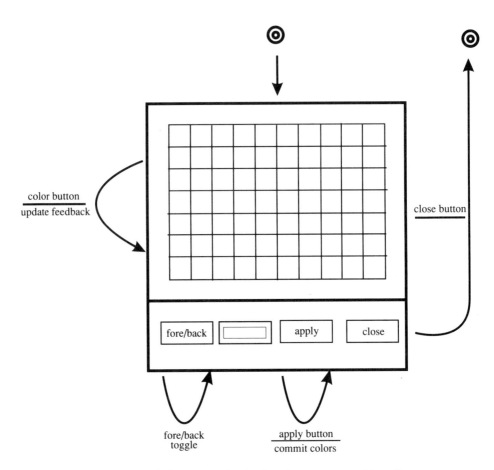

Figure 7.7   The two to eight bit color selection interface, state transition diagram.

creation of the widget hierarchy designed in Figure 7.9 involves the creation of an indeterminate number of *pushButton* widgets all of which will have the name '*color button*'. One button will be required for each entry in the color map, and the number of entries in the colormap is equal to 2 to the power of the depth (number of z planes) of the screen. The depth of the screen can be obtained by retrieving the value of the *depth* resource of the *parent* widget supplied to the creation function.

Having determined the number of buttons, the *static* widget pointer, called *csd_buttons*, is initialized to point to an allocated area of memory which can contain sufficient widgets. This area of memory is then treated as an array of widgets, one for each required *pushButton*. As each button is created, as a child of a *form* widget, its *attachment* resources are computed and installed. The border width is set to 2 pixels and the border color set to white. The border color

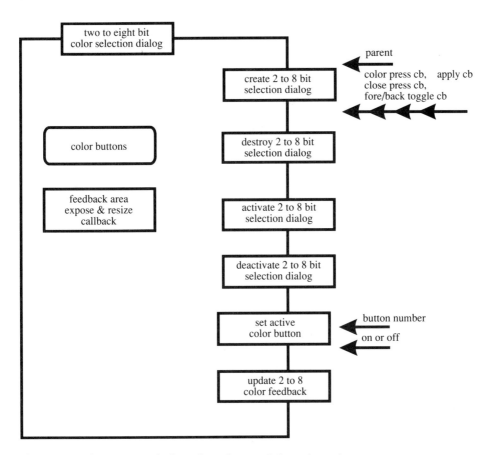

Figure 7.8   The two to eight bit color selection dialog, object diagram.

resource will be set to black during the dialog's operation to indicate the currently selected button. The label string resource of each *pushButton* is set to a null string and the background color value set to the button's position in the array. This *background* resource, of type *Pixel*, will be used by the intrinsics as an index into the *colormap*, allowing the button to present itself with its color indicating the color to be selected.

After creating and managing the buttons, the *color_selection_callback* function provided by the translation module is installed as the *activateCallback* resource, with the *client_data* parameter set to the button's index. Thus when the callback is called, the *client_data* parameter can be examined to determine precisely which button was pressed and thus which color the user is indicating.

The creation of the array of color buttons from the *create_2_to_8_bit_color_selection_dialog* is given in Listing 7.1. This would be a very suitable situation for the use of *gadgets* instead of *widgets*. With an eight bit

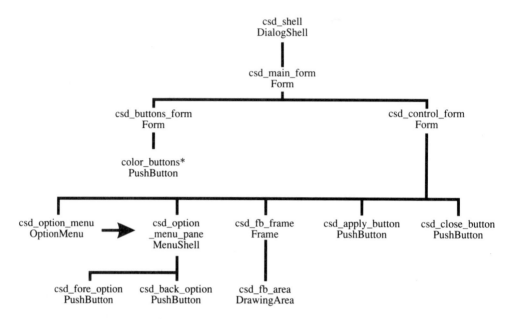

Figure 7.9   The two to eight bit color selection dialog, application widget hierarchy.

display, 256 *pushButton* widgets would be required. The time taken to create them during program initiation and the server resources required to support them are not insignificant. However it is not possible to use *gadgets* in this situation as a *gadget* has to use the same foreground and background colors as its parent.

Careful examination of this function will reveal a potential flaw. The number of buttons required is computed as two to the power of the depth of the window. These are then presented as a square matrix of buttons using the square root of the number of buttons to determine the number of buttons on each side of the square. This will produce an appropriate display for a depth of eight bits, with 256 buttons in a sixteen by sixteen matrix. An appropriate display will also be produced for two, four and six bit depths. However for odd values of bit depths the number of buttons per side would be computed as a non-integer value which, when truncated to an integer value, would imply that an incorrect number of buttons would be created. This apparent problem is rarely an actual problem as windows supporting an odd number of z planes are uncommon.

The *foreground/ background* toggle is implemented as a Motif *option menu*. An *option menu* is a composite widget containing a specialized *rowColumn* and a *label* widget, which posts a *pull down* menu pane when it is activated. The *menu pane* contains a number of *pushButton* widgets, activation of any one of which will cause it to be displayed as the currently selected option when the menu pane is unposted.

Listing 7.1   The creation of a pushButtons array from create_two_to_eight_bit_color_
           selection_dialog

```
 1   /* white is of type Pixel with value of white color of screen      *
 2      depth is of type int with value set to depth of screen.         *
 3      csd_buttons is of type Widget * with no value.                  *
 4      num_buttons, buttons_per_side, this_button_index, this_button_y, *
 5      this_button_x are integers with no value.                       *
 6   */
 7
 8      num_buttons = (int) pow( 2, depth);
 9      buttons_per_side = (int) sqrt( num_buttons)
10      null_str = XmStringCreateSimple( "");
11
12      /* allocate memory for the array of buttons */
13      csd_buttons = (Widget *) malloc( num_buttons * sizeof( Widget ));
14
15      /* iterate through the array of buttons, creating each button *
16       * with computed attachment resources and a background color  *
17       * based upon its position in the array                       *
18       */
19      buttons = csd_buttons;  /* pointer to each button in sequence */
20      this_button_index  = 0;
21      for( this_button_y = 0;
22            this_button_y < buttons_per_side;
23            this_button_y++){
24        for( this_button_x = 0;
25              this_button_x < buttons_per_side;
26              this_button_x++){
27
28            num_args = 0;
29            XtSetArg( args[num_args], XmNlabelString,
30                                      null_str); num_args++;
31            XtSetArg( args[num_args], XmNleftAttachment,
32                                      XmATTACH_POSITION); num_args++;
33            XtSetArg( args[num_args], XmNleftPosition,
34                     (this_button_x * (256/buttons_per_side ))); num_args++;
35            /* omitted right, top and bottom attachments similarly set */
36            XtSetArg( args[num_args], XmNborderWidth,
37                                              2); num_args++;
38            XtSetArg( args[num_args], XmNborderColor,
39                                        white); num_args++;
40            XtSetArg( args[num_args], XmNbackground,
41                      ((Pixel) this_button_index)); num_args++;
42            /* create the button in the array */
43            buttons[this_button_index] =
44                       XmCreatePushButton( csd_buttons_form,
45                                      "color button",
46                                      args, num_args );
47            XtManageChild( buttons[this_button_index]);
48            /* pass the button's index in the call data parameter */
49            XtAddCallback( buttons[this_button_index],
50                      XmNactivateCallback,
51                      color_button_press_callback,
52                        (XtPointer) this_button_index );
```

continued

\\\

Listing 7.1 *continued*

```
53              this_button_index++;
54          } /* end x loop */
55      } /* end y loop   */
```

It would seem that a *radio box* might be more appropriate here, but an *option menu* has been used for two reasons. Firstly it provides an opportunity to introduce *option menus*. Secondly, and more importantly, it provides for future extendibility. A revised version of the *graphplot* application might allow the user to select different colors for the axes, data points, graph title, axes titles, etc. The use of an *option menu* will allow these options to be introduced without destroying the integrity of the visual design.

The construction of an *option* menu is similar to the construction of a *pull down* menu, first introduced in Chapter 4. The *menu pane* is created first using the utility function *XmCreatePullDownMenu* and the contents of the menu created as *pushButton* children of the *menu pane*. Having created the menu, it is installed into the *optionMenu* composite widget by specifying the *menu pane's* widget identity as the *subMenuId* resource of the *optionMenu* created with the *XmCreateOptionMenu* utility function. The *optionMenu* and the *menu pane* must both be children of the same parent; the relationship between them is indicated on the application widget hierarchy by an arrow. The label used for the option menu is determined by the value of the *labelString* resource of the *optionMenu*. In the menu used in this dialog the *labelString* has been set to a null string and consequently is not visible in Figures 7.4 and 7.5.

By default the option presented by the *optionMenu* when it is first created is the first created option of the *menu pane*. The default can be changed by setting the value of the *menuHistory* resource of the *optionMenu* to the widget identity of the required option. The *menuHistory* resource can also be queried by the application should it have a requirement to determine the current state of the menu. In this example the *activateCallbacks* of the option menu *pushButtons* are used to monitor the state of the menu. The code used in the creation of the *optionMenu* is presented in Listing 7.2.

The remaining components of the *two to eight bit* color selection dialog are created using mechanisms similar to those which have been introduced in previous chapters. The activation and deactivation of the dialog is accomplished by managing and unmanaging the *csd_2_to_8_main_form* widget which is the child of the *dialogShell* widget at the root of the application's hierarchy.

There remain two public functions and one private function of the dialog to be considered. The *set_active_color_button* function uses the *button_number* parameter as an index into the *pushButtons* array and uses the *on_or_off* parameter to decide between setting its *borderColor* resource black or white respectively. As this function reinforces the understanding of the array of *pushButtons*, it is presented in its entirety in Listing 7.3.

Listing 7.2   The creation of an option menu, from create_two_to_eight_bit_color_
selection_dialog

```
1    /* create the pull down menu pane before the option menu */
2
3    num_args = 0;
4    csd_option_menu_pane = XmCreatePulldownMenu( csd_control_form,
5                                      "csd option menu pane",
6                                      args, num_args);
7
8    /* install the options (as pushButtons)into the menu pane, */
9    num_args = 0;
10   csd_fore_option = XmCreatePushButton( csd_option_menu_pane,
11                                     "csd fore option",
12                                     args, num_args);
13   XtManageChild( csd_fore_option);
14   XtAddCallback( csd_fore_option, XmNactivateCallback,
15                  fore_back_toggle_callback, (XtPointer) NULL );
16
17   num_args = 0;
18   csd_back_option = XmCreatePushButton( csd_option_menu_pane,
19                                     "csd back option",
20                                     args, num_args);
21   XtManageChild( csd_back_option);
22   XtAddCallback( csd_back_option, XmNactivateCallback,
23                  fore_back_toggle_callback, (XtPointer) NULL );
24
25   /* create the option menu itself, specifying the identity *
26    * of the menu pane as the subMenuId of the option menu   */
27   num_args = 0;
28   XtSetArg( args[num_args], XmNsubMenuId,
29                 csd_option_menu_pane); num_args++;
30   csd_option_menu = XmCreateOptionMenu( csd_control_form,
31                                     "csd option menu",
32                                     args, num_args);
33   XtManageChild( csd_option_menu);
```

Listing 7.3   The set_active_color_button function

```
1   extern void set_active_color_button( int     button_number,
2                                        Boolean on_or_off   ){
3
4   /* a slight misnomer in the name, the function is called twice  *
5    * when a button is activated, once to turn the existing button *
6    * 'off', and once to turn the new button 'on'                  *
7   */
8
9   Widget   the_button;
10  Pixel    white_pixel, black_pixel;
11
12  Arg args[ MAX_ARGS ];
13  int num_args;
14
15    /* activate or deactivate by setting border color *
```

continued

\\\

Listing 7.3 *continued*

```
16      * resource black or white respectively          */
17      the_button = csd_buttons[button_number];
18      white_pixel = WhitePixelOfScreen( XtScreen( the_button));
19      black_pixel = BlackPixelOfScreen( XtScreen( the_button));
20      num_args =0;
21      if (on_or_off){
22         XtSetArg( args[num_args], XmNborderColor,
23                                      black_pixel); num_args++;
24      }else{
25         XtSetArg( args[num_args], XmNborderColor,
26                                      white_pixel); num_args++;
27      } /* end if */
28      XtSetValues( the_button, args, num_args );
29   } /* end fun set active button */
```

The remaining public function, *update_color_feedback*, is implemented as an explicit call to the private callback function *color_feedback_expose_and_resize_callback*, which has already been installed into the *expose* and *resize* callback resources of the feedback *drawingArea* widget. This callback function obtains the value of the working foreground and background colors from the support module before redrawing the entire feedback area using *X library* drawing calls. The effect is to update the feedback area to reflect the current state of the dialog.

The only point of note is the private *graphics context* maintained by this function. The graphics context variable is declared as a local static variable and initialized to a null value. The first action of the function is to examine the value of the *gc* variable and, if it is null, to create a graphics context using the *XCreateGC* function introduced in the previous chapter.

This is a useful technique for implementing once only private actions. The declaration of a static variable with a null value and testing for this value at the start of the function will indicate that this is the first time that the function has been called. Once only initialization actions can then be included within the function's code, usually involving the creation of a resource. The drawback of using this technique is that a routine to destroy the resource when it is no longer required cannot easily be implemented. The alternative technique would have been to declare the variable static and global to the entire module. The resource could then be created within the module's creation function and destroyed within the module's destruction function. However this second technique increases the number of encapsulated static variables, which should be kept to a minimum.

7.2.2 The other presentation modules

The other two presentation modules, the *one bit* module and the *more than eight bit* module, are relatively straightforward. The *more than eight bit* module is very similar to the *two to eight bit* module described in detail above. It differs primarily in providing a color *swathe,* within a scrolled drawing area, from which the user can select the required color. It is anticipated that a display which has more than eight bits per pixel will maintain a static colormap which is logically laid out. Thus the colors in the swathe will be ordered in some manner which makes visual sense to the user; e.g. all the various shades of reds will be grouped together and ordered according to their intensity. Should the display have a dynamic colormap the ordering of colors in the swathe may not be convenient, but the interface will still be usable. The object diagram for the *more than eight bit* color selection dialog is given in Figure 7.10.

The swathe is drawn onto a static *pixmap* which is associated with a *drawingArea* widget by the use of a callback function attached to the *drawingArea*'s *exposeCallback.* This private function of the presentation module, called *color_swathe_expose_callback*, is virtually identical to the callback function introduced in the last chapter which associated a *pixmap* with a *drawingArea.* The size of the *pixmap* and of the *drawingArea* is related to the number of z planes in

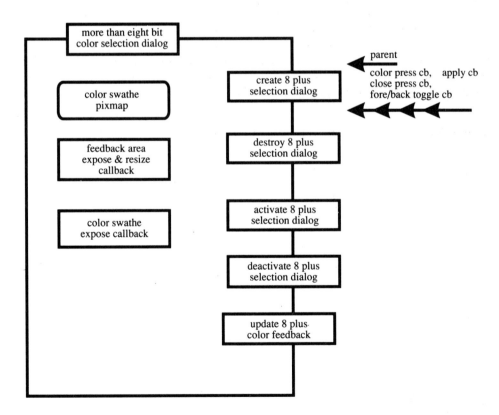

Figure 7.10   The more than eight bit color selection dialog, object diagram.

\\\

the display. Each color from the colormap is drawn onto the *pixmap* as a two by two pixel area using four calls to *XDrawPoint*. A single call to *XFillRectangle* could have been used but for such a simple rectangle the overhead of drawing a filled rectangle would outweigh four calls to draw a point.

The *drawingArea* is implemented as a child of a *scrolledWindow* widget, as described in detail in the last chapter. When the user manipulates the scrollBars to view the color swathe, an *expose* event is generated in the *drawingArea* which will cause the newly exposed area of the *swathe* to be copied from the *pixmap* to the window. The *drawingArea's inputCallback* resource has the *color_selection_callback* function parameter function attached to it. This callback function is provided by the color selection interface translation module and is implemented in a similar manner to the *mouse_click_callback* used in the previous chapter. The function will respond only to *ButtonRelease* events, will determine where in *drawingArea* the button was released and from this information determine which color is being indicated by the user.

The salient parts of the creation of the *more than eight bit* color selection dialog are presented in Listing 7.4. One point to note from this listing is that the *graphics context* created to draw the color swathe is destroyed using *XFreeGC* when it is no longer required. The creation of the remaining parts of the *more than eight bit* color selection dialog is very similar to the construction of the corresponding parts of the *two to eight bit* color selection dialog. Likewise, the other public and private functions of the module are implemented using techniques similar to the techniques used above.

Listing 7.4   The creation of the color swathe within create_8plus_cs_dialog

```
 1   extern void create_8plus_bit_color_selection_dialog(Widget parent,
 2                        XtCallbackProc       color_select_callback,
 3                        XtCallbackProc     fore_back_option_callback,
 4                        XtCallbackProc   apply_button_press_callback,
 5                        XtCallbackProc   close_button_press_callback){
 6
 7
 8   Widget csd_shell, csd_swindow, csd_swathe,
 9          csd_control_form, csd_option_menu_pane, csd_option_menu,
10          csd_fore_option, csd_back_option, csd_fb_frame,
11          csd_apply_button, csd_close_button, temp;
12
13   unsigned int depth, num_of_cells, cells_per_side, length_of_side;
14   unsigned int this_cell, this_x_cell, this_y_cell;
15   GC           csd_8plus_gc;
16
17   Arg args[ MAX_ARGS ];
18   int num_args;
19
20      /* omitted get the depth of the screen, create shell & main form  */
21
22      /* compute total number of cells & from it other requirements */
```

continued

Listing 7.4 *continued*

```
23    num_of_cells  = (int) pow( 2, depth );
24    cells_per_side = (int) sqrt( num_of_cells );
25    length_of_side = cells_per_side *2;
26
27    csd_8plus_gc = XCreateGC( XtDisplay( parent),
28                              DefaultRootWindow( XtDisplay( parent )),
29                              0, NULL );
30
31    /* create the scrolled window with essential resources set */
32    num_args = 0;
33    XtSetArg( args[num_args], XmNscrollingPolicy,
34                              XmAUTOMATIC);          num_args++;
35    XtSetArg( args[num_args], XmNscrollBarDisplayPolicy,
36                              XmSTATIC); num_args++;
37    XtSetArg( args[num_args], XmNleftAttachment,
38                              XmATTACH_FORM);        num_args++;
39    XtSetArg( args[num_args], XmNtopAttachment,
40                              XmATTACH_FORM);        num_args++;
41    XtSetArg( args[num_args], XmNrightAttachment,
42                              XmATTACH_FORM);        num_args++;
43    XtSetArg( args[num_args], XmNbottomAttachment,
44                              XmATTACH_POSITION);    num_args++;
45    XtSetArg( args[num_args], XmNbottomPosition,
46                              85);                   num_args++;
47    csd_swindow = XmCreateScrolledWindow( csd_main_form,
48                                    "csd 8plus swindow",
49                                    args, num_args );
50    XtManageChild( csd_swindow )
51
52    /* create drawing area of required size as child of scrolled window */
53    num_args = 0;
54    XtSetArg( args[num_args], XmNwidth,
55                              (Dimension) length_of_side); num_args++;
56    XtSetArg( args[num_args], XmNheight,
57                              (Dimension) length_of_side); num_args++;
58    csd_swathe = XmCreateDrawingArea( csd_swindow,
59                                    "csd 8plus swathe",
60                                    args, num_args );
61    XtAddCallback( csd_swathe, XmNinputCallback,
62                   color_select_callback,     (XtPointer) NULL );
63    XtAddCallback( csd_swathe, XmNexposeCallback,
64                   color_swathe_expose_callback, (XtPointer) NULL );
65
66    /* and pixmap with identical dimensions */
67    csd_color_swathe = XCreatePixmap( XtDisplay( parent ),
68                              DefaultRootWindow( XtDisplay( parent )),
69                              length_of_side, length_of_side, depth );
70
71    XtManageChild( csd_swathe );
72
73    /* inform the scrolled window of its work area child */
74    num_args = 0;
75    XtSetArg( args[num_args], XmNworkWindow,
```

continued

\\

Listing 7.4 *continued*

```
76                                csd_swathe); num_args++;
77     XtSetValues( csd_swindow, args, num_args );
78
79     /* plot the color cells onto the pixmap */
80     this_cell = 0;
81     for( this_x_cell =0; this_x_cell < cells_per_side; this_x_cell++ ){
82        for( this_y_cell =0; this_y_cell < cells_per_side; this_y_cell++ ){
83           XSetForeground( XtDisplay( parent), csd_8plus_gc, (Pixel) this_cell );
84           XDrawPoint( XtDisplay( parent), csd_color_swathe, csd_8p_gc,
85                               this_x_cell*2, this_y_cell*2);
86           XDrawPoint( XtDisplay( parent), csd_color_swathe, csd_8p_gc,
87                               this_x_cell*2+1, this_y_cell*2);
88           XDrawPoint( XtDisplay( parent), csd_color_swathe, csd_8p_gc,
89                               this_x_cell*2, this_y_cell*2+1);
90           XDrawPoint( XtDisplay( parent), csd_color_swathe, csd_8p_gc,
91                               this_x_cell*2+1, this_y_cell*2+1);
92           this_cell++;
93        } /* end for this_y_cell */
94     } /* end for this x cell */
95
96     /* dispose of the gc */
97     XFreeGC( XtDisplay( parent) , csd_8plus_gc );
98
99  /* details of the creation of the rest of the dialog omitted */
100
101 } /* end fun create_8plus_bit_color_selection_dialog */
```

The *one bit* color selection dialog's object diagram is given in Figure 7.11. The color selection part of the dialog consists of a *rowColumn* widget configured as a *radioBox* and created using the convenience function *XmCreateRadioBox*. Its children are two *toggleButton* widgets, configured to offer a *1 of many* selection. The major resources of the *toggleButton* widget class are given in Table 7.4. The *color_select_callback* function supplied by the translation module is installed in the *toggleButton*'s *valueChangedCallback* resource, using the *client_data* parameter to indicate if the normal or inverse toggle button has been pressed. The salient parts of the creation of the *one bit* color selection dialog are presented in Listing 7.5. The remaining parts of the *one bit* color selection dialog are straightforward; details can be found in Appendix C.

7.2.3 The color selection dialog, support module

The color selection dialog support module implements four encapsulated variables, the *working foreground color*, the *working background color*, the *screen type* and the *foreground or background selection* state of the dialog. Suitable set value and get value functions are supplied for these variables and for the *screen type* and *fore/ background selection* state variables suitable manifest values are defined.

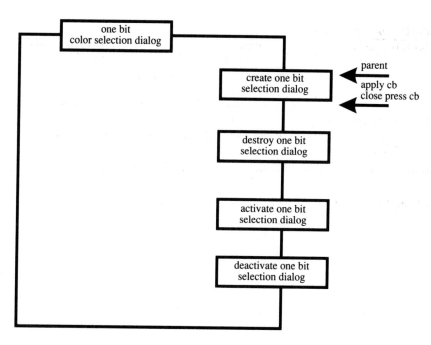

Figure 7.11   The one bit color selection dialog, object diagram.

Table 7.4   *ToggleButton* widget class major resources

Resource name	type	(default) values
armCallback	CallbackList	null
the actions to be performed when the button is armed		
disarmCallback	CallbackList	null
the actions to be performed when the button is disarmed		
fillOnSelect	Boolean	varies
if true will fill the toggle indicator with color specified in selectColor		
indicatorOn	Boolean	True
if true causes the toggle indicator to be drawn		
indicatorSize	Dimension	varies
if set causes the size of the indicator to remain fixed, otherwise it will change size to match the labeltext or Pixmap size		
indicatorType	manifest (unsigned char)	XmONE_OF_MANY XmN_OF_MANY
determines the shape of the toggle indicator (diamond or square respectively)		
selectColor	Pixel	varies
color to fill the toggle indicator with when it is selected		
selectInsensitivePixmap	Pixmap	XmUNSPECIFIEDPIXMAP
pixmap to be used when the button is selected and insensitive		
selectPixmap	Pixmap	XmUNSPECIFIEDPIXMAP
pixmap to be used when the button is selected and sensitive		

continued

||||||||||||||||||||||||||||||||||||||||||||||||||||||||||||||||||||||||||||||||||||||||||||||||||||||||||||||||||||||||||||||||||||||||||||||||||||||||||||

Table 7.4 *continued*

Resource name	type	(default) values
set	Boolean	False
determines the selection state of the button		
spacing	Dimension	4
the spacing in pixels between the indicator and label or pixmap		
valueChangedCallback	CallbackList	null
the actions to be taken when the toggle is selected or deselected		
visibleWhenOff	Boolean	varies
if true the indicator is visible when the toggle is unselected		

Listing 7.5   The creation of a radiobox from the create_1_bit_cs_dialog function

```
1   /* Part of create_1_bit_cs_dialog from csi_1_pm.c, illustrating  *
2    * the creation of a 1 of many radio box.                         *
3    * foreground and background are of type Pixel and have been set *
4    * to the foreground and background resource of the parent       *
5    * widget supplied. The main form has been created.              *
6    */
7       num_args = 0;
8       csd_radio_box = XmCreateRadioBox( csd_main_form,
9                                         "csd radio box",
10                                        args, num_args);
11      XtManageChild( csd_radio_box );
12
13      /* Create normal button with toggle indicator set.       *
14       * The manifest value NORMAL_TOGGLE used to identify the *
15       * button is supplied by the support module.            */
16      num_args = 0;
17      XtSetArg( args[num_args], XmNforeground,
18                                foreground);    num_args++;
19      XtSetArg( args[num_args], XmNbackground,
20                                background);    num_args++;
21      XtSetArg( args[num_args], XmNindicatorType,
22                                XmONE_OF_MANY); num_args++;
23      XtSetArg( args[num_args], XmNset,
24                                True);          num_args++;
25      csd_normal_toggle = XmCreateToggleButton( csd_radio_box,
26                                        "csd normal toggle",
27                                        args, num_args);
28      XtManageChild( csd_normal_toggle );
29      XtAddCallback( csd_normal_toggle,
30                     XmNvalueChangedCallback,
31                     color_select_callback,
32                     (XtPointer) NORMAL_TOGGLE );
33
34      /* Create inverse button with toggle indicator set. */
35      num_args = 0;
36      XtSetArg( args[num_args], XmNforeground,
37                                background);    num_args++;
38      XtSetArg( args[num_args], XmNbackground,
39                                foreground);    num_args++;
```

continued

\\\

Listing 7.5 *continued*

```
40    XtSetArg( args[num_args], XmNindicatorType,
41                          XmONE_OF_MANY); num_args++;
42    XtSetArg( args[num_args], XmNset,
43                          False);             num_args++;
44    csd_inverse_toggle = XmCreateToggleButton( csd_radio_box,
45                               "csd inverse toggle",
46                               args, num_args);
47    XtManageChild( csd_inverse_toggle );
48    XtAddCallback( csd_inverse_toggle,
49                   XmNvalueChangedCallback,
50                   color_select_callback,
51                   (XtPointer) INVERSE_TOGGLE );
52  /* creation of the apply and close buttons omitted */
```

The working foreground and background variables are used to store the currently selected foreground and background colors. During the creation of the interface they are initialized to the value of the *foreground* and *background* resources of the *parent* widget supplied. During operation of the dialog they may be used to reset the state of the dialog when it is toggled between foreground and background selection. When the *apply* button is activated the values are communicated to the application data layer.

The *screen type* variable is set during creation of the interface to a value determined by the value of the *depth* resource of the parent widget supplied. The value is used subsequently by the translations when knowledge of the type of dialog in use is required. The *fore/ background state* is likewise set to foreground during creation and toggled in response to the user's interaction with the dialog.

The object diagrams for the four variables are given in Figure 7.12 and the header file derived from them in Listing 7.6. The header file also contains two manifest values to support the operation of the *one bit* dialog. The associated code file is straightforward and can be located in Appendix C.

Listing 7.6   The color selection interface support module header file

```
1  /* filename color select interface support module header    *
2   * file (csi_sm.h).                                          *
3   *                                                           *
4   * Written for Motif book Chapter 7, see text.               *
5   *                                                           *
6   * Fintan Culwin v1.0 Oct 92 revised Jan 94                  *
7   */
8
9  #ifndef CSI_SM
10 #define CSI_SM
11
12 #include <X11.h>
13
```

continued

\\\

Listing 7.6 *continued*

```
14  /* support for the working foreground & background */
15  extern void  set_working_foreground_color( Pixel new_foreground );
16  extern void  set_working_background_color( Pixel new_background );
17  extern Pixel get_working_foreground_color( void );
18  extern Pixel get_working_background_color( void );
19
20  /* support for the type of screen *./
21  #define ONE_BIT              0
22  #define TWO_TO_EIGHT_BIT     1
23  #define MORE_THAN_EIGHT_BIT  2
24  extern void set_screen_type( int the_screen_type );
25  extern int  get_screen_type( void );
26
27  /* support for the state of the dialog */
28  #define FOREGROUND_SELECT 0
29  #define BACKGROUND_SELECT 1
30  extern void set_selection_mode( int new_selection_mode );
31  extern int  get_selection_mode( void );
32
33  /* support for the one bit toggle */
34  #define NORMAL_TOGGLE        0
35  #define INVERSE_TOGGLE       1
36
37  #endif /* ifndef CSI_SM */
```

7.2.4 The color selection dialog, translation module

The translation module is the only part of the *color selection interface* which is aware that there are three different possible dialogs which may be presented to the user. Each of the dialogs is aware only of its own existence and, although the support module stores the dialog state information, it does not change its behaviour in response to this information.

The public aspects of the translation module are comprised of the four expected functions *create_color_selection_interface*, *destroy_color_selection_interface*, *activate_color_selection_interface* and *deactivate_color_selection_interface*. The creation function initializes the working foreground and background state variables of the support module and the foreground and background state variables of the application layer to the values of the *foreground* and *background* resources of the *parent* widget supplied to the creation function. It sets the support module *fore/ background state* variable to the foreground selection state and sets the support module *screen type* variable to a value which is determined by the value of the *depth* resource of the *parent* widget supplied.

Having initialized the state variables it then creates one of the color selection dialogs by calling the appropriate creation function, passing as parameters the appropriate private callback functions for its controls. Some of the callback functions passed are common to all dialogs, for example the

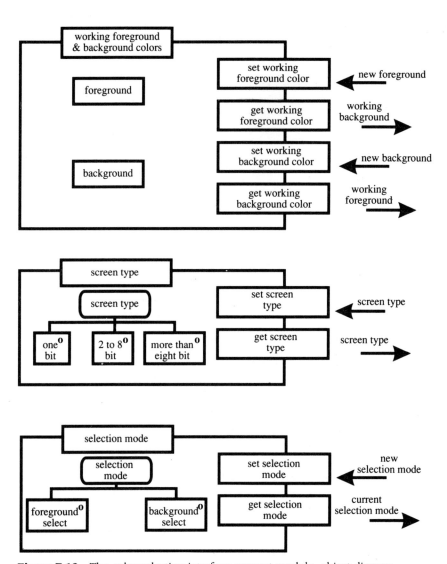

Figure 7.12   The color selection interface support module, object diagram.

apply_button_callback. Some are common to two of the dialogs, for example the *fore_back_option_select_callback* is used by both dialogs which use an option menu. Others are particular to the dialog, for example the *color_select_callback* passed to the *two to eight* bit dialog and the *color_select_callback* passed to the *more than eight bit* dialog differ. The prototype declarations of the private callback functions are given in Listing 7.7 and a section of the interface creation function is given in Listing 7.8.

\\\

Listing 7.7   The private declarations of the translation module

```
1   /* filename color select interface translation module   *
2    * code file (csi tm.c).                                 *
3    *                                                        *
4    * Written for Motif book Chapter 7, see text.           *
5    *                                                        *
6    * Fintan Culwin v1.0 Oct 92 revised Jan 94              *
7   */
8
9   #include "csi_tm.h"
10  #include "csi_2pm.h"
11  #include "csi_28pm.h"
12  #include "csi_8ppm.h"
13
14  #include "csi_sm.h"
15
16  /* private prototype declarations */
17
18  /* function to be installed as the 2 to 8 bit *
19   * color select callback                      */
20  static void color_button_press_callback( Widget widget,
21                                            XtPointer client_data,
22                                            XtPointer call_data);
23
24  /* function to be installed as the 8 plus bit *
25   * color select callback                      */
26  static void color_swathe_press_callback( Widget widget,
27                                           XtPointer client_data,
28                                           XtPointer call_data);
29
30  /* function to be installed as the 1 bit color select callback */
31  static void color_toggle_activate_callback( Widget widget,
32                                              XtPointer client_data,
33                                              XtPointer call_data);
34
35  /* function to be installed as the 2 to 8 &  *
36   * 8 plus bit fore/ back option callback      */
37  static void fore_back_option_select_callback( Widget widget,
38                                                XtPointer client_data,
39                                                XtPointer call_data);
40
41  /* function to be installed in all dialog's apply buttons */
42  static void apply_button_press_callback( Widget widget,
43                                           XtPointer client_data,
44                                           XtPointer call_data);
45
46  /* function to be installed in all dialog's close buttons */
47  static void close_button_press_callback( Widget widget,
48                                           XtPointer client_data,
49                                           XtPointer call_data);
```

Listing 7.8   Part of the color selection interface creation function

```
1   /* filename color select interface translation module    *
2    * code file (csi_tm.c).                                  *
3    * Written for Motif book Chapter 7                        *
4    * Fintan Culwin v1.O Oct 92 revised Jan 94               *
5    */
6   extern void  create_color_selection_interface(Widget parent){
7
8   Pixel         default_fg, default_bg,
9   unsigned int  depth;
10
11      /* omitted: get the value of foreground, background and    *
12       * depth resources of the parent widget using XtGetValues. */
13
14      /* initialize the support & application layers *
15       * with values obtained                       */
16      set_working_foreground_color( default_fg);
17      set_working_background_color( default_bg);
18      set_application_foreground_color( default_fg);
19      set_application_background_color( default_bg);
20
21      /* set the selection mode in the support layer */
22      set_selection_mode( FOREGROUND_SELECT );
23
24      /* set the dialog type in the support layer and *
25       * create the appropriate dialog.               */
26      if ( depth == 1) {
27         set_screen_type( ONE_BIT );
28         create_1_bit_color_selection_dialog(parent,
29                         apply_button_press_callback,
30                         close_button_press_callback);
31      } else {
32         if ( depth <= 8) {
33            set_screen_type( TWO_TO_EIGHT_BIT );
34            create_2_to_8_bit_color_selection_dialog(parent,
35                               color_button_press_callback,
36                               fore_back_option_select_callback,
37                               apply_button_press_callback,
38                               close_button_press_callback );
39         } else {
40            set_screen_type( MORE_THAN_EIGHT_BIT );
41            create_8plus_bit_color_selection_dialog(parent,
42                               color_swathe_press_callback,
43                               fore_back_option_select_callback,
44                               apply_button_press_callback,
45                               close_button_press_callback );
46         } /* end if */
47      } /* end if */
48   } /* end fun create_color_selection_interface */
```

The interface activation and deactivation functions are trivial. Each is implemented by retrieving the *screen type* value from the support module and calling the appropriate dialog activation or deactivation function. The color selection interface activation function is given in Listing 7.9. The deactivation and destruction functions of the color selection interface can be found in Appendix C.

Listing 7.9   The color selection interface activation function

```
 1  extern void activate_color_selection_interface( Widget widget,
 2                                                  XtPointer client_data,
 3                                                  XtPointer call_data ){
 4
 5  /* public callback function of the color selection interface    *
 6   * translation module. Used to activate the appropriate dialog  *
 7   * in the appropriate state.                                    */
 8
 9  int   screen_type;
10  int   current_selection_mode;
11  Pixel current_working_foreground, current_working_background;
12
13      /* obtain the current state from the support module */
14      screen_type             = get_screen_type();
15      current_selection_mode  = get_selection_mode();
16      current_working_foreground = get_working_foreground();
17      current_working_background = get_working_background();
18
19      switch ( screen_type ){
20
21        case ONE_BIT :
22           activate_1_bit_color_selection_dialog();
23           break;
24
25        case TWO_TO_EIGHT_BIT :
26           if ( current_selection_mode == FOREGROUND_SELECT ){
27              set_active_color_button( (int)current_working_foreground ,True );
28           } else {
29              set_active_color_button( (int)current_working_background ,True );
30           } /* end if */
31           activate_2_to_8_bit_color_selection_dialog();
32           break;
33
34        case MORE_THAN_EIGHT_BIT :
35           activate_8plus_color_selection_dialog();
36           break:
37      } /* end switch */
38  } /* end fun activate color selection interface */
```

The *apply_button_press_callback* private function is supplied from the translation module to all of the presentation components. The requirements of this function are to communicate the current working foreground and background values stored in the support module to the application layer. The effect of this, as will be explained later in this chapter, is to define the colors which will be used by other parts of the application. The implementation of the function is straightforward and is presented in Listing 7.10.

Listing 7.10   The apply_button_press_callback function

```
 1  static void apply_button_press_callback( Widget widget,
 2                                           XtPointer client_data,
 3                                           XtPointer call_data ){
 4
 5  /* function from color selection interface translation module   *
 6   * to be installed into all three color selection dialogs.       *
 7   * Implemented by transferring the values from the support       *
 8   * module to the application layer.                              *
 9   */
10
11  Pixel temp_foreground, temp_background;
12
13     /* get the values from the support module */
14     temp_foreground = get_working_foreground_color();
15     temp_background = get_working_background_color();
16
17     /* and send the values to the application layer */
18     set_application_foreground_color( temp_foreground );
19     set_application_background_color( temp_background );
20
21  } /* end fun apply button press callback */
```

The *color_selection_callback* supplied to each of the three dialogs differ. The actual *color_selection_callback* parameter passed to the *create_2_to_8_cs_dialog* function is called *color_button_press_callback* and is defined in the translations module. It implements the required behaviour by extracting the ordinal position of the button from the *client_data* parameter, casting it to a *Pixel* value, setting the value of the working foreground or background color in the support module depending on the current selection state and finally updating the color feedback area in the dialog. The implementation of the function is given in Listing 7.11.

Listing 7.11   The color_button_press_callback installed into the two to eight bit color selection dialog

```
 1  static void color_button_press_callback( Widget widget,
 2                                           XtPointer client_data,
 3                                           XtPointer call_data){
 4
 5  /* function from color selection interface translation module   *
 6   * to be installed into the two to eight bit color selection     *
 7   * dialog. The client_data parameter indicates the ordinal       *
 8   * position of the button which has been pressed.                *
 9   */
```

continued

\\

Listing 7.11 *continued*

```
10  Pixel active_pixel, new_pixel;
11
12      /* cast the ordinal button number to a Pixel value */
13      new_pixel = (Pixel) client_data;
14
15      /* change the appropriate value in the support module */
16      if ( get_selection_mode() == FOREGROUND_SELECT )  {
17         active_pixel = get_working_foreground_color();
18         set_working_foreground_color( new_pixel );
19      } else {
20         active_pixel = get_working_background_color();
21         set_working_background_color( new_pixel );
22      } /* end if */
23
24      /* change the appropriate values in the display component, *
25       * by switching current button off and new button on.      */
26      set_active_color_button( (int)active_pixel, False );
27      set_active_color_button( (int)new_pixel,    True );
28      update_2_to_8_color_feedback( get_working_foreground_color(),
29                                    get_working_background_color() );
30  } /* end fun color button press callback */
```

The *color_selection_callback* supplied to the *create_8plus_cs_dialog* is implemented in the translation module as *color_swathe_press_callback*. This function differs from the *color_button_press_callback* only in the manner by which it determines which color the user is indicating. It does this by extracting the *x* and *y* co-ordinate values of the mouse pointer when a *ButtonRelease* occurs, from the event structure passed as part of the *call_data* parameter. Once obtained, the co-ordinate values can be converted into the appropriate *Pixel* value. The remaining parts of the *color_swathe_press_callback function* are identical to the corresponding parts of the *color_button_press_callback*. The implementation of the function is given in Listing 7.12.

Listing 7.12   The color_swathe_press_callback function

```
 1  static void color_swathe_press_callback( Widget widget,
 2                                     XtPointer client_data,
 3                                     XtPointer call_data){
 4
 5  /* function from color selection interface translation module   *
 6   * to be installed into the more than eight bit color selection  *
 7   * dialog.                                                       *
 8   */
 9
10  Pixel          new_pixel;
11  XEvent       * event;
12  Position       mouse_x, mouse_y;
13  int    width;
```

continued

\\\

Listing 7.12 *continued*

```
14
15  XmDrawingAreaCallbackStruct * call_details;
16
17  Arg args[ MAX_ARGS ];
18  int num_args;
19
20     call_details = (XmDrawingAreaCallbackStruct *) call_data;
21     event = call_details->event;
22     /* only respond to button release events */
23     if ( event->xany.type == ButtonRelease){
24         mouse_x = event->xbutton.x;
25         mouse_y = event->xbutton.y;
26         num_args = 0;
27         XtSetArg( args[num_args], XmNwidth,
28                                  &width ); num_args++;
29         XtGetValues( widget, args, num_args );
30
31         /* each color cell is a 2 by 2 square, so convert *
32          * the button location to a Pixel value           */
33         new_pixel = (Pixel) (mouse_y * (width/2)) + (mouse_x/2);
34
35         /* pass the value to the support module and update *
36          * the feedback on the dialog.                     */
37         if ( get_selection_mode() == FOREGROUND_SELECT )  {
38             set_working_foreground_color( new_pixel );
39         } else {
40             set_working_background_color( new_pixel );
41         } /* end if */
42         update_8plus_color_feedback( get_working_foreground_color(),
43                                      get_working_background_color());
44     } /* end if */
45  } /* end fun color_swathe_press_callback */
```

The *color_selection_callback* passed to the *one bit* color selection dialog is called *color_toggle_activate_callback* and is significantly different from the other two *color_selection_callbacks*. It is attached to the *valueChanged* callback of the *toggleButtons* in the *radioBox*. Should the change in value indicate a change in the state of the interface, the callback implements its required behaviour by reversing the working foreground and background values in the support module.   The implementation of the function is given in Listing 7.13.

Listing 7.13   The color_toggle_activate_callback function

```
1  static void color_toggle_activate_callback( Widget widget,
2                                              XtPointer client_data,
3                                              XtPointer call_data){
4
5  /* function to be attached to the one bit toggle button's *
6   * activate callback. If toggle indicates a change,       *
```

continued

\\\

Listing 7.13 *continued*

```
7   * update the support module.                                    *
8  */
9
10  XmToggleButtonCallbackStruct * call_details;
11  Pixel                          old_foreground, old_background;
12
13     call_details = (XmToggleButtonCallbackStruct *) call_data;
14
15     /* only react if button is being turned on */
16     if ( call_details->set) {
17        /* if change of state is requested */
18        if ( /* normal requested, background set */
19             (( (int)client_data      == NORMAL_TOGGLE) &&
20                (get_selection_mode() == BACKGROUND_SELECT))
21            ||
22              /* or inverse requested, foreground set */
23              (((int) client_data     == INVERSE_TOGGLE) &&
24               (get_selection_mode() == FOREGROUND_SELECT))
25           ){
26           /* toggle the colors */
27           old_foreground = get_working_foreground_color();
28           old_background = get_working_background_color();
29           set_working_foreground_color( old_background );
30           set_working_background_color( old_foreground );
31
32           /* toggle the state */
33           if ( get_selection_mode() == BACKGROUND_SELECT ){
34              set_selection_mode( FOREGROUND_SELECT );
35           }else{
36              set_selection_mode( BACKGROUND_SELECT );
37           } /* end if */
38        } /* end if */
39     } /* end if */
40  } /* end fun  color_toggle_activate_callback */
```

7.2.5 The color selection interface, example application layer

Having described the color selection interface an example of its use will be given by attaching it to the *graphplot* application described in the previous chapter. As was mentioned above, the application layer encapsulates static foreground and background *Pixel* variables, and supplies suitable set and get value functions to manipulate them. The callback attached to the *apply* button in all color selection dialogs uses these set value functions to set the values of the application foreground and background colors to those stored in the color selection interface's support module.

For the color selection dialog to be effective in an application, all parts of the application which draw with the colors selected by the *color selection interface* must retrieve the colors from the application layer every time an *X library* drawing call is made. One way to accomplish this is for each drawing module to maintain its own private *graphics context*. The drawing module would then retrieve the foreground and background *Pixel* values from the application data layer and install them into its private *graphics context* prior to drawing.

There are two disadvantages with this mechanism, the first of which is that it will proliferate the number of graphic contexts created on the server. The resource capability of the server should be regarded as limited and thus needless proliferation of any resource should be avoided. The second disadvantage is that components of the *graphics context* other than colors may have to be set prior to it being used. If this mechanism is extended, then the drawing module will have to retrieve a number of resource values from the application layer and install them into its private *graphics context* before drawing. This will complicate the construction of the drawing module and increase the amount of traffic between the client and the server.

The alternative mechanism is to maintain a number of *graphics contexts* in the application layer and for the drawing module to retrieve the identity of the graphics context prior to its use. The functions which set color values in the application data layer will also have to change the values of the appropriate component of the relevant *graphics contexts*.

The *graphplot* main application module will have to be changed to comply with this mechanism. The encapsulated private global *graphics context* which was maintained within the module in the original version will have to be replaced with local *graphics context* pointer variables within each function. This *graphics context* pointer variable will have to be initialized to the identity of a *graphics context* variable maintained within the application layer using a get value function supplied by the application layer called *get_normal_graphics_context*.

The application layer will implement the *set_foreground_color* and *set_background_color* functions by setting the value of the encapsulated foreground and background *Pixel* variables, and by setting the foreground and background component values of an encapsulated graphics context variable called *normal_gc*. As implied by the name '*normal_gc*' a number of other *graphics contexts* may have to be maintained in the application data layer. For example an *inverse_gc* with inverted foreground and background colors may be required by some applications. The relationship between the *color_selection_interface*, the *application_main_module* and the appropriate parts of the *application layer* is illustrated in Figure 7.13.

As shown in the diagram, the communication of information from the *color_selection_interface* to the *application_main_module* takes place only via the *application layer*. This makes each module totally independent of each other. The *color_selection_interface* will be able to operate with any *application layer* which supports the protocol, allowing it to manipulate foreground and background values. The *application_main_module* is likewise unaware of the *color_selection_interface* and is able to operate with any *application layer* which supplies it with a normal *graphics context*.

Application main menu

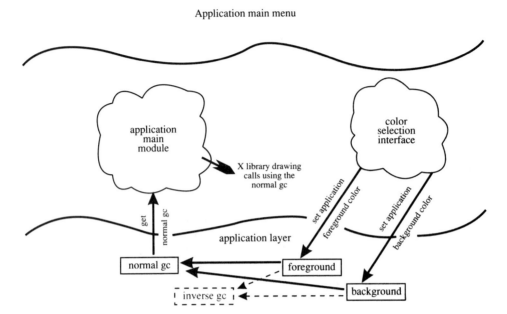

Figure 7.13   The relationship between the color selection interface, the application main module and the application layer.

7.3 The font selection and text entry interface

The use of alternative fonts was introduced in Chapters 1 and 3, where the use of font specifications and font list specifications in resource files was introduced. This section will continue consideration of the use of fonts, with the introduction of a reusable *font selection and text entry* interface, for brevity referred to as the *font and text* interface. As with the color selection interface introduced in the first part of this chapter, the integration of the interface with the *graphplot* application will be described.

The *font and text* interface will be used in the *graphplot* application to add a title to the graph, and to select the font which should be used to display it. Other applications may only have a requirement to select a font without having to input any text, consequently the interface is designed to allow reconfiguration during reuse to support this requirement.

The visual appearance of the font selection interface is shown in Figure 7.14. It consists of a *preview area* where the entered text can be previewed in the currently selected font. If the interface is being used only for font selection, or should the user not have entered any text into the text area, a default text is used in the preview area. The *text area* is where the user can enter the text which is to be displayed. This implementation separates the *text area* from the *preview* area in

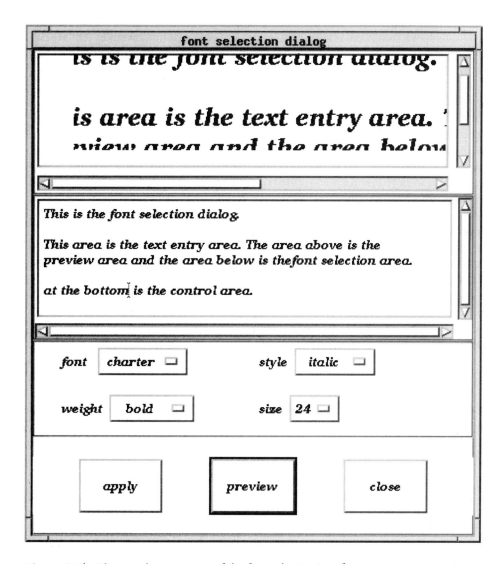

Figure 7.14 The visual appearance of the font selection interface.

order to facilitate the use of large, small or symbol fonts which would be inconvenient to edit in the text area. It is also separated to facilitate the reuse of the interface when text input is not required and to emphasize the distinction between *selecting* and *loading* a font, a distinction which will be made clear shortly.

The *font selection area* consists of four option menus allowing the *font, style, weight* and *point size* of the font to be selected. The *font* determines the overall shape and the *point size* determines the size of each character. The *weight* determines the boldness of the characters and the *style* determines the slant of each character. This sub-set of the available characteristics of fonts is appropriate for most applications. Should a particular application have a requirement to select fonts on the basis of other characteristics additional menus could be added to the four illustrated.

The final area contains the dialog's controls. The *apply* button will commit the currently selected font, if it is available, and the currently entered text to the application layer. It may also cause actions to be performed in the part of the application from which the interface was activated. In the *graphplot* application the *color selection interface* caused future drawing requests to change the colors used and thus had no immediate effect upon the application main area. The use of the *font selection and text entry interface* to select a font and enter a title for the graph should result in the graph being redrawn with the newly entered title when the *apply* button is activated. The mechanism by which this is effected will be explained when the construction of the interface is described.

The *preview* button will cause the currently entered text to be displayed in the preview area using the currently selected font. Should the user not have entered any text, or should the text entry component not be available to the user, a default text string is shown in the preview area. The *close* button closes the dialog after a check is made that the currently selected font is available and the user warned if it is not.

The selection of a set of font attributes does not guarantee that a suitable font is available to the server. Fonts are a server resource of type *Font* which are loaded into the server and shared between applications. A request to load a particular font into the server may fail because the font is not available to the server or because the server does not have sufficient resources available for the requested font. The activation of the *preview* button, or of the *apply* button, may result in an *information dialog* informing the user that the requested font is not available. The appearance of the *font not available* dialog is illustrated in Figure 7.15. The activation of the *close* button may result in an *alternative font possible* dialog warning the user that the currently selected font is not available and informing the user which font is currently available. This allows the user to deny or confirm the request to close the interface. The appearance of the *alternative font possible* dialog is illustrated in Figure 7.16.

As a change in any of the *option menus* may result in the selection of a font which is not available, the preview area will be cleared whenever a new option is selected. The usability design of the font selection interface is given in Figure 7.17. Figure 7.18 illustrates the appearance of the font option menu when the button labels are displayed using a standard font, and when they are displayed using an example of the font which they offer. It is clearly preferable to use example fonts, which can be easily accomplished using suitable *fontList* specifications in the resource file for the application.

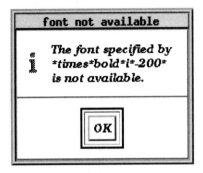

Figure 7.15 The font selection interface, font not available dialog.

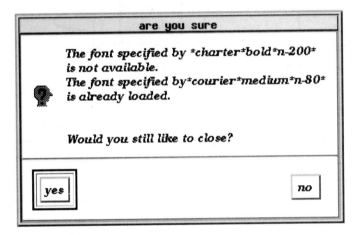

Figure 7.16 The font selection interface, close confirmation dialog.

7.3.1 The font selection interface, presentation module

The *font_and_text* interface presentation module is straightforward. It contains the three required dialogs, the *font and text* dialog, the *font not available* dialog and the *alternative font possible* dialog. Each of these dialogs has the expected *creation, destruction, activation* and *deactivation* functions exported from the module.

The *font and text* dialog creation function requires six callback functions to be supplied for installation as the dialog is created. Four of the callbacks will be installed into the option menus and two into the control buttons. Only the *apply* and *close* button require a callback from the translations; the callback attached to the *preview* button is private to the presentation module. The object diagram for

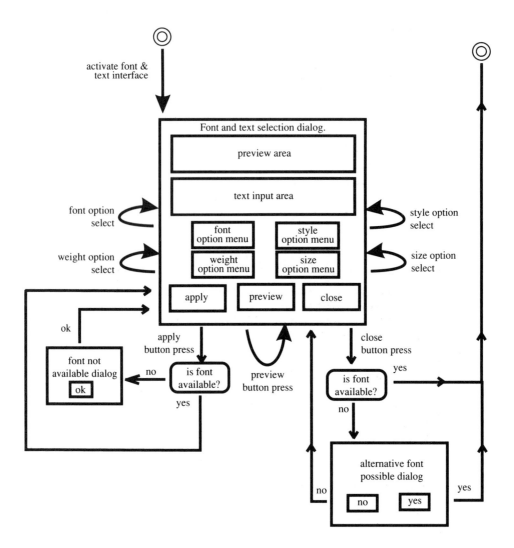

Figure 7.17   The font selection interface, usability design.

the *font and text* dialog is given in Figure 7.19 and the appropriate parts of the presentation module header file derived from it in Listing 7.14.

The implementation of the four standard functions contains no new concepts and can be located in Appendix C. The *show_preview_callback* function illustrates the techniques by which Motif programs can render strings onto the display using fonts specified within the program. The string entered into the text input area is rendered by these techniques into the preview area by this function. The preview area is implemented by *drawingArea,* a widget which, as explained in the last

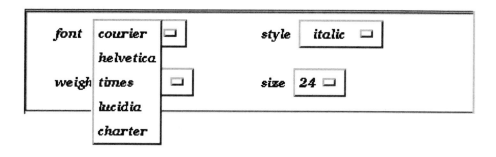

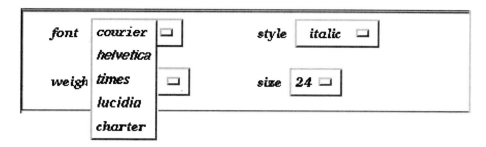

Figure 7.18   The alternative appearances of the fonts option menu.

chapter, has no *save under* capability. Consequently a static pixmap variable called *preview_pixmap* is maintained which will contain a copy of the image in the preview area, and will be used by the *preview area expose callback* to update the area when it is exposed. The construction of this function is identical to the expose callback function introduced in the last chapter. There is no requirement for a resize callback function to be attached to the *drawingArea,* as resizing of the window will have no effect upon the size of the rendered text.

Listing 7.14   The text and font selection dialog parts of the presentation module header file

```
1   /* filename font select interface color presentation   *
2    * module header file (fsi_pm.h).                       *
3    * Written for Motif book Chapter 7, see text.          *
4    * Fintan Culwin v1.0 Dec 92.                           *
5    */
6
7   #ifndef FSI_PM
8   #define  FSI_PM
9
10  /* inclusion of required Motif header files omitted */
```

continued

Listing 7.14 *continued*

```
11
12
13  extern void create_font_and_text_selection_dialog( Widget parent,
14                      XtCallbackProc  font_option_select_callback,
15                      XtCallbackProc  weight_option_select_callback,
16                      XtCallbackProc  style_option_select_callback,
17                      XtCallbackProc  size_option_select_callback,
18                      XtCallbackProc  apply_button_press_callback,
19                      XtCallbackProc  close_button_press_callback);
20  /* function to create the dialog installing the callback parameters *
21   * into the appropriate components of the dialog                    */
22
23  extern void   destroy_font_and_text_selection_dialog( void );
24
25  /* The parameter to the activation function is a pointer to a *
26   * callback function which will be indirectly called as part  *
27   * of the dialog's apply actions.                             */
28  extern void   activate_font_and_text_selection_dialog(
29                      XtCallbackProc * apply_action_callback );
30  extern void deactivate_font_and_text_selection_dialog( void );
31
32  char * get_current_text( void );
33  /* function to obtain the text from the text component of the dialog.*
34   * Returns a copy of the text which the calling environment is       *
35   * responsible for freeing.                                          */
36
37  /* creation, destruction, activation and deactivation prototypes  *
38   * for the font_not_available and the alternative_font_possible   *
39   * dialogs omitted.                                               */
40
41  #endif /* ifndef FSI_PM */
```

The first action of the *show_preview_callback* function is to call the support module enquiry function *is_font_available* and if not terminate after activating the *font_not_available* dialog. If the font is available, the font identity is retrieved from the support module using the *get_current_fid* function. To conclude the preparatory part of the function, any existing pixmap is destroyed with *XFreePixmap* and the text entered in the text area is obtained using *XmTextGetString*. Should the string obtained from the *text* widget be a null string, a default string is substituted.

The rendering of the string will require the asciiz string to be converted into an *XmString* and a font list of type *XmFontList* to be created. As was explained in Chapter 3, an *XmString* can contain a number of components, each of which can be rendered in a different font. The fonts are specified within the *XmString* using an arbitrary fontname, which is associated with an actual font contained within a *FontList* as the string is rendered. In this application only a single font is required, consequently an *XmFontList* containing a single font, which has been obtained

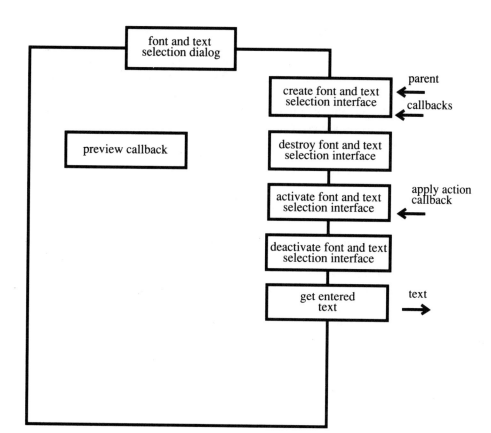

Figure 7.19   The font selection and text input dialog, object diagram.

from the support module, has to be created. The Motif function *XmFontListCreate* can be used to create a suitable *fontList*. The prototype of this function is:

```
XmFontList XmFontListCreate( XFontStruct * the_font_to_use,
                             char        * arbitrary_fontname );
```

A *font identity* identifies a font on the server but contains no details of the actual font; a *font structure* contains full information about the font. In general fonts should be manipulated using font identities and full font structures retrieved from the server only when they are required. A *font structure* can be obtained from the server by specifying the font identity using the library function *XQueryFont*, whose prototype is:

```
XFontStruct * XQueryFont( Display * display,
                          Font      font_identity );
```

This function will allocate space in the client for a font structure record, initialize it with details retrieved from the server and return a pointer to the structure. The

\\

application program which calls the function is responsible for destroying the structure using *XFreeFont*.

The arbitrary fontname used for a *fontList* which contains a single font can most conveniently be specified as XmDEFAULT_CHARSET, which can subsequently be used when the asciiz string is converted into an *XmString*, using *XmStringCreateLtoR*. Having prepared the *fontList* and the *XmString*, the size of the string when it is rendered can be determined using the *Motif* function *XmStringExtent*, whose prototype is:

```
void XmStringExtent ( XmFontList   font_list,
                      XmString     the_string,
                      Dimension * width,
                      Dimension * height );
```

This function will return in the *width* and *height* parameters the dimensions of the string when it is rendered, using the fonts in the *fontList* specified. Having obtained the size of the rendered string, the size of the *drawingArea* widget can be adjusted to contain it and the *preview pixmap* can be created with the required size. Using the default graphics context, the *drawingArea* and the *pixmap* can be cleared. Finally the string can be rendered using the *XmStringDrawImage* function. The prototype of this function is:

```
void XmStringDrawImage ( Display *       display,
                         Drawable        drawable,
                         XmFontList      font_list,
                         XmString        the_string,
                         GC              gc,
                         Position        x, y,
                         Dimension       width,
                         unsigned char alignment,
                         unsigned char layout_direction,
                         XRectangle      clip_area);
```

This function will render *the_string* using the *font_list* supplied with appropriate components of the *graphics context*, at the *x,y* co-ordinates on the *drawable*. The alignment parameter can take one of the values XmALIGNMENT_BEGINNING, XmALIGNMENT_CENTRE or XmALIGNMENT_END, which will align the string within the *width* given. The *layout_direction* can take one of the values XmSTRING_DIRECTION_L_TO_R or XmSTRING_DIRECTION_R_TO_L, controlling the direction in which the string will be laid out. The final parameter can be used to specify a clip rectangle, or can be specified as NULL if no clipping is required. Having imaged the string, the function can terminate after releasing any allocated resources. The implementation of the function *show_preview_callback* is given in Listing 7.15.

Listing 7.15 The show_preview_callback function

```
1   static void show_preview_callback( Widget  widget,
2                                       XtPointer  client_data;
3                                       XtPointer  call_data  ){
4
5   char           * the_text, * text_to_use, * the_font_name;
6   XmString       x_text_to_use;
7   char           default_text[] = "ABCDEFGHIJKLMNOPQRSTUVWXYZ\n"\
8                                    "abcdefghijklmnopqrstuvwxyz\n"\
9                                    "0123456789!£$%^&*()+-=@#?<>"\
10  int            is_font_available;
11  Font           the_font;
12  Dimension      text_width, text_height;
13  int            screen_depth;
14  GC             gc;
15  XFontStruct *  font_structure;
16  XmFontList     font_list;
17
18  Arg args[ MAX_ARGS ];
19  int num_args;
20
21      /* check to make sure the font is available and abend if not */
22      is_font_available = load_working_selection( widget );
23      if (!is_font_available) {
24          get_working_formatted_font_string( &the_font_name );
25          activate_font_not_available_info_dialog( the_font_name );
26          free( the_font_name);
27          return;
28      } /* end if */
29
30      the_font = get_current_fid();
31      /* destroy any existing pixmap */
32      if ( preview_pixmap != (Pixmap) NULL ){
33          XFreePixmap( XtDisplay(widget), preview_pixmap );
34          preview_pixmap = (Pixmap) NULL;
35      } /* end if */
36
37      /* decide upon the string to use */
38      the_text = XmTextGetString( fsi_text_area) ;
39      if (strlen( the_text ) != 0){
40          text_to_use = the_text;
41      }else{
42          text_to_use = default_text;
43      } /* end if */
44
45      /* make a font list */
46      font_structure = XQueryFont( XtDisplay( widget ),
47                                   the_font );
48      font_list = XmFontListCreate( font_structure,
49                                    XmSTRING_DEFAULT_CHARSET);
50      x_text_to_use = XmStringCreateLtoR( text_to_use,
51                                    XmSTRING_DEFAULT_CHARSET);
52
53      /* get the size of the imaged string */
```

continued

\\

Listing 7.15 *continued*

```
54    XmStringExtent( font_list,    x_text_to_use,
55                        &text_width, &text_height );
56
57    /* resize the drawing area to accommodate */
58    num_args = 0;
59    XtSetArg( args[num_args], XmNwidth,
60                              text_width); num_args++;
61    XtSetArg( args[num_args], XmNheight,
62                              text_height); num_args++;
63    XtSetValues( fsi_preview_area, args, num_args );
64
65    /* create the pixmap */
66    num_args = 0;
67    XtSetArg( args[num_args], XmNdepth,
68                              &screen_depth); num_args++;
69    XtGetValues( fsi_preview_area, args, num_args );
70    preview_pixmap = XCreatePixmap( XtDisplay( widget),
71                                    XtWindow( widget),
72                                    text_width, text_height,
73                                    screen_depth );
74
75    /* prepare the gc */
76    gc = DefaultGC( XtDisplay( widget),
77                    DefaultScreen( XtDisplay( widget)));
78    XSetBackground( XtDisplay( widget), gc,
79                    WhitePixel( XtDisplay( widget),
80                    DefaultScreen( XtDisplay( widget))));
81    XSetForeground( XtDisplay( widget), gc,
82                    WhitePixel( XtDisplay( widget),
83                    DefaultScreen( XtDisplay( widget))));
84
85    /* clear the window & pixmap */
86    XFillRectangle( XtDisplay( widget),
87                    XtWindow( fsi_preview_area),
88                    gc, 0, 0, text_width, text_height );
89    XFillRectangle( XtDisplay( widget),
90                    preview_pixmap,
91                    gc, 0, 0, text_width, text_height );
92
93    /* finally draw the string! */
94    XSetForeground( XtDisplay( widget), gc,
95                    BlackPixel( XtDisplay( widget),
96                    DefaultScreen( XtDisplay( widget))));
97
98    XmStringDrawImage( XtDisplay( widget),
99                       preview_pixmap,
100                      font_list, x_text_to_use,
101                      gc, 0, 0, text_width,
102                      XmALIGNMENT_BEGINNING,
103                      XmSTRING_DIRECTION_L_TO_R,
104                      (XRectangle *) NULL );
105   XmStringDrawImage( XtDisplay( widget),
106                      XtWindow( fsi_preview_area),
```

continued

Listing 7.15 *continued*

```
107                         font_list, x_text_to_use,
108                         gc, 0, 0, text_width,
109                         XmALIGNMENT_BEGINNING,
110                         XmSTRING_DIRECTION_L_TO_R,
111                         (XRectangle *) NULL );
112      /* and release resources */
113      XtFree( the_text );
114      XFreeFont( XtDisplay( widget), font_structure );
115      XmStringFree( x_text_to_use );
116      XmFontListFree( font_list );
117  } /* end fun show_preview */
```

The *font and text* dialog part of the presentation module contains a related private callback function called *clear_preview_area_callback*. This function is attached to the *activate* callback resource of all option menu *pushButtons* in order to clear the preview area whenever the requested font is changed. The implementation of this function is trivial; details can be located in Appendix C.

The remaining components of the presentation module, the *font not available* dialog and the *alternative font possible* dialog, are both based upon *messageBox* widgets. Their construction is very similar to the *messageBox* based dialogs introduced in Chapter 5 and will not be explained further here.

7.3.2 The font selection interface, support module

The object diagram for the support module is given in Figure 7.20. It contains the working *family*, *size*, *weight* and *style* values and a set value function for each of them; formatted versions of the working and loaded font, with a get value function for each of them; and an encapsulated font identity variable of type *Font* with a function to retrieve its value.

The module also provides a function to attempt to load the current working font returning true or false as appropriate. This is the only function of the module which deserves any further explanation. The *X library* supplies a function called *XLoadQueryFont* which requests the server to return the font structure of the specified font, loading it into the server if it is not already loaded. The prototype of *XLoadQueryFont* is:

```
XFontStruct * XLoadQueryFont( Display * display,
                             char    * font_name);
```

The *font_name* parameter is a font specification string identical in format to the font specification string used in resource files. The function will return details of the font if it is available or NULL if it is not available. The returned structure contains a large number of fields giving details of the font; the only one required by this module is the font identity which is contained in a field called *fid*.

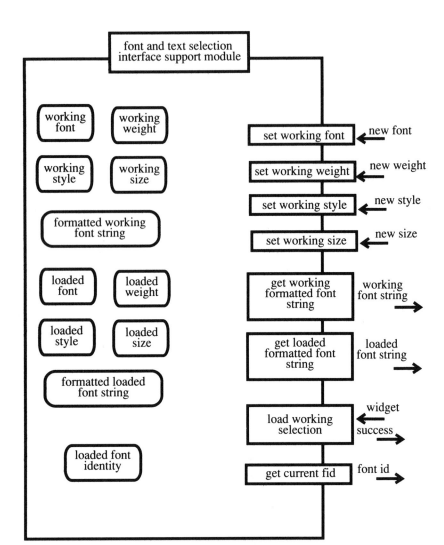

Figure 7.20   The font selection interface support module, object diagram.

The *load_current_font* function is thus implemented by transforming the *working font*, *style*, *weight* and *size* values into a formatted string, and attempting to load the specified font. If the font is available the *loaded font*, *style*, *weight* and *size* values are updated and the font identity contained in the *XFontStruct* is stored in the encapsulated *Font* variable. The transformation of a set of *font*, *style*, *weight* and *size* values into a formatted string is accomplished by the public function *get_working_formatted_font_string*. Before the function terminates, the resources used by the font structure, allocated by *XLoadQueryFont*, are released using the

XFreeFont library function. The implementation of the *load_working_selection* function is given in Listing 7.16.

The remaining aspects of the support module are implemented using encapsulated string variables and do not contribute anything further to the understanding of Motif concepts. The complete code of the module can be found in Appendix C.

Listing 7.16   The load_working_selection function

```
 1   /* the encapsulated font identity variable */
 2   static Font loaded_font_id = (Font) NULL;
 3
 4   extern int  load_working_selection( Widget any_widget ){
 5
 6   char         * the_working_font;
 7   int            font_is_available;
 8   XFontStruct  * font_structure;
 9
10      /* attempt to load the font */
11      get_working_formatted_font_string( &the_working_font );
12      font_structure = XLoadQueryFont( XtDisplay( any_widget ),
13                                        the_working_font );
14      free( the_working_font );
15
16      /* update the loaded vars and the font identity *
17       * if the font is available                     */
18      font_is_available = ( font_structure != (XFontStruct *) NULL);
19      if ( font_is_available ){
20          loaded_font_id = font_structure->fid;
21          strcpy( loaded_font, working_font );
22          strcpy( loaded_weight, working_weight );
23          strcpy( loaded_style, working_style );
24          strcpy( loaded_size, working_size );
25          XFontFree( XtDisplay( any_widget ), font_structure);
26      } /* end if */
27
28      return font_is_available;
29   } /* end fun load_working_selection */
30
```

7.3.3 The font selection interface, translation module

The translation module implements the six callback functions which are installed into the *text and font* dialog. The first four of these which are to be attached to the *pushButtons* within the option menus are straightforward. During their installation the *client data* parameter of each callback is set to a string value which will be used within the support module to produce a part of the formatted font specification string. The purpose of the callback function is therefore to extract the string from the *client data* parameter and pass it onto the support module, where it will update the appropriate working value.

The option callback function is not the only callback function attached to the option menu *pushButton*s. As explained above a private callback of the presentation module called *clear_preview_area_callback* is also attached in order to clear any invalid representation when the requested font option is changed.

One final point to note here is that during the construction of the option menus within the creation of the *font and text* dialog, the state of the support module is set to reflect the initial settings of each menu. This is accomplished by direct calls of the set working value functions, from the presentation module to the support module, passing the default values of the menu.

The *close_button_press_callback* will ensure that the current working font is available by calling the support module *load_working_selection* function. If the font is available the *font and text* dialog is deactivated, causing the interface to terminate. If the font is not available the *alternative font possible* dialog is activated passing it the current values of the working and loaded formatted font strings. This dialog has two translation module callback functions installed into it as it is created. The callback attached to the *yes* button, indicating that the interface should terminate, deactivates the *alternative font possible* dialog and the *font and text* dialog causing the interface to terminate. The callback attached to the *no* button, indicating that the interface should not terminate, only deactivates the *alternative font possible* dialog.

Finally the callback attached to the *font and text* dialog's *apply* button also checks to ensure that the current working font is available and if it isn't it activates the *font not available* dialog, passing the formatted working font string. If the font is available, the function has two operations to perform. The first of these is straightforward; the current font identity, which can be obtained from the support module, and the current entered text, which can be obtained from the presentation module, have to be communicated to the *application layer*. This is conceptually comparable to the committing of the *foreground* and *background* *pixel* values to the *application layer* from the *color selection dialog*, which was discussed in detail earlier in this chapter.

The second action of the *apply* button callback is a little more difficult. The selection of colors with the *color selection* interface specified the colors which were to be used for future drawing requests but had no effect upon the current state of the application. However the entering of text and selection of a font may have to have an immediate effect upon the application. For example, when the interface is attached to the *graphplot* application allowing a title for the graph to be entered, pressing the *apply* button should cause the graph to be redrawn showing the newly entered title. To accomplish this the activation function of the interface requires an *apply_action_callback* function parameter to be supplied. The interface will call this function during the *apply_button_callback,* causing the requisite actions to be performed. Should the interface be being used where there is no requirement to immediately perform actions when the *apply* button is pressed, a dummy callback function with a null body can be passed; execution of this dummy function will have no effect upon the application.

The callback function to be used during the *apply* transition is passed as a parameter of the interface activate function, not as a parameter of the interface creation function, as the required behaviour may change during operation of the application. For example in the *graphplot* application the interface is currently used to install a title for the graph. In an extended version of the application it may also be used to provide titles for the axes. By supplying the required behaviour as the interface is activated, not when it is created, the interface can be configured to install a graph title, axes titles, or any other annotations which may be required.

7.3.4 The font selection dialog, example application layer

As discussed above, when the *text and font selection interface* is installed into the *graphplot* application, pressing the apply button in the *text and font* dialog should cause the *application main area* to redraw itself, with the newly entered title displayed at the top of the graph. This can be accomplished by passing the *application main area*'s publicly available *redraw graph callback* function to the *text and font* interface's creation function, where it will be installed into the *apply* button's callback. This will cause the graph to redraw itself at the appropriate point, but changes will have to be made to the *graphplot application main module* to make it aware of the existence of the title.

The *points graph* functions, introduced in Chapter 6, assumed that the entire *drawingArea* was available for drawing the graph. If a title is introduced into the graph, then a region of the *drawingArea* at the top of the window has to be reserved for the title. The width of this region is always equal to the width of the window, but the height of the region will vary depending upon the text and font selected. To support this requirement an encapsulated variable called *title_height* will have to be introduced into the *points_graph* component. If this is given a default value of zero, it will have no effect upon the normal operation of the *points_graph* until a title is entered.

The redrawing of the *points_graph* commences with a call to a private function called *draw_axes*, which is an appropriate place to render the title onto the graph. Following the clearing of the *drawingArea*, the application layer get value functions are used to retrieve the *title text* and the *current font*. The creation function of the *text and font selection interface* would have set these two encapsulated variables to null, and the *apply* callback of the *text and font selection dialog* may subsequently have changed their values. Should they have non-null values, the *draw_axes* function can render the graph's title onto the top of the *drawingArea*, setting the value of the encapsulated variable *title_height* to the height of the rendered text using the *height* value returned from *XmStringExtent*.

The remaining parts of the *draw_axes* function will have to take into account the rendering of the title text. The usable height of the graph is now not the height of the window but the height of the window minus the value of the *title_height* variable. The other functions which also rely upon the size of the window for their operation, the *mouse_click_callback* and the *plot_point* function, will require a similar amendment.

7.4 Activities for Chapter 7

1. An alternative color selection interface can be constructed using the contents of the rgb ascii text database. This is contained within the X11 environment as a file called *rgb.txt*. A color selection interface could read this file to determine the list of colornames to be offered to the user in a *list* widget. When the user selects an entry from the list the interface could translate the ascii color name into a Pixel value using the appropriate function. Implement this alternative interface.
2. Extend the font selection part of the *font and text* dialog, by adding additional option menus to extend the characteristics by which a font can be selected.
3. Extend the *two to eight bit color selection* interface by adding a contained interface within the color selection dialog, which allows the user to manipulate the red, green and blue color components of a read–write color cell using three sliders.
4. Extend the *graphplot* application to add titles to the axes of the graph. Implement the required changes to the *font selection and text entry interface* allowing the user to enter the required changes.

\\

Other X/Motif resources

Case study

Unfortunately it is not possible to include details of a realistic application in this book as it would probably add another two or three chapters. There are two major considerations, *cut/ copy/ paste* and *undo/ redo,* which a realistic application would be expected to provide which consequently have had to be omitted. A case study of a realistic sized application called *yaged* (*yet another graphics editor*) has been prepared and is available from the author. Please contact:

fintan@uk.ac.sbu.vax

for further details. The case study illustrates how the techniques introduced in this book can be applied to produce a complete application, introduces further details of the Xlibrary drawing primitives and introduces the design rationales for reusable *cut/ copy/ paste* and *undo/ redo* modules.

Books

The definitive guides to Motif are the official OSF/Motif series published by Prentice Hall:

OSF/Motif User's Guide Release 1.2	ISBN 0-13-643131-3
OSF/Motif Style Guide Release 1.2	ISBN 0-13-640616-5
OSF/Motif Programmer's Guide Release 1.2	ISBN 0-13-643107-0
OSF/Motif Programmer's Reference Release 1.2	ISBN 0-13-643115-1

The definitive guides to the Xlibrary and intrinsics are published by O'Reilly:

Volume 0 *X Protocol Reference Manual*, Third Edition
Adrian Nye, 1992   ISBN 1-56592-008-2

Volume 1 *Xlib Programming Manual*, Third Edition
Adrian Nye, 1992   ISBN 1-56592-002-3

Volume 2 *Xlib Reference Manual*, Third Edition
Valerie Quercia and Tim O'Reilly, 1992   ISBN 1-56592-006-6

Volume 3 *X Window System User's Guide*, Motif Edition
Adrian Nye and Tim O'Reilly, 1991   ISBN 0-937175-61-7

Volume 4 *X Toolkit Intrinsics Programming Manual*, Motif Edition
David Flanagan, 1992   ISBN 1-56592-013-9

\\

Volume 5	*X Toolkit Intrinsics Reference Manual*, Third Edition Dan Heller, 1992	ISBN 1-56592-007-4
Volume 6	*Motif Programming Manual* Dan Heller, 1991	ISBN 0-937175-70-6
Volume 7	*XView Programming Manual*, Third Edition Dan Heller, 1991	ISBN 0-937175-87-0
Volume 8	*X Window System Administrator's Guide* Ellie Cutler, Daniel Gilly and Tim O'Reilly, 1992	ISBN 0-937175-83-8
	The X Window System in a Nutshell David Flanagan, 1992	ISBN 1-56592-017-1
	Programmer's Supplement for R5 of the X Window System Tom Gaskins, 1991	ISBN 0-937175-86-2
	PHIGS Programming Manual, 3D Programming in X Linda Kosko, 1992	ISBN 0-937175-85-4

There are many other books published on X and Motif. My favourite three are:

Xlibrary	*Introduction to the X Window System*, seventh printing Oliver Jones, Prentice Hall, 1989	ISBN 0-13-499997-5
Intrinsics	*X Window System: Programming and Applications with Xt* Douglas Young, Prentice Hall, 1989	ISBN 0-13-972167-3
Motif	*Visual Design With OSF/Motif* Shiz Kobara, Addison Wesley, 1991	ISBN 0-201-56320-7

This is the book on Motif visual design referred to in Chapter 3.

Software

The X Window system, including the Motif toolkit, is now considered standard system software by most Unix vendors and as such is supplied as part of the system software.

For 486 based personal computers a free of charge Unix-like system called Linux is available. The easiest way of obtaining a copy of Linux is to purchase an installation, which includes the X Library and intrinsics from:

> Softlanding Software (SLS)
> 910 Lodge Avenue,
> Victoria,
> B.C. V8X 3A8
> Canada

The cost at the time of writing is $99 (U.S.) for a 30 disc (or CD rom or QIC tape) distribution. Alternatively the distribution can be obtained over the internet, free of charge, from *tsx-11.mit.edu* or *nic.funet.fi*.

Unfortunately the Motif toolkit is not available free of charge. SLS can supply a Motif toolkit for Linux at a cost of $400 (U.S.). The cheapest Linux Motif distribution which I am aware of costs $150 (U.S.) and is available from:

> Soft*Star s.r.l.
> Via Camburzano 9
> 10143 Torino
> Italy

Addendum to Appendix A

Books on C, Unix and OOP

There are a large number of books published on C, many of which are of a dubious quality. My recommendation for an introductory book suitable for experienced programmers is:

> *The Joy of C*
> Miller & Quilici
> Wiley 1993 0 471 59967 0

Likewise there are many books concerned with introducing Unix, my favourite is:

> *The Waite Group's Unix Primer Plus*
> Waite, Martin & Prata
> Sams 1990 0 672 22729 0

There are also an increasing number of books concerned with object oriented programming. The most authoritative which describes the notation used in this book is:

> *Object Oriented Analysis and Design with Applications*
> Grady Booch
> Addison Wesley 0 805 35340 2

\\

X/Motif reference material

This appendix contains reference information for X/Motif. Although this collection only represents a very small fraction of the facilities available, it is sufficient for the construction of moderately complex clients, as introduced in this book. The appendix is divided into seven parts:

B1   An explanation of X fontnames.
B2   A selection of colornames.
B3   A selection of standard cursors.
B4   A selection of standard bitmaps.
B5   A selection of X library resources.
B6   A selection of intrinsic resources.
B7   A selection of Motif resources.

B1   An explanation of X fontnames

A font can be specified using a full fontname, for example:

```
-adobe-helvetica-medium-r-normal--10-100-75-75-p-56-iso8859-1
```

A full fontname consists of the following fields:

foundry	the supplier of the font	eg	*adobe*
family	the style of the font	eg	*helvetica*
weight	intensity medium or bold	eg	*medium*
slant	roman (upright), italic or oblique	eg	*r*(oman)
set width	proportionate width	eg	*normal*
pixels	size in pixels	eg	*10*
points	size in tenths of a point	eg	*100*
horizontal	resolution in dpi	eg	*75*
vertical	resolution in dpi	eg	*75*
spacing	mono, proportional or fixed	eg	*p*(roportional)
average	width in tenths of a pixel	eg	*56*
character set		eg	*iso8859-1*

A font can also be specified by using a wildcarded font specification, where parts of the full fontname are replaced with an asterisk '*'. The X server will search the list of available fontnames and select the one which first matches the wildcarded specification.

Figure B1   A selection of the standard cursors.

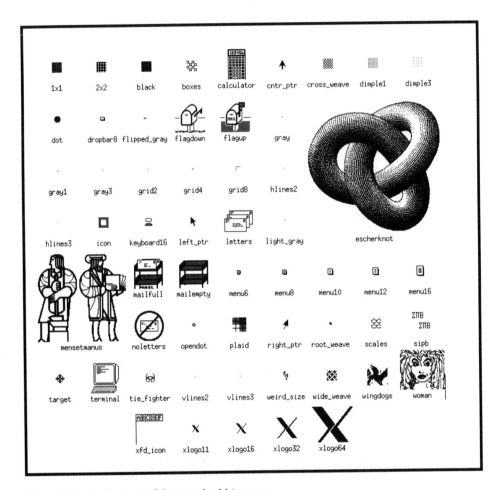

Figure B2   A selection of the standard bitmaps.

In addition it is also possible to use font aliases, such as *'fixed'*, which are predefined to match a particular font. The standard client *xlsfonts* can be used to obtain a list of all the fontnames which will be recognized by the server; the predefined aliases will appear at the end of the resulting list.

When a wildcarded fontname is being specified on the command line it should be enclosed in quotes as the asterisk may be interpreted by the command processor.

B2   A selection of colornames

The *X Window system* allows colors to be specified from the command line, and with certain functions, using ascii text colornames. This section gives an illustrative list of the colornames available. The complete list can normally be located on Unix systems in the file /usr/lib/X11/rgb.txt.

snow	royal blue	tan
ghost white	blue	chocolate
white smoke	sky blue	firebrick
floral white	steel blue	brown
old lace	powder blue	salmon
linen	pale turquoise	orange
antique white	dark turquoise	dark orange
blanched almond	turquoise	coral
navajo white	cyan	light coral
cornsilk	light cyan	tomato
ivory	aquamarine	orange red
seashell	dark green	red
mint cream	sea green	hot pink
azure	pale green	pink
alice blue	spring green	light pink
lavender	lawn green	pale violet red
misty rose	green	violet red
white	chartreuse	magenta
black	green yellow	violet
dark slate gray	yellow green	plum
dim gray	forest green	orchid
slate gray	olive drab	dark violet
light slate gray	khaki	blue violet
gray	light yellow	purple
grey	yellow	
light grey	gold	gray0
midnight blue	rosy brown	
navy	indian red	gray100
cornflower blue	saddle brown	
dark slate blue	sienna	grey0
slate blue	wheat	
medium blue	sandy brown	grey100

B3 A selection of standard cursors

The standard cursors are illustrated in Figure B1. Each cursor can be identified using a name from the list below. The functions by which the default cursor can be changed to one of the standard cursors, XCreateFontCursor and XDefineCursor, are described in Section B5. Some clients allow the cursor to be specified in resource files, for example to change the cursor used in the xterm client to the *gumby* cursor the following line can be included in a suitable resource file:

```
XTerm*pointerShape:    gumby
```

For details of which clients will allow their cursors to be changed the *man* page for the client should be consulted.

\\\

X_cursor	fleur	sailboat
arrow	gobbler	sb_down_arrow
based_arrow_down	gumby	sb_h_double_arrow
based_arrow_up	hand1	sb_left_arrow
boat	hand2	sb_right_arrow
bogosity	heart	sb_up_arrow
bottom_left_corner	icon	sb_v_double_arrow
bottom_right_corner	iron_cross	shuttle
bottom_side	left_ptr	sizing
bottom_tee	left_side	spider
box_spiral	left_tee	spraycan
center_ptr	leftbutton	star
circle	ll_angle	target
clock	lr_angle	tcross
coffee_mug	man	top_left_arrow
cross	middlebutton	top_left_corner
cross_reverse	mouse	top_right_corner
crosshair	pencil	top_side
diamond_cross	pirate	top_tee
dot	plus	trek
dotbox	question_arrow	ul_angle
double_arrow	right_ptr	umbrella
draft_large	right_side	ur_angle
draft_small	right_tee	watch
draped_box	rightbutton	xterm
exchange	rtl_logo	

B4 A selection of standard bitmaps

The standard bitmaps are illustrated in Figure B2. The techniques by which a bitmap can be specified as a background bitmap for a client are described in Chapter 3. All clients allow the background bitmap for all or part of the client to be specified in resource files; for example, to change the background used in the graphplot client to the *scales* bitmap the following line can be included in a suitable resource file:

```
Graphplot*backgroundPixmap:   scales
```

B5 A selection of X library resources

BlackPixel

```
Pixel BlackPixel(Display * display,
                 int      screen_number);
```
BlackPixel is a macro, not a function. It returns the Pixel value for black on the screen specified.

\\\

DefaultColormap

```
Colormap DefaultColormap(Display * display,
                         int        screen_number);
```

DefaultColormap is a macro, not a function. It returns the default Colormap for the screen specified.

DefaultDepth

```
int DefaultDepth(Display * display,
                 int        screen_number);
```

DefaultDepth is a macro, not a function. It returns the default depth of the specified screen.

DefaultGC

```
GC  DefaultGC(Display * display,
              int        screen_number);
```

DefaultGC is a macro, not a function. It returns the default graphics context of the specified screen.

DefaultScreen

```
int DefaultScreen(Display * display);
```

DefaultScreen is a macro, not a function. It returns the screen number (not the screen pointer) of the default screen of the specified display.

DefaultScreenOfDisplay

```
screen_ptr DefaultScreenOfDisplay(Display * display);
```

DefaultScreenOfDisplay is a macro, not a function. It returns the screen pointer (not the screen number) of the default screen of the specified display.

DefaultRootWindow

```
Window DefaultRootWindow(Display * display);
```

DefaultRootWindow is a macro, not a function. It returns the identity of the root window of the server's default screen.

DisplayCells

```
unsigned int DisplayCells(Display * display,
                          int        screen_number);
```

DisplayCells is a macro, not a function. It returns the maximum number of colormap cells on the specified screen. This should not be relied upon; the depth resource of a widget should be used in preference.

\\

RootWindowOfScreen

```
Window RootWindowOfScreen(Screen * screen);
```

RootWindowOfScreen is a macro, not a function. It returns the identity of the root window of the screen specified.

WhitePixel

```
Pixel WhitePixel(Display * display,
                 int       screen_number);
```

WhitePixel is a macro, not a function. It returns the Pixel value for white on the screen specified.

XAllocColor

```
Status XAllocColor(Display  * display,
                   Colormap   colormap,
                   XColor   * colorcell_definition);
```

Request to allocate a shareable colorcell. The definition contains the requested rgb values before the call, and the allocated pixel value and actual rgb values upon return. The requested and allocated values may not be identical. The function returns 0 if no allocation could be made and 1 otherwise.

XAllocColorCells

```
Status XAllocColorCells(Display  * display,
                        Colormap   colormap,
                        Boolean    contiguous,
              unsigned long        plane_mask[num_planes],
              unsigned int         num_planes,
              unsigned long        pixels[num_colors],
              unsigned int         num_colors);
```

Request to allocate a number of private colorcells. The function returns 0 if no allocation could be made and 1 otherwise.

XAllocColorPlanes

```
Status XAllocColorPlanes(Display  * display,
                         Colormap   colormap,
                         Boolean    contiguous,
               unsigned long        pixels[num_colors],
               int                  num_colors,
               int                  num-reds,
                                    num_greens,
                                    num_blues,
               unsigned long      * red_mask,
                                  * green_mask,
                                  * blue_mask)
```

Request to allocate a number of private colorcells. The function returns 0 if no allocation could be made and 1 otherwise.

XAllocNamedColor

```
Status XAllocNamedColor(Display  * display,
                        Colormap   colormap,
                        char      * color_name,
                        XColor    * colorcell_definition,
                        XColor    * colorcell_requested);
```

Request to allocate a shareable colorcell by name. The color_name identifies the ascii name of the requested color. colorcell_definition contains the rgb values of the allocated cell and colorcell_definition the rgb values from the colorname database. The function returns 1 if the colorname exists in the database and 0 otherwise.

XBell

```
void XBell(Display * display,
           int        loudness);
```

Causes the terminal to bleep. Display identifies which terminal and loudness, in the range 0 to 100, determines how loud.

XChangeGC

```
void XChangeGC(Display       * display,
               GC              gc,
               unsigned long  ·valuemask,
               XGCValues     * values);
```

Changes the values of the components of the graphics context specified by the valuemask to the values contained within the values structure.

XCopyArea

```
void XCopyArea(Display      * display,
               Drawable       source, destination,
               GC             gc,
               int            sourceX, sourceY,
               unsigned int   width, height,
               int            destinationX, destinationY);
```

Copies the area specified from the source drawable to the destination drawable, placing it at the position specified, using the gc specified. Both drawables must have the same depth and be children of the same root window.

XCopyColormapAndFree

```
Colormap XCopyColormapAndFree(Display  * display,
                              Colormap   old_colormap);
```

\\

Creates a new virtual colormap, copying and releasing all private colorcell definitions from the old colormap.

XCopyGC

```
void XCopyGC(Display      * display,
             GC             source,
             unsigned long  valuemask,
             GC             destination);
```

Copies the values of the components of the source graphics context specified by the valuemask to the destination graphics context. To copy all components specify 0XLFFFF for the valuemask.

XCreateColormap

```
Colormap XCreateColormap(Display * display,
                         Window    window,
                         Visual  * visual,
                         int       alloc);
```

Creates a new virtual colormap, suitable for the screen upon which the specified window exists and for the visual specified. alloc can be either of the manifest values AllocNone or AllocAll.

XCreateFontCursor

```
Cursor XCreateFontCursor(Display      * display,
                         unsigned int   shape);
```

Creates a cursor from a set of pre-defined cursor shapes. For details of the possible shapes and their names see Appendix B3.

XCreateGC

```
void XCreateGC(Display       * display,
               Drawable        drawable,
               unsigned long   valuemask,
               XGCValues     * values);
```

Creates a GC suitable for use on the screen associated with the drawable, setting the components to the default values, or to the values in the values structure if the appropriate bit is set in the valuemask.

XCreatePixmap

```
Pixmap XCreatePixmap(Display      * display,
                     Drawable       drawable,
                     unsigned int   width,
                     unsigned int   height,
                     unsigned int   depth);
```

Creates and returns a Pixmap with the size and depth specified, suitable for use on the display specified and on the screen associated with the drawable.

XCreatePixmapCursor

```
Cursor XCreatePixmapCursor(Display      * display,
                           Pixmap         shape,
                           Pixmap         mask,
                           XColor       * foreground,
                           XColor       * background,
                           unsigned int   x_hot,
                           unsigned int   y_hot );
```

Creates a cursor from the shape given, with the colors and hotspots as specified; the Pixmaps must have a depth of 1. The shape defines the shape of the cursor and the mask the area around, or inside, the cursor which will be shown on the screen. In general the mask shape should extend the cursor shape by a single pixel.

XCreatePixmapFromBitmapData

```
Pixmap XCreatePixmapFromBitmapData(Display   * display,
                                   Drawable    drawable,
                                   char      * bitmap_data,
                                   int         width,
                                   int         height,
                                   Pixel       foreground,
                                   Pixel       background,
                                   int         depth); .
```

Creates and returns a Pixmap composed of the bitmap data, possibly obtained from the bitmap client. Display identifies the server, drawable any drawable on the server (use the root window), bitmap_data, width and height are obtained from the bitmap header file, foreground and background can be obtained from the BlackPixel and WhitePixel macros, depth can use the DefaultDepth macro.

XDefineCursor

```
void XDefineCursor(Display * display,
                   Window    window,
                   Cursor    cursor);
```

Installs the cursor supplied as the window's cursor. If XDefineCursor is not called the window inherits its cursor from its parent.

XDestroyImage

```
int XDestroyImage(XImage * image);
```

Releases the client resources used by the XImage.

\\

XDrawArc

```
void XDrawArc(Display      * display,
              Drawable       drawable,
              GC             gc,
              int            start_x, start_y,
              unsigned int   width, height,
              int            start_angle, end_angle );
```

Draws an arc on the drawable (window or pixmap), within a rectangle delineated by start_x, start_y, width and height, using the graphics context supplied. Angles are expressed in 64ths of a degree, with the 3 o'clock direction as an arbitrary zero. A full circle is 23040 64ths of a degree.

XDrawLine

```
void XDrawLine(Display   * display,
              Drawable     drawable,
              GC           gc,
              int          startX, startY,
              int          endX,   endY );
```

Draws a line on the drawable (window or pixmap), between the co-ordinates specified, using the graphics context supplied.

XDrawPoint

```
void XDrawPoint(Display   * display,
               Drawable     drawable,
               GC           gc,
               int          x, y);
```

Draws a single point on the drawable (window or pixmap) at the co-ordinates specified, using the graphics context supplied.

XDrawRectangle

```
void XDrawRectangle(Display      * display,
                    Drawable       drawable,
                    GC             gc,
                    int            topLeftX, topLeftY,
                    unsigned int   width, height);
```

Draws a rectangle on the drawable (window or pixmap) specified, using the graphics context supplied, bounding the area defined by the co-ordinates supplied.

XFillRectangle

```
void XFillRectangle(Display      * display,
                    Drawable       drawable
                    GC             gc,
```

```
                         int              topLeftX, topLeftY,
                         unsigned int  width, height);
```

Fills the area specified, on the drawable (window or pixmap) specified, using the graphics context supplied.

XFree

```
void XFree(caddr_t no_longer_required);
```

Releases resources which have been previously allocated by Xlib calls and which do not have an explicit function to release them.

XFreeColormap

```
void XFreeColormap(Display  * display,
                   Colormap   colormap);
```

Releases the server resources occupied by the colormap.

XFreeColors

```
void XFreeColors(Display        * display,
                 Colormap         colormap,
                 unsigned long    pixels[],
                 int              num_pixels,
                 unsigned long    planes);
```

Releases colorcells which have been previously allocated.

XFreeGC

```
void XFreeGC(Display * display,
             GC        no_longer_required);
```

Releases the resources associated with the GC which is no longer required.

XFreeFont

```
void XFreeFont(Display      * display,
               XFontStruct * no_longer_required);
```

Releases the client resources associated with the font structure which is no longer required.

XFreePixmap

```
void XFreePixmap(Pixmap no_longer_required);
```

Releases the server resources associated with the Pixmap which is no longer required.

\\

XGetImage

```
XImage * XGetImage(Display      * display,
                   Drawable       drawable,
                   int            x, y,
                   unsigned int   width, height,
                   int            plane_mask,
                   int            format);
```

Obtains the area of the drawable specified as an XImage data structure in the client. The plane_mask determines which z planes should be used; specify -1 for all. The format can take one of the values XYBitmap, XYPixmap or ZPixmap.

XGetPixel

```
unsigned long XGetPixel(XImage * image,
                        int      x, y);
```

Returns the pixel value of the location specified on the XImage specified.

XGetStandardColormap

```
Status XGetStandardColormap(Display         * display,
                            Window            window,
                            XStandardColormap * colormap_info,
                            Atom              property );
```

Returns information concerning colormap of the type identified by property, suitable for use in the screen on which the window exists. Returns 1 if the property can be supported and 0 otherwise.

XImage

```
typedef struct _XImage{
                int             width, height;
                int             xoffset;
                int             format;
                char *          data;
                int             byte_order;
                int             bitmap_unit;
                int             bitmap_bit_oder;
                int             bitmap_pad;
                int             depth;
                int             bytes_per_line;
                int             bits_per_pixel;
                unsigned long   red_mask;
                unsigned long   green_mask;
                unsigned long   blue_mask;
                char *          obdata;
                struct funcs {
                    struct _XImage * (*create_image) ();
                    unsigned long    (*get_pixel) ();
```

```
                          int              (*put_pixel)();
                          struct _XImage *(*sum_image)();
                          int              (*add_pixel)();
                      } f;
        } XImage;
```

The detailed structure of an XImage.

XInstallColormap

```
void XInstallColormap(Display * display,
                      Colormap   colormap);
```

Installs the colormap specified into the display specified and possibly activates it.

XListInstalledColormaps

```
Colormap * XListInstalledColormaps(Display *  display,
                                   Window     window,
                                   int     *  num_maps);
```

Returns a list of the colormaps installed for the screen of the specified window. The number in the list is returned in num_maps. The list should be released with XFree when no longer required.

XLoadFont

```
Font XLoadFont(Display * display,
               char    * font_name );
```

Loads the font specified by font_name into the server; the function returns NULL if the font could not be loaded.

XLoadQueryFont

```
XFontStruct * XLoadQueryFont( Display * display,
                              char    * font_name );
```

Loads the font specified by font_name into the server and creates a FontStructure in the client containing the font's details. The function returns NULL if the font could not be loaded.

XLookupColor

```
Status XLookupColor(Display  * display,
                    Colormap   colormap,
                    char     * color_name,
                    XColor   * colorcell_definition,
                    XColor   * colorcell_possible);
```

Function to obtain the rgb values of a named color from the ascii colorname database and the closest possible hardware values. Color_name contains the ascii color name,

\\

colorcell_definition the rgb values from the database and colorcell_possible the closest rgb definition possible on the hardware. The function returns 1 if the colorname exists in the database and 0 otherwise.

XParseColor

```
Status XParseColor(Display    * display,
                   Colormap     colormap,
                   char        * color_spec,
                   XColor      * colorcell_definition);
```

Function to obtain the rgb values of a named color from the ascii colorname database or by translating the hexadecimal code. color_spec contains either an ascii colorname or a hexadecimal color specification. colorcell_definition contains on return the rgb values from the database or the hexadecimal values suitably converted. The function returns 1 if the specification could be parsed and 0 otherwise.

XPutImage

```
void XPutImage(Display    * display,
               Drawable     drawable,
               GC           gc,
               XImage     * image,
               int          source_x, source_y,
               int          destination_x, destination_y,
        unsigned int        width, height);
```

Puts the specified section of the image onto the drawable specified. Care should be taken to ensure that the characteristics of the XImage are compatible with those of the screen.

XPutPixel

```
int XPutPixel(XImage * image,
              int       x, y,
        unsigned long   pixel);
```

Puts the pixel value at the *x,y* location of the XImage.

XQueryColor

```
void XQueryColor(Display    * display,
                 Colormap     colormap,
                 XColor      * colorcell_definition);
```

Function to obtain the rgb values of a specified pixel. On entry the colorcell_definition pixel component contains the requested pixel value; on return the red, green and blue components contain the defined values.

XQueryColors

```
void XQueryColors(
          Display  *  display,
          Colormap    colormap,
          XColor      colorcell_definitions[num_colors],
          int         num_colors);
```

Function to obtain the rgb values of a number of specified pixels; details as for XQueryColor above.

XQueryFont

```
XFontStruct * XQueryFont(Display * display,
                         Font       font_identity);
```

Returns details of the characteristics of the font_identity supplied; the function will return NULL if the font has not been loaded. The calling environment is responsible for releasing the storage allocated by calling XFreeFont.

XSetArcMode

```
void XSetArcMode(Display  * display
                 GC         gc,
                 int        arc_mode);
```

Sets the arc_mode component of the graphics context to the arcmode value specified. Arcmode can be ArcChord or ArcPieSlice.

XSetBackground

```
void XSetBackground(Display * display
                    GC         gc,
          unsigned long        background);
```

Sets the background component of the graphics context to the background pixel value specified.

XSetClipMask

```
void XSetClipMask(Display  * display
                  GC         gc,
                  Pixmap     clip_mask);
```

Sets the clip_mask component of the graphics context to the clip_mask value specified.

XSetClipOrigin

```
void XSetClipOrigin(Display  * display
                    GC         gc,
                    int        clip_x_origin,
                    int        clip_y_origin);
```

\\

Sets the clip x origin and clip y origin components of the graphics context to the values specified.

XSetClipRectangles

```
void XSetClipRectangles(Display    * display
                        GC          gc,
                        XRectangle  rectangles[],
                        int         num_rectangles,
                        int         ordering);
```

Sets the clip_mask component of the graphics context to the union which encompasses the list of rectangles supplied. The ordering parameter can always be set to unsorted.

XSetDashes

```
void XSetDashes(Display   * display
                GC          gc,
                int         dash_offset,
                char        dash_list[],
                int         num_in_list);
```

Sets the dash_offset and dash_list components of the graphics context to the values specified. The list is a list of ascii digits, with the first digit indicating an initial number of off pixels.

XSetFillRule

```
Void XSetFillRule(Display   * display
                  GC          gc,
                  int         fill_rule);
```

Sets the fill_rule component of the graphics context to the value specified. The value WindingRule will fill the entire area.

XSetFillStyle

```
void XSetFillStyle(Display   * display
                   GC          gc,
                   int         fill_style);
```

Sets the fill_style component of the graphics context to the value specified. The value FillSolid will fill the entire area.

XSetForeground

```
void XSetForeground(Display   * display
                    GC          gc,
                    unsigned long    foreground);
```

Sets the foreground component of the graphics context to the pixel value specified.

XSetFunction

```
void XSetFunction(Display   * display
                  GC          gc,
                  int         function);
```

Sets the function component of the graphics context to the value specified. The value GXcopy will copy from the source to the destination. The value GXxor will logically xor the source with the destination, allowing the drawing to be removed with a second identical call.

XSetGraphicsExposures

```
void XSetGraphicsExposures(Display   * display,
                           GC          gc,
                           Boolean     graphics_exposures);
```

Sets the graphics_exposures component of the graphics context to the value specified. The value true will cause exposure events to be generated when copying to the window is performed.

XSetLineAttributes

```
void XSetLineAttributes(Display   * display
                        GC          gc,
                        int         line_width,
                        int         line_style,
                        int         cap_style,
                        int         join_style);
```

Sets the line_width, line_style, cap_style and join_style components of the graphics context to the values specified.

XSetPlaneMask

```
void XSetPlaneMask(Display    * display
                   GC           gc,
                   unsigned long  plane_mask);
```

Sets the plane_mask component of the graphics context to the value specified. The value controls which z planes will be affected by drawing actions.

XSetState

```
void XSetState(Display    * display,
               GC           gc,
               unsigned long  foreground,
               unsigned long  background,
               int            function,
               unsigned long  plane_mask);
```

Sets the foreground, background, function and plane_mask components of the graphics context to the values specified.

\\\

XSetStipple

```
void XSetStipple( Display   * display,
                  GC          gc,
                  Pixmap      stipple);
```

Sets the stipple component of the graphics context to the value specified. The stipple is a pixmap with a depth of one.

XSetSubWindowMode

```
void XSetSubWindowMode(Display   * display,
                       GC.         gc,
                       int         subwindow_mode);
```

Sets the subwindow_mode component of the graphics context to the value specified.

XSetTile

```
void XSetTile(Display   * display,
              GC          gc,
              Pixmap      tile);
```

Sets the tile component of the graphics context to the value specified.

XSetTSOrigin

```
void XSetTSOrigin(Display   * display
                  GC          gc,
                  int         ts_x_origin,
                  int         ts_y_origin);
```

Sets the ts_x_origin and ts_y_origin components of the graphics context to the values specified. The ts components determine the placement of the tile or stipple pattern.

XSetWindowColormap

```
void XSetWindowColormap(Display   * display,
                        Window      window,
                        Colormap    colormap);
```

Sets the specified colormap as the specified window's colormap attribute.

XStoreColor

```
void XStoreColor(Display   * display,
                 Colormap    colormap,
                 XColor      colorcell_definitions);
```

Function to request to change the rgb values of the colormap colorcell identified by the pixel component of the colorcell_definition, to the rgb values in the red, green and blue components. On exit the red, green and blue components contain the values actually allocated.

XStoreColors

```
void XStoreColors(
        Display  * display,
        Colormap   colormap,
        XColor     colorcell_definitions[num_colors],
        int        num_colors);
```

Function to request a change to the rgb values of a number of colorcells. Details as for XStoreColor above.

XStoreNamedColor

```
void XStoreNamedColor( Display       * display,
                       Colormap        colormap,
                       char          * colorname,
                       unsigned long   pixel,
                       int             flags);
```

Looks up the rgb definition of the named color storing the definition in the read/write colorcell of the colormap. The flags parameter is a bitwise ORed combination of DoRED, DoBLUE and DoGREEN, determining which components are to be changed.

XUndefineCursor

```
void XUndefineCursor(Display  * display,
                     Window     window);
```

Uninstalls any cursor previously installed with XDefineCursor, restoring the cursor to that inherited from the window's parent.

XUninstallColormap

```
void XSetWindowColormap(Display  * display,
                        Colormap   colormap);
```

Uninstalls the specified colormap from the display, if possible.

XUnloadFont

```
void XUnloadLoadFont(Display  * display,
                     Font       no_longer_required);
```

Indicates to the server that the client no longer requires the font specified. If no other clients require the font then it may be unloaded from the server.

B6 A selection of intrinsic resources

XtAddCallback

```
void XtAddCallback(Widget        widget,
                   String        callback_name,
                   XtCallbackProc callback,
                   XtPointer     client_data);
```

Adds a callback to a widget. widget and callback_name identify which widget and which callback, callback is the callback function and client_data is the identity of the client_data parameter for the callback function.

XtAddEventHandler

```
XtAddEventHandler(Widget        widget,
                  EventMask     event_mask,
                  Boolean       maskable,
                  XtEventHandler event_handler,
                  XtPointer     client_data);
```

Adds the event handler to the widget specified. The event_mask specifies which events are to be responded to, and maskable if it is to respond to nonmaskable events (for simple applications it should always be set False).

XtAppAddTimeOut

```
XtIntervalId XtAppAddTimeOut(
                  XtAppContext        app_context,
                  unsigned long       interval,
                  XtTimerCallbackProc timeout_procedure,
                  XtPointer           client_data);
```

Causes the timeout_procedure to be called after the interval which is expressed in milliseconds. The client_data will be passed to the timeout_procedure in its client_data parameter. The value returned by the function can be used to cancel the timeout before it is called.

XtAppInitialize

```
Widget XtAppInitialize(XtAppContext * context,
                  String              application_class,
                  XrmOrdinalDescList  options,
                  Cardinal            num_options,
                  Cardinal          * argc_in_out,
                  String            * argv_in_out,
                  String            * fallback_resources,
                  ArgList             args,
                  Cardinal            num_args);
```

Initializes an Xapplication and returns the application shell. Context is a context to identify the application instance, application_class identifies the client's class name to the resource database (the client's instance name is taken from the command on the command line, unless a -name option is given). options and num options can be used to specify any client specific command line options. argc and argv are the command line identifiers from main(). fallback_resources can be used to specify the values of any resources not explicitly specified on the command line. args/ num_args are widget resources to be communicated to the application shell.

XtAppMainLoop

```
void XtAppMainLoop(Context context);
```

Implements the main event loop for the application specified in the context. The main loop will process events from the user, identifying the widget to receive the event, calling the appropriate widget methods and then any callback functions registered for that event and widget.

XtDestroyWidget

```
void XtDestroyWidget(Widget widget);
```

Marks the specified widget for destruction. Widgets which are not explicitly destroyed will be destroyed when the application terminates.

XtDisplay

```
Display * XtDisplay(Widget widget);
```

Returns the display pointer of the display upon which the widget's window is realized.

XtFree

```
void XtFree(XtPointer resource);
```

Releases resources previously allocated by an intrinsics function.

XtIsShell

```
Boolean XtIsShell(Widget widget);
```

XtIsShell is a macro, not a function. Returns True if the widget specified is an instance of any subclass of the shell widget class.

XtIsTopLevelShell

```
Boolean XtIsTopLevelShell(Widget widget);
```

XtIsTopLevelShell is a macro, not a function. Returns True if the widget specified is an instance of any subclass of the topLevelShell widget class.

\\

XtLastTimestampProcessed

```
Time XtLastTimestampProcessed(Display  * display);
```

Returns the timestamp contained in the last event which was dispatched.

XtManageChild

```
void XtManageChild(Widget widget);
```

Manages the widget specified. Managed widgets will take part in geometry negotiations and will have space reserved for them on the screen. If the widget's mapWhenManaged resource is True (which is the default), the widget will also be mapped as a result of the call when it or any of its ancestors are realized.

XtParent

```
Widget XtParent(Widget widget);
```

Returns the identity of the parent widget of the widget specified.

XtRealizeWidget

```
void XtRealizeWidget(Widget widget);
```

Causes any managed widgets within the widget tree whose root is given to become visible upon the terminal. Usually called once in a program, with the top_level widget as a parameter, immediately prior to the call to XtAppMainLoop.

XtRemoveTimeout

```
void XtRemoveTimeout(XtIntervalID id);
```

Cancels the timeout identified before it is called.

XtSetArgs

```
XtSetArg(Arg        argument,
         Manifest   resource_class,
         (various)  resource_value);
```

XtSetArg is a macro, not a function. It is used to construct each entry in an argument list, which is subsequently used to communicate resource values to a widget upon creation, to change the resource values of a created widget (XtSetValues) or to enquire of the values of a created widget (XtGetValues).

XtSetSensitive

```
void XtSetSensitive(Widget  widget,
                    Boolean sensitivity);
```

\\

Sets the sensitivity resource of the widget specified to the value specified. Insensitive widgets, and their children, are presented in a greyed out style and cannot be used by the user.

XtSetValues

```
void XtSetValues(Widget   widget,
                 ArgList  args,
                 Cardinal num_args);
```

Used to change the resource values of the widget, using the args/ num_args argument list.

XtTimerCallbackProc

```
void XtTimerCallbackProc(XtPointer     client_data,
                         XtIntervalId * id);
```

The required prototype for timeout procedures.

XtUnmanageChild

```
void XtUnmanageChild(Widget widget);
```

Unmanages the widget specified.

XtWindow

```
Window XtWindow( Widget widget );
```

Returns the window identity of the widget specified; should only be called after the widget has been realized.

B7 A selection of Motif resources

XmClipboardCopy

```
int XmClipboardCopy(Display       * display,
                    Window          window,
                    long            item_id,
                    char          * format_name,
                    XtPointer       buffer,
                    unsigned long   length,
                    long            private_id,
                    long          * data_id);
```

Transfers the data, of size length, from the buffer to the clipboard, using format_name to identify the format. The item_id is obtained from XmClipboardStartCopy and data_id is returned to uniquely identify this combination of format and data. Additional data can be supplied in the private_id parameter. Returns ClipboardFail, ClipboardLocked or ClipboardSuccess.

\\

XmClipboardEndCopy

```
int XmClipboardEndCopy(Display  * display,
                       Window      window,
                       long        item_id);
```

Terminates the copy operation started with XmClipboardStartCopy, unlocking the clipboard to other clients. Returns ClipboardFail, ClipboardLocked or ClipboardSuccess.

XmClipboardEndRetrieve

```
int XmClipboardEndRetrieve(Display  * display,
                           Window      window);
```

Terminates the retrieve operation started with XmClipboardStartRetrieve, unlocking the clipboard to other clients. Returns ClipboardLocked or ClipboardSuccess.

XmClipboardInquireLength

```
int XmClipboardInquireLength(Display        * display,
                             Window           window,
                             char           * format_name,
                             unsigned long  * size);
```

Returns, in size, the length of any data stored in the clipboard in the format identified by format_name. Returns ClipboardLocked, ClipboardNoData, ClipboardSuccess.

XmClipboardRetrieve

```
int XmClipboardRetrieve(Display          * display,
                        Window             window,
                        char             * format_name,
                        XtPointer          buffer,
                        unsigned long      buffer_length,
                        unsigned long    * bytes_transferred,
                        long             * private_id);
```

Transfers data in the format_name from the clipboard to the buffer whose size is specified. The number of bytes actually transferred is returned in bytes_transferred and private_id contains any private data stored with the data and format. Returns ClipboardLocked, ClipboardNoData, ClipboardSuccess or ClipboardTruncate.

XmClipboardStartCopy

```
int XmClipboardStartCopy(Display       * display,
                         Window          window,
                         char          * clip_label,
                         Time            time_stamp,
                         Widget          widget,
                         XmCutPasteProc  cut_paste_callback,
                         long          * item_id);
```

Prepares the clipboard to receive data from the application and locks the clipboard to other clients. clip_label is an arbitrary string (the format name can be used). The time_stamp can be obtained with XtLastTimestampProcessed. The widget and cut_paste_callback parameters only need be supplied if the data is to be provided upon request, and can be specified null otherwise. The item_id is returned and needs to be stored for use when the data is actually transferred. Returns ClipboardLocked or ClipboardSuccess.

XmClipboardStartRetrieve

```
int XmClipboardStartRetrieve(Display  * display,
                             Window      window,
                             Time        time_stamp);
```

Prepares the clipboard to transfer data to the application and locks the clipboard to other clients. The time_stamp can be obtained with XtLastTimestampProcessed. Returns ClipboardLocked or ClipboardSuccess.

XmCreate{whatever}

```
Widget XmCreate{whatever}(Widget      parent,
                          String      name,
                          ArgList     args,
                          Cardinal    num_args );
```

Creates and returns an instance of the widget class specified. Parent identifies the parent, name identifies the name and args/ num_args any resources to be set upon creation.

XmDrawingAreaCallbackStruct

```
typedef struct {
        int       reason;
        Xevent  * event;
        Window    window;
} XmDrawingAreaCallbackStruct;
```

Structure passed as call_data parameter of the DrawingArea's inputCallback functions. Xevent union component will be of type xbutton for mouse button events, containing x and y components which indicate location on the window.

XmFileSelectionBoxCallbackStruct

```
typedef struct {
        int       reason,
        Xevent  * event,
        XmString  value,
        int       length,
        XmString  mask,
        int       mask_length,
        XmString  dir,
        int       dir_length,
        XmString  pattern,
        int       pattern_length,
} XmFileSelectionBoxCallbackStruct;
```

Structure passed as call_data parameter of the FileSelectionBox's callback functions. The value component contains the currently selected file.

XmFileSelectionDoSearch

```
Void XmFileSelectionDoSearch(Widget     file_selection_box,
                             XmString   new_filter);
```

Causes the fileSelectionBox to update its contents after performing a file and directory search. If the new_filter specified is null the existing directory mask is used.

XmFileSelectionBoxGetChild

```
Widget XmFileSelectionBoxGetChild(Widget file_select_box,
                                  int     widget_literal);
```

Returns the identity of the specified widget component of the composite fileSelectionBox instance supplied. Widget_literal can take one of the values:

```
XmDIALOG_APPLY_BUTTON          XmDIALOG_CANCEL_BUTTON
XmDIALOG_DEFAULT_BUTTON        XmDIALOG_DIR_LIST
XmDIALOG_DIR_LIST_LABEL        XmDIALOG_FILTER_LABEL
XmDIALOG_FILTER_TEXT           XmDIALOG_HELP_BUTTON
XmDIALOG_LIST                  XmDIALOG_LIST_LABEL
XmDIALOG_OK_BUTTON             XmDIALOG_SELECTION_LABEL
XmDIALOG_SEPARATOR             XmDIALOG_TEXT
XmDIALOG_WORK_AREA
```

XmFontListCreate

```
XmFontList XmFontListCreate(XFontStruct * the_font_to_use,
                            char        * arbitrary_fontname);
```

Creates and returns a new FontList structure containing a single font as supplied with the arbitrary fontname supplied. For simple usage the fontname XmSTRING_DEFAULT_CHARSET (or XmSTRING_DEFAULT_TAG in Motif 1.2) can be used.

XmFontListFree

```
void XmFontListFree(XmFontList no_longer_required);
```

Releases resources occupied by the FontList structure.

XmMessageBoxGetChild

```
Widget XmMessageBoxGetChild(Widget file_select_box,
                            int     widget_literal);
```

Returns the identity of the specified widget component of the composite messageBox instance supplied. Widget_literal can take one of the values:

```
XmDIALOG_CANCEL_BUTTON          XmDIALOG_DEFAULT_BUTTON
XmDIALOG_HELP_BUTTON            XmDIALOG_MESSAGE_LABEL
XmDIALOG_OK_BUTTON             XmDIALOG_SEPARATOR
XmDIALOG_SYMBOL_LABEL
```

XmScrollBarSetValues

```
void XmScrollBarSetValues(Widget  scroll_bar_widget,
                          int     new_value,
                          int     new_slider_size,
                          int     new_increment,
                          int     new_page_increment,
                          Boolean notify);
```

Sets the values of the scrollBar widget specified to the values supplied. If notify is True expose events may be generated, otherwise they are suppressed.

XmScrollBarGetValues

```
void XmScrollBarGetValues(Widget   scroll_bar_widget,
                          int    * value,
                          int    * slider_size,
                          int    * increment,
                          int    * page_increment);
```

Convenience function to obtain the specified resource values of the scrollBar widget.

XmSelectionBoxGetChild

```
Widget XmSelectionBoxGetChild(Widget file_select_box,
                              int    widget_literal);
```

Returns the identity of the specified widget component of the composite selectionBox instance supplied. Widget_literal can take one of the values:

```
XmDIALOG_APPLY_BUTTON           XmDIALOG_CANCEL_BUTTON
XmDIALOG_DEFAULT_BUTTON         XmDIALOG_HELP_BUTTON
XmDIALOG_LIST                  XmDIALOG_LIST_LABEL
XmDIALOG_OK_BUTTON             XmDIALOG_SELECTION_LABEL
XmDIALOG_SEPARATOR             XmDIALOG_TEXT
XmDIALOG_WORK_AREA
```

XmStringConcat

```
XmString XmStringConcat(XmString first_string,
                        XmString second_string);
```

Joins second XmString onto the end of first XmString and returns the combined XmString.

XmStringCreate

```
XmString XmStringCreate(char *          asciiz_string,
                        XmStringCharSet charset);
```

\\

Creates and returns a single segment XmString, containing the asciiz_string supplied using the charset specified. The charset should be identified within an associated XmFontList; XmSTRING_DEFAULT_CHARSET (or XmSTRING_DEFAULT_TAG in Motif 1.2) can be specified which will use the first charset in the font list.

XmStringCreateLtoR

```
XmString XmStringCreateLtoR(char *          asciiz_string,
                            XmStringCharSet charset);
```

Creates and returns an XmString, parameters as for XmStringCreate above. XmStringCreateLtoR differs from XmStringCreate in that XmStringCreate will only create a single segment. XmStringCreateLtoR will scan the asciiz string for new line characters and create multiple segments.

XmStringExtent

```
void XmStringExtent(XmFontList   font_list,
                    XmString     the_string,
                    Dimension  * width,
                    Dimension  * height);
```

Determines and returns the width and height of the XmString supplied as it would be rendered by the FontList specified.

XmStringDrawImage

```
void XmStringDrawImage(Display    * display,
                       Drawable     drawable,
                       XmFontList   font_list,
                       XmString     the_string,
                       GC           gc,
                       Position     x, y,
                       Dimension    width,
            unsigned char          alignment,
            unsigned char          layout_direction,
                       XRectangle   clip_area);
```

Renders the XmString on the drawable, using the FontList and GC, at the *x,y* co-ordinates, with width defining the rectangle for alignment. Alignment can take one of the values:

```
XmALIGNMENT_BEGINNING  XmALIGNMENT_CENTRE  XmALIGNMENT_END
```

layout_direction can take one of the values:

```
XmSTRING_DIRECTION_L_TO_R      XmSTRING_DIRECTION_R_TO_L
```

clip_area can be used to define an area which clips the rendered string.

XmStringFree

```
void XmStringFree(XmString an_Xmstring);
```

Releases the resources associated with an XmString.

XmTextBlock

```
typedef struct {
        char        * ptr;
        int           length;
        XmTextFormat  format;
} XmTextBlockRec, XmTextBlock;
```

Specifies a block of text within a text widget, most notably as a component part of an XmTextVerifyCallbackStruct. The format component can indicate eight bit or sixteen bit format.

XmTextGetLastPosition

```
XmTextPosition XmTextGetLastPosition(Widget widget);
```

Returns the last position (in characters) of the text in the text widget specified.

XmTextGetString

```
char * XmTextGetString(Widget widget);
```

Returns a copy of the text contained within the text widget specified. The calling environment is responsible for releasing the resources occupied by the returned text.

XmTextReplace

```
void XmTextReplace(Widget         widget,
                   XmTextPosition  fromPos,
                   XmTextPosition  toPos,
                   char          * newString);
```

Replaces the text specified in the widget with the text supplied. If fromPos is equal to toPos an insertion is effected. If newString is a null string a deletion is effected. The text widget's modifyVerifyCallback functions will be called prior to the replacement.

XmTextSetInsertionPosition

```
void XmTextSetInsertionPosition(Widget         widget,
                                XmTextPosition position );
```

Moves the insertion cursor of the text widget specified to the position specified. The text in the widget will scroll if necessary. If the new position differs from the old position the text widget's motionVerifyCallback functions will be called.

XmTextVerifyCallbackStruct

```
typedef struct {
        int             reason;
        Xevent        * event;
        Boolean         doit;
        XmTextPosition  currentInsert;
        XmTextPosition  newInsert;
        XmTextPosition  startPos;
        XmTextPosition  endPos;
        XmTextBlock     text;
} XmTextVerifyCallbackStruct, *XmTextVerifyPtr;
```

Structure passed as the call_data parameter of focusCallback, losingFocusCallback, modifyVerifyCallback and motionVerifyCallback. reason is XmCR_FOCUS for focusCallback, XmCR_LOSE_FOCUS for losingFocusCallback, and XmCR_MODIFYING_TEXT_VALUE for modifyVerifyCallback. Remaining parameters specify the current and proposed position of the cursor for motionVerifyCallback; or location and value of the new text to be inserted. If startPos is equal to endPos then an insertion is implied, otherwise a replacement is implied. If the textBlock is empty then a deletion is implied.

\\\

Selected source code

This appendix contains details of all the source code which is presented in the book. Listings are identified either by their chapter and sequence number in the text, e.g. Listing 5.2, or by their chapter and sequence number in the appendix, e.g. Listing C3.1. The source code is freely available from the author via e-mail; please contact:

fintan@uk.ac.sbu.vax

for further details.

\\

Listing C2.1   The String date time module (sdtime)

```
1   /* filename sdtime.c (string date and time)        *
2    * Utility module to package the standard <time.h>  *
3    * standard facilities and return a string of the   *
4    * form "Day dd Mon yyyy" eg "Tue 17 may 1993"      *
5    * or a string of form "HH:MM" eg "12:24"           *
6    *                                                   *
7    * Developed for Motif book chapter 2               *
8    *                                                   *
9    * Fintan Culwin Jun 1992 v1.0, checked Jan 94      *
10  */
11
12  #include "sdtime.h"
13  #include <time.h>
14
15  extern int sdate( char * buffer ){
16
```

continued

Listing C2.1 *continued*

```
17  int          index;
18  time_t       time_now;
19  struct tm * the_time;
20
21     if ( time( & time_now ) != -1 ) {
22         the_time = localtime( &time_now );
23         strftime( buffer, MAX_DATE_LENGTH, "%a %d %b %Y\0", the_time );
24         return 1;
25     }else{
26         *buffer = '\0';
27         return 0;
28     } /* end if */
29  } /* end fun sdate */
30
31
32  extern int stime( char * buffer ) {
33
34  int          index;
35  time_t       time_now;
36  struct tm * the_time;
37
38     if ( time(& time_now ) != -1 ) {
39         the_time = localtime( &time_now );
40         strftime( buffer, MAX_TIME_LENGTH, "%H:%M\0", the_time);
41         return 1;
42     }else{
43         *buffer = '\0';
44         return 0;
45     } /* end if */
46  } /* end fun stime */
```

Listing C3.1   The click counter presentation code file

```
1   /* filename click_counter_presentation.c (cl_cnt_p.c)    *
2    *                                                        *
3    * Code file for the click counter presentation module.   *
4    * Written for Motif book chapter 3.                       *
5    *                                                        *
6    * Fintan Culwin version 1.0 Feb 1992, checked Jan 94     *
7    */
8
9   #include <X11/Shell.h>
10  #include <Xm/PushB.h>
11  #include <Xm/RowColumn.h>
12  #include <Xm/Label.h>
13  #include <Xm/Frame.h>
14  #include <Xm/Form.h>
15
16  #include "c_c_t.h"
17
18  #define MAX_ARGS     10
19
20  void main ( int argc, char *argv[]){
```

continued

\\\

Listing C3.1 *continued*

```
21
22   char * application_class = "Click_counter";
23
24   XtAppContext      context;
25
26   Widget      toplevel,
27               main_form, value_frame, value_display,
28               control_form, plus_button, zero_button, minus_button;
29
30   Arg         args[ MAX_ARGS ];
31   int         num_args;
32
33
34       num_args = 0;
35       XtSetArg( args[num_args], XmNallowShellResize, True );
36       num_args++;
37       toplevel = XtAppInitialize( &context,
38                                   application_class,
39                                   NULL, 0,
40                                   &argc, argv,
41                                   NULL,
42                                   args, num_args );
43
44       /* create the main form */
45       num_args = 0;
46       main_form = XmCreateForm( toplevel, "main_form", args, num_args );
47       XtManageChild( main_form );
48
49       num_args = 0;
50       XtSetArg( args[num_args], XmNtopAttachment, XmATTACH_FORM);
51                                                   num_args++;
52       XtSetArg( args[num_args], XmNleftAttachment, XmATTACH_FORM);
53                                                   num_args++;
54       XtSetArg( args[num_args], XmNrightAttachment, XmATTACH_FORM);
55                                                   num_args++;
56       XtSetArg( args[num_args], XmNbottomAttachment, XmATTACH_POSITION);
57                                                   num_args++;
58       XtSetArg( args[num_args], XmNbottomPosition, 55);
59                                                   num_args++;
60       value_frame = XmCreateFrame( main_form, "text_frame",
61                                    args,      num_args );
62       XtManageChild( value_frame );
63
64       /* create the value widget*/
65       num_args = 0;
66       value_display = XmCreateLabel( value_frame, "value_frame",
67                                    args, num_args );
68       XtManageChild( value_display );
69
70       num_args = 0;
71       XtSetArg( args[num_args], XmNleftAttachment,  XmATTACH_FORM );
72                                                   num_args++;
73       XtSetArg( args[num_args], XmNrightAttachment, XmATTACH_FORM );
```

continued

\\\

Listing C3.1 *continued*

```
74                                                               num_args++;
75     XtSetArg( args[num_args], XmNtopAttachment,   XmATTACH_WIDGET );
76                                                               num_args++;
77     XtSetArg( args[num_args], XmNbottomAttachment, XmATTACH_FORM );
78                                                               num_args++;
79     XtSetArg( args[num_args], XmNtopWidget, value_frame);
80                                                               num_args++;
81     control_form = XmCreateForm( main_form, "control_form",
82                                  args,       num_args );
83     XtManageChild( control_form );
84
85     num_args = 0;
86     XtSetArg( args[num_args], XmNleftAttachment,   XmATTACH_FORM );
87                                                               num_args++;
88     XtSetArg( args[num_args], XmNrightAttachment, XmATTACH_POSITION );
89                                                               num_args++;
90     XtSetArg( args[num_args], XmNtopAttachment,   XmATTACH_FORM );
91                                                               num_args++;
92     XtSetArg( args[num_args], XmNbottomAttachment, XmATTACH_FORM );
93                                                               num_args++;
94     XtSetArg( args[num_args], XmNrightPosition, 33 );
95                                                               num_args++;
96     plus_button = XmCreatePushButton( control_form, " + ",
97                                  args,            num_args );
98     XtManageChild( plus_button );
99    XtAddCallback( plus_button, XmNactivateCallback,
100                                 increment_callback,
101                                 (XtPointer) value_display );
102
103    num_args = 0;
104    XtSetArg( args[num_args], XmNleftAttachment,   XmATTACH_WIDGET
105                                                               num_args++;
106    XtSetArg( args[num_args], XmNrightAttachment, XmATTACH_POSITION );
107                                                               num_args++;
108    XtSetArg( args[num_args], XmNtopAttachment,   XmATTACH_FORM );
109                                                               num_args++;
110    XtSetArg( args[num_args], XmNbottomAttachment, XmATTACH_FORM );
111                                                               num_args++;
112    XtSetArg( args[num_args], XmNleftWidget, plus_button );
113                                                               num_args++;
114    XtSetArg( args[num_args], XmNrightPosition, 67 );
115                                                               num_args++;
116    zero_button = XmCreatePushButton( control_form, " 0 ",
117                                  args,            num_args );
118    XtManageChild( zero_button );
119    XtAddCallback( zero_button, XmNactivateCallback,
120                                 zero_callback,
121                                 (XtPointer) value_display );
122
123    num_args = 0;
124    XtSetArg( args[num_args], XmNleftAttachment,   XmATTACH_WIDGET );
125                                                               num_args++;
126    XtSetArg( args[num_args], XmNrightAttachment, XmATTACH_FORM );
```

continued

\\\

Listing C3.1 *continued*

```
127                                                          num_args++;
128     XtSetArg( args[num_args], XmNtopAttachment,    XmATTACH_FORM );
129                                                          num_args++;
130     XtSetArg( args[num_args], XmNbottomAttachment, XmATTACH_FORM )
131                                                          num_args++;
132     XtSetArg( args[num_args], XmNleftWidget, zero_button );
133                                                          num_args++;
134     minus_button = XmCreatePushButton( control_form, " - ",
135                                        args,          num_args );
136     XtManageChild( minus_button );
137     XtAddCallback( minus_button, XmNactivateCallback,
138                                  decrement_callback,
139                                  (XtPointer) value_display );
140
141     /* set the initial state using an explicit call to the *
142      * zero callback.                                      */
143     zero_callback( NULL, (XtPointer) value_display , NULL );
144
145     /* realize the widgets then get and dispatch events */
146     XtRealizeWidget(toplevel);
147
148     XtAppMainLoop( context );
149 } /* end fun main */
```

Listing C3.2   The version demo code file

```
1  /* filename version demo   (ver_demo.c)                        *
2   *                                                             *
3   * Introductory X/Motif program to illustrate visual design    *
4   * considerations, written for X/Motif book chapter 3.         *
5   * Although documentation refers to the shell as a             *
6   * DialogShell, it is implemented here as an                   *
7   * ApplicationShell. The changes to use it as version dialog   *
8   * are trivial.                                                *
9   *                                                             *
10  * Fintan Culwin June 92 v1.0 revised Jan 94                   *
11  */
12
13  #include <Xm/Xm.h>
14  #include <Xm/Form.h>
15  #include <Xm/Frame.h>
16  #include <Xm/Label.h>
17  #include <Xm/PushB.h>
18
19  #include "fractree.h"
20
21  #define MAX_ARGS      10
22  #define XIFS_TITLE      "Xifs - iterated function system viewer \n\n"
23  #define XIFS_PROGRAMMERS "Fintan Culwin & \n" \
24                          "Ninh Quoc Chu\n\n"
25  #define XIFS_VERSION    "V1.0 Aug 1991"
26
27  /* prototype */
```

continued

Listing C3.2 *continued*

```
28  void create_version_dialog( Widget toplevel );
29
30  void main ( int argc, char *argv[]){
31
32  char * application_class = "Version_demo";
33  XtAppContext   context;
34
35  Widget         toplevel;
36  Arg            args[ MAX_ARGS ];
37  int            num_args;
38
39     num_args = 0;
40     XtSetArg( args[num_args], XmNallowShellResize, True ); num_args++;
41     XtSetArg( args[num_args], XmNmwmDecorations,
42                              XM_DECOR_BORDER | XM_DECOR_TITLE);
43                                                 num_args++;
44     toplevel = XtAppInitialize( &context,
45                                 application_class,
46                                 NULL, 0,
47                                 &argc, argv,
48                                 NULL,
49                                 args, num_args );
50
51     create_version_dialog( toplevel );
52
53     /* realize the widgets then get and dispatch events */
54     XtRealizeWidget( toplevel );
55
56     XtAppMainLoop( context );
57  } /* end fun main */
58
59
60  void create_version_dialog( Widget toplevel ){
61
62  Widget version_form, version_pixmap_frame, version_pixmap,
63         version_text_frame, version_text, version_button;
64
65  static Pixmap   fract_pix = (Pixmap) NULL;
66  /* static as the widget does not take copy */
67  Display * display;
68  XmString  title_segment, name_segment, version_segment,
69            temp_string, version_string;
70
71
72  Arg    args[ MAX_ARGS ];
73  int    num_args;
74
75   /* create the form widget */
76     num_args = 0;
77     version_form = XmCreateForm( toplevel, "version form",
78                                  args, num_args);
79     XtManageChild( version_form );
80
```

continued

Listing C3.2 *continued*

```
81    /* create the pixmap and install into the version pixmap *
82     * widget as it is created                              */
83    num_args = 0;
84    version_pixmap_frame = XmCreateFrame( version_form,
85                                          "version pixmap frame",
86                                          args, num_args );
87    XtManageChild( version_pixmap_frame );
88
89    display = XtDisplay( toplevel);
90    fract_pix = XCreatePixmapFromBitmapData( display,
91                      DefaultRootWindow( display ),
92                       fractree_bits, fractree_width, fractree_height,
93                        BlackPixel( display, DefaultScreen( display )),
94                        WhitePixel( display, DefaultScreen( display )),
95                      DefaultDepth( display, DefaultScreen( display)));
96
97    num_args = 0;
98    XtSetArg( args[num_args], XmNlabelType, XmPIXMAP); num_args++;
99    XtSetArg( args[num_args], XmNlabelPixmap, fract_pix); num_args++;
100   version_pixmap = XmCreateLabel( version_pixmap_frame,
101                                   "version pixmap",
102                                   args, num_args);
103   XtManageChild( version_pixmap );
104
105   /* create the version text widget  */
106   num_args = 0;
107   version_text_frame = XmCreateFrame( version_form,
108                                       "version text frame",
109                                       args, num_args );
110   XtManageChild( version_text_frame );
111
112   /* create the Xm string from the ascii strings */
113   title_segment   = XmStringCreateLtoR( XIFS_TITLE,       "fancy");
114   name_segment    = XmStringCreateLtoR( XIFS_PROGRAMMERS, "italic");
115   version_segment = XmStringCreateLtoR( XIFS_VERSION,     "bold");
116   temp_string     = XmStringConcat( title_segment, name_segment);
117   version_string  = XmStringConcat( temp_string,   version_segment);
118   XmStringFree( title_segment);
119   XmStringFree( name_segment);
120   XmStringFree( version_segment);
121   XmStringFree( temp_string);
122
123   num_args = 0;
124   XtSetArg( args[num_args], XmNlabelString, version_string);
125                                               num_args++;
126   XtSetArg( args[num_args], XmNleftWidget,  version_pixmap );
127                                               num_args++;
128   version_text = XmCreateLabel(version_text_frame ,
129                                "version text",
130                                args, num_args);
131   XtManageChild( version_text );
132   XmStringFree( version_string);
133
```

continued

Listing C3.2 *continued*

```
134     /* create the push button */
135     num_args = 0;
136     version_button = XmCreatePushButton( version_form,
137                                          "version button",
138                                          args, num_args);
139     XtManageChild( version_button );
140  } /* end fun create version dialog */
```

Listing C5.1   The save/ save as interface support module code file

```
1   /* filename save demo translations support code file    *
2    * (s_d_t_s.c).                                          *
3    *                                                       *
4    * Written for Motif book chapter 5.                     *
5    * fintan culwin v1.0 March 92 revised Jan 94            *
6    */
7
8
9   #include "s_d_t_s.h"
10  #include <stdio.h>
11
12  static int save_state = S_D_UNCREATED;
13
14  extern void set_save_state( int new_state ){
15  /* possibly over-defensive implementation, but it makes *
16   * the point (which will not be repeated!)              */
17  const char * msg = "Program error in set save state. \n"
18                     "Attempt to set state to value %u.\n"
19                     "Program abending!\n\n";
20
21       switch ( new_state ) {
22          case S_D_UNCREATED :
23          case S_D_AVAILABLE :
24          case S_D_SAVE      :
25          case S_D_SAVE_AS   :
26                             save_state = new_state;
27                             break;
28          default:
29                             fprintf( stderr, msg, new_state );
30                             exit( -1 );
31       } /* end switch */
32  } /* end set save state */
33
34
35  extern int  get_save_state( void ){
36     return save_state;
37  } /* end fun get save state */
38
39
40  /* filenames support */
41  static char temp_filename[ MAX_FILE_NAME_SIZE ] = "\0";
42  static char      filename[ MAX_FILE_NAME_SIZE ] = "\0";
43
```

continued

\\\

Listing C5.1 *continued*

```
44  extern char * set_temp_filename( char * new_filename ){
45    strncpy( temp_filename, new_filename, (size_t) MAX_FILE_NAME_SIZE);
46    return temp_filename;
47  } /* end fun set temp filename */
48
49
50  extern char * get_temp_filename( void ){
51    return temp_filename;
52  } /* end fun get temp filename */
53
54
55  extern char * set_filename( char * new_filename ){
56    strncpy( filename, new_filename, (size_t) MAX_FILE_NAME_SIZE);
57    return filename;
58  } /* end fun set temp filename */
59
60
61  extern char * get_filename( void ){
62      return filename;
63  } /* end fun get filename */
64
65
66  extern int does_file_exist( char * filename ){
67  /* this may not be elegant, but it is portable! */
68
69  FILE * temp_file;
70  int     it_does;
71
72    it_does = ((temp_file = fopen( filename, "r")) != NULL );
73    if ( it_does ){
74        fclose( temp_file );
75    } /* end if */
76    return  it_does;
77  } /* end fun does file exist */
```

Listing C5.2   The save/ save as example application layer code file

```
1   /* filename save demonstration application layer code     *
2    * file (sv_dmo_a.c). Supplies demonstration application save  *
3    * and load functions for the save/ save as interface.     *
4    * See Motif book chap 5.                                   *
5    * fintan culwin v1.0 March 92  revised Jan 94.             *
6    */
7
8
9   #include "sv_dmo_a.h"
10  #include <stdio.h>
11  #include <string.h>
12
13  #define FAIL_MESSAGE "an unknown error".
14
15
16  extern int save_app_workspace( char *  filename,
```

continued

Listing C5.2 *continued*

```
17                                char ** message){
18  /* dummy implementation only */
19     fprintf( stderr, "\nApplication layer called to save as %s\n",
20             filename );
21     *message = (char *) NULL;
22     return 0;
23
24  /* alternative for testing the failure option *
25   * (void) strcpy( *message, FAIL_MESSAGE );    *
26   * return 1;                                   *
27   */
28  } /* end fun save app workspace */
29
30  extern int load_app_workspace( char * filename ){
31  /* dummy implementation only */
32     fprintf( stderr, "\nApplication layer called to load from %s\n",
33             filename );
34     *message = (char *) NULL;
35     return 0;
36
37  /* alternative for testing the failure option *
38   * (void) strcpy( *message, FAIL_MESSAGE );    *
39   * return 1;                                   *
40   */
41  } /* end fun load app workspace */
```

Listing C5.3   The help interface support module code file

```
 1  /* filename help interface support code file.         */
 2   * (help_i_s.c)                                        *
 3   * Supplies and supports help topic list and records  *
 4   * state of the topic selection dialog                 *
 5   *                                                     *
 6   * Written for Motif book chapter 5.                   *
 7   *                                                     *
 8   * fintan culwin v1.0 July 92, revised Jan 94.         *
 9   */
10
11  #include "help_i_s.h"
12
13  #define BUFFER_LENGTH   255
14
15  static int    num_topics = 0;
16  static char * topics[ MAX_TOPICS * 2 ];
17
18  static int get_file_for_topic( char * topic, char ** filename );
19  /* function which looks up a topic from the list and returns the *
20   * topic and the filename separated by a \n in the filename       *
21   * parameter and true (-1) as result of function. If the topic    *
22   * cannot be found returns false (0)                              *
23   */
24
25  extern int create_help_list( void ){
```

continued

Listing C5.3 *continued*

```
26
27  char    topic[ BUFFER_LENGTH ];
28  char    fname[ BUFFER_LENGTH ];
29  FILE *  topic_file;
30  int     success;
31  int     num_read = 0;
32
33      success = ((topic_file = fopen( "help.index", "r")) != NULL );
34
35      /* get each pair of strings from the file */
36      while( success && (num_read < MAX_TOPICS) && !feof(topic_file)){
37          success = ( fgets( topic, BUFFER_LENGTH, topic_file ) != NULL);
38          if ( topic[ strlen(topic)-1] == '\n' ){
39           topic[strlen(topic)-1] = '\0';
40          } /* end if */
41
42          if ( success ){
43           success = ( fgets( fname, BUFFER_LENGTH, topic_file ) !=NULL);
44           if ( fname[ strlen(fname)-1] == '\n' ){
45              fname[strlen(fname)-1] = '\0';
46           } /* end if */
47          } /* end if */
48
49          /* two strings got - so store them */
50          if ( success) {
51              success = ( (topics[ num_read *2] = (char *)
52                               malloc( strlen(topic) +1)) != NULL);
53              if (success){
54                  strcpy( topics[ num_read *2], topic );
55              } /* end if */
56          } /* end if */
57
58          if (success ) {
59              success = ( (topics[ num_read *2 +1] = (char*)
60                               malloc( strlen(fname) +1)) != NULL);
61              if (success){
62                  strcpy( topics[ num_read *2 +1], fname );
63              } /* end if */
64          } /* end if */
65
66          if( success ){
67              num_read++;
68          } /* end if */
69      } /* end while */
70      num_topics = num_read;
71      return num_read;
72  } /* end fun create help list */
73
74
75  extern void destroy_help_list( void ){
76
77  int index;
78      for ( index = 0; index < num_topics; index++){
```

continued

Listing C5.3 *continued*

```
 79            free( topics[ index *2]);
 80            free( topics[ index *2 +1]);
 81       } /* end for */;
 82  } /* end fun destroy help list */
 83
 84
 85  static int get_file_for_topic( char * topic, char ** filename ){
 86
 87  int index   = 0;
 88  int located = 0;
 89
 90       /* search for the topic */
 91       while( !located && (index < num_topics )){
 92          located = (strcmp( topics[ index *2], topic) == 0);
 93          if (!located){
 94             index++;
 95          } /* end if */
 96       } /* end while */
 97
 98       /* if found get the filename */
 99       if (located){
100          *filename = (char*) malloc( strlen( topics[ index *2 +1]) +1);
101          located = (*filename) != NULL;
102       } /* end if */
103       /* and return it */
104       if (located ){
105             strcpy( *filename,  topics[ index *2+1] );
106       } /* end if */
107       return located;
108  } /* end fun get file for topic */
109
110
111  extern int get_topic_list( char * topiks[] ){
112
113  int index = 0;
114  int success = -1;
115
116       /* do each topic in the list */
117       while( success && (index < num_topics)){
118          success = ((topics[ index ] = (char *)
119                        malloc( strlen(topics[ index*2] +1))) != NULL);
120          if (success){
121             strcpy( topiks[ index], topics[ index*2] );
122             index ++;
123          } /* end if */
124       } /* end while */
125       return index;
126  } /* end fun get topic list */
127
128
129  extern int get_topic_info( char * topic, char ** info ){
130
131  FILE * info_file;
```

continued

Listing C5.3 *continued*

```
132  char * filename;
133  int    success;
134  int    file_extent ;
135
136      /* get the filename */
137      success = get_file_for_topic( topic, & filename );
138
139      /* open the file *.
140      if ( success ) {
141          success = ((info_file = fopen( filename, "r")) != NULL );
142      } /* end if */
143
144      /* get the size of the file */
145      if ( success ) {
146          fseek( info_file, 0L, SEEK_END );
147          success = ((file_extent = ftell( info_file)) != -1L);
148      } /* end if */
149
150      /* allocate memory */
151      if ( success ) {
152          *info = (char *) malloc( file_extent * sizeof( char) + 1);
153          success = (*info != NULL);
154      } /* end if */
155
156      /* read the contents */
157      if ( success ) {
158          fseek( info_file, 0L, SEEK_SET);
159          fread( *info, sizeof( char ), file_extent, info_file );
160      } /* end if */
161
162      return success;
163  } /* end fun get topic info */
164
165
166  /* topic dialog support functions */
167  static char topic_view_state = TOPIC_VIEW_INACTIVE;
168
169  extern void set_topic_view_state( int new_state ){
170     topic_view_state = new_state;
171  } /* end fun set_topic_view_state */
172
173  extern int is_topic_view_active( void ){
174     return topic_view_state == TOPIC_VIEW_ACTIVE;
175  } /* end fun is_topic_view_active */
```

Listing C6.1   The replace_all_point and merge_new_points functions from the graphplot
translations module

```
1  extern void replace_all_points ( char * new_points ){
2
3      /* remove all existing points */
4      clear_points_graph();
5      clear_all_text_points();
```

continued

Listing C6.1 *continued*

```
 6
 7     /* add the new points */
 8     redraw_all_points( new_points );
 9  } /* end replace_all_points */
10
11
12  extern void merge_new_points ( char * new_points ){
13
14  int    num_points, this_point;
15  int    virtual_x, virtual_y;
16  char * this_line;
17  int    all_ok;
18
19      this_line = new_points;
20      all_ok = True;
21      /* extract the number of points in the list */
22      all_ok = (sscanf( this_line, " %i ", &num_points)) == 1;
23      /* traverse the list processing all points */
24      while ( (all_ok) && (num_points-> 0)){
25         /* find the start of the next line */
26         while( *this_line != '\n' ){
27            this_line ++;
28         } /* end while */
29         this_line ++;
30         /* extract the co-ordinate pair */
31         all_ok = (sscanf( this_line, " %i , %i ",
32                           &virtual_x, &virtual_y)) == 2;
33         if ( all_ok) {
34            /* add the point to the list */
35            add_text_point( virtual_x, virtual_y );
36         } /* end if */
37      } /* end while */
38  } /* end merge_new_points */
```

Listing C7.1   The color selection translation module header file

```
 1  /* filename color select interface translation module   *
 2   * header file csi_tm.h.                                 *
 3   * Written for Motif book Chapter 7 revised Jan 94       *
 4   * Fintan Culwin v1.0 Oct 92                             *
 5   */
 6
 7  #ifndef CSI_TM
 8  #define  CSI_TM
 9
10  #include <Xm/Xm.h>
11  #include "yag_adl.h"
12
13  extern void  create_color_selection_interface(Widget parent);
14
15  extern void destroy_color_selection_interface( void );
16
17  extern void activate_color_selection_interface(Widget widget,
```

continued

\\

Listing C6.1 *continued*

```
18                                                   XtPointer client_data,
19                                                   XtPointer call_data);
20
21  extern void deactivate_color_selection_interface( void );
22
23
24  #endif /* ifndef CSI_TM */
```

Listing C7.2   The color selection presentation module header file

```
1   /* filename color select interface color presentation    *
2    * module header file csi c pm.h.                         *
3    * Written for Motif book Chapter 7.                      *
4    * Fintan Culwin v1.0 Oct 92 revised Jan 94              *
5    */
6
7   #ifndef CSI_C_PM
8   #define CSI_C_PM
9
10  #include <Xm/Xm.h>
11  #include <Xm/Form.h>
12  #include <Xm/Frame.h>
13  #include <Xm/PushB.h>
14  #include <Xm/DialogS.h>
15  #include <Xm/RowColumn.h>
16  #include <Xm/DrawingA.h>
17  #include <Xm/ScrolledW.h>
18  #include <Xm/ToggleB.h>
19
20
21  /* **** one bit dialog functions **** */
22  extern void create_1_bit_color_selection_dialog(Widget parent,
23                  XtCallbackProc  color_selection_callback,
24                  XtCallbackProc  apply_button_press_callback,
25                  XtCallbackProc  close_button_press_callback);
26
27  extern void    destroy_1_bit_color_selection_dialog( void );
28  extern void   activate_1_bit_color_selection_dialog( void );
29  extern void deactivate_1_bit_color_selection_dialog( void );
30
31
32  /* **** two to eight bit  dialog functions **** */
33  extern void create_28_bit_color_selection_dialog(Widget parent,
34                  XtCallbackProc  color_select_callback,
35                  XtCallbackProc  fore_back_option_callback,
36                  XtCallbackProc  apply_button_press_callback,
37                  XtCallbackProc  close_button_press_callback);
38
39  extern void    destroy_28_bit_color_selection_dialog( void );
40  extern void   activate_28_bit_color_selection_dialog( void );
41  extern void deactivate_28_bit_color_selection_dialog( void );
42  extern void set_active_color_button( int     button_number,
43                                       Boolean on_or_off    );
```

continued

Listing C7.2 *continued*

```
44   extern void update_28_color_feedback( Pixel foreground,
45                                         Pixel background );
46
47
48   /* **** more than eight bit  dialog functions **** */
49   extern void create_8plus_bit_color_selection_dialog(Widget parent,
50                     XtCallbackProc  color_button_press_callback,
51                     XtCallbackProc  fore_back_toggle_callback,
52                     XtCallbackProc  apply_button_press_callback,
53                     XtCallbackProc  close_button_press_callback);
54
55   extern void    destroy_8plus_bit_color_selection_dialog( void );
56   extern void    activate_8plus_bit_color_selection_dialog( void );
57   extern void deactivate_8plus_bit_color_selection_dialog( void );
58   extern void update_8plus_color_feedback( Pixel foreground,
59                                            Pixel background );
60
61   #endif /* ifndef CSI_C_PM */
```

Listing C7.3   The font and text interface translation module header and code files

```
1    /* filename font select interface translation module      *
2     * interface header file (fsi_tm.h).                       *
3     * Written for Motif book Chapter 7                        *
4     * Fintan Culwin v1.0 Dec 92 revised Jan 94                *
5     */
6
7    #ifndef FSI_TM
8    #define FSI_TM
9
10   #include <Xm/Xm.h>
11
12   extern void  create_font_and_text_selection_interface(Widget parent);
13   extern void destroy_font_and_text_selection_interface( void );
14
15   extern void activate_font_and_text_selection_interface(
16                                            Widget    widget,
17                                            XtPointer client_data,
18                                            XtPointer call_data);
19
20   extern void deactivate_font_and_text_selection_interface( void );
21
22
23   #endif /* ifndef FSI_TM */
```

```
1    /* filename font select interface translation module      *
2     * interface code file (fsi_tm.c).                         *
3     * Written for Motif book chapter 7                        *
4     * Fintan Culwin v1.0 Dec 92                               *
5     */
```

continued

\\

Listing C7.3 *continued*

```
 6
 7
 8  #include "fsi_tm.h"
 9  #include "fsi_pm.h"
10  #include "fsi_sm.h"
11
12
13  /* callback functions for the font and text dialog */
14  static void font_option_select_callback( Widget    widget,
15                                    XtPointer client_data,
16                                    XtPointer call_data );
17  static void weight_option_select_callback( Widget    widget,
18                                      XtPointer client_data,
19                                      XtPointer call_data );
20  static void style_option_select_callback( Widget    widget,
21                                     XtPointer client_data,
22                                     XtPointer call_data );
23  static void size_option_select_callback( Widget    widget,
24                                    XtPointer client_data,
25                                    XtPointer call_data );
26
27  static void apply_button_press_callback( Widget    widget,
28                                    XtPointer client_data,
29                                    XtPointer call_data );
30  static void close_button_press_callback( Widget widget,
31                                    XtPointer client_data,
32                                    XtPointer call_data );
33
34  /* callback functions for the other dialogs */
35  static void font_unavailable_ok_button_callback( Widget widget,
36                                        XtPointer client_data,
37                                        XtPointer call_data );
38
39  static void alternative_possible_ok_callback( Widget widget,
40                                     XtPointer client_data,
41                                     XtPointer call_data );
42
43  static void alternative_possible_not_ok_callback( Widget widget,
44                                         XtPointer client_data,
45                                         XtPointer call_data );
46
47  /* declaration of a pointer to a function returning void *
48   * taking void arguments. To be installed as part of the *
49   * text and font apply button's actions                  */
50  static void (*text_tool_apply_action)(void) = NULL;
51
52  extern void  create_font_and_text_selection_interface(Widget parent){
53
54      /* create the dialogs */
55      create_font_and_text_selection_dialog(parent,
56                      font_option_select_callback,
57                      weight_option_select_callback,
58                      style_option_select_callback,
```

continued

Listing C7.3 *continued*

```
59                         size_option_select_callback,
60                         apply_button_press_callback,
61                       preview_button_press_callback,
62                        close_button_press_callback);
63
64      create_font_not_available_info_dialog( parent,
65                      font_unavailable_ok_button_callback);
66
67      create_alternative_possible_question_dialog( parent,
68                        alternative_possible_ok_callback,
69                        alternative_possible_not_ok_callback);
70   } /* end fun create_font_and_text_selection_interface */
71
72
73   extern void destroy_font_and_text_selection_interface( void ){
74
75      destroy_font_and_text_selection_dialog();
76      destroy_font_not_available_info_dialog();
77      destroy_alternative_possible_question_dialog();
78   } /* end fun destroy_font_and_text_selection_interface */
79
80
81   extern void activate_font_and_text_selection_interface(
82                                          Widget    widget,
83                                          XtPointer client_data,
84                                          XtPointer call_data){
85
86      activate_font_and_text_selection_dialog();
87
88      /* the client_data is a function - so assign it to    *
89       * the function pointer. This function will be called *
90       * as part of the apply button's actions              */
91      text_tool_apply_action =  client_data;
92   } /* end fun activate_font_and_text_selection_interface */
93
94
95   extern void deactivate_font_and_text_selection_interface( void){
96
97      /* null - no actions required */
98   } /* end fun deactivate_font_and_text_selection_interface */
99
100
101  /* the actions attached to the various option menu callbacks */
102  static void font_option_select_callback( Widget    widget,
103                                          XtPointer client_data,
104                                          XtPointer call_data ){
105      set_working_font( (char*) client_data);
106  } /* end fun font_option_select_callback */
107
108
109  static void weight_option_select_callback( Widget    widget,
110                                          XtPointer client_data,
111                                          XtPointer call_data ){
```

continued

\\

Listing C7.3 *continued*

```
112        set_working_weight( (char*) client_data);
113  } /* end fun weight_option_select_callback */
114
115
116  static void style_option_select_callback( Widget      widget,
117                                            XtPointer client_data,
118                                            XtPointer call_data ){
119      set_working_style( (char*) client_data);
120  } /* end fun style_option_select_callback */
121
122
123  static void size_option_select_callback( Widget     widget,
124                                           XtPointer client_data,
125                                           XtPointer call_data ){
126      set_working_size( (char*) client_data);
127  } /* end fun size_option_select_callback */
128
129
130  static void apply_button_press_callback( Widget     widget,
131                                           XtPointer client_data,
132                                           XtPointer call_data ){
133
134  char * font_name;
135  Font    font_id;
136  char * text;
137
138    if (!(load_working_selection( widget ))){
139        get_working_formatted_font_string( &font_name );
140        activate_font_not_available_info_dialog( font_name );
141        free( font_name );
142    } else {
143        /* get the font id from the support module */
144        font_id = get_current_fid();
145        /* get the text from the presentation module */
146        get_current_text( &text );
147        /* communicate font & text to application layer */
148        set_application_font( font_id );
149        set_application_text( text );
150        free(text );
151        deactivate_font_and_text_selection_dialog();
152
153        /* call the function passed as part of the activate action */
154        text_tool_apply_action();
155    } /* end if */
156  } /* end fun apply_button_press_callback */
157
158
159  static void close_button_press_callback( Widget widget,
160                                           XtPointer client_data,
161                                           XtPointer call_data ){
162
163  char * working_font_name, loaded_font_name;
164  Font    font_id;
```

continued

Listing C7.3 *continued*

```
165  char * text;
166
167     if (!(load_working_selection( widget ))){
168        get_working_formatted_font_string( &working_font_name );
169        get_loaded_formatted_font_string( &loaded_font_name );
170        activate_alternative_possible_question_dialog(
171                                      working_font_name,
172                                      loaded_font_name );
173        free( working_font_name );
174        free( loaded_font_name );
175     } else {
176        deactivate_font_and_text_selection_dialog();
177     } /* end if */
178  }/* end fun close_button_press_callback */
179
180
181  static void font_unavailable_ok_button_callback( Widget widget,
182                                      XtPointer client_data,
183                                      XtPointer call_data ){
184     deactivate_font_not_available_info_dialog();
185  } /* end fun font_unavailable_ok_button_callback */
186
187
188  static void alternative_possible_ok_callback( Widget widget,
189                                      XtPointer client_data,
190                                      XtPointer call_data ){
191
192     deactivate_alternative_possible_question_dialog();
193     deactivate_font_and_text_selection_dialog();
194  } /* end fun alternative_possible_ok_callback */
195
196
197  static void alternative_possible_not_ok_callback( Widget widget,
198                                      XtPointer client_data,
199                                      XtPointer call_data ){
200     deactivate_alternative_possible_question_dialog();
201  }/* end fun alternative_possible_not_ok_callback */
```

Listing C7.4   The font and text interface support module header and code files

```
1   /* filename font select interface support module       *
2    * header file (fsi_sm.h).                              *
3    * Written for Motif book Chapter 7.                    *
4    * Fintan Culwin v1.0 Dec 92                            *
5    */
6
7   #ifndef FSI_SM
8   #define FSI_SM
9
10  #include <Xm/Xm.h>
11
12  /* support for the working attributes */
13  extern void set_working_font(  char *  new_font );
```

continued

\\\

Listing C7.4 *continued*

```
14  extern void get_working_font(   char ** the_working_font );
15  extern void set_working_weight( char *  new_weight );
16  extern void get_working_weight( char ** the_working_weight );
17  extern void set_working_size(   char *  new_size );
18  extern void get_working_size(   char ** the_working_size );
19  extern void set_working_style(  char *  new_style );
20  extern void get_working_style(  char ** the_working_style );
21  extern void get_working_formatted_font_string(
22                              char ** the_working_font_string );
23
24  /* support for the loaded attributes */
25  extern void set_loaded_font(   char *  new_font );
26  extern void get_loaded_font(   char ** the_loaded_font );
27  extern void set_loaded_weight( char *  new_weight );
28  extern void get_loaded_weight( char ** the_loaded_weight );
29  extern void set_loaded_size(   char *  new_size );
30  extern void get_loaded_size(   char ** the_loaded_size );
31  extern void set_loaded_style(  char *  new_style );
32  extern void get_loaded_style(  char ** the_loaded_style );
33  extern void get_loaded_formatted_font_string(
34                              char ** the_loaded_font_string );
35
36  /* support for the fid */
37  extern int  load_working_selection( Widget any_widget );
38  extern Font get_current_fid( void );
39
40  #endif /* ifndef FSI_SM */




1   /* filename font select interface support module     *
2    * code file (fsi sm.c).                             *
3    * Written for Motif book chapter 7.                 *
4    * Fintan Culwin v1.0 Dec 92 revised Jan 94          *
5    */
6
7   #include <stdio.h>
8   #include <string.h>
9
10  #include "fsi_sm.h"
11
12  #define FSI_SMALL_BUFFER_SIZE 40
13  #define FSI_LARGE_BUFFER_SIZE 200
14
15  /* private prototypes */
16  static char * catenate_font_string( char * font,
17                                      char * weight,
18                                      char * size,
19                                      char * style );
20
21  /* support for the working attributes */
22  static char working_font[   FSI_SMALL_BUFFER_SIZE ] = "\0";
23  static char working_weight[ FSI_SMALL_BUFFER_SIZE ] = "\0";
```

continued

Listing C7.4 *continued*

```
24  static char working_size[  FSI_SMALL_BUFFER_SIZE ] = "\0";
25  static char working_style[  FSI_SMALL_BUFFER_SIZE ] = "\0";
26
27
28  extern void   set_working_font(   char * new_font ){
29     strncpy( working_font, new_font, FSI_SMALL_BUFFER_SIZE);
30  } /* end fun set_working_font */
31
32
33  extern void get_working_font( char ** the_working_font ){
34
35     (*the_working_font ) = (char *) malloc( strlen(working_font) + 1);
36     strcpy( (*the_working_font), working_font );
37  } /* end fun get_working_font */
38
39  /* Omitted the remaining working set and get functions which *
40   * manipulate the other components in an identical manner.    */
41
42  /* support for the loaded attributes */
43  static char loaded_font[ FSI_SMALL_BUFFER_SIZE ] = "\0";
44  static char loaded_weight[ FSI_SMALL_BUFFER_SIZE ] = "\0";
45  static char loaded_size[ FSI_SMALL_BUFFER_SIZE ] = "\0";
46  static char loaded_style[ FSI_SMALL_BUFFER_SIZE ] = "\0";
47
48  /* Omitted the loaded set and get functions which are *
49   * identical to the working components above.         */
50
51
52  extern void get_loaded_formatted_font_string(
53                            char ** the_loaded_font_string ){
54
55     (* the_loaded_font_string) = catenate_font_string(
56                            loaded_font, loaded_weight,
57                            loaded_size, loaded_style );
58  } /* end fun get_loaded_formatted_font_string */
59
60
61  extern void get_working_formatted_font_string(
62                            char ** the_loaded_font_string ){
63  /* omitted, essentially identical to *
64   * get_loaded_formatted_font_string  */
65  } /* end fun get_working_formatted_font_string */
66
67
68  static char * catenate_font_string( char * font,
69                                      char * weight,
70                                      char * size,
71                                      char * style ){
72
73  char buffer[ FSI_LARGE_BUFFER_SIZE ] = "*\0";
74  char * dy_buffer;
75
76     /* catenate the components and transfer to *
```

continued

\\\

Listing C7.4 *continued*

```
77        * a dynamically allocated string.          */
78        strcat( buffer, font );
79        strcat( buffer, "*" );
80        strcat( buffer, weight );
81        strcat( buffer, "*" );
82        strcat( buffer, style );
83        strcat( buffer, "*-" );
84        strcat( buffer, size );
85        strcat( buffer, "0*\0" );
86        if( strcmp( buffer, "****-0*") == 0) {
87          *buffer = '\0';
88        } /* end if */
89
90        dy_buffer = (char *) malloc( strlen(buffer) + 1);
91        strcpy( dy_buffer, buffer );
92        return dy_buffer;
93    } /* end fun catenate_font_string */
94
95
96    /* support for the fid */
97    static Font loaded_font_id = (Font) NULL;
98
99    extern int  load_working_selection( Widget any_widget ){
100
101   char        * the_working_font;
102   int           font_is_available;
103   XFontStruct  * font_structure;
104
105       /* attempt to load the font */
106       get_working_formatted_font_string( &the_working_font );
107       font_structure = XLoadQueryFont( XtDisplay( any_widget ),
108                                        the_working_font );
109       free( the_working_font );
110
111       /* update the loaded vars and the font identity *
112        * if the font is available                     */
113       font_is_available = ( font_structure != (XFontStruct *) NULL);
114       if ( font_is_available ){
115            loaded_font_id = font_structure->fid;
116            strcpy( loaded_font, working_font );
117            strcpy( loaded_weight, working_weight );
118            strcpy( loaded_style, working_style );
119            strcpy( loaded_size, working_size );
120            XFontFree( XtDisplay( any_widget ), font_structure);
121       } /* end if */
122       return font_is_available;
123   } /* end fun load_working_selection */
124
125
126   extern Font get_current_fid( void ){
127       return loaded_font_id;
128   } /* end fun load working selection */
```

Index

\\

\\

\\\

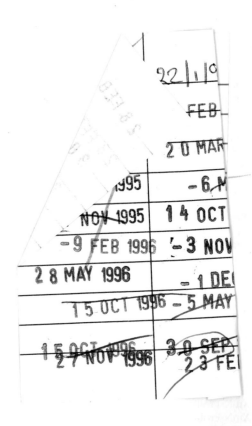